Praise for

"*The Foreigner's Gift* is the wo... — to some extent embedded in—the American enterprise in Iraq. The book will both inform and provoke. In style and substance, this book is vintage Ajami. He crisply presents characters and anecdotes, using them as springboards for musings on larger issues before moving on to different details that in turn lead him to address other big issues."

—L. Carl Brown, *Foreign Affairs*

"A ruined Iraq, March 2003, is where Ajami's tale begins, and there is no one more qualified to tell it. What distinguishes this book from the late sandstorm of volumes on Iraq is that Ajami is at once a graceful writer and a man steeped in the ways of the Arab world."

—Joseph Tartakovsky, *Claremont Review of Books*

"Mr. Ajami is a gifted storyteller, and a brutally honest one."

—Jonathan Karl, *The Wall Street Journal*

"This important book represents the well-informed and deeply personal reflections of a major Arab-American intellectual—a man with a deep feeling for the grand causes and passions that have driven Arab politics for the last six decades."

—R. Stephen Humphreys, *The Washington Post Book World*

"Renowned scholar and political commentator Fouad Ajami delves deep into the lives of Iraqis to create this profound portrayal of a confused country that has emerged as a crucial battleground between American power and Arab extremism."

—*The Globe and Mail* (Toronto)

"*The Foreigner's Gift* offers a beautifully written account, based on six trips [Ajami] made to Iraq in the aftermath of the defeat of Saddam Hussein's regime, of the alternating moods, hopes, fears, and disillusionments among Iraqis, and Arabs more generally, since this momentous event."

—*The New York Sun*

"[A]t a time when the atmosphere of the debate on Iraq is being poisoned by the toxic fumes of partisan politics, Ajami's book comes as a breath of fresh air. Don't miss it!"
—Amir Taheri, *New York Post*

"Few other Americans have Ajami's distinctive qualifications for reflecting on the Iraq war . . . [H]is extraordinary level of access in Washington is reflected in *The Foreigner's Gift*."
—Noah Feldman, *The New York Times Book Review*

"[Ajami] has an enviable gift for charting those invisible lines of clan, tribe, and faction that structure the Arabic-speaking world."
—Christian Caryl, *The Washington Monthly*

Praise for *The Dream Palace of the Arabs*

" . . . beautifully written (Mr. Ajami has poetic flair as both author and translator), yet somehow dispiriting . . . Mr. Ajami's strength is that he can pose convincingly as both outsider and insider . . . [His] insights are revealing."
—*The Economist*

"Ajami is deeply schooled in his subject. His writing is smooth, evocative, richly cadenced . . . Ajami has written an important and illuminating book . . . a valuable testament to a tragic generation that tried to bridge the Arab past with modern ideals."
—Richard Bernstein, *The New York Times*

"*The Dream Palace of the Arabs* is an absorbing and sadly moving account of what political and economic failures on a grand scale have meant in human terms and at an individual level."
—*The Washington Post Book World*

"Eloquent . . . A clear-eyed look at the lost hopes of the Arabs. It opens the door to the thought processes of a society whose motivations have been little understood and often feared. *The Dream Palace of the Arabs* is a courageous book."
—*The Christian Science Monitor*

*f***P**

Also by Fouad Ajami

The Arab Predicament
The Vanished Imam
Beirut: City of Regrets
The Dream Palace of the Arabs

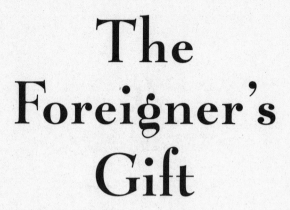

The Foreigner's Gift

THE AMERICANS, THE ARABS, AND THE IRAQIS IN IRAQ

Fouad Ajami

FREE PRESS

New York   London   Toronto   Sydney

FREE PRESS
A Division of Simon & Schuster, Inc.
1230 Avenue of the Americas
New York, NY 10020

First Free Press trade paperback edition June 2007

FREE PRESS and colophon are trademarks of Simon & Schuster, Inc.

For information about special discounts for bulk purchases,
please contact Simon & Schuster Special Sales:
1-800-456-6798 or business@simonandschuster.com

DESIGNED BY ERICH HOBBING

Manufactured in the United States of America

10   9   8   7   6   5   4   3   2   1

The Library of Congress has catalogued the hardcover edition as follows:
Ajami, Fouad.
The foreigner's gift: the Americans, the Arabs, and the Iraqis in Iraq / Fouad Ajami.
p.   cm.
Includes bibliographical references and index.
1. Iraq War, 2003–. 2. Iraq—Politics and government—2003–. 3. United States—
Military relations—Iraq. 4. Iraq—Military relations—United States. I. Title.
DS79.76.A373   2006
956.7044'3—dc22   2006045813

ISBN-13: 978-0-7432-3667-6
ISBN-10: 0-7432-3667-X
ISBN-13: 978-0-7432-3668-3 (pbk)
ISBN-10: 0-7432-3668-8 (pbk)

For my twin nephews
Chris Couch and Jake Couch

We spent year after year after year watching
Thunderous, lightning clouds with no rain
And winds like storms which neither pass as a storm
Nor lie quiet—we sleep and wake up in fear of them.

Badr Shakir al-Sayyab, "The Song of Rain," 1960
(Translated by Issa Boullata)

Contents

Introduction to Paperback Edition
June 2007

There was mayhem at the gallows, and there was justice at the gallows. Saddam Hussein had divided Iraqis and Arabs—and others—while he lived, and he was to do so again on the day of his execution. In the best of worlds, Saddam's executioners would have been "clinical" about the thing and subdued; they would have given the event the dignity it deserved. Iraq's rulers might have even waited for Saddam's victims in Kurdistan to have had their day in court. The Kurds could complain, as they did, that Saddam was being sent to the gallows for the murder of 148 men and boys from the Shia town of Dujail, while his campaign of genocide in Kurdistan had not yet been given a hearing. But this was a despot who had cut a swath of terror through the land, and the prime minister who had come to power from the Shia underground was determined to bring the matter of Saddam Hussein to a fitting end. It wasn't pretty, that spectacle of execution, and there should have been no cell phone video recording of the deed; but the truth at the heart of what played out at the execution bloc in the early hours of December 30, in Saddam's old military intelligence headquarters, was plain and simple justice and retribution. Men are not angels, and the dictator had reaped what he had sown.

Aides to Prime Minister Nuri al-Maliki say that the pen with which he signed Saddam Hussein's death warrant had been in his possession for well over a quarter-century. He had carried this pen with him to a long exile in Syria and Iran after he had fled the terrors of Saddam Hussein. He had waited for that moment, and truth be told there was perhaps relish in the way the death sentence was signed, before the cameras, a message to Maliki's Shia kinsmen. He had rushed through the ceremony and the reception of his son's wedding the day before to prepare for what was to come. The American regency in Baghdad had underestimated Maliki. There was more steel in the man than our commanders and diplomats on the scene had suspected. He had been an unlikely choice for prime minister. He was through and through a man of the Shia traditional classes; unlike his peers in the political class, he spoke not a word of English. He had never really taken to the Americans or fully trusted them. His predecessor, Ibrahim al-Jaafari, who hailed from the same political party, had been removed from office through American pressure in the spring of last year. Maliki had been the beneficiary of that American decision, but there lingered in him a suspicion that he could conceivably suffer the same fate.

It did not help that a memo by National Security Advisor Stephen Hadley, made public the preceding month, had questioned Maliki's ability to rule and to rein in the Shia militias. Hadley had made a brief visit to Baghdad and the portrait he drew of Maliki was not flattering:

> His intentions seem good when he talks with Americans, and sensitive reporting suggests he is trying to stand up to the Shia hierarchy and force positive change. But the reality on the streets of Baghdad suggest Maliki is either ignorant of what is going on, misrepresenting his intentions, or that his capabilities are not yet sufficient to turn his good intentions into action.

American power had bet heavily on reconciling the Sunni insurgents, and Maliki had read the diplomacy of the preceding year as a steady effort to court the Sunni Arabs within Iraq, and to appease the neighboring Arab regimes as well. The man led to the gallows may have been a shadow of his old self, but he still haunted the imagination of his fervent supporters and his haters alike. For Maliki it was important that all these doubts be stilled.

It was said in the Sunni strongholds of Iraq, and in the Arab capitals, that it had been bad form that the dictator had been dispatched at dawn, on the first day of Id al-Adha, the feast of sacrifice marking the end of the annual pilgrimage to Mecca. There was a measure of truth in that complaint; but there was willfulness as well. Those protests had come from a people who had never shed a tear for Saddam's victims. There was no conceivable way of conciliating the crowds in Amman and Ramallah, reconciling them to the truth of Saddam's brutal legacy. Those mourners among the Palestinians and the Egyptians and the Jordanians who proclaimed Saddam a "hero martyr" of the Arab nation were beyond moral judgment and argumentation. Their sympathies lay with the tyrant and not with his victims. Their loyalties were atavistic: they were motivated by a dread of the Shia and by a reflexive, unthinking anti-Americanism. For them the horror at an execution on Id al-Adha was an affectation and a canard. For those Saddam devotees in Amman who mobbed his oldest daughter when she turned up among them there would have been no proper day for serving justice on the despot.

A big thing happened, it has to be conceded, when Maliki affixed his signature to that death sentence. Sunni rulers had been hounding Shia rebels for centuries in Arab lands; they had been sending them to the gallows or to rot and die in prison for as long as this terrible feud has raged. Now the ground had shifted and a Shia man of government was signing the death warrant of a condemned man. Saddam himself had put to death, it will be recalled, some great men of standing in the Shia religious establishment. In April 1980, in a deed that is still recalled with terror by the vast majority of Shiites within (and beyond) Iraq, a great figure of the Shia seminaries, Ayatollah Muhammad Baqir al-Sadr, was put to death by the Saddam regime. His immensely talented sister, Bint al-Huda, a poetess and a writer of exquisite sensibility, was killed alongside him. Sadr had become the great martyr of Iraqi Shi'ism; he is said to have been the intellectual inspiration behind the Daawa Party to which Maliki belongs. The execution of Saddam was an act of fealty to that beloved man. For the Shia faithful, justice had been slow in coming.

It had taken a foreign war to decapitate that tyrannical regime in Baghdad, it is true. Then, too, the despot had been held in captivity by American soldiers who had handed him over to the Iraqis only two hours before he met his fate. But the judgment that mattered was an affair of the Iraqis. American officials had been asking them to claim responsibility for their country, bemoaning their political abdication. That leaked Hadley memo had asked the American envoy in Baghdad to "move into the background and let Maliki take more credit for positive developments." Quite ironically in light of what was to come, Hadley added: "We want Maliki to exert his authority—and demonstrate to Iraqis that he is a strong leader—by taking action against extremists, not by pushing back on the United States and the Coalition." On that morning in Baghdad, three years after he had been flushed out of his spider hole, Saddam Hussein came face-to-face with the wrath and hurt he had bequeathed Iraqis. Those vengeful men taunting him as he fell through the gallows' trapdoor were in the most direct way the children of his cruel reign of terror.

It was vintage Saddam to fall back on Islamic piety when the end came. This had always been his way when calamities struck. The heir of Baath secularism, the bearer of the ideology of the Greek Orthodox theorist Michel Aflaq, in a note prior to the execution, appealed to the "merciful God who helps those who take refuge in him and who will never disappoint any honest believer." Three years earlier, there had been that scene of Saddam's meek surrender to American forces, and that surrender had traumatized those taken in by the image he had peddled of his heroism and toughness. The true believers of his cult had recoiled from the scene—some had insisted that he had been drugged, that the spectacle of abject surrender was a hoax. This time, the "knight of Arabism" was determined to leave behind a more flattering legacy; he refused the black hood offered him and accepted his fate with composure.

The paradox of the man's legacy was easy to see. Had Saddam been possessed of a scant measure of introspection he might have wondered at the ironic turn of fate that had made Iraq—and a good deal of the region around it—a battleground between Pax Americana and Persian power. By the time of his execution, there was a virtual absence of the Arabs from the contest of nations. From Iraq and the Gulf to Beirut and the Mediterranean, the Arabs now seemed like spectators to their destiny, as a great struggle played out between Pax Americana and Iran. In no small measure, this was due to the adventurism and obtuseness of Saddam Hussein. Even before the Anglo-American invasion had decapitated his regime in 2003, the country he had put forth as the Prussia of the Arabs, destined to unite them, lay at the mercy of the Powers, its oil and trade subject to an international regime, its air space and a good chunk of its land mass under the control and supervision of outsiders. He had wanted to herd his Arab neighbors into a sphere of influence under his dominion; frightened by his aggression, they had scurried for cover in search of Western protection. The standard-bearer of the Arabs had delivered them into a new age of tutelage and dependence. Deluded to the last, he told the men who had taunted him as he was being led to the gallows that he had made Iraq, that "backward country, into an advanced and prosperous nation."

The American debate about the war had not waited on Saddam's execution. The scaffolding of the war had come under intense attack in the run-up to the midterm elections of November. Those elections would serve as a verdict on the Bush presidency and on that war that had become the centerpiece of that presidency. On September 8, the case against the war was to acquire a new canonical document: a report by the Senate Select Committee on Intelligence. The report's title, overly long and ponderous, *Postwar Findings About Iraq's WMD Programs and Links to Terrorism and How They Compare with Prewar Assessments,* gave away its central message: the war had been an unnecessary endeavor, based on a faulty reading both of the arsenal of weapons in Saddam's possession and of the connection between Saddam's regime and the terrorists of Al Qaeda. Opponents of the war— to use their own language—would now "cherry-pick" this report, finding in it the damning verdict against the war that had been their conviction all along. It was revealed that Tariq Aziz, once Goebbels to his master, now in captivity, said that Saddam had only had "negative sentiments" about Osama bin Laden, and that the former leader had issued a decree "outlawing Wahhabism and threatening offenders with execution." On the narrowest of grounds, it was the verdict of this report that there had been no operational links between the "secular" regime of Saddam Hussein and the jihadists of Al Qaeda.

Intended or not, the release of this report, around the fifth anniversary of 9/11, was read as definitive proof that the Iraq war now stood alone, that the terrors that had come America's way had nothing to do with the origins of the war. It is safe to say, few readers made their way through the turgid, bureaucratic prose of the report. Fewer still would step forth to ask a virtually incomprehensible Arab-Islamic world that has eluded America for so long to now yield its secrets to a congressional committee. America's enemies were full of cunning and good at dissimulation, hunkering down when needed. No one in the coffeehouses of the Arab world (let alone in the safe houses of the terrorists) would be led astray by that distinction between "secular" and "religious" movements emphasized by the Senate Intelligence Committee. Arabs live in a world where the enemies of order move with remarkable ease from outward religious piety to the most secular of appearances. It did not really matter that there had been no meeting in Prague between Mohamed Atta and Iraqi intelligence operative Ahmad al-Ani. The men and women of the Arab world have a grasp of such matters given them by the life they lead. But this battle was being waged in the court of American opinion, and this Senate report was to play its part in undermining the case for the war.

On the heels of this report came another blow. In the same month, a National Intelligence Estimate depicted Iraq as a breeding ground of a new generation of terrorists. Islamic terror had not waited on Iraq, but the NIE's assertion that that brand of terror had "metastasized and spread across the globe" because of Iraq was to find broad acceptance. (It was odd that the intelligence agencies that had been mocked by liberal opinion for their reporting on Iraq before the war were to suddenly acquire the aura of infallibility.) Strictly speaking, the NIE estimates were not a "finding"; they were a reading of what the jihadists themselves were posting on their websites. It stood to reason that the Islamists would trumpet their attachment to the cause of Iraq, and that American analysts, glued to jihadist cyberspace and lacking intimate knowledge of Arab ways, would take the jihadists at their word.

The declassified portions of the NIE were not particularly profound in their reading of Islamism. Their sociologese was of a piece with a big body of writings on Islamist movements. There was nothing particularly novel or compelling in the assertion that the wrath of the Islamists sprang from "anger, humiliation, and a sense of powerlessness" in the face of the West. I dare guess that were Ayman Zawahiri or the leaders of Al Qaeda in Iraq to make their way through these findings, they would marvel at the naïveté of those who had offered that reading of their motives. But the damage was done, and the critics of the war could be forgiven the satisfaction they derived from the NIE's estimates.

These bureaucratic documents were what they were—weapons in the inevitable bureaucratic-political struggle of a power that had struck into a foreign land which had proven more treacherous and difficult by the day. The struggle that truly mattered was of course unfolding in Iraq itself. "After we invaded Iraq, Iraq invaded itself," *The New Republic*'s Leon Wieseltier would observe with his customary clarity and turn of phrase. America had hoped for a better Iraq, he wrote, and what it found was only "communitarian love and communitarian hatred." Working with the title of this book, he added: "Gifts must not be only given, they must also be received." The blame for

Iraq's frenzied recoil from "the foreigner's gift," he concluded, lay with the Iraqis themselves.

The enemies of this new Iraq had proven unusually brutal, and truth be known, unusually skilled in the war they had waged against the new order of things in Iraq. In retrospect, the bombing of al-Askariya Shrine, with its golden dome, in the town of Samarra in February of 2006 was the starting gun, as it were, of a bitter new war between the Sunnis and the Shia. Faith is peculiar; there had been relentless violence directed against the Shiites the preceding three years, but this attack against one of Shiism's great shrines—and the one located in a predominantly Sunni town—was to goad the Shia to do what the attackers must have hoped for: to be drawn into this sectarian war as they had not been before. The restraint that Grand Ayatollah Ali al-Sistani had tried to impose on the Shia since the fall of the despotism would now give way. If some old, inherited notions had played on the Sunnis about the "meekness" of the Shia, and their lack of a "martial spirit," this would now be cast aside. And if the bombing of the shrine and its psychic violation had not sufficed, the Sunni insurgents were to feed the flames. In the months that followed, the weapon of choice, booby-trapped cars, would be pushed into the Shia stronghold of Sadr City, the home of the underclass and of the brigades of Muqtada al-Sadr. Around this self-designated avenger there had clustered the young and the disoriented; and the ranks of his followers included brigands who had once been in the terror squads of the old regime. They had reincarnated now as warriors of the Shia faith. They were eager for loot, and they knew no other way save the way of terror and intimidation.

The battle was now fully joined. And as the fourth year of the American presence in Iraq unfolded, the violence of the Shia militias had become no less deadly than that of the old regime's remnants and their allies among the Arab jihadists. The demographic advantage of the Shia being what it is, the odds were stacked against the Sunni insurgents. But this was not a time, or a place, of reason and sober calculation. To begin with, the Sunni Arabs had never accepted that they were a minority, nor were they convinced that the tide of battle had turned against them. They had their memory of their old dominion, and it still sustained them. They had "the cover"—as one of Prime Minister Maliki's younger aides, Sadiq al-Rikabi, put it to me—given them by the weight of the Sunni world. No Arab cavalry from Egypt or Jordan

or the Peninsula was riding to the rescue of the Sunni Arabs. But the
old Baathists and the Sunni Arabs fought on, carried along, it seemed
at times, by that expectation. Now and then a Saudi pundit, or a Jordanian, would beat the drums of Sunni Arab intervention in Iraq
against the Persians—read the Shiites of Iraq. And this was enough to
give determination to the diehards. Stiffer dosages of violence would
be administered to Sadr City, as the sectarian "cleansing" of mixed
areas did its work. On November 23, there came the deadliest sectarian attack since the American-led invasion. Five powerful car bombs
exploded in Sadr City in the afternoon, taking a toll of some 200 lives.
The revenge was swift: the next day there were retaliations against the
Baghdad Sunni neighborhood of Adhamiya. Sunni mosques were
stormed there and in other parts of the city as well. Four mosques were
attacked in the Sunni neighborhood of Hurriya; two were completely
destroyed.

That political process that had been the pride of Iraqis a year or so earlier—those elections celebrated in this book's hardcover edition, I
have to add—was overwhelmed by the violence. There was a National
Assembly but the flames of sectarian violence were mightier. Iraqis were
dying in large numbers. In 2006, the Iraqi authorities reported that
12,000 people had been killed, 5,000 of them in the last three months
of the year. There were higher estimates by the United Nations—
27,000 people in the first nine months of the year. Either way, Iraq was
becoming terrifying to its own people. And Iraqis were in flight—fleeing their homes in mixed neighborhoods within Iraq to places of
their sect, and fleeing Iraq itself for safer lands. No one knows the precise numbers of the internal migration, or of the flight out of Iraq. It
was a cruel irony: Iraqis had taken to the road under the old tyranny,
and now the chaos and the brutality were pushing them out of their
homeland yet again. The November 2006 Iraq Displacement Report
by the United Nations High Commissioner for Refugees estimated that
there were 700,000 Iraqis in Jordan, at least 600,000 in Syria, 100,000
in Egypt, 54,000 in Iran. On a daily basis, Syria and Jordan in particular were flooded with new arrivals: 2,000 a day in Syria; 1,000 a day
in Jordan. Iraqis with skill and social capital and savings were building
new lives in Dubai, and in any other land that would take them. They
were laying siege to foreign embassies and consulates. They were once
again a people of exile, fated to dream in foreign lands of their tor-

mented homeland. Was it a surprise that no reprieve had been given Saddam Hussein? Mercy had drained out of the land, and men fighting in his name, under his old banner, had brought about a hellish world in their own image.

"The situation in Iraq is grave and deteriorating" was the opening sentence of a much-awaited report by the Iraq Study Group, which was headed by two "wise men" of the foreign policy establishment: former secretary of state James Baker and the former Democratic congressman from Indiana Lee Hamilton. "There is no path that can guarantee success, but the prospects can be improved." This was December 2006, and there had been much anticipation of this report. This was the moment of the realists, it was said, their return to their place of primacy in foreign policy, a rescue effort for an administration given to ideology and redemptionism.

The principal figure in the Study Group—five Democrats and five Republicans, some with very little if any knowledge of foreign policy or of the Islamic world—was of course James Baker himself. He had had his turn under Bush the Elder; he had been there, the steward of American foreign policy, when the Kurdish and Shia rebellions his president had called for, in 1991, were abandoned to the tender mercy of Saddam Hussein. Bush the Elder had walked away from those rebellions, and Baker had headed to the Madrid summit conference in October of that year; the "authority" gained in Iraq would be used, Baker was determined, to bring about a settlement between Israel and the Palestinians. He had been tone-deaf to history's anguish; he was the quintessential diplomatic fixer. He would miss the ordeal in Iraq, as he had failed to read the drama of communism's collapse in the former domains of the Soviet Union and in the Balkans. In April of 1991, he had flown to the Turkish-Iraqi border. He had seen a massive humanitarian disaster—the Kurds abandoning their hill country, fleeing the helicopter gunships of the Iraqi regime. A petition had been submitted to him by a Kurdish delegation: "All Iraqis were waiting for freedom and democratic regime in Iraq. But the mistakes and wrong decisions that allowed the Iraqi regime to use tanks and helicopters caused this tragedy." He was in the inner sanctum of power, a party to decisions that mattered, but he wrote, in his memoirs, as a man unimplicated in the calamity. In the south the killer squads of the regime, thrown on the defensive by the war against the American-led coalition, had

rebounded. Spared by the victors, told that they could use their helicopter gunships so long as they kept grounded their "fixed wing aircraft," they had struck into Karbala, into Najaf and Basra, with a
brutality that still haunts victims and perpetrators alike.

Baker returned a generation later, a man unchanged by all that had
played out in the intervening years. The center of gravity in the region
had shifted from the Mediterranean to Iraq and the Persian Gulf. The
fury of Iraq and the push of Iran into Arab affairs had "de-linked" the
Gulf from the Mediterranean, but Baker had returned with an old prescription: a settlement of the Israeli-Palestinian conflict, and the
Rolodex diplomacy of his years in power. In his view, redemptionism
had failed, and it was time to return to the courts of Arab monarchs
and rulers, and to the incrementalism of diplomacy. Peace between
Israel and the Palestinians had nothing to do with peace in Ramadi
and Sadr City. The insurgents in Iraq were not fighting for Palestine,
but for their lost hegemony. Beyond the old obsession with Palestine,
Baker's recommendations were an odd mix. There would be peace
offerings to the rogues (Syria and Iran), and an invitation to the
"moderate" Arab governments to bail out the American effort in Iraq.

America had struck into Iraq, full of confidence. In truth, none of Iraq's
neighboring states—the Arabs in particular—had the slightest interest in coming to the rescue of the American effort there. For their part,
the Syrians and the Iranians had been doing their best to thwart
America in Iraq. They had been relieved to see the frustration of
American power. The Syrians had paid dearly in 2005; they had quit
Lebanon under the threat of American power, and had to abandon the
vast extortion racket their dominion in Lebanon had become. Too
timid to confront American might directly, they had done what they
could to make Iraq ungovernable. The Syrian rulers—by the logic of
the Sunni jihadists, Alawite heretics and schismatics—had made their
border with Iraq a passage of choice for Arab jihadists on their way to
Iraq. Iran's ambitions and means were more formidable than those of
the Syrians. From the vantage point of the Iranian regime, Iraq was the
most convenient place to take on American power. The Iranians could
be opportunistic: they could pick and choose, they could harass the
Americans, and play the spoiler's game. Thus the call by the Iraq
Study Group to "engage" these two regimes was idle.

Nor did the "moderate" Arab regimes have much to contribute to the struggle in Iraq. They had kept their distance from the entire American project; they had been convinced that it was destined to fail. For the rulers in Egypt, Jordan, and the Arabian Peninsula, the rise of a Shia-led government in Baghdad was anathema. In the long scheme of things, they would have no choice but to accommodate the kind of order that sticks on the ground in Iraq. But no one in the Arab constellation of power was rushing to the aid of the Americans—or to the aid of the Iraqis, for that matter. The whole weight of the neighboring Arab states—their preachers railing against the Americans and against Iraq's rulers, their media saturated with hostility to Iraq's Shiites and growing increasingly strident, and those diehards from their midst turning Iraq into a new battleground for the jihad—was arrayed against the success of America in Iraq. In more confident days, Iraq under the Americans for a brief, shining moment was a rebuke to the Arab autocrats. What autocrat was going to throw it a lifeline in its time of turmoil?

The mountain had brought forth mice: The Baker-Hamilton recommendations had been released to sky-high expectations, and had been hollow. In Iraq itself, they were destined to be badly received by the Kurds and the Shia. There was no patience there with the "realism" of James Baker and his colleagues. These two populations had "known" James Baker during their terrible ordeal in 1991. The Shia tell their history in metaphors of justice and betrayal; a diplomatic fixer at ease with the old order in Arab lands had triggered in them the understandable fear that the power that had come their way in their country could be bargained away in a deal with the Arab rulers. The Kurds were quick to respond in defense of their own interests. They had done well by federalism, and the Baker-Hamilton report was biased in favor of central control. Throughout the report, "emphasis was placed on strengthening the central government and weakening the regional one," read a note issued by Massoud Barzani on December 8. "This is contrary to the principles of federalism and the constitution that forms the basis upon which the new Iraq was built." Barzani could see through the deference of Baker and his colleagues to the status quo in the neighborhood. "In a few sections of the report, the interest and concerns of the neighboring countries were taken into account and there are calls for a bigger role for them. We think that this is contrary to the interests of the people of Iraq in general and of Iraqi Kurdistan in particular."

That order of power in the region, benign to the American members of this study group, had heaped upon Kurdistan and its people a history of indifference and outright grief. Several members of the Baker-Hamilton group had made a perfunctory visit to the Green Zone in Baghdad; they had never bothered to turn up in Kurdistan, and this, too, had fed the Kurdish sense that these realists were no friends of theirs. Baker had not thought much of the promise of democracy in Iraq, but that promise was all the Kurds and the Shia had to sustain them in the midst of great brutality.

For the Bush administration, the Baker-Hamilton report turned out to be a gift of deliverance. Its very weakness gave the administration more running room, if only because the alternatives to its own course seemed so defective. There was no need to do battle with this report: it had its burst of attention, and was then consigned to oblivion. It was grim in Iraq, but Americans still recoiled from the prospect of abdication, and the president calling the shots had two years of office left him. He could still defend the battle for Iraq as the pillar of a broader effort to maintain stability in the Arab world and the Persian Gulf.

In early January 2007, as of this writing, he had signaled that he would not abandon the war he had launched. Neither he nor the people around him were using the term "staying the course" any longer. But there would be no quick exit from Iraq. There would be a surge in troops, and some new emergency funds as well, for the military commanders to provide employment and quick relief for the Iraqi poor. Indeed, were the new direction of the American policy to be divined, there were indications that the Pax Americana had finally come to terms with the very Iraq it had midwifed. The doubts and the reservations about Shia power were giving way. Instead of cutting the Maliki government adrift—as Maliki and his aides and the entire Shia political class had feared—the Bush administration now seemed more determined to sustain it.

True enough, there was still anxiety about Iran's sway with the Shia political class, and there were the representations made by Cairo, Riyadh, and Amman about the dangers of the Shia bogeyman. But the policy seemed more steady. Where Maliki, as late as November 2006, had complained that he could not move a "single company without coalition approval," even though he was the commander of the armed forces, a greater acceptance of his authority was taking hold in American official circles. It was an open secret that Maliki had always been

wary of the American envoy, Zalmay Khalilzad, and that a good
number of the Shia political class were convinced that Khalilzad had
been unduly solicitous of the Sunni insurgency and of the Sunni
Arab politicians empowered by that insurgency. Khalilzad had played
his hand, and was now assigned to the United Nations. One of the
dramatis personae of the early course of this war—and of the early edition of this book—was Lt. Gen. David Petraeus. The big assignment
now came his way: he would be sent back to Iraq as overall commander of the American forces. The reprieve in Fort Leavenworth,
Kansas, and the big house with the porch overlooking the Missouri
were not to his taste. In the interim, he had been restless, and the
details and the news of Iraq were an obsession. Those in the know of
military strategy prophesied that this meant a sure shift from "force
protection" to counterinsurgency.

In the November 7 midterm elections, the American public voted
its disenchantment with the course of things in Iraq, and the Democrats could maintain that the election had been a warrant for a phased
withdrawal, or at least for a de-escalation of the American role in Iraq.
But a different policy appeared to be taking shape. Its elements were
stoicism and acceptance of the burden of this war. The project in Iraq
would not be mortgaged to the Iranians and the Syrians, nor would it
be bartered to the Arab rulers in the orbit of American power. Deliverance would be sought in Baghdad, and among Iraqis. And America
would give the Iraq it had brought forth a little more time in the hope
that those expectations that had carried America to that country in the
first place could yet be redeemed.

There were no trumpets and drums to announce the "new" policy.
Unveiled in a presidential address on January 10, it had in it both the
promise of resolve and commitment and a warning to the Iraqi leaders that this was their last chance to pull their country back from the
brink. "I have made it clear to the prime minister and Iraq's other leaders that America's commitment is not open-ended. If the Iraqi government does not follow through on its promises, it will lose the support
of the American people—and it will lose the support of the Iraqi
people." This was the proverbial "extra mile," more American grief and
burden in the hope of an honorable exit. For once, there was no
promise of success. "Victory will not look like the ones our fathers and
grandfathers achieved. There will be no surrender ceremony on the
deck of a battleship." Iraq had hardened its liberators, and worked its

terrible disappointments on them. What sustained this mission now
were the American sacrifices incurred in that country and the bleak
prospect of walking away under the gaze, and the scrutiny, of an
Arab-Islamic world that had been sure, from the start, that the foreign
power was bound to falter.

Preface

Those nineteen young Arabs who assaulted America on the morning of 9/11 had come into their own after the disappointments of modern Arab history. They were not exactly traditional men: they were the issue, the children, of disappointment and of the tearing asunder of modern Arab history. They were city people, newly urbanized, half educated. They had filled the faith with their anxieties and a belligerent piety. They hated the West but were drawn to its magnetic force and felt the power of its attraction; they sharpened their "tradition," but it could no longer contain their lives or truly answer their needs. I had set out to write a long narrative of these pitiless young men—and the culture that had given rise to them. But the Iraq war, "embedded" in this cruel history, was to overtake the writing I was doing.

A war fated and "written," *maktoob,* as the Arabs would say, this Iraq war turned out to be. For the full length of a decade, in the 1990s, the anti-American subversion—and the incitement feeding it—knew no respite. Appeasement had not worked. The "moderns," with Bill Clinton as their standard-bearer, had been sure we would be delivered by the marketplace and the spread of the World Wide Web. History had mocked them, and us all. In Kabul, and then in Baghdad, America had taken up sword against these troubles.

"The justice of a cause is not a promise of its success," Leon Wieseltier wrote in the pages of *The New Republic,* in a reassessment of the Iraq war. For growing numbers of Americans, the prospects for "success" in Iraq look uncertain at best. Before success, though, some words about the justice of this war. Let me be forthright about the view that runs through these pages. For me this was a legitimate and, at the beginning, a popular war that issued out of a deep American frustration with the "road rage" of the Arab world and with the culture of terrorism that had put down roots in Arab lands. It was not an iso-

lated band of misguided young men who came America's way on
9/11. They emerged out of the Arab world's dominant culture and
malignancies. There were the financiers who subsidized the terrorism.
There were the intellectuals who winked at the terrorism and justified
it. There were the preachers—from Arabia to Amsterdam and Fins-
bury Park—who gave it religious sanction and cover. And there were
the Arab rulers whose authoritarian orders produced the terrorism and
who looked away from it so long as it targeted foreign shores.

Afghanistan was the setting for the first battle against Arab radicalism. That desperate, impoverished land had been hijacked, rented if
you will, by the Arab jihadists and their masters and financiers. Iraq
followed: America wanted to get closer to the source of the troubles in
the Arab world. It wasn't democracy that was at stake in Iraq. It was
something more limited but important and achievable in its own
way: a state less lethal to its own people and to the lands and peoples
around it. Iraq's political culture had been poisoned by a crude theory
of race and a racialist Arabism that had wrecked and unsettled Arab
and Muslim life in the 1980s and 1990s. The Tikriti rulers had ignited
a Sunni-Shia war within and over Islam. They had given Arabs a
cruel view of history—iron and fire and bigotry. They had, for all practical purposes, cut off the Arab world from the possibility of a decent,
modern life.

It is easy to say that the expedition in Iraq is the product of American innocence. And it is easy to see that the American regent, L. Paul
Bremer, didn't find his way to the deep recesses of Iraqi culture. Sure
enough, it has proven virtually impossible to convince the people of
Fallujah to take to more peaceful ways. It is painfully obvious that at
the Abu Ghraib prison some of America's soldiers and military police
and reservists broke the codes of war and of military justice. But
there can be no doubting the nobility of the effort, for Abu Ghraib
isn't the U.S. war. With support for the war hanging in the balance,
Abu Ghraib has been an unmitigated disaster. But for all the terrible-
ness of Abu Ghraib and its stain, this war has not been some "rogue
operation" willed by the White House and by the Department of
Defense. It isn't Paul Wolfowitz's war. It has been a war waged with
congressional authorization and fought in the shadow of a terrible
calamity visited upon America on 9/11. Sure enough, the United
States didn't have the support of Kofi Annan or of Jacques Chirac. But
Americans can be forgiven a touch of raw pride: the American rescue

of Bosnia, in 1995, didn't have the approval of Boutros Boutros-Ghali (or of the head of his peacekeeping operations at the time, the same Kofi Annan) or of François Mitterrand either.

My sense of Iraq, and of the U.S. expedition, is indelibly marked by the images and thoughts that came to me on six trips that I made to that country in the aftermath of the destruction of the regime of Saddam Hussein. A sense of America's power alternated with thoughts of its solitude and isolation in an alien world. The armies and machines—and earnestness—of a great foreign power against the background of a big, impenetrable region: America could awe the people of the Arab-Muslim world, and that region could outwit and outwait American power. The foreign power could repair the infrastructure of Iraq, and the insurgents could wreck it. America could "stand up" and train civil defense and police units, and they could disappear just when needed. In its desire to redeem its work, America could entertain for Iraqis hopes of a decent political culture, and the enemies of this project could fall back on a bigotry sharpened for combat and intolerance. Beyond the prison of the old despotism, the Iraqis have found the hazards and uncertainties—and promise—of freedom. An old order of dominion and primacy was shattered in Iraq. The rage against this American war, in Iraq itself and in the wider Arab world, was the anger of a culture that America had given power to the Shia stepchildren of the Arab world—and to the Kurds. This proud sense of violation stretched from the embittered towns of the Sunni Triangle in western Iraq to the chat rooms of Arabia and to jihadists as far away from Iraq as North Africa and the Muslim enclaves of Western Europe.

In the way of people familiar with modern canons of expression—of things that can and cannot be said—the Arab elites were not about to own up in public to the real source of their animus toward this American project. The great Arab silence that greeted the terrors inflicted on Iraq by the brigades of Abu Musab al-Zarqawi gave away the wider Arab unease with the rise of the Shia in Iraq. For nearly three years, that Jordanian-born terrorist brought death and ruin to Iraq. There was barely concealed admiration for him in his native land and in Arab countries beyond. Jordan, in particular, showed remarkable sympathy for deeds of terror masquerading as Islamic acts. In one Pew survey, in the summer of 2005, 57 percent of Jordanians expressed support for suicide bombings and attacks on civilians. It was only when the chickens came home to roost and Zarqawi's pitiless warriors struck three hotels in Amman on November 9, 2005, killing sixty people, that Jordanians drew back in horror. In one survey, conducted a week after these attacks by a public opinion firm, Ipsos Jordan, 94 percent of the people surveyed now said that Al Qaeda's activities were detrimental to the interests of Arabs and Muslims; nearly three out of four Jordanians said that they had not expected "at all" such terrorist attacks in Jordan. Abu Musab al-Zarqawi's own tribe now disowned him and broke ties with him. He had "shamed" them at home and placed in jeopardy their access to the state and its patronage. But even as they mourned their loss, the old habits persisted. "Zionist terror in Palestine = American terror in Iraq = Terror in Amman," read a banner held aloft by the leaders of the Engineers' Syndicate of Jordan who had come together to protest the hotel bombings. A country with this kind of political culture is in need of repair; the bureaucratic-military elite who run this realm have their work cut out for them. The Iraqi Shia were staking a claim to their country in the face of a stubborn Arab refusal to admit the sectarian bias at the heart of modern Arab life.

It would have been heady and right had Iraqis brought about their own liberty, had they demolished the prisons and the statues on their own. And it would have been easier and more comforting had America not redeemed their liberty with such heartbreaking American losses. There might have been greater American support for the war had the Iraqis not been too proud to admit that they needed the stranger's gift and had the United States come to a decent relationship with them. But the harvest of the war has been what it has been. In Kurdistan, Anglo-American power has provided protection to a people who have made good use of this new order. There is no excessive or contrived religious zeal in Kurdistan, and the nationalism that blows there seems free of chauvinism and delirium. There's a fight for the city of Kirkuk, where the Kurds will have to show greater restraint in the face of competing claims by the Turkomans, and by the Arabs who were pushed into Kirkuk by the old regime. But on balance Kurdistan shows that terrible histories can be remade. In the rest of the country, America rolled history's dice. There is a view that sees Shia theocracy stalking this new Iraq, but this view, as these pages will make clear, is not mine. Iraq may not provide the Pax Americana with a base of power in the Persian Gulf that some architects and proponents of the war hoped for. America can live without that strategic gain. It is the Iraqis who will need the saving graces of moderate politics.

I am keenly aware that for many Baghdad was not the right return address for a war against terror. But the Iraq war inexorably unfolded out of the American reading of the Arab-Muslim world in the aftermath of 9/11. Three years after these attacks, there would settle upon America doubts about the wisdom and the urgency of the war. In the autumn of 2004, the chief U.S. arms inspector for Iraq, Charles A. Duelfer, came forth with a definitive report that confirmed that Saddam Hussein had possessed no stockpiles of weapons of mass destruction and no active weapons programs. In January 2005, Duelfer's Iraq Survey Group officially folded up its work. The pursuit of a menacing dictator had shifted: Saddam was now a pathetic figure, a delusional man idling his time away writing bad novels and reading Hemingway's *The Old Man and the Sea.* But this was hindsight and bore no resemblance to the fears that played upon Americans when the decision to go to war had been made.

Much has been said about the "Bush Doctrine" of preemptive war. But after Iraq, caution will be the animating principle of American conduct abroad. Iraq put on display the things that military power can and cannot do. The expedition unnerved Syria and Iran, to be sure. But the Pax Americana now shared borders with these two regimes, as it were. The dictators in the Arab-Muslim world could now rest easier. The Syrian dictator was not about to be chased into a spider hole, deep into the Alawite strongholds in the mountains. And the Iranian theocracy was not going to be sacked by soldiers from West Virginia and Indiana and Vermont. The Iranians would have to secure their own liberty; Americans now knew better than to provide it to strangers sure to second-guess on the morning after.

An officer in the Marine Corps, Colonel Stephen Ganyard (a former student of mine), trying to speak to my anxieties about this war, offered a soldier's consolation—the clarifying power of time and of patience. "Tell me in twenty years," he wrote, "how this war will have turned out, for it will take that long for it to reveal its full harvest." We judge quicker. Without the soldiers' mission, without their poise, we ride the roller coaster of a war whose justice and heartbreak alternate in endless succession. Nowadays you dread the Department of Defense releases of the mounting number of those predominantly young men lost in the "Iraq theater of operations." Nowadays you look away in hurt from the crawl at the bottom of the TV screen bringing news of another roadside bomb and another American fatality. There was a stirring Iraqi election on December 15, 2005—the third in eleven months—and eleven million Iraqis cast their ballots. But on that day the Department of Defense's tally of American service members killed in Iraq reached 2,142. It hasn't been easy and it hasn't been cheap, this new military campaign brought about by the coming apart of an Arab-Muslim world unwilling to deal with its despotisms and purveyors of terrorism. It would be a consolation were we to think that, after Kabul and Baghdad, there would be repose and an end to vigilance. But we should know the burning grounds of the Arab-Muslim world better by now. And one can be forgiven the premonition that this isn't the end of the matter.

In a work of penetrating insight, *al-Iraq al-Amriki (American Iraq)*, a highly respected Iraqi intellectual and diplomat, Hassan al-Alawi, observes that it is proper to speak of an American Iraq as one does of a Sumerian, a Babylonian, an Abbasid, an Ottoman, and then a British Iraq. The time of the Americans, he notes, is destined to be exceedingly short but of great impact. Where British Iraq was Sunni, American Iraq can be said to be Shia. During the time of British primacy, the Sunnis were shrewd and accepted the logic of power, and of defeat; they got a homeland, a political kingdom, embassies, and official positions, while the Shia were left with the legend of the resistance to British rule and the "rusty, old rifles" of the Marsh Arabs. Iraq could have done better for itself, Alawi writes, had it accepted American power, had it turned away from violence and from rebellion. The Shia have not been as brilliant and cunning in the time of the Americans as the Sunnis were under British rule and tutelage, he adds. But a beginning has been made, and the old order has been shattered for good.

Alawi—himself a Shia, and a "soft" Baathist who broke away from the regime in 1979 to join the opposition to Saddam's rule—sees this American era as a time of transition. There is an "explosion of freedoms" in today's Iraq, the pent-up energy of a people long repressed. It is too early to see in this time of transition genuine political parties and adherence to the law. That kind of transformation will require a confident middle class that will carry the banner of freedom under the law. It will not be easy, Alawi says, to bring about this kind of historical shift, and it will be immensely important for the Shia to go beyond the memory of those "martyred" by the old regime, beyond the partisanship of the established Shia movements keen to consolidate their hold on power. These Shia movements bear the burden of their birth outside the soil of Iraq: they were formed in exile and have functioned away from the land of Iraq for more than a quarter-century. "I am a Shia," he forthrightly says, "and the Shia state that forms political parties is Iran and I will never be with Iran." A new Iraq would draw on the rich Shia heritage, but that heritage itself will have to come to terms with both the specificity of Iraq and its pluralism.

The future of this Iraq will have to be "federal and democratic," for no force can bring back the old order. For their part, the Sunni Arabs, with the skills of authority and administration given them by a long history of rule, will have to break with the Sunni jihadists from Arab lands who have come to Iraq armed with a warrant to kill the Shia "apostates." In a clever turn of phrase, Alawi writes that the Sunni jihadists, Zarqawi among them, have their gaze fixed on the "green fields of paradise," while the Sunni leaders of Iraq are focused on the Green Zone, the headquarters of the American regency. The Shia could help bring about the break of Iraq's Sunni Arabs from the wider currents of Arab jihadism were they to accept a role for the Sunnis of Iraq disproportionate to their numbers. This is a bow to the logic of necessity and of realism.

A federal, democratic Iraq will have to accept the uniqueness of Kurdistan and the historical conditions that have forced the Kurds into a country they did not want in the first place. No one would have wanted the Kurds in Iraq had they been Shia, Alawi writes. They were pressed into this country to balance the demographic weight of the Shia. The Arabs of Iraq will have to concede that the Kurds, though Muslims, have never been Arabized. A prudent country would do its best to understand why the Kurds have never taken to the Iraqi flag; a prudent country would add to its flag the yellow color of Kurdistan. And a country keen to succeed would not expect the Kurds to accept a nation that slights their rights and their history. In the cruel play of the region's history, the Kurds have been the sacrificial lamb at the altar of Kemalist Turkey, Pahlavi Iran, and the Iraq of the monarchy. Now the Kurds are done with that history of subjugation, and the attempt to Arabize their region has resulted in failure. There are "extremists" among the Kurds, Alawi warns, and their map will have to yield to the logic of things, for American power—which sheltered the Kurds—is sure to distance itself from a bid for a Greater Kurdistan. This new world can't bear "frightening maps," and a reasonable Iraqi polity that comes to terms with these realities will have America as a "guarantor" of its place in the region against the ambitions of Turkey, and of Iran.

Hassan al-Alawi has given his country the gift of clarity. He has given the American project in his country its due. He is wistful, but resigned, that his country has not followed the lead of Germany and Japan in the aftermath of the Second World War—accepting America's stewardship and making the best of it. And he is unerringly accurate that the Americans are not in Iraq for the long haul. Three years after America struck into Iraq, there would be new limits on the scale of the American commitment. The budget request for fiscal 2007 included no new reconstruction funds for Iraq. The three-year $18.4 billion U.S. rebuilding effort had a mixed record: there had been corruption, contractor overcharges, and the burden of a virtually impossible security situation. And an audit of contracts that the United States had undertaken with $5.8 billion of Iraqi money was to expose a pattern of widespread waste and unfinished work. The accent now was on Iraq's ability to fend for itself. Fatigue and disillusionment with the corruption rampant in Iraq and with the virulence of the insurgency had done their damage. And over the horizon loomed new limits on the size of the American force in Iraq. The Iraqis would have to secure their own defense; no one had intended for this American expedition to "own" and claim Iraq.

As March 2006 came, the Iraq war acquired another marker, its third anniversary. It was hard to recall, amid the retrospects, that this war, now practically an orphan in the court of public opinion, was once a popular war. Seventy-seven percent of Americans surveyed in January 2003 had favored military action to remove Saddam Hussein. Now a minority of just 29 percent thought the war in Iraq was worth the cost. Revisionism had taken hold, as people abandoned what they had once written and advocated.

This wasn't the war they had signed up for, some of the new opponents of the war asserted. Recent American military interventions had been forgiving. There had been those interventions in the Persian Gulf in 1991, Bosnia in 1995, Kosovo in 1999, and there had been that swift campaign against the Taliban launched in the shadow of 9/11. These were virtual wars, affairs of technological mastery. (A lone suicide bomber, a boy in a Mercedes truck loaded with TNT, in Beirut, had inflicted more fatalities upon American forces on October 23, 1983, when he attacked the marine barracks on the outskirts of that city than had the army of Saddam Hussein in 1991.) This new campaign in Iraq was different. It was the war after the war that was to frustrate American will. And it was not just the insurgency and the combat. A foreign power good at releasing communities from the burden of the past, and from the limits and confines of narrow identity, found itself deep in the thicket of a culture defined by sectarian loyalties. An innately optimistic America had struck into a land steeped in a history of sorrow. In Baghdad, a thoughtful man of the Iraqi political class, Zuhair Chalabi, the minister of human rights—and a Sunni Arab from Mosul at that—assured me some weeks before this somber third anniversary that his country felt deep appreciation for this American war, but he cautioned that it would take time for this gratitude to come to the surface. The time left for this expedition would be determined the only way it could be in a democratic society—by popular tolerance and support. The custodians of American power were under great pressure to force history's pace.

On the Abandoned Lover's Bridge:
The Sorrow of Mussayib

I went to Mussayib, on the Euphrates, some forty miles south of Baghdad, two days after a terrorist had driven a fuel truck to the town square and detonated himself next to the cistern of the truck, killing nearly one hundred people in this Shia farming town. This was mid-July, in the summer of 2005; on my way to Iraq, I had read about Mussayib's calamity in a dispatch in the *Jordan Times.* In the article I read that fifty-nine of Mussayib's people had perished, that the terrorist had struck in the evening as people had come out of their homes to catch a break from the day's heat. By the time I got to Mussayib, the death toll had risen, and the town looked like the movie set for a scene of utter mayhem. There was soot everywhere, puddles of fuel and blood, and the hulk of burnt cars and the cistern of the fuel truck that had done the terrible damage. There were the black funeral banners of the Shia faith with the names of the victims. Overlooking the square, the balconies were charred and covered with soot. The flames had been horrific, more deadly than the shrapnel. Mothers had thrown infants from the balconies to escape the flames.

I had come to Mussayib with the deputy prime minister of the Iraqi government, Ahmad Chalabi. Our convoy had driven through the "triangle of death," a notorious stretch of land south of Baghdad, where the insurgents from the restive Anbar province routinely ambush passengers on the way to the Shia south and plant roadside bombs that target American convoys. Ahmad Chalabi knew the risks of this road: four of his bodyguards had been killed on it some months earlier. We came in a heavily guarded convoy, a fleet of Land Cruisers. After the main highway the road to Mussayib was paved in fits and starts. This had not been a place favored by the Baathist regime; with a touch of irony, Chalabi said that this must have been the way the countryside looked during Babylon, and perhaps it was even better then. No great history had played here. Hitherto, the town had been known for a timeless song about the abandoned lover lamenting his fate on the bridge to Mussayib. The song was in part a play on words, for the word *mussayib* itself meant an abandoned place, and the jilted lover was made to weep for himself on the "bridge of abandonment." In the lyrics, a male lover laments his fate: "After you my eyes know no sleep/In the book of fate it is written that after you my soul is parched/I stay awake, I watch the stars and wonder why my beloved never comes/I befriend the night and my worries come and my soul withers." The song's most accessible line, *"ala Jisr al-Mussayib Sayyaboni* (on the bridge of abandonment they abandoned me)," had been this town's claim to fame. Now an unknown man in a fuel truck had given Mussayib a new kind of recognition.

No one knew the identity of the assailant. He had left no will or testament. He may have been a man of Saudi Arabia, for the Saudi border was nearby; he could have come from Arab countries further afield, for the neighboring Anbar province provided sanctuary and support for jihadists eager to kill and be killed in a campaign against Shia "heretics" and against the Americans who had made possible the Shia rise out of subjugation. (It is an article of faith in Iraq that suicide operations are the preserve of the Arab jihadists, that the local insurgents rarely if ever commit suicide.)

Ahmad Chalabi had come to console this town. Though a man of Baghdad, he knew this world of the Middle Euphrates, shared the Shia faith of its population. One of the towns in the badlands of the triangle of death, Latifiyya, had been a childhood haunt of his, the location of a vast agricultural estate owned by his father. There had been endless grief in Iraq, and these stoic people were glad for the visit, oddly grateful that their sorrow had been noticed by a big man of the Baghdad government. Trailed by a phalanx of bodyguards and aides, as well as local officials and policemen, he came to the hospital, where the spectacle was one of unmitigated misery, the smell of the dead unmistakable through its wards. There were rows of people being treated for burns, and there were victims of shrapnel. A young Arab-American reporter for Knight Ridder, who, like me, had been given a ride to Mussayib, read my mind: she had been here two years and had seen suffering before and told me that these patients here at least had bedsheets and that in other places the burn victims had to lie on sheets of plastic. Chalabi made the rounds, and there was a discreet and quick visit to the women's ward; the visiting politician asked his entourage to stay outside that ward.

In the wards I walked through, every patient had his tale of grief. A young bearded man on his cot, heavily bandaged, Sattar Hamza, said that he had lost his brother, and that the body had not been found and identified, for many had been incinerated beyond recognition by the flames. Another man, Imad Abdulamir Ibrahim, said that he lost eleven members of his extended family. It was a strain for him to talk, and you could tell that he was a proud man, that he was uncomfortable with the prying eyes, and with the physical exposure of much of his body. A woman clad in black sat by her brother's bed and wept for a nephew she had lost. "Find us a way out of this," another wounded man pleaded with the visiting politician. Chalabi had no wand with which he could ward off the terror; the man pleading for a way out must have known that. Still, the plea was made, and this official visit was all this town had.

"Our blood is *halal,*" permissible and cheap, "because we are Shia; we are singled out for this violence," said an agitated man who had pushed his way to the front of a crowd that had followed Chalabi to the police headquarters. A young Shia cleric with a white turban, Muqdad Kazim al-Janabi (his tribe has Sunni and Shia "branches"; he came from the "good Janabis," a policeman standing next to me said) laid out the grief and the needs of this town. With a cleric's command of the language, he said that he represented the office of Grand Ayatollah Ali al-Sistani of Najaf. "Mussayib desperately needs fire trucks and hoses and an emergency service. We could have saved a large number of victims, at least eased the suffering of the wounded." He wanted "respect" from the police, a change in their ways, an acknowledgment of the abuses of the old order. But even this cleric knew the limitations of the army and police units: they were heavily infiltrated by the insurgents; they turned a blind eye to the perpetrators of terror, supplied intelligence to the insurgency. They were outgunned in this swath of the country, the forces of order. The insurgents had better cars, better weapons, the chief of police ruefully conceded. He spoke of a town not so far from here, a Sunni town, Kafr al-Sakhr, as a place where the insurgents and the jihadists plot their deeds of terror, a place that aids and abets this terrible work. The forces of order could not cope with this terror: their own ranks had been among the victims of the terror.

We left the town by the bridge with the famed name. Down below, the Euphrates flowed, wide and full by this town, offering a contrast of its own to the grief of Mussayib. And by the foot of the bridge, I caught a glimpse of a solitary man standing there casting his reel into the water.

Before returning to Baghdad, the convoy drove to a power plant nearby: it was under construction; a big Texas firm with the initials STIS was building this plant. It was "state of the art," nothing like it even in the United States, the chief technician, Carl Bloomfield, told us with the drawl and manner of the rural South. He had been here for four months, he said. He planned no vacations; there would be more months to come. He had done this kind of work in other Third World lands, and this place "is as dangerous as they come." When it kicks in, he said, this plant will give a big boost to the country's electricity grid. The solitude and desolation were overwhelming. We had found the power plant at the end of a side road of gravel and dust. Bloomfield and his technicians were not the only Americans on the premises. There was a military contingent of the 155th Separate Armored Brigade. There were Iraqi soldiers as well, sandbags and heavy fortifications all around, and there were the signature American trailers behind the barricades. We might have been the first visitors in a long time; the young army captains who received us were glad for the visit, and for the interruption of the routine. I could not help feeling a touch of melancholy, thinking of these young Americans away from everything familiar to them. I knew that this was the life they had chosen, but I could not shake off the feeling of sadness that came upon me. They were unfailingly polite and curious. They had seen and heard the explosion in Mussayib and spoke of this region and its people with tenderness and pity. Many of their workers hailed from the devastated town: the soldiers did not yet know how many of them were killed, what became of their families, and how many would turn up for work after the obligatory period of mourning.

The technicians from Texas and the American soldiers were walk-ons in a battle as old as this landscape. In one of the trailers, there was a billboard, in Arabic, meant to instill hope in the Iraqi soldiers. Its words mourned for the "martyrs of Mussayib" but proclaimed that terror was a sign of weakness, that its perpetrators had already lost the battle for the new Iraq. Doubtless, in villages and towns not so far from here, beyond the stretch of desert and the palm groves, there were men in safe houses biding their time, possessed of an entirely different reading of this battle for Iraq.

• • •

A fortnight later I traveled the same road southward out of Baghdad. I was going to the Shia holy city of Najaf. I was to get an audience with the reclusive Grand Ayatollah Ali al-Sistani. Ahmad Chalabi was to see him and I was to come along. I did not quarrel with that piece of fortune, and the pessimist in me assumed that the arrangement might fall through. I was content that in the worst of cases I would see Najaf and get a reprieve from Baghdad's confinement.

Nowadays Baghdad is a sore to the eye, a place of cement barriers and barricades. Nothing relieves the senses here. The discarded junk and machinery and abandoned weapons of the old regime add to the desolation. A traveler taking the road southward is treated to the unsentimental logic of the Baathist regime. The approaches in and out of the city were places that Saddam Hussein had been careful to control. By the side of the road there were towns and housing settlements for his praetorian guard and for the men of his regime. The Saddam regime would have lasted a thousand years had the Americans not come in and decapitated it. The system of control had left nothing to chance: the capital was like a city under siege. And the drive past these suburban outposts is a drive through a hostile land. Some of the housing gave away the alienation of the regime, its separateness from the land: in a country with precious little stone, where houses are made of brick, there were ostentatious houses of stone, obscene against the background.

After the triangle of death, and the stark desert road, we drove deeper into the Middle Euphrates. Now the landscape altered; this was historic Babylon. After Baghdad, this landscape was a gift. We drove past rice paddies and groves of palm trees, and the earth grew gentler. There were kilns for firing the mud into bricks—an inheritance that no doubt dated back to the Sumerians. And there were houses of great simplicity with gardens pleasing to the eye, and thatched huts where fruits and vegetables and cans of soda were sold. The old tyranny had given this people precious little; one of Saddam's big palaces stood there, large and mute, out of place in the land.

Before long, after the bustling town of Hilla, we arrived in Kufa. We were now in the cradle of Shiism. It was in this town, in its very mosque standing there like a buttressed fortress, that the first of the revered twelve imams of the Shia, Imam Ali, the Prophet's cousin and son-in-law, had been assassinated in AD 661. It was to this place that his son, Imam Hussein, was traveling, at the invitation of its people, when he was abandoned and cut off at the plains of Karbala, and where he was beheaded in the year 680. The chroniclers of early Islam assign a big role to this city in the spread, and early political troubles, of Islam. It was from this place, for all practical purposes a garrison town of the Arabs, that much of the conquest of Persia was launched. This had been a volatile town, its rivalry with Damascus in the first century of Islam a centerpiece of the fight between orthodox Islam and the partisans (the literal meaning of the word *shia*) of Imam Ali and his successors. The imprint of Shiism was everywhere—in the black banners of mourning announcing the deaths and the deeds of the departed, in the graffiti on the walls denouncing the crimes of the Baath Party and proclaiming loyalty to the Shia movements. There was a martyr's square and a place commemorating Ayatollah Muhammad Baqir al-Hakim, a political-clerical leader who had returned from a long exile in Iran to be struck down by a huge bomb in the summer of 2003. The portraits of Grand Ayatollah Sistani were everywhere, and so were sketches of the early saints of the Shia faith. Sunni Islam bans visual representation, but the Shia faith is altogether different. And by now, those figures of the seventh century are represented and known in a fashion that approximates photography. The faithful willed the features of these saintly men.

The holy city of Najaf was not far; it was an extension of the sprawl of Kufa, and the golden dome of the Shrine of Ali could be seen glittering in the sun. A place of memory and faith, the holy city is associated with all sorts of legends. In one pretty story, one of Noah's sons refused to board the Ark, choosing instead to stay atop a mountain that covered present-day Najaf. Then the mountain crumbled, drowning Noah's son, and a river appeared. Eventually the river dried up, giving the city its name—*najaf*, or dry river. In a specifically Shia legend, after the assassination of Imam Ali in the mosque of Kufa, his body was loaded on a camel, and the believers agreed that he would be buried where the camel knelt down. The camel wandered into the desert, then rested on a little rise. And there the city of Najaf was born. History was to bring this city all the sanctity and all the heartbreak of Shiism.

We drove to a simple lane in the souk. I was not prepared for the simplicity of Sistani's house; it was a few steps removed from the shops, in the middle of an ordinary alleyway. A young cleric was waiting for us; with him were three or four younger men. There was nothing on the premises to announce the presence of the country's most powerful man. A piece of white and blue batik hanging from a line was all that separated Sistani's house from the street outside.

Beyond the steps of the house, there were two adjacent rooms, one full of visitors, the other completely empty. We were met by Sistani's principal aide, his son Muhammad Reda, forty-two years of age, a wiry man with stylish glasses. He wore no flowing *abaya*, but a tight-fitting black tunic, a white *thoub*, and the black turban of a sayyid; this was the attire of a young cleric at work, announcing a kind of serious simplicity. He greeted us warmly; he embraced me as though we had known each other for ages. I needed this comfort, for the sanctity of the town and the prospect of meeting the great figure of Iraqi Shiism had unsettled me. After we took off our shoes, Muhammad Reda led us to the empty room.

The room itself was airy and spacious, painted in a soft white, with a high ceiling, an air conditioner humming overhead, and a white fan. There were no chairs or tables; Persian carpets covered the entire floor. I had grown up in and around houses that displayed Persian carpets, and these were of middling quality. On the floor, against the walls, there were two rows of cushions; the walls were stark, with no adornment save for a glass frame with a calligraphy that read, "Blessed are those who listen and from what they hear abide by that which is good."

Baghdad had come to Najaf; a politician from the highest reaches of the government had come to call on the jurist. Sistani's son sat straight up on his knees facing us and spoke with candor of the state of affairs in the country. "We are disappointed in the performance of the government. We supported the emergence of this government, held out high hopes for it, told our people to support it. Now we can't show our faces to the public, because we are so embarrassed by the condition of the country. This is an ordinary home; when the electricity is cut off from other homes, it is cut off from this house. There is no security in the country. The forces of order can't be trusted, and the Americans will not let them defend the people and do their duties." He found it "strange and inappropriate" that the members of the National Assembly had voted for themselves an allotment of $50,000 each at a time of "widespread need and misery." He had no patience with those calling for an end to subsidies on the price of gasoline; "the people are in distress, and they won't take to this measure."

Sistani's son had delivered his father's message. He had done it skillfully, but he had spoken as a friend of the deputy prime minister, and he warded off with no small subtlety Chalabi's query whether he, Chalabi, should resign from the government. The son now left the room through a back door that led to his father's private quarters. We were meant to wait. He had not said that we would be given an audience, but it was a safe assumption now that there would be a meeting with the ayatollah. I had been given this experience through no great effort of my own, and I was eager for it to come about.

We were not to wait long—just long enough, it was obvious in retrospect, for the son to brief his father about his meeting with Chalabi. Sistani's entrance was majestic and simple at the same time. Great, powerful men rarely if ever let us in on how they view themselves, but surely this man knew the reverence millions have for him. I had seen the photograph of Sistani available everywhere—the visage stern, perhaps unapproachable. In person, the face was entirely different, friendly and welcoming, the cheekbones and features recognizably Persian. Sistani is said to be in failing health, but I saw no evidence of that. He was a man of medium height, quite trim, and the white beard against the black *abaya* and turban added to his striking aura. He did not hold himself aloof. He embraced Chalabi, whom he knew quite well, and he greeted me in the same way. I was being received as a man of faith, my American nationality perhaps regarded as secondary to my birth to a Shia family. He then sat down in a corner on a cushion clearly marked for him. A silence settled on the room. He might have been praying, I thought, but there was not the murmur of prayer. It was a moment of privacy for him. He put his hands on his folded knees and welcomed us, thanked us for making the trip from Baghdad.

When Sistani spoke, the voice was steady, the Arabic rigorous, and the words were carefully chosen. But I heard Persian intonations and a Persian way of pronouncing Arabic letters. The jurist had come to Arabic as a second language, a language of learning. His care with the language was that of an immensely learned man.

Chalabi told the jurist of our visit to Mussayib, of the grief he had seen. The sorrow of Shiism was endless, the politician said, and it has been like this for a long time. He thought, he added, of a great book on the martyrdom of the Shia written in the tenth century by a celebrated author, Abu al-Faraj al-Isfahani (899–966). That author had not been a Shia partisan; he had been moved by that deep Shia sorrow that persists to the present. The scholar in Sistani took the bait, but only slightly. He talked of that author and of the Shia inheritance. "But *azizi,* my dear, let us not talk of history. Let us talk of the present." The country was in the throes of a decisive fight over a new constitution, and Sistani's message to the man of the government was unambiguous. "I want you to do everything you can to bring our Sunni Arab brothers into the fold." That community had stayed out of the national elections that had taken place nearly six months earlier, and the national balloting had not worked to its advantage. Sistani pressed for a change in the nation's electoral laws to give the Sunni provinces a greater share of the national power. "You are the elected government; the people voted for you; they went to the polls under mortar rounds." He spoke of this democracy with reverence; he would take no credit for that democratic opening, "for the credit belongs to the people." He spoke with feeling of what the people had endured before the fall of the Baath dictatorship. "I myself was here for thirty-five years. I saw how the people were treated; I saw the abuse. It was not the life of human beings that they had lived. For myself, I want nothing. *Azizi,* my dear, I live in a rented house, and you know how I live. It is important to go on, to do all we can for this tormented country." No, he did not seek the resignation of this government, he only wanted greater competence in the service of the Iraqis.

I had no burning questions of my own. I had come for a sense of the man, not for an interview. I asked him about the terror at play in the world of Islam, of the use of religion in the service of a cult of violence; I added that there were many people in the Islamic world grateful for the mercy and the moderation he has continued to preach. He sidestepped the compliment and spoke about the terror. He listed recent deeds of terror with precision, in their sequence—deeds in Iraq, the transit bombings in London, the terror attacks in the Egyptian resort of Sharm al-Sheikh. He would provide no names of preachers who winked at the terror. But he hoped that the Islamic world would shake off this scourge. He returned to Iraq; he had faith, he said, in the good judgment and decency of the Iraqi people, in their desire to be done with the violence. I asked him if he had been surprised by the enthusiasm for democracy shown by the Iraqi people in their national elections. No, he said, it had not come as a surprise; they had yearned for it, and it was they who deserved the credit for that break with the terrible past.

We took leave of Sistani and then bade his son farewell. Alleyways

keep no secrets, and this was no ordinary alleyway: we came out to
find a bank of microphones and television cameras waiting to report
on the politician's visit to the religious leader. Chalabi has mastered this
art form: he had come, he said, to visit Sayyid Sistani, and to consult
with him about the state of public affairs: it was natural to come to
Najaf to seek Ayatollah Sistani's advice and to brief him about the
business of the government, and to seek his opinion. The politician
was a secular man through and through, but there had been a profound change in Najaf's fortunes, and these people crowded in this
alleyway knew that. There had come reverence to the jurist; there
would be no Baathist terror squads in the streets of the holy city. Sistani had confined himself to his residence for a number of years during the terror, not even setting foot in the shrine of Imam Ali, just
across the street from his home. Now the secular rulers came to
acknowledge the role of the clerical institution of Najaf in the governance of the land. A worldly politician with the best of Western education and a huge fleet of Land Cruisers and armed bodyguards had
come to the door of the ascetic man of religion. By the strictures of the
faith this was the way the world ought to be ordered. The jurist
would not govern; the men of religion would "enjoin the good and
forbid evil," as the tradition had it. They would advise but keep a discreet distance from the rulers. In their turn, these rulers would not
trample over the religious and moral scruples of the faith.

"For fourteen centuries, no ruler has given us justice, but we have
endured. Above all we are repelled by the shedding of blood, because
our blood was shed for so long and by so many." The man providing
these reflections was Sayyid Muhammad Reda al-Ghurayfi, the influential overseer of the shrine of Imam Ali. We were inside the shrine, in
the overseer's private quarters. Ghurayfi was a widely published scholar,
fifty-one years of age, short and portly with a gray beard, his brown
abaya hanging indifferently over his shoulders. Where his mentor, Sistani, exuded calm and elegance, Ghurayfi communicated enormous
joy and a love of storytelling.

We had come to see Ghurayfi and to pay the shrine a respectful
visit. The bodyguards with their weapons were to stay outside the
main gate. The sun bounced off the white marble floors of the courtyard, and the place was bathed with light. It was a two-story structure
with calligraphy on the arches of the balconies, and white and blue

tiles. The place was not particularly large: the feeling was one of intimacy rather than awe. The effect was one of great serenity: an old woman clad in black huddled in a corner as children played about her. An old man found a place in the shade and sat there taking in the coming and going around him.

The overseer's private chambers had a touch of casual elegance. There was a huge sketch of Imam Ali; there were comfortable seats set in a rectangular arrangement against the walls, and the obligatory white fan overhead. Ghurayfi filled this room with his buoyancy; a book manuscript he was working on was piled up in front of him. There was to be no formality in this man's presence. A group of young seminarians, devotees of Ghurayfi, added to the casualness of the atmosphere.

Still, the history Ghurayfi gave us was the sorrowful Shia narrative. "The Shia of Imam Ali are born to suffering. We have to be in a constant state of agitation. This agitation made us what we are. We are born oppositionists." A new power had come to the Shia, but Ghurayfi seemed averse to giving up the agitation. He was sure that the world would always deny the Shia; to him this agitation was precious, the scorching brand of the faith. He gave me his personal history—the adversity he recounted at odds with the joy of the man. "Go ahead, write it down," he said as he saw my hesitation, caught as I was between the protocol of listening to him and the desire to put down in my notepad what he had to say. "I was born in 1954, in Baghdad, to a family from Najaf of Bahraini origins. My family has branches in all Arab countries. I am a son of this religious institution. I have been thoroughly immersed in it since I was six years old. I lived right here in this sacred place throughout the long years of oppression. I went nowhere else. Since childhood, I have distributed leaflets and scribbled graffiti on the walls. I have had no other passion save the life of this place." He took pride in this personal history; he narrated it to the appreciation of the young seminarians, who clearly relished being in his presence and loved his mastery of the language, his knowledge of religious subjects and modern poetry alike.

I threw him a predictable remark about the influence of Iran, in the form of a question about Iran's weight in the affairs of the Shia of Iraq. The question was less weighty than his reflections, and he fielded it with an edge of impatience. "We have nothing to do with Iran. We share the same faith, but we are different. We don't want Iran to rule

us." He beheld the world beyond Najaf with a sense of confident supe-
riority. "Najaf is the sun, it transcends all, and all the other cities of the
Shia world revolve around it, live off its illumination." He did not like
political Islamists, whether Shia or Sunni. He told me that an envoy
had come to Najaf from Beirut on behalf of the leader of the Party of
God, Sayyid Hassan Nasrallah. A breach had opened between the
Party of God, with its virulent anti-Americanism, and the Shia clerical institution in Najaf; the Shia of Lebanon had not supported the
coming of this new order in Iraq. "We told him to go back and to tell
his leader that we are constantly praying for his undoing and his eternal damnation. We used to respect him as a resister to Israel's occupation of his land; Najaf always stood with Lebanon. But we are through
with the likes of Nasrallah."

Of Iraq, he spoke with cautious hope. "Nothing could be worse
than what we have seen under the Baath. After 1991, the secret police
had the run of our city. Their agents were everywhere. People of
unknown origins turned up in our seminaries as seekers of religious
knowledge. Turbans covered heads of people with black hearts and evil
intentions. We preserved and purified this place. This country will
have to be healed. I told Muhsin Abdul Hamid [a leader of a Sunni-
based political party] that we are in the same boat, but that people on
his side were busy puncturing this boat, and that we will all drown
together if he didn't do all he could to stop the subverters. These Sunnis are a people of power; they are accustomed and addicted to it. They
will have to change to accept the new reality."

The conversation had lasted into prayer time. For me, this was a
moment of delicacy. I am of the Shia faith, but I have never prayed,
nor did I know the ritual washing that precedes the prayer. I was
tempted to dissimulate, but I was spared. He read my hesitation, and
he and the people in his entourage left for the prayer hall. On his
return, he offered me the ritual invocation given to those who perform
prayer, *"Qiballah,"* may God accept our prayers. "We have no compul-
sion in religion," he said. "We ask only for discretion. If people want
to sin, then do it in private. If people want to drink, let them do it
without great noise. If a woman wants to unveil, let her assume the
burden of her decision."

We had stayed long, but we were not to be released. He extended to
us the rare honor of lunch on this sacred ground. He does not normally eat on the grounds of the shrine, he said, but this was a special

occasion. A lunch was laid out on the carpet, on the other side of a low divide in the room, a simple fare of chicken and rice and watermelons and soft drinks. He had held us with his delivery; for me, it had been easy, the straight man providing promptings and openings for his pronouncements. Now he wanted me to display what I knew. He wanted to know what America "intended for Iraq." I circled his question, told him that I was writing a book and that I myself was wondering about the same thing. I said that my sense was that the Bush administration wanted a release from Iraq's burden. His response came as no surprise to me: he did not look with favor on the prospect of American withdrawal. I don't have his exact words, for I had set my notepad aside for the lunch. But he phrased his sentiment artfully in the form of a question: Why should we assume, he said, that the American withdrawal would be a good thing? As a religious scholar, he would not trumpet support for an occupying power. But he was a shrewd man; he had been here—he had insisted on that—as his people and his sacred city suffered. In the course of this conversation, he would offer no diatribe against the Americans. He was full of curiosity about American society; he displayed a keen interest in the cultural fault line between the "red" and the "blue" states in the United States. He wanted to know where I had been on the morning of 9/11, and he spoke of that day with dread and with sympathy for the victims.

It was time to depart: he handed me a white manila envelope in which he had put two of his books and some postcard-size photographs of the shrine. He gave me as well a slab of marble, wrapped in a green cloth—a sacred gift, a prayer stone. I carried the books back to Baghdad and brought them with me to New York City. I thought I would read the books to honor the author, to better understand him. The marble with the green cloth I left in Baghdad, on the dresser, in the place where I had been staying.

On a flight out of Baghdad to Amman, I was given one of those fragments of Iraq's history, pained but easily available, that offer themselves everywhere. Across the aisle from me sat a dignified man, formal in the way of people of small towns, well dressed in a brown suit and a tie with a wide knot. We had met in Suleimaniyah the year before, he told me. His name was Adel Karim, and he was a deputy minister in the Iraqi government. He was a Kurd, so we fell into a conversation about Kurdistan. I told him that I had gone to Halabja, the town that had been on the receiving end of Baathist terror in 1988, where chemical weapons and nerve gas had murdered no fewer than five thousand people; I told him that I had seen the monument erected in memory of the victims of Saddam Hussein. Quietly, and with great reserve, he said that his older brother, Omar Khawar, was the man in perhaps the most searing image to reach the world from Halabja: a man clutching a bundled infant in his arms, struck down by the nerve gas. I recalled that photograph, but this man of forty-five, sitting across the aisle, had a different knowledge of it. His older brother had been a man of fifty-eight then. He had fathered eight daughters, loved them all, but had tried without success to have male children. He had been on the verge of giving up, late in life, when luck delivered him twin boys. He named them Ahmad and Mohammed, and doted on them. It was never known which of the twins he had been holding when the tyrant's forces struck. It was never known where he was buried. All his children, male and female, had perished with him.

The man across the aisle was traveling to Amman on government business. It was hard, he said, to root out Saddamism from Iraq's public life, but he and his colleagues were trying. In the way he told the story, he offered me another variant of Iraq's gift that I found repeated time after time: the reminder that life renews. For odd reasons I can't explain, he reminded me of the man I had caught a glimpse of at the foot of the bridge in Mussayib, casting his reel into the water after the terror and the flames had engulfed his town. I had had an anxious ride to Baghdad's airport. I had nearly missed my flight, I had overstayed my visa, and this had given me more grief, another obstacle. Now this fellow passenger had given me this tale—a reminder of where I had been, and what furies and real grief had blown through that land.

CHAPTER 1

"Tell Me How This Ends"

T he stranger does not have to be unduly curious: the sorrow of Iraq offers itself easily and is everywhere. In August 2004, on my third visit to Iraq since the fall of Saddam Hussein's regime, on the grounds of the American compound where I was staying, a young Iraqi Army officer, Abbas Fadel Abdul Sahib, a man of rugged good looks and quiet intensity, treated me to the details of his life. He was in the midst of a hectic—and futile—search for his dearest friend. The friend had had a new American car, and he and the car had disappeared a fortnight earlier. The officer spoke of his friend with great sorrow. He had warned him about the hazards of owning an American car amid the banditry and the breakdown—and the envy. Abdul Sahib described him as a man of gentle disposition: the officer feared the worst for his friend and dreaded visits to the man's family, the heartbreaking news that there was nothing new to report on yet another day.

Then the grief for his friend flowed into his own. Several months earlier, Abdul Sahib had been asked to tape an appeal on television calling on former army officers to return to the service of the country. It was easy to see why he had been chosen for that assignment. He had not only good looks but, as I could see immediately, a way with the Arabic language: melodic and fluent, gracefully mixing precision with evocative power. He had not hesitated when he was asked to perform this task. He loved his country, he said, and was eager to do right by its new possibilities. With that television broadcast, he had become a marked man. His house was attacked, an infant daughter had been killed, and his mother had lost her eyesight in the attack. A volley of gunfire aimed at him had gone astray and he had survived, living on his nerves, staying a step ahead of the insurgents and the potential assassins.

His country bewildered him, Abdul Sahib said, and he felt pity for it. "Foreigners have come our way, Americans who have sacrificed their sons and daughters, and still Iraq does not rest and know repose. The world over, people yearn for progress, but look at us: the electricity we sabotage; the oil pipelines we blow up; the foreign businesses we drive away. After thirty-five years of tyranny, we were given a chance, but it is on the verge of slipping away. There is no governmental authority anywhere, and everywhere it is the law of the gun and the masked men." He did not know if sanity would ever come to his country. Above all, he told me, what he would love most now was some distance between himself and this volatile land. He was desperate to leave and had no way out. He wondered aloud if there was a foreign assignment available somewhere, but he had little hope that an escape would materialize.

The desire for escape was to be the theme of a conversation with Laith, a younger man, in his midtwenties, a graduate student of industrial design in Baghdad. He had waited and pined for the war, he admitted, in the hope that the toppling of the regime would enable him to quit the country for a foreign land. He told me that he and his friends lived with the anxiety that the Americans may not carry through with the war, and that the dictator may be spared yet again. The war had come as a great relief, he said. But the hope of emigration had not been fulfilled. "No one wants us now that the world outside thinks we are terrorists and saboteurs and murderers," he said. He was working for the Americans while waiting for the chance to find a new home outside Iraq, in "safe and prosperous lands." The access to the American compound in the Green Zone was a nightmare, he said. The security was tight, and he would have to wait in a long queue. The long lines were a boon to the insurgents: they could identify those working with the Americans, take down their license plates, target them for assassination. He had given up on commuting by car after one attack on him. He now varied his route, in a steady effort to outwit the would-be assailants. The war came; it had given him a break. But as we sat down for breakfast, there played upon this young man's face a mix of relief and disappointment. This country could not give him what he wanted, and the Americans could not open up the borders of the world for him. His needs—the needs of youth in a country that no longer met the expectations of its sons and daughters—were bigger and older than this war. Laith and the lucky few of his peers working for the Americans would take the foreign power's money, but gratitude was another matter, and an open recognition of it always hard to come by.

Iraq never yields a tidy truth: In the shadow of insurgencies by Shia and Sunni alike, on an August morning preceded by a night when the mortar shells had been steady and ominously close—"They're getting better out there," a veteran soldier in my trailer park had said of the insurgents and their fire—I had been given the chance to visit with the country's interim president at that time, Sheikh Ghazi al-Yawar, a tribal Sunni Arab leader from Mosul. Sheikh Ghazi hailed from the Shammar tribe, one of the great tribal federations comprising no fewer than five million people in Iraq, Syria, Saudi Arabia, Kuwait, and the United Arab Emirates. (The Shammar had a substantial Shia branch, and this was of no small consequence to the identity of Yawar.) No proof could be more convincing that a new world was in the making in Iraq than an audience with this immensely gregarious and engaging man. If this new order of things sought to demonstrate its break with Saddam Hussein and his megalomania and cult of terror, Sheikh Ghazi was something of a casting director's dream. Of all of Iraq's principal leaders, he was the only one who dressed in the traditional Arab garb—a white kaffiyeh, a *thoub,* and an *abaya;* yet, for all this attire's traditionalism, there was something familiar and accessible about him and, dare I say, a measure of Americanism given him by his graduate education in engineering at George Washington University. He had the ease of a natural politician; his tribal background had given him that touch. I had come to see him with a colleague of his, Deputy Prime Minister Barham Salih. We navigated an obstacle course of checkpoints—Iraqi police cars, American Humvees, a zigzag of barriers. Nothing had been left to chance. The man himself could not have been more casual. There was no official pomp, no great pretension, in him; he was at ease with himself. His residence within the Green Zone was being readied for him; in the meantime we found a quiet, small room of great simplicity. There was pounding upstairs, so he called on an aide and asked for it to stop. But after a brief interruption, the pounding resumed, and he was thoroughly and genuinely amused that his presidential authority was light enough that the construction crew could defy it.

The geniality of Sheikh Ghazi was deceptive: he had great political dexterity. I had been told he was engaged to marry a Kurdish woman; I had been assured by the Shia politicians that the man was free of any taint of anti-Shia bigotry. If there was a new Iraq, this man was a good embodiment of it. He had run a successful business in Saudi Arabia; in Iraq, he was without enemies. He had a thorough command of the region's politics. He was unsentimental but still oddly optimistic about Iraq's neighbors and strategic environment. He was preparing for a state visit to Turkey; he knew the details of Saudi and Syrian politics. He had confidence in Iraq's ability to emerge intact and as a "big player" in the politics of the Arab world. He had a lucid reading of recent Arab history, of the place of Iraq in the Arab balance of forces. He saw a "natural" rivalry between Egypt and Iraq, with Syria and Saudi Arabia always pulled into that fight. These neighboring states, he believed, would come around, for the stakes for them in an Iraq that would come apart were huge indeed. In strict constitutional terms, this man was Saddam Hussein's successor. I was aware of this thought; I could not drive it away. And the modernism and the modesty and the warmth of the man were for me an unintended but powerful vindication of this war.

I was to see Sheikh Ghazi again, a couple of days later, over dinner. He had invited a relatively small group of people, ten or so guests—journalists, Deputy Prime Minister Barham Salih, the Iraqi-American author and academic Kanan Makiya, who had gone back to Iraq to document the cruelties of the despotism of Saddam Hussein, and Fouad Masoum, the newly elected chairman of the Pan-Iraqi National Conference. The group was as varied as Iraq itself—Kurds, Sunnis, and Shia—and their comfort with one another was easy to see. The heat of the day had given way, and there was to the evening a surprising casualness and informality. The conversation flowed about Sheikh Ghazi; he never dominated it. He loved gossip, and he had an irrepressible sense of humor. A thorny battle against Moqtada al-Sadr had entered a critical phase. There were worries that some Shia members in the cabinet had been holding back from a decisive showdown with Sadr's militia; there was truculence in the Sunni triangle, an unwillingness on the part of Sheikh Ghazi's own community to partake of this new order. But there was serenity in the man, and among his guests there was the spirit of a cultured elite with a chance at a new world.

Taking leave of Sheikh Ghazi and his guests, I waited outside for the security people to give me a ride home. It would take a while, but as I stood there with Fouad Masoum, I could only wish for this order to stick—and to prevail. The manners and elegance of Masoum—a

Kurdish politician and former academic in his midsixties, a highly educated man with a doctorate from Cairo University—were of this old culture at its best. A man with an open face and an easy smile, he was now at the center of things, with the convening of the National Conference. He spoke of Iraq's "factions" with patience and entertained decent hopes for the success of a parliamentary-pluralist undertaking in Iraq. He was not given to illusions about Iraq; as one of the founders of the Patriotic Union of Kurdistan, he had seen plenty of disorder around him. But a new possibility appeared within reach, and he looked at the prospects over the horizon with some optimism.

Fair enough, these men had not by their own effort brought down the Tikriti tyranny. Mosul, the hometown of Sheikh Ghazi himself, was being contested now by the insurgents. The fragile peace that had held in that city was breaking down. There was agitation within Mosul, and there could be felt there the subversive reach of the neighboring Syrian regime winking at the jihadists and granting them easy access to Iraq. And no one could say with confidence what would become of this new order were the American protectors to pack up and leave, were the Nepalese Gurkhas and the young American soldiers guarding the homes of these interim leaders to be withdrawn. But for anyone who knows the ways of Arab politics—for anyone with even a scant familiarity with the courts of the Egyptian and Saudi and Syrian rulers—this order in Iraq was a decent undertaking. It was a sad commentary on contemporary Arab political life that this embattled experiment had become a repository of the hopes of Arab liberals and secularists, but such was the landscape of the Arab world.

It was not just this decent man at the helm of the state who provided a measure of hope and a break with the past. In the Shia holy city of Najaf, as the battle with the young cleric Moqtada al-Sadr threatened to overwhelm the interim government, rescue came from the revered jurist Grand Ayatollah Ali al-Sistani. Things were stretched to the breaking point: Sadr had ignited the crisis in early August when he ordered an attack on a police station after the arrest of one of his aides. He then sought sanctuary in Najaf, turning the mosque of Imam Ali into a virtual fortress. The rebel had warmed up to his role: he goaded the government and challenged the Americans. At one point he appeared in public with one hand bandaged, saying that he had been injured in the fighting. But if Sadr had worked his crowd to a fever pitch, there was mastery to Sistani's performance as well. He had been in London for emergency medical care, but Najaf needed his authority, so he cut short his stay in England. In truth, Sistani had been double-crossed by the interim government of Iyad Allawi. He had gone to London with the assurance that no attack would be ordered in his absence. For all practical purposes, this betrayal sealed the fate of Allawi's government with the jurist. Sistani was now done with Allawi; he returned via Basra, made his way back to Najaf in a motorcade. Tens of thousands had converged on Najaf to welcome him back and to proclaim his primacy over the holy city.

Moqtada al-Sadr had gambled and lost and was looking for a way out. He had put into the field untold numbers of followers, the over-whelming majority of them ill-equipped and with only the most rudimentary military training. There were unofficial estimates that no fewer than a thousand of his followers had been killed in this round of fighting—by all accounts, the heaviest since the end of "major combat." In the American compound, there were American officers who spoke with resignation and dismay of the cynicism of Sadr, of the uneven fight their soldiers had had with the Mahdi Army, of the lack of mercy Sadr had shown his own men. It was estimated that a vast bulk of Sadr's fighting force consisted of young boys, thirteen to fifteen years of age. Sistani's intervention couldn't have been more timely. The word had gone out that an Iranian delegation had called on Sistani when he was still in London and had tried to convince him of the legitimacy of an Iranian role in Najaf's—and Iraq's—affairs, but that he would have none of it; it was said that the meeting had ended in acrimony. Sistani's pride, perhaps the very source of his authority, lay in his independence. And his return to Najaf was presented to the faithful as the deed of a man who had consulted neither the Americans nor the interim government about his plans or the timing of his return. He had done it for his religious guild, for the peace of the holy city, and for Iraq. In an ideal world, it would have been better, a secularist leader in this government confided to me, had Sadr been thwarted by the interim government itself. But there was hesitation within the cabinet, and this had made Sistani's intervention the only way out of this crisis of Najaf.

I had come to Iraq from Kuwait City. I had been given a lift on the C-130 transport plane that makes the trip three or four times a week between the military airport in Kuwait and Baghdad International Airport. I had made this run before; now again I was given an intimation of America's great power and reach, and the isolation of its efforts so far away from home.

There were the KBR people—Kellogg Brown & Root—who did the paperwork and processed the passengers. In America, I would have seen the KBR people as ordinary people at home, going about their normal lives. But there they stood out, and for me, I was always thrown back on my memories of when I was a boy in Lebanon and the Americans were a breed apart. Years in America—the bulk of my adult life—had taken away from me that sense of the differentness of Americans. Amid the heat of Kuwait, against the desert background, the Americans stood out again. A country of extraordinary reach had pushed deep into this region: its people moved men and machines, put up "pizza inns" and sandwich shops and calling centers and blue U.S. mail boxes, but the foreignness of the effort, and of the men and women doing the work, was impossible to shake off.

This war, this undertaking, had speed and surprise. America did not have an imperial edifice in Araby. It had paid this region attention intermittently. It had known little about Iraq. Yet a full-blown imperial venture had been "stood up" with breathtaking speed. The passengers who made the C-130 flight with me—having arrived by bus, from a Hilton resort hotel with bungalows and a Starbucks coffee shop—were a varied lot. There was a State Department official, an Egyptian-born Arabist and interpreter dispatched on a temporary assignment to help the American embassy bring its interpreters and Arabic language people "up to speed." He was a man of enormous ability and deep knowledge of this region. There was an intelligence operative who had known Beirut in its better days: he had kicked around this region and was in the know about its ways. There was a cop, a Kansan, who was returning to Mosul from home leave. He was not a worldly man; he had a contract working to train Iraqi police units. He would not question, he told me, the rationale of this war. Leaders in the know, men and women whose authority he would never question, had called up this war, and this policeman, who had had an earlier career in the military, had ended up in Mosul.

The C-130 arrived in Baghdad at midday: the heat was elemental and fierce. The wind whipped up the desert dust. There was to be more waiting here for the armed convoy that would take us to the American compound—once Saddam Hussein's Republican Palace, then the headquarters of the Coalition Provisional Authority, now home to the American embassy. There was little shade to be had: I sheltered in the shadow of the PX, alongside two young soldiers, army privates—a soldier who hailed from Louisville, another from Arkansas. Weather was the natural topic for three perfect strangers. It was terrible here, they both said, but they had just returned from Qatar, where the heat was merciless. Their ease of manners was amazing given the place and the assignment they had drawn. The young soldier from Louisville had plans for attending college in his hometown when this assignment was over; his counterpart from Arkansas was not so sure, but he was proud of the football prowess of the Razorbacks, the team of the University of Arkansas, and he could see making his way there after Iraq. There was challenge and danger, they said, on patrols through Baghdad, but the young man from Louisville said that he was partial to the children of Baghdad, that he delighted in their company, and that they deserved something better than they had known. I had seen this earnestness among the soldiers many times before, and I would see it again in the days to come. But it always lingered with me—the soldiers' clarity of mind, their ability to stay true to their tasks amid the dangers and the hell of this war.

In the fortnight that followed, I was to stay in the American compound, in a trailer park. My neighbors were the soldiers and the civilians manning this American enterprise in Iraq. I had no fixed assignment. The traveler's luck would see me through: I would see what I would see. It was important for me to be here, to see for myself the play of things. Two prior visits—in October 2003, then in March 2004—had given me snapshots of this war and this country. But the ground had shifted in the intervening months, and from afar I could not be sure that the truth of what I had seen had held. There was a "sovereign" Iraqi government in place now; the American regency had been (nominally at least) brought to an end. But the violence of Iraq, and its difficulties, had multiplied. One of the military's genuine stars, the soldier-scholar Lieutenant General David H. Petraeus, had been sent back to Iraq for his second tour of duty (in the preceding year, as a major general, he had been commander of the 101st Airborne and had run the affairs of the northern city of Mosul and the larger Nineveh province around it). He had been given the make-or-break assignment of this war: leadership of the Multinational Security Transition Command, charged with the "standing up" and training of 250,000 Iraqi soldiers and police units and border guards. I had gotten to know General Petraeus: he had earned a PhD in international relations at Princeton University; he had done teaching of his own at West Point. He had a tolerance for curiosity and was willing to let a "low-maintenance" observer hang around on the outer margins of his work.

There were truths the American compound revealed. On days when I could spare the time, I would take in the wide range of people pulled into this American enterprise. There was a huge cafeteria, in the ballroom of this sprawling palace, which fed more than two thousand soldiers and civilians a day. The people in this bubble within the Green Zone took their meals here. There were soldiers of fortune (this was my label for them), security people—Lebanese, South Africans— who had come here for the money, providing security details for those venturing beyond the confines of the compound. The Lebanese were no doubt alumni of the wars of Lebanon: they were young men who had done a fair amount of bodybuilding, and they kept their own company. There was a South African, beefy and heavily bearded, with a T-shirt a size or two too small for him, and the muzzle of a gun artfully showing through the top of his backpack. There were former ambassadors, Arabists who knew this region, rotated into Iraq from postings in other lands. There were people who had worked on the Hill, back in Washington, who had brought their skills here, applying them to the care and maintenance of visiting members of Congress. There was a Department of Justice lawyer working with the Iraqi Criminal Court, a Minnesotan with zeal for the law, sure that the American legal tradition was a boon and a potential inspiration for the Iraqis.

There was earnestness and devotion aplenty. A polite and self-effacing middle-aged man, a naturalized American citizen of Lebanese background, Bassem Houssami, in the political section, spoke with feeling of his work: "We can't take twenty-five million Iraqis to America, so we bring America to them." He had come to America late in his life, and its optimism and openness had been a great gift, and he knew, he told me, that were Iraqis to give themselves this chance, they would emerge better off than their neighbors and they would shake off the deadly habits of their past.

By chance, in this compound, in the same trailer park where I lived, I was to meet one of the best of my former students, from Johns

Hopkins, Clifford Russell. A man in his early thirties, even in his graduate school days courteous and polite beyond his years, he had been drawn to development work. He had worked in Cambodia and Africa; he was now an adviser to the Iraqi Ministry of Transportation. He had been here three months. His work was dangerous; it took him outside the Green Zone. He had ridden the trains throughout the country. He had come to terms with his work. He would let the Iraqis he encountered on his projects know who he was; there was no need, and no advantage, in trying to conceal his identity. He had his way of coping with it all: he read no daily papers, watched no television broadcasts. He worked in the field, returned to his trailer, and kept his head down. His sympathy for the Iraqi people was of a piece with his temperament, and with my sense of him from his student days. He gave the Iraqis high marks for industry and skill, for their desire to improve their lives. He knew the dangers on the road, but he beheld a kind of optimism that this effort would not come to grief.

This was a twilight war, a thin line between ordinary life and mayhem, and the life of the compound showed it. There was a swimming pool and a clubhouse under tall palm trees. (The despot had been kind to himself and his own.) At times, by the pool, there was a colonial overhang, a tropical feel. At dusk there would be young men and women, soldiers and civilians, doing laps in the pool, grilling steaks under the trees, trading stories of their day outside the bubble. But Baghdad was not the tropics: for several nights, at the beginning of my stay, the false peace by the pool was shattered by mortar rounds, and sirens ordering everyone to take cover indoors. Invariably, the evenings ended up like that: peace in the late afternoon and at dusk, then shelling at night.

"Tell me how this ends": this was one of David Petraeus's mantras. Superbly articulate and confident, he had a way of flinging about his more revealing utterances as he went about his daily work. Leadership is a gift, something you recognize when you see it but cannot quite render. Petraeus came by his sense of command in a natural way. Intense and wiry—physical fitness was a personal code—he moved about with speed and restlessness. He had "cannibalized" the best of the American military to put together his command. There was Elizabeth Olivia Young, a Rhodes scholar, an impish young captain, the star of her class at West Point. There was a lieutenant colonel, a military lawyer, Mark Martins, with dazzling academic credentials; Martins, on loan from his work for the chairman of the Joint Chiefs of Staff, General Richard Myers, had an intellectual curiosity matched by his decency and grace of manners. There was the public affairs officer, my guide through this maze, Captain Steve Alvarez, from the Florida National Guard, a man of striking looks and intellect, who had put on hold a successful career in information technology back home and the plans for a second child. And there was Petraeus's steady companion, his shadow, a Palestinian-American translator by the name of Sadi Othman. In this compound, Sadi was known everywhere and to everyone by his first name alone. "Translator" does not quite capture the full sense of what he did; he was more like a cultural interpreter of the ways of the Arabs, his leader's bridge, at times, to the Iraqis. Sadi, orphaned as a young boy, had made his own way in the world. A lanky six-seven, he had played basketball in Jordan, had made his way to a Mennonite college in Kansas, had worked as a New York City cabbie. Answering an advertisement for translators, he bonded with Petraeus in his command in Mosul, hooked up with him again on this second tour of duty.

Sadi knew the cast of characters—Iraqis and Americans—caught up in this drama. He had seen plenty in his time in Iraq. He had been there when two helicopters crashed in Mosul, had seen the wreckage and the maimed and the dead. He had held an Iraqi policeman, spoken to him, as the man expired in his arms. He never used the word exactly, but he had a sense of pity for Iraq. Loyal to his boss in a kind of eastern way, he amplified his boss's optimism, but doubts always broke through the reports of progress and accomplishments.

Amid the hectic motion, Petraeus kept his cool—and his own counsel. The inner workings of his mind, I came to suspect, he never quite revealed. He knew the hopes invested in his work; his mission was the linchpin of America's exit strategy. He would train the Iraqis, a national army would stand and fight for its country, and Americans would be able to make an honorable exit. The country's borders were porous—terrible borders with Syria and Iran, more ambiguous but still troubled borders with Jordan and Saudi Arabia. There were estimates that a force of thirty-two thousand border guards would be needed, and the country barely had a fraction of that available to it.

"This is not April" was another of Petraeus's favorite declarations. The reference was to the searing American experience the preceding

April when Iraqi units trained (barely so) and equipped by the Americans melted away or switched sides and joined the insurgents in Fallujah and Sadr City. This time, Petraeus had vowed, would be different: the troops would fight, they would not "cut and run," the training would be better, the vetting of officers more thorough, and these soldiers would withstand the call of their clans and sects.

I accompanied General Petraeus on his excursions to the field. On one occasion, he had a congressional delegation, five members of the House of Representatives who were touring the region. He took the visitors to see the training of an Iraqi intervention unit, an elite special force. Despite the barrier of language—and Sadi always did a masterly job of rendering his boss's exhortations and battle sermons—the bond of Petraeus with these Iraqi units was quite special. The training was being done in an old military compound, an officers' training college. There was dereliction everywhere: a hothouse was run-down and its glass ceiling shattered, the vegetation around it wild and unkempt; a clock tower that harked back to a simpler age stood amid the decay.

An Iraqi brigadier and a young lieutenant colonel proudly displayed the military maneuvers of their young recruits. The brigadier was from Mosul, Petraeus's old base, a Sunni Arab, and was clearly a protégé of the American commander. The lieutenant colonel, Safeen Abdul Majid, a Kurd in his midthirties, had an easier way about him than his more senior colleague from Mosul. He was articulate, and he knew this was a group of some importance. "Don't leave," he said in Arabic, with Sadi translating. "We are not yet ready for independence. If you take a man deep into the sea who does not know how to swim and leave him there, he is sure to drown. The Iraqi people are not used to freedom. They have been deprived of it for four decades. They took freedom to mean the right to commit murder and arson: they need to be firmly governed, and then they will be ready, and you will have done well by us, and we shall be grateful." From afar, there were the standard public opinion polls that Iraqis were done with American tutelage. Two months earlier, in one such poll by the Independent Institute for Administrative Civil Society Studies, 92 percent of Iraqis had reportedly described the Americans and their coalition partners as "occupiers," and only 2 percent had embraced them as "liberators." This officer—and many Iraqis encountered along the way—gave voice to a sentiment at variance with the public disaffection with the American presence.

If this occasion was meant to be a pep rally, something happened to give it a solemn and serious edge. Wayne Gilchrest of Maryland, a quiet congressman, older than his colleagues, with nothing flashy or sunny about him, spoke to the Iraqi recruits. More than three decades earlier, Gilchrest had seen combat in Vietnam. He had been wounded, and thirty-six hours had passed before he could be evacuated from the field. He spoke to the Iraqis as "fellow soldiers," told them that they were his "brothers," in the way that all patriotic soldiers are brothers. He recognized in them, he said, and saw in their eyes the same courage and love of comrades and fear that he had seen among American soldiers in Vietnam. "You will make your country proud," he told them. Americans will soon be on their way out, he said, and Iraqis and Americans would be friends, and Americans would look back on this "friendly nation" as a vindication of their effort here. "We have no schemes on your country. We want to see you make your way in the world and succeed."

In the evening, there came to the American compound reports that this unit had seen combat in the afternoon in Sadr City and that three of the men had sustained injuries. "This is the way of combat; this is the way combat culture is formed," Petraeus said to me as I ran into him making his way to his trailer at the end of a long day. "We want to recede into the background," he said. (This too was one of his favorite maxims.) Few Americans had been looking for an imperial burden in Iraq, but here it had been acquired in the aftermath of a lightning victory. The foreigners were determined to transmit to Iraqis the ways of professional combat and the ethics of soldiers, but Americans were learning things in the bargain. A captain spoke to me of the clash between the way he had been trained, the attitudes he had brought with him, and the surprising ways of Iraq. "They stab each other in the back," he said of the Iraqis. "You train them, assume all is well, then they slip back into the ways of their sects and clans. They don't trust themselves, and they don't trust their fellows." I had known this young officer a while. There was a streak of perfectionism in him; he was hard on himself. He had wanted this assignment, pined for it. It was his first exposure to foreign lands and foreign ways. He conceded that he had to rein in his "idealism" as he went about his work.

For all the soldiers of fortune and the contractors such wars attract, there was no shortage of idealism in this undertaking. I think of

Richard Shammas, an Iraqi-American interpreter who was hit by a
mortar round. It was the randomness of war. He had sustained, while
in his trailer park, a terrible injury to his shoulder and a minor one in
his leg. The word had gone out in his circle of friends and acquain-
tances. I went with General Petraeus and Sadi Othman to see him at
the hospital. He was about to be taken out of the country to Germany,
then home to the United States. Sedated and heavily bandaged, he still
showed a grace, gratitude for the visit, and an odd acceptance of
what had happened. In Petraeus he had the ideal visitor: in 1991 the
general had been shot in the chest in a training exercise when an
infantryman had tripped and discharged his M-16 rifle. It had been a
very close brush with death, and Petraeus drew on that experience to
buck up Shammas's spirit. "You will be as good as new before long,
maybe better with physical training and therapy. Believe me, I know."
There was no hesitation in Shammas: he said that he had not told his
family back home about his injury, and he was certain that after his
recovery he would be back to resume his work.

There was cruel irony to Shammas's injury: it had come after several
nights of mortar attacks. The next day, unexpectedly, the night came
and it was still and quiet in the Green Zone. That night the insurgents
were not heard from.

Knowledge of a different kind about Iraq and about Iraqis came to me
when I went north to Kurdistan. I flew with then Deputy Prime
Minister Barham Salih to his hometown and political base in
Suleimaniyah. This political leader and technocrat, born in 1960,
the son of a judge, had made his mark in that part of the country in
the Kurdish regional government. He had known brief imprisonment under the Baath, then had made his way to Britain, where he
completed a doctorate in statistics and computer modeling. Having
represented the Kurds in London and Washington, he knew the world
beyond the hill country of Kurdistan. He spoke Arabic, Kurdish, and
English with equal ease. A can-do man and an optimist of enormous
will and talent, he had left his base in Suleimaniyah to be part of this
interim government. He was going to visit his family and be with his
mother and to call on his political leader, Jalal Talabani.

After the checkpoints and the gunfire and the mortars of Baghdad,
the tranquility of Suleimaniyah came as a surprise. There was peace in
the streets and normalcy, a boom of sorts in the building trade, houses

going up everywhere, a public park with gardens and a lake where Iraqi military barracks and facilities had once stood, a sunlit library of exquisite design with books tumbling out of the shelves, computer terminals, a children's reading room. A kind of modernity was being grafted onto the place, the peace of a people who know that fate can turn cruel at any time.

On my first day there, I was invited for a private lunch with one of Kurdistan's most accomplished writers, Noshirwan Mustafa Emin, a man who straddles the worlds of literature and politics. Graceful and reserved, perhaps oddly shy for someone so political, Emin had been born in Baghdad in 1944 and had come into his own in a bicultural world: the culture and language of his home were Kurdish; the politics at the University of Baghdad, where he had studied, were those of Iraqi and Arab nationalism.

We were joined by two of his children, young men seventeen and nineteen years of age, who were home for the summer holiday from their studies in England. This was good family life, and it showed. The boys were glad to be in Suleimaniyah. "We are mountain people, and we love the light of this place," one of the boys said. He said it with some shyness, as one offers an unexpected thought. He wearied, he said, of the darkness of London. We were at the foot of the mountains. From the large windows, the hills were near, and the settled life seemed like a way of staying close to the mountains.

Emin and I spoke in English: it was his choice and mine as well, though every now and then an Arabic expression or phrase offered itself. (His sons, like so many young Kurds, knew no Arabic, for the Kurds had made a life for themselves in their own language, in the years of their estrangement from the rest of Iraq.) I asked him if Kurdistan was enough for the Kurds: the question was a stranger's response to the mountains and the isolation of the place. He did not hesitate. No, he said, it was too small and vulnerable. Baghdad would be useful for the Kurds as a counter to the weight of Iran and Turkey and Syria. Iraq had been cruel to the Kurds, he observed, but it was important for the Kurds to hold on to the idea of a federal state based in Baghdad. "It is good for the Kurds to have a port in Basra, pipelines that reach into Syria and Saudi Arabia. It is both wise and good to work through a larger government based in Baghdad." He cited the success that the Kurds had had when they turned back a proposal by the Bush administration to introduce forty thousand Turkish troops into Iraq. "Had we been alone," he said, "we would have had quite a struggle with the Americans. But we were not alone in wanting nothing to do with this scheme: we were joined by the whole Governing Council—Sunnis and Shia alike—and that proposal was turned back."

This man knew the Arab world as it was: he spoke with sorrow and disappointment of the indifference of the Arab states to the suffering of the Kurds. He said that the Arabs were now on the ropes, in the grip of a deep crisis, but it was still important for the Kurds to have access to that Arab world, if only to have wider horizons as a people. This man had not lived a sheltered life, but he spoke of Iraq's prospects with measured hope. He would not allow himself a severe judgment of American policies in Iraq. "No one here," he said, "had the power to topple the regime, and this must be remembered as we speak of particular American deeds." He spoke, but with irony, and free of shrillness, of the Americans' shoring up U.S. borders while leaving Iraq's borders open to the infiltrators from Iran and Syria. He would not offer a precise view of Iraq's prospects, but he thought the political center would hold, that the sheer brutality of the alternatives would bring Iraqis to their senses.

In their heart of hearts, my hosts in Suleimaniyah preferred the purity of their world: they spoke Kurdish during the Friday lunch that brought together family and close friends at the home of Barham Salih's mother. In deference to me, they would switch to Arabic or English, but I assured them that I would not feel left out and that I preferred to see them at ease during a family gathering. They had made a world of their own—small but theirs. They had gone, so to speak, to Baghdad, sent the best of their own—Barham Salih from this part of Kurdistan, the foreign minister Hoshyar Zebari from the town of Arbil to the west, and others as well—to give this new order a chance. But a line of retreat was open to them. They wanted nothing to do with a Shia theocracy or a pan-Arab Sunni state. They were doomed to live with ambiguity, in this halfway house between independence and a federal Iraq. The flags on public display gave away the ambivalence at the heart of their political life: now and then an Iraqi flag was displayed, but everywhere there was the flag of Kurdistan—a yellow sunburst on red, white, and green stripes.

"We're two separate nations: everything about us is different—language, culture, history." This was the view put to me by the celebrated Kurdish poet Sherko Bekas. I had come to visit him in a publishing house over which he presided. I was told that he was a poet with a remarkable feel for the language—and the geography, and the pain—of his people. His Arabic—the medium of our conversation; he knew no English—was melodic. I could imagine the beauty of the language of his daily life and his craft.

There was a hardness to his view of the border, the separation, between Arabs and Kurds. Though he presided over an Arabic edition of a literary magazine, *Sardam Al-Arabi,* he had arrived at an acceptance of Kurdistan's estrangement from the Arabs. At my request, he gave a brief rendition of his political and personal odyssey. He was a "son of this town," he said, born in 1940. His father had been a celebrated poet in his own right. He himself, educated in Baghdad, had started writing poetry in the early 1960s. In that decade, he drifted into Kurdish politics and the cause of autonomy for the Kurds. He then made his way to the mountains and to the "armed struggle." In 1975, when history turned cruel to the Kurds and a rebellion supported by the shah of Iran was abandoned and betrayed by that monarch, the Kurdish resistance had collapsed, and Sherko Bekas had been sent into "internal exile" in Ramadi. He was to know another period in the mountains in 1984, with the forces of the preeminent leader of this region, Jalal Talabani. Four years later, he sought a period of peace in Sweden, where he lived for three years and knew a measure of literary success. When Anglo-American power provided Kurdistan with protection in the aftermath of Desert Storm, the poet was back in his town, serving for a brief period as minister of information and culture. The place he worked, the publishing house, was modest and dimly lit, but it was his and his colleagues'. I could not see this man trading this world for the uncertainties, and the hazards, of Baghdad. (Six months later, I would read of Bekas taking the lead in a nonbinding plebiscite in which Kurds were asked to choose between Iraq or an independent state of their own. No surprise, 99 percent of those surveyed had chosen independence.)

The independence of this world was made clear to me on an evening drive into the hills to visit Jalal Talabani. A narrow road snaked into the mountains. The hills below and around looked majestic, stark, and endless. These hills would be wild with vegetation come spring, I was told. Fog was blowing in, and it was getting cooler. At the roadside, families had congregated for picnics and dinner.

There were fires being readied for the preparation of the meals. There was no privacy here, and no great need of it.

Talabani's heavily guarded residence was elegant but within the bounds of taste. This was no palace in the Saudi mold and size. A gregarious, overpowering man in his midseventies, Talabani was surrounded by a dozen or so of his colleagues. He filled the gathering with his presence. No host could have been more attentive: he urged more food on me. We sat in his garden under a starlit sky, enveloped by the mountains. The heat—and the insurgency—of Baghdad seemed worlds away. There was no trace here of the anti-Americanism that dominates many an evening in Arab lands. Talabani spoke of America and Americans with genuine fondness; he wanted more Americans in Kurdistan. This man had known combat; in his youth, he had been a Marxist. But in his mountain lair, he harked back to an older role, a chief of his people. He took pride in the peace of Kurdistan: a Chinese restaurant had opened in Suleimaniyah, and he took pleasure in that. Indeed, he had some of that restaurant's dishes added to an already huge dinner. Talabani exuded optimism. In the scramble for this new Iraq, he had a seat at the table. He had his younger colleagues represented in the interim government. But he had these hills, and the town below, and the armed militiamen defending this turf as well; they were what he relied upon.

The next day I was to go to the town of Halabja, little more than an hour's drive away. This was where the Baath despotism had committed mass murder with chemical weapons in 1988; the Kurds had turned the place into a monument of Kurdish sorrow and memory. The landscape alternated—patches of green, fields of sunflower seeds and pomegranates and corn broken by fields of wheat and barley and by the threshing floors of peasants. (I knew and loved those threshing floors from my childhood in Lebanon; politics yielded in my thoughts to the timeless ways of the land.) The villages by the road were forlorn and poor places that the Baath utopia of power and progress had never reached. I had not been prepared for this neglect. I had seen rural poverty in other Middle Eastern lands, but these villages dug into the hillsides with houses of rough stone and flat mud roofs were poor even by those standards. The satellite dishes atop the shacks and the mud houses were an ironic reminder that the "timeless" rhythm of the countryside had been broken.

There was something else that broke the rhythm and stood out against the landscape: mosques of a bluish color, large and elaborate, by the shacks. I did not count the mosques, but practically every village had one. They were the gift of the "charities" of Saudi Arabia: the plaques at the entrance to these mosques acknowledged the names of the charities and of the donors. Deildar Kittani, a secular Kurdish woman—with years of education in England behind her—heaped scorn on these charities. These villages were bereft of roads and clinics and schools, she said, but no one had come to their rescue. This organized religious drive had blown here, bringing disputes and bigotry in its wake.

On a clearing at the foot of the hills, a monument to the victims of Halabja had been erected. It was elegant and subdued. Inside— inspired by the Vietnam War Memorial—on a black wall were inscribed the names of the five thousand people who perished when the Iraqi Army struck in March 1988. There was installation art and black-and-white photography that honored the dead. The director, a dignified, quiet man, led me through the monument.

I then went through the town itself—a small, bustling place. The commerce in the shops offering the usual fare of out-of-the-way places was an odd consolation that life renews itself. I paid a visit to the cemetery on the town's outskirts. Rows of neatly arranged headstones suggested method and care. One plot was reserved for a family of twenty-four people who had been cut down that day in 1988. This was the burden of Kurdistan's—and Iraq's—history.

It was on our flight back to Baghdad—by Black Hawk, courtesy of the American forces—that the land below yielded hints and suggestions. At first we flew over the pastoral lands of the Kurds, hills and meadows. The farmers tilling the soil, the men on tractors, and the children could be seen greeting the choppers. The gunners on both sides of the helicopters invariably waved back, and there was a discernible ease in the way they scanned the ground below. Then the landscape altered: we flew over the Zagros Mountains, a stark brown moonscape of stone and desolation. Before long we would be over Kirkuk—a town rich with oil and ethnic tension. The flares of the oil wells burned against a merciless sun. There was another kind of desolation here— the junk of the old regime, its discarded trucks and tanks. To refuel, we landed at an air base, and its dereliction spoke of a regime that could purchase modern technologies but could never maintain them or connect them to the larger life of the land. "God, Country, Leader" was the slogan emblazoned on a decaying hangar.

More desert stretched out beneath us: the machines of a great power flew over an occasional mud village, shepherds with their flocks, herds of camels. Now and then we came upon ponds of bluish water, surprises amid the desert. Then the land shifted again: we had come to western Iraq, and the thick groves of palm trees were like a sudden gift after the hard earth. They were achingly beautiful, and the mind could imagine a tranquil life amid those groves. This was Baquba, in the Sunni Triangle, I was told. The gunners grew more attentive. Gone now were the children waving at the choppers. A group of young boys could be seen below, in their long white *dish-dashas*. They gestured in the motion of throwing stones at the choppers. Within minutes, we would be over Baghdad, flying low and fast, in a zigzag pattern, over the clutter and the rooftops of a huge, sprawling city, on the banks of the Tigris, shimmering in the sun. The Americans (when they could dodge the missiles) controlled the skies, and the native city stretched out beneath us, dense and impenetrable.

"Heartbreak and heartening moments do go hand in hand here," General David Petraeus wrote to me, in a note of December 22, 2004. A day earlier there had occurred one of those grim episodes of terror that punctuated this war. A homicide bomber had struck in Mosul, in a mess tent, as soldiers had gathered at lunchtime. It was not a mortar round that had struck the mess hall, as earlier reports had indicated. There was material evidence consistent with a "suicide vest, as well as ball bearings," investigators were quick to conclude. Fourteen American soldiers, four U.S. civilians, three Iraqi guardsmen, and an unidentified foreign worker had been killed in the attack. Petraeus had known the scene well—this was Mosul, after all, his first command in Iraq; the American troops who were there had replaced his own 101st Airborne Division—and apparently, he knew the "non-Americans" on the scene as well. In his note, he wrote, "We lost three of 'our' Iraqi troopers who were doing well up there in that tough environment and also one of our advisors."

Nothing was easy here; the sense of comradeship had to be balanced against the harsh insecurity. In my limited time in Iraq, I had many a meal in these mess tents. The fare, and the salad bars, and the presentation were all American through and through. They spoke at times, these mess tents, of a power eager to reproduce the culture and the diet of home in an alien, unsettling place. Iraqis and others drawn from foreign lands the world over had access to these places. There was no safety here and there were no clear front lines. Wholesale trouble had come to Mosul: the city—Iraq's third largest—was no stranger to disorder. In the aftermath of the subduing of Fallujah, Mosul had become the epicenter of the insurgency. No fewer than two hundred Iraqi recruits into the army and the police, one knowledgeable source estimated, had been murdered in cold blood here for their collaboration with the Americans. There had been desertions from the ranks, as recruits balanced their needs for a new life and for steady wages against the terrors. The city's police force had disintegrated as insurgents opened a new front here, a substitute for Fallujah. The country's interim president, Sheikh Ghazi al-Yawar, had ducked that fight in—and over—his hometown. He promised he would go there to help in the restoration of order. But he had stayed away, and the hope that this Sunni Arab leader would step forth as a national leader—the hope, I have to concede, that I had entertained when I met him several months earlier—had been dashed. In the aftermath of the bloodletting in Mosul, the Americans would conduct the obligatory sweep of the city. It was doubtful that they would find their way into the inner reaches of Mosul, that the place would yield its secrets, turn in the insurgents, and turn its back on the underground and on the purveyors of terror.

It was not an American investigation that revealed the workings of the terror attack in Mosul. News from Saudi Arabia laid out what had transpired at the mess tent. A young Saudi medical student studying in the Sudan, Ahmad al-Ghamdi, twenty years of age, had pulled off the deed. There had been held for him a funeral ceremony in Riyadh, and his family received throngs of people who had come to offer their condolences. There was nothing unusual about this homicide bomber or about the sorts of things his family said about him; by now the profiles of these jihadists and the statements of their parents had become repetitious. The young man was in the second year of medical school. He couldn't have been a particularly promising student; the Sudan would not be the place of choice for a young Saudi of talent or means. His family had given him enough money to complete his academic year. But he had withdrawn the money a mere fortnight before the terror attack and had made his way to Iraq through "one of the neighboring states." The point of crossing was left unspecified; this was a Saudi paper doing the reporting, so discretion was in order, but it was important to make it clear that the jihadist had not crossed to Iraq from Saudi Arabia itself. No one had noticed that he had grown particularly zealous or fanatical about the faith, his family claimed. In his family's narrative, he had succumbed to the call of "the extremists" because he was "young and alone" in the Sudan. Once in Iraq, he had had a single telephone conversation with his father. He had made clear to his father that he had come to Iraq to pursue the holy struggle; his father had tried to dissuade him but had not been able to do so. (America had encountered young men from the Ghamdi clan before. Two Ghamdis, Ahmad and Hamza, were among "the muscle" aboard United Airlines flight 175 that crashed into the South Tower on 9/11. Another Ghamdi, Said, was aboard United Airlines flight 93 that was forced down in Pennsylvania by its heroic passengers.)

This tale of the Saudi jihadist spoke to the broader breakdown in Iraq—and in Mosul, to be exact. A stranger with no knowledge of the geography or the social milieu of Mosul had been able to penetrate an American base. No doubt there had been careful preparation for this deed of terror, and there had been help for him from the Iraqi security forces themselves. Mosul was Baathist country now; the old security operatives, with Syrian help and connivance, had their way in this city. They could wear the uniforms of this interim government and take its salaries while providing intelligence to the insurgents. A young man from Saudi Arabia—speaking a wholly different dialect of Arabic—had to be taken and guided through the maze of Mosul. The peace had come apart; the rise of the Kurds in and around Mosul had triggered the wrath of the Sunni Arabs of this brittle city. A foreign jihadist willing to kill and be killed walked into a receptive environment. The perpetrators of this deed of terror played to the audience within and beyond Iraq. They had videotaped the entire operation. They must have been ominously close to the base, on its perimeter, as their camera caught the sound and the picture of the blast.

"I would welcome a civil war," an astute Iraqi with a thorough knowledge of the country's politics said to me from his home in Baghdad. I had reached him, by phone from New York, after news of another terrible day in Iraq. On January 4, 2005, the governor of Baghdad, Ali Haidari, had been killed, along with several of his bodyguards. It was a killing in broad daylight. The insurgents had grown increasingly brazen. The man in Baghdad who would welcome a civil war was speaking with bitter irony, but only partly so. In a civil war, he said, there would be a "balance of terror" in which armed groups would check each other. A measure of restraint would come if men and neighborhoods were left to fend for themselves. But Iraq was stranded in no-man's-land; the insurgents struck with abandon, and the interim government was powerless or unwilling to stop them. My informant described what had befallen the governor of Baghdad: his convoy had come under "concentrated fire" for fifteen minutes; the insurgents had not been timid or eager to flee. No one had come to the rescue of this high official; there had been a prior attempt on his life, and this time the insurgents succeeded where they had failed before. The forces of order—the battalions of police and commandos the Americans were training—were heavily infiltrated by the insurgents; the Ministry of Interior had become a stronghold of operatives of the old regime. The bureaucracy kept no secrets; the whereabouts of officials, and the routes they took on official business, were conveyed to the insurgents. The system was riddled with bribes and corruption, and there was rampant insecurity throughout the society. And there was official abdication: at any time, he added, a good number of the ministers were out of the country. He gave the example of a cabinet minister who had spent several months living in a hotel in Amman.

In this man's telling, the interim government and its American patrons were leaning over backward in their desire to accommodate the disaffected elements of the old regime. What aggrieved him was the indulgence given to the operatives of the old regime who showed no signs of remorse, no indications of a willingness to change their ways. The American regency had come to a decision that de-Baathification had not worked, and this decision was a boon to elements of the old regime. He gave the example of the head of the security services, one Muhammad Abdallah Shahwani, as a man of the former regime now fully rehabilitated and back in the swing of things. There was one case in which rogue elements within the security services settled old scores that my informant found particularly galling: the security services had raided the home of a legendary leader of the Marsh Arabs in the south, Sheikh Abdul Karim al-Mohammedawi. A follower of this man, who had been a bitter and celebrated foe of the Saddam Hussein regime, had asked the officer conducting this raid if he knew who Mohammedawi was. "Yes, we know him well. We had many clashes and confrontations with him and his forces when we were in the Fourth Corps," he said, referring to his old army unit.

The man describing the chaos then turned a corner in our conversation. The elections were four weeks away, and he was thoroughly immersed in their details, passionate about their promise. The American stewardship of Iraq may not have been brilliant, but he conceded the gains the country had made, was grateful that President Bush had held firm in the face of suggestions that the elections ought to be postponed. He was in his country—he had known years of exile—and he was free to speak on an open phone, without fear that the "visitors of dawn" would haul him off to prison or worse. He was a claimant to his country, and he could see something better taking hold amid the insecurity and the chaos. Two or three days earlier, in his neighborhood, a little after midnight, he had seen two policemen going around tearing down election posters and placards. He had expected better from the police; he saw this as evidence of the ability of the Baath Party apparatus to make its way into the new state. Still, he allowed himself a note of satisfaction that this was the new Iraq and that there were election posters and banners in the streets of his country. He was proud of the tumult of these elections—the wide range of political parties competing for places in the National Assembly—and took it all as evidence that his deeply wounded country could still find its way.

By happenstance, the day before that episode in Mosul, President George W. Bush had been forced to speak to Iraq's troubles in a rare press conference. His reelection behind him, he offered a subdued reading of Iraq. "Now, I would call the results mixed in terms of standing up Iraqi units who are willing to fight. There have been some cases where when the heat got on, they left the battlefield. I fully understand that. . . . On the other hand, there were really some fine units in Fallujah, for example, in Najaf, that did their duty. And so our military trainers, our military leaders have analyzed what worked and what didn't work." It was the better part of wisdom to be cautious. Iraq's surprises knew no end. He was "wise enough," he said, not to give a "specific moment in time" when the mission in Iraq would be seen to have reached a successful outcome, and when Iraqi units would be ready to secure their own liberty. The next day would bring news of Mosul's calamity. The stakes in this war had grown with the sacrifices, and the gains had become harder to pin down, abstract perhaps in the face of concrete sorrow.

Some eight decades earlier, in 1922, Winston Churchill, then Britain's colonial secretary, had spoken with despair of the new Iraqi polity British power had willed and put together. The Hashemite monarch, Faisal I, imposed on this realm by British power, had proved hard to manage, and Churchill had penned a memorandum to his prime minister. "I am deeply concerned about Iraq. The task you have given me is becoming nearly impossible. . . . Faisal is playing the fool, if not the knave. . . . There is scarcely a single newspaper—Tory, Liberal, or Labour—which is not consistently hostile to our remaining in this country. . . . At present we are paying eight million a year for the privilege of living on an ungrateful volcano." Had he had Churchill's gift for the language, the American president entangled in Iraq might have allowed himself sentiments of a similar kind. But by the appearance of things, this American leader was wholly different. He would not quarrel with history or argue about its verdict. He had prevailed in an election in the midst of this Iraq war, and he had been vindicated. "We had an accountability moment, and that's called the 2004 election. And the American people listened to different assessments made about what was taking place in Iraq, and they looked at the two candidates, and chose me, for which I am grateful."

These remarks were made five days before his second inaugural. With mayhem in Iraq, there was no stirring oratory about Mesopotamia. On the eve of this inaugural, a news poll conducted by the *Wall Street Journal* and NBC News delivered the sobering news that a 52 percent majority of the American public now believed that the Iraq war was not worth the human and financial costs, and that 54 percent of those surveyed believed that America's standing in the world had eroded. Bush's doubts—if they existed—had to be hidden, for this was a president who insisted that he led by "gut and instinct," that he would stand on principle. The war in Iraq was now folded into a wider campaign on behalf of liberty and freedom. Though the inaugural speech had not a single reference to Iraq, that difficult war hovered over the occasion and the president's larger abstractions. "Our country has accepted obligations that are difficult to fulfill, and would be dishonorable to abandon." No relief was in sight: a stoical American public was being asked for patience. Nothing was said about

Iraq's mayhem, or about its readiness for liberty. The inevitable change had taken place. What had begun as a contest over Iraq's ways had become a verdict on America's will.

"I firmly planted the flag of liberty," President Bush said of the message of his inaugural, and of what he was attempting to do in Iraq. This was on January 26, in that brief interlude between his second inaugural address and the first Iraqi elections of January 30, 2005. Freedom was not a policy, the realists were quick to point out, and even the American leader himself seemed to seesaw between putting tyrannies on notice that America would be the friend of their dissidents and opponents, and then sending messages of reconciliation that there would be moderation and care in the conduct of America's policies abroad. There remained of course the sobering truths of Iraq and its heartbreak, and Winston Churchill's refrain: that flag of liberty had been planted atop a volcano; Iraq was its unforgiving self. The president's remarks about the flag of liberty had been made on yet another harrowing day in Iraq. Hours earlier, a marine helicopter had crashed in a desert sandstorm near the Jordanian border, and all thirty-one service members aboard had been killed, while six other American soldiers had died in combat that same day. This would be the single deadliest day for American troops since the beginning of the American invasion twenty-two months earlier. Iraq's roads were filled with danger, and the marines were being ferried by helicopter to provide security for Iraq's elections. The broad assertions about the spread of liberty battled with the steady carnage.

The Iraq war seemed to present the odd spectacle—a veritable reversal of intellectual galaxies—of a conservative American president proclaiming the gospel of liberty, with liberals falling back on a surly belief that liberty can't spread to Muslim lands. Leave aside American liberalism's hostility to this venture and consider America's critics in European and Arab intellectual circles. It is they who were now propagating a view of peoples and nations fit—and unfit—for democracy. It is they who were now speaking of Iraq's innate violence.

In their condescension, people given to dismissing Iraq's elections—dismissing the entire venture into Iraq as a doomed enterprise—said of Iraq that this was the wrong country for a Jeffersonian democracy. (Forgive the emptiness of this remark, for America itself is more of a Hamiltonian creation, but that is another matter.) No Jeffersonianism was needed, as these elections showed. The bluff of the insurgents and the jihadists was called. On a dramatic day, Iraqis seemed to reclaim their political life. The insurgents hadn't gone away; Iraq's troubles had not been healed. But it took no literacy in the writings of Locke and Mill to know the self-respect that comes with choosing one's rulers.

A kind of wisdom had been given ordinary Iraqis, an eagerness to be rid of the culture of terror and statues and informers. And that wisdom was on dramatic display as Iraqis went to the polls. There were men and women who brought to the voting centers memories of fathers and mothers and sons lost to the terror of the Saddam regime. Their vote was their revenge, a belated answer to the time of the great terror. An Arab reporter who flew from Amman to Baghdad on the day before Iraq's election recorded this conversation with a simple Iraqi woman, fifty-three years of age, who had made the hazardous flight to cast her vote in her homeland. "I don't know how to speak about polit-ical matters, but I will speak from the bottom of my heart. Under the former regime we would be herded to the voting stations like cattle to say 'yes' to Saddam even though in our depths we harbored a deep hatred of him. Under the former regime I lost two sons and always wished that I could stand in public, amid the people, and shout 'no' to Saddam. Now the time has come to say 'no' to all the oppression we endured in the past. That is why I am going to Baghdad to take part in these elections."

Perhaps the exuberance couldn't redeem this war; for the war's opponents, of course it could not. But set this election against the background of Iraq's historical torment—and against the background of an Arab world thrashing about for a new political way—and one could be forgiven the sense that this was a signal day in Iraq's history. A fortnight earlier, it had been the people of Ukraine with their Orange Revolution who had supplied evidence of liberty's appeal. But Ukraine was, for Arabs, a world away. Now in Iraq, the men and women proudly displaying their forefingers dipped in purple ink were participants in an Arab experiment. The "democratic wave" that had remade other regions had previously bypassed the Arabs; nationalism here had trumped the demand for democracy and civil liberties. Iraq supplied proof that liberty needn't be the aspiration of the upper orders and the bourgeois classes. Ordinary Iraqis, men and women, were eager to be counted. No surprise, democracy was for them about self-respect. A circle was closed. Two years earlier, there was the exhil-aration that had greeted the demolition of the statue of Saddam Hussein in Baghdad's Firdos Square. Then the Iraqis and the Americans had drifted apart. There were, to be sure, Americans on the scene in Baghdad and Mosul and Kirkuk possessed of genuine sympathy for Iraqis. But from a distance the American mood had darkened; fewer and fewer Americans liked what they saw of Iraq and Iraqis; there were even conservatives now, former supporters of the war, writing off the surly, violent country they saw on their television screens. Now Iraqis were performing the most American of political acts—casting their ballots, making their way, at that, past the threats of violence and terror. America's truth had not suddenly blossomed in Iraq, but here was proof, just when needed, that this expedition had not all been in vain.

It was, of course, the American regency in Iraq that protected these courageous people and made the elections possible. It took faith in the power and the discipline of the soldiers of the American-led coalition for Iraqis to brave their way to the polling stations in Basra and Mosul and Kirkuk. From Kirkuk, there came a "warrior note" from Colonel Lloyd "Milo" Miles addressed to his Second Brigade Combat Team, on the eve of these elections. This commander, whom I had gotten to know in the course of this war, told his soldiers of a meeting he had held with local leaders. One of these leaders had heard a rumor that the U.S.-led forces would be confined to their bases on the day of the elections and that security would be provided by Iraqi military and police units. The man was distraught and demoralized. "I beg of you, you must help us, do not let us walk alone on that day." We know that the Iraqis did not walk alone on that signal day in their country's history.

There was no need to dwell on the demonstration effect of this election, on its meaning to other Arabs. Iraq had already become the battleground between Arab authoritarianism and participatory politics. This election was taking place under the gaze of other Arabs. Saudi women could see for themselves their Iraqi counterparts voting, and running for public office. The autocrats in the Arab world, and in Iran, had already placed their (nervous) bets that Iraq and the American venture in it were destined to fail. America was a "wounded beast" in Iraq, the clerical custodians of the Iranian regime announced, and had its hands full in that country, and was thus incapable of challenging the order of power in the region. America's Arab allies in Amman, Cairo, and Riyadh were more subtle than their counterparts in the

Iranian theocratic republic. But these men were no fans of liberty; they were given to a belief that political life divides in a simple way: autocracy on one side, anarchy on the other. Those streets in Baghdad and Mosul and Fallujah set ablaze by the insurgents and the remnants of the old dictatorship were, to these Arab rulers, a gift of deliverance, proof that men and women who venture beyond heavily monitored political orders were bound to wander into a kind of political wilderness.

The American president could trumpet the cause of liberty and the holders of power in the Arab world would wait him out, trusting that the flames in Baghdad would drive all but the most foolhardy of their populations back into the fold of authoritarian rule. A man of the Egyptian regime, Hosni Mubarak's prime minister, Ahmed Nazif, speaking from the watering hole of the global elite in Davos, at the World Economic Forum, gave away the view of the entrenched Arab autocracies: Iraq's elections, he asserted, would mean little to Egypt, for every Middle Eastern country was "unique," and Iraq was a "devastated" country with its own burden to bear. Egypt was not worried, he said, for it had a "close working relationship with Washington." There was reform in Egypt, he claimed, thirty years of it, a "steady process that has been going forward." Egypt was already being held up as a test case of this doctrine of spreading liberty, and this man of the regime knew that; the custodians of the Pax Americana were caught between business as usual and this new campaign of spreading liberty's gospel.

Iraqis given to anxiety about their country were not eager to proclaim it a model for other Arabs. They had no patience with those who spoke of Iraq's showing other Arabs the way out of authoritarianism. But for the first time in a very long stretch of history, Iraq was at the center of Arab political life. It was a statement on the political sterility of other Arab lands that an election held under the protection of a foreign power, right alongside a raging insurgency, had come to be viewed as the herald of a new Arab political way.

The newness of this Iraqi history was there to see on a day I spent at the Iraqi National Assembly in April 2005. By happenstance, this was the second anniversary of the fall of Baghdad and the destruction of Saddam's regime. This was my fourth visit to the country. I had come with a colleague and close friend, one of America's most accomplished foreign policy practitioners and analysts, Leslie Gelb, former president of the Council on Foreign Relations and a former columnist for the *New York Times*. We were there to give some lectures and to meet with Iraqi academics and political figures. The State Department had invited us for this undertaking, the first of its kind. We would visit Baghdad, Kirkuk, Suleimaniyah, and Arbil. We must have talked to literally dozens of Iraqi leaders and journalists—Sunni and Shia Arabs, Kurds, Turkomans, clerics and secularists, provincial legislators. But that day in the National Assembly stood out as the most consoling and comforting experience of that visit. From afar, there had been reports of the "acrimony" of Iraq, of the long interlude between the elections of January 30 and the interminable negotiations over the formation of a new cabinet. But that day in the Assembly, these concerns seemed like a quibble with history. We saw the spectacle of democracy: men and women doing democracy's work, women cloaked in Islamic attire right alongside more emancipated women, the technocrats and the tribal sheikhs, and the infectious awareness among these people of the precious tradition bequeathed them after a terrible history. One of the principal leaders of the Shia movement the Supreme Council for the Islamic Revolution in Iraq, Sheikh Humam Hamoudi, an elegant, thoughtful cleric in his early fifties, brushed aside the talk of a Shia theocracy. This man, who knew a smattering of English, offered his own assurance that the example and the power of Iran shall be kept at bay: "My English is better than my Farsi, even though I spent twenty years in Iran." He was proud of his Iraqi identity, proud of being "an Arab." He was sure that the Najaf school of Shia jurisprudence would offer its own alternative to the culture and the worldview of Qom, across the border. He wanted no theocratic state in Iraq: Islam, he said, would be "a source" of legislation, but the content of politics would be largely secular. The model, he added, with a touch of irony, would be closer to the American mix of religion and politics than to the uncompromising secularism of French public life.

Hamoudi was no ordinary political cleric: he had been selected to lead the committee of the National Assembly that would draft Iraq's constitution. He spoke with approval of Grand Ayatollah Ali al-Sistani's worldview. He took it as an article of faith that a "turbaned man should not be head of state, for religion would then be made to bear the burden of executive decisions." In his view, Islam had left a whole range of social and political and economic questions to the "requirements of time and place and to human reason." The "Najaf way" with the faith was to him appropriately restrained. The one sole

Iraqi among the four grand ayatollahs, Ayatollah Muhammad Said al-Hakim, he added, had been deeply ambivalent about the simple act of casting a ballot in the Iraqi elections, so keen had been his determination to keep politics and the faith as separate endeavors.

"We have yet to assume power," Hamoudi said, shifting the discussions to the worldly political realm. He was speaking as an Iraqi political man; he dispensed with the standard demand for American withdrawal. The country was not ready for that, he said. "You could have a schedule of withdrawal—a set date for withdrawal—or you could have conditions for American withdrawal. The second strategy is better, and withdrawal could come when our forces are ready to assume their responsibility. You should not fear the power of the Shiites. The Arabs are afraid of that power, but they will make their adjustment to that change in due time."

Hamoudi's delivery had been polished; he was eager to talk, eager for his side to be understood. He had spent three years in one of Saddam's prisons, and there had been his years in exile in Iran. But he spoke with serenity, and he looked forward to the work of drafting a new constitution. There was no dogmatism in the way he spoke, nothing of the obscurantism and righteousness that other political clerics are given to. "My door is open to you," he told his two American visitors.

The insurgents were busy with their bombs and their plots of mayhem. Georgian troops guarded the National Assembly and controlled access to it. (The Georgians, of course, spoke neither Arabic nor English. I dreaded going past them, because I never had the badges and identification cards they required. They were part of the Coalition, and I always wondered what they thought of their mission and of the country that the political winds had sent them to.) Meanwhile a people were taking to a new political way. A woman garbed in black, a daughter of a distinguished clerical Shia family, made the rounds among her fellow legislators. Religious scruples decreed that she could not shake the hand of a male stranger. She covered her hand with the sleeve of her *abaya* to shake my hand. But she was proud and wily, a free woman in a newly emancipated polity. She let me know how much she knew about the culture and the ways and the literature of the West. American power may have turned on its erstwhile ally Ahmad Chalabi, but his appearance in the delegate lounge drew to him parliamentarians of every stripe. He too had about him the

excitement of this new politics. He had been given up for dead, politically, after Washington and the American regency in Iraq had broken
with him. But he had made a remarkable comeback; he had been
instrumental in putting together the big electoral list blessed by Grand
Ayatollah Ali al-Sistani that had won 140 seats (out of 275) in the elections. He was in the thick of negotiations over a place for himself in
the new cabinet. He would be named deputy prime minister, and both
the American regency and his critics in the Arab world would have to
acknowledge democracy's verdict and deal with him.

The Speaker of this National Assembly was a Sunni Arab, Hajem
Hassani, who aspired, he was to tell both Les Gelb and myself, to be
the Tip O'Neill of Iraq. The reference to Tip O'Neill was no accident.
Hassani, a charming, stocky man in his early fifties, had spent more
than two decades in the United States; he had earned a doctorate in
industrial organization at the University of Connecticut. He had
worked in Silicon Valley. He had returned to Iraq with the dream of
doing what he could for his country. He did not hail from a big
tribe, nor did he share in the rage of his sect against this new order. He
was sure that this new democratic way would stick, and he was proud
of the parliamentary procedures he had begun to master.

That same confidence that a better world beckoned was the steady
companion of the country's newly elected president, Jalal Talabani.
Iraq had turned to him, and an abrupt change had taken place in the
country's history with the selection of a Kurdish politician for the presidency. The same informality, the friendly banter, that had been his
hallmark all along had not deserted him. Over a casual dinner in the
garden of his younger colleague Barham Salih, he plied his guests with
food, filling our plates with mounds of mushrooms from his beloved
Kurdistan. He was in a nostalgic mood; he recalled his struggles as a
young fighter in the Kurdish hills. There had been a time, he said,
when mushrooms in the hill country were the only sustenance for him
and his fighters. They had been cut off in the mountains without
bread, without meat. He had never thought that Iraqi history would
turn this way, that a Kurd would assume the presidency of Iraq. He
delighted in the knowledge that Saddam Hussein, in his prison cell,
had watched the presidential inauguration ceremony and had been
outraged that his Kurdish nemesis now claimed the highest office in
the land. Amid the mayhem, Talabani too beheld the future of Iraq
with no small measure of optimism.

Beyond the National Assembly, and the presidency of Talabani, a lively press has sprouted in Iraq: there are an astonishing number of newspapers and weeklies, more than 250 in all. There are dozens of private television channels and radio stations. The journalists and the editors speak of a press free of censorship. Admittedly, the work is hard and dangerous, the logistics a veritable nightmare. In a gathering that drew the country's leading journalists, the diversity of this country— at once its malady and its richness—was on display. There were Shia publishers and Kurdish publishers, an Assyrian editor; there were exiles who had brought their publications with them. There was clear sectarianism, but no single truth claimed this country, no "big man" sucked the air out of its public life. By a twist of fate, the one Arab country that had seemed marked for brutality and sorrow now stood on the cusp of a new political world. No Iraqis I met looked to the neighboring Arab lands for political inspiration: they were scorched by the terror and the insurgency, but a better political culture seemed tantalizingly close.

There is light in Iraq, and there is darkness. And they alternate in ways that play tricks on the mind. This passage to Iraq was no exception. Leslie Gelb and I had gone to the Kurdish town of Arbil to give a lecture at the local university. We had drawn an earnest group of academics and journalists and politicians; the lunch spread out for us had been generous by any measure. Our hosts had been remarkably candid: they would live within Iraq, but independence was their first choice. It had been a friendly gathering. Our convoy—this is Iraq; we moved about courtesy of a security detail of former marines and army rangers—had driven through what seemed to be a quaint, quiet town, past the headquarters of the Kurdish Democratic Party. A week or so later, terror struck Arbil; a homicide bomber turned up among a throng of job applicants lined up at the party's headquarters. No fewer than 60 people were killed, 150 wounded. On the television screen, I watched the grim spectacle: the grief of the survivors, the blood being swept into the drainpipes. This too was Arbil, and the alternating reality of Iraq.

In his headquarters in Baghdad, the indefatigable Lieutenant General Petraeus—now beginning his third year in Iraq, away from his family—has been overseeing the military training of the Iraqis. He treated us, one evening, to a PowerPoint presentation about the progress of his work. One slide had a quotation he was fond of, a passage borrowed from T. E. Lawrence about his experience among the Arabs in the First World War. "Do not try to do too much with your own hands. Better the Arabs do it tolerably than you do it perfectly. It is their war, and you are there to help them, not win it for them." A stranger given the gift of a limited time among the Iraqis can only wish them well and glimpse them, amid the violence, building a better country.

The period of this trip had been relatively orderly. Iraqis, it was said, had begun to provide better intelligence on the insurgents. The training of Iraqis had turned a corner. "Knock on wood," General Petraeus said, as he talked of Iraqi soldiers taking up the defense of their country. But the American commanders were under no illusions; they would draw no big conclusions about the course of the insurgency. The top American commander, General George Casey, a handsome, possessed man not given to idle hopes or idle chatter, had spoken of this reprieve with caution; he did not know how long it would last. The caution was in order. The month to come turned out to be one of sheer mayhem, as though the insurgents had gathered strength to puncture the optimism. May 2005 was a month of sorrow. The car bombs—150 in all that month—struck throughout the country. There were 77 American fatalities, and 750 Iraqis paid with their lives as well. The intelligence from Iraq—both American and Iraqi—told of growing numbers of Arab jihadists crossing into Iraq, with Saudi Arabia, Syria, Egypt, Jordan, and Sudan as leading countries of origin. The forensic evidence disclosed that up to 20 percent of the suicide car bombers came from Algeria. That North African country, worlds away, was now spilling into Iraq. It had had its own terrible war between the secular autocrats in the saddle and the Islamists. The rulers had won in a scorched-earth war. Now the thwarted Islamists had found a new battleground. Iraq had its own hurt—and troubles. This Iraqi effort to be rid of a terrible legacy carried the added burden of a wider Arab disorder.

CHAPTER 2

Chronicle of a War Foretold

The month of November 2003—seven months, that is, after the fall of Saddam Hussein's regime—appeared to offer a partial fulfillment of the dreams of those in the Arab world who foresaw calamity and frustration for the American military campaign in Iraq. The American helicopters had begun to fall out of the sky, it seemed. In the battle for Baghdad, back in April, a legend had spread that a helicopter had been brought down by an Iraqi peasant using an old hunting rifle. The peasant and his rifle had become a big Arab story, proof that faith and patriotism would outdo the foreigner's technological mastery. But the regime had fallen, and the peasant's tale had been forgotten. Now in November, fulfillment had come: on the second day of the month, in the town of Fallujah, a Chinook helicopter was shot down, taking a toll of sixteen American lives. Then on November 7, another helicopter fell over Tikrit, and seven American soldiers were lost. The day of greatest American sorrow came in Mosul on November 15, when two Black Hawks collided and crashed, killing seventeen American soldiers.

It was idle to debate whether this was a war of choice or of necessity. American power had decapitated the old regime and pledged to build a better order in its place. And America's truth was being redeemed in the most painful of ways—by predominantly young men and women carrying the heaviest of burdens. The great big question of whether a single national society exists in Iraq was yet to be answered. The insurgency in the Sunni Triangle was the rebellion and the rearguard action of people eager to restore their own hegemony and the reign of terror that came with it. To a great, liberal country free of tribal and sectarian feuds had fallen the grim task of putting down a rebellion of the darkest atavism. Imperial power has always carried with it heartbreak. In the shade of these palm trees of Mesopotamia, a vast American expedition was trying to bring order to a fractious land. The young Tikritis and Fallujans celebrating the downing of American helicopters, displaying the helmets of fallen soldiers, wanted nothing of the foreign power's redemption.

For America, the heartbreak in Iraq came after the war of liberation and the fall of the regime. War had been easy, and the Anglo-American forces had been good at it. Beyond the clear field of battle lay the alleyways of an Arab society, and a culture inaccessible to the foreigners who came into temporary custodianship of it. There was no script to follow. Afghanistan had provided some intimations of things to come in Iraq—the sudden collapse of an enemy whose martial prowess had been held up as a warning against American intervention, the happiness of men and women liberated from brutal rule, and then the encounter with the decimation and chaos that poverty and brigandage had wrought.

But the lessons of Afghanistan were of limited value: the strike into Iraq had come so soon after the war in Afghanistan that the truths taught there had not really sunk in. At any rate, there were deep differences between these two countries: where Afghanistan had been an anarchic realm of bandits, Iraq was a more developed tyranny, wealthier, a predominantly urban society tightly held by a despot who had had all the time in the world to construct a formidable system of control.

The details of Iraq's situation under Saddam had been unavailable to outsiders. Neither neighboring Muslims and Arabs nor Westerners had any appreciable knowledge of the place. For both the proponents and opponents of this war, the strike into Iraq, and its hazards, were a leap into the void. No one could be sure whether Iraqis would fight for the despot or embrace their liberators. The regime itself was a great unknown: would it crack or treat the Arabs to an epic tale of resistance? There was no end to the speculation about the Shia, but it was reasonable to assume that they would celebrate their release from a long subjugation. Amid all the speculations about the intentions of the Shia, few bothered to wonder how the Sunni Arabs would conduct themselves in the new order of things. The Coalition forces were overthrowing not only a man but a ruling sect, a minority community whose idea of normalcy was the claim to political power and to the spoils of the state.

There would be surprises in store for hawks and doves alike. Slowly and methodically, without mercy or qualms, Saddam Hussein had taken his country apart, leveled its political life. Iraq had been wild and tempestuous: Communists had had their play in Iraq, tribal sheikhs, Arab nationalists, Kurdish warriors, isolated bands of constitutionalists drawn from the modern professions. But Saddam Hussein had tamed the place, broken its spirit, turned it into a large prison. He had not resolved the ethnic and sectarian feuds of the country; he had suppressed them. In an apt metaphor that the late Isaiah Berlin used for Communist dictatorships, and for the dark fury of nationalisms that greeted us when the "captive nations" returned to history after the fall of Communism, here too the tombstone would be rolled back, and from the grave there would spring the old atavisms awaiting release and satisfaction.

A fortnight after the fall of Baghdad, the Shia self-flagellations and religious processions banned under Saddam Hussein made their return. The Shia were staking a claim to the new order of things: the displays of religious devotion were an announcement that *taqiyya* (dissimulation) and fear were being cast aside by a community that had known a bitter legacy of disinheritance and terror.

The people of the Sunni Triangle soon struck back. The violence and the ambushes of American soldiers in the towns of Fallujah and Tikrit expressed the anger of a people whose entire political universe had been overthrown. The Baath regime of Saddam Hussein had both implicated the Sunni Arabs in its crimes and enfranchised them. The foreigner's swift justice came at their expense. Old habits of dominion die hard. The collective mind of the Sunni Arabs was easy to read. Harassed by a guerrilla campaign, the foreign forces would leave, and the world would then be reconstituted, with those reviled Shia—and Kurds—returned to their previous subjugation.

Beyond Iraq's borders, and the great, open questions posed by the country's sectarian troubles and by the tyrant's legacy, Arabs watched the war and responded to the new American push into their world. One principal rationale for the war was the American desire to reform the Arab political condition, to take American power deeper into the affairs of the Arab world. The American campaign in Afghanistan had been fought far away from the Arab world. The drive against the Taliban had struck at Arab jihadists who had hijacked Afghanistan for their own purposes. In retrospect, the "Arab Afghans" had for all practical purposes rented a country from the Taliban at the paltry rate of $20 million a year. (The figure is supplied by the Joint Congressional Inquiry on Terrorism; money from the Persian Gulf and the Arabian Peninsula had secured that terrorist haven for the Arab jihadists.) But the jihadists had drawn on the wider sympathies of the Arab world, and it was important to take the fight to the Arab world itself. In the punishment administered to the Iraqi regime, other Arab radicals would see the specter of their own undoing. That punishment, it was thought, would tip the scales in favor of those Arabs eager to see their world rid of its deadly yarns and delusions, of its political malignancies. No one was quite sure that there was a reliable constituency for political reform in Arab lands. But it was hoped that the politics of the Palestinians, and the politics of the Gulf and of Syria and Iran, would be transformed by a dramatic display of American power.

The road to Iraq led through the terror attacks of September 11. True, no compelling case had linked Iraq to the terror attacks. But the targets were rolled together—Al Qaeda, the Taliban, and Iraq. No satisfaction was to be had solely from decapitating the Taliban regime. The nineteen young men who shattered the American psyche and brought the hubris and economism of the 1990s to a close were Arabs. Iraq offered a way, geographically and psychologically, into the Arab world. The conviction that took hold at the highest reaches of the Bush administration that Afghanistan was not a "target-rich" environment was both literally and figuratively true. You could pound the Afghan Arabs into the caves, deny them sanctuary, take away from them the bandit state they had secured in Afghanistan (with a mix of money obtained from Arabia and the Gulf and the prestige, compared to the simpler, more earnest Afghans, of being Arabs who had direct access to the sacred text). But this still remained a war fought away from the Arab world. Iraq presented itself as a more appropriate battleground, a place where Phase Two of the war on terror could be fought out. There were targets aplenty in Iraq: weapons of mass destruction (or so it was thought), a dictator in a pivotal Arab state, an unfinished war against an adventurer who had defied the obituaries written for him by American war planners and leaders who had spared him a dozen years earlier.

There were major players within the administration who had long had Iraq on their minds. It would be safe to say that the civilian leadership at the Pentagon partook of this view of Iraq as a menace to American security. It was common knowledge that the deputy secretary of defense, Paul Wolfowitz, was an unapologetic hawk on Iraq.

And it would be safe to state by now that the secretary of defense shared his deputy's outlook. The bureaucratic balance of power, so the first draft of history would seem to suggest, had shifted in favor of a war against Iraq with the shift in Vice President Richard Cheney's outlook. A dozen years earlier, in the first campaign against Saddam Hussein, Cheney had been the quintessential practitioner of realpolitik. As secretary of defense, he had executed a limited war, bereft of zeal and ideological claims. He was comfortable with the order of power in the Arabian Peninsula and the Persian Gulf. He had been there, in 1991, with enormous, bureaucratic authority, when Baghdad was declared off-limits and American power let the dictator be. Balance of power had sufficed then; this was not a man given to Wilsonian redemptionism. He took the Arab world, and the Persian Gulf and its order of princes and merchants, as it was. He had headed into corporate life, and oil services—hardly the breeding grounds of ideological redemptionism. September 11, it would seem, altered Cheney's thinking. He was convinced now that America was in the midst of a war, that enemies and dangers stalked it, that no mercy, and no weakness, ought to be shown America's enemies.

There may have been no operational links between Iraq and Al Qaeda; Mohamed Atta, the lead hijacker in the September 11 attacks, may or may not have met with an Iraqi intelligence operative in Prague; Al Qaeda may have been "religious" whereas Baghdad was "secular" in its ways. These distinctions did not matter: the connection had been made in American opinion. A distinct minority was willing to take it on faith that America was done with dangers that emanated from Arab lands. A broader consensus—no less powerful for being inchoate and unstated—beheld the Arab world with great reserve and suspicion. The terrors had originated in Saudi Arabia and Egypt, but no wars could be waged against these regimes. They were "problematic allies" (the term the 9/11 Commission Report had chosen to describe the Saudi-American relationship), and no credible scenario had America loading up the gear to sack these regimes. True, some deep hostility had welled up in the American polity against the Saudi state. But this was enmity within limits, and no easy solution presented itself for the troubles of the Saudi realm. The facts of dependence on Saudi oil were stark and sobering, and those facts reined in the wrath against that state. As for the Egyptian despot, he and his regime were spared intense scrutiny. No one followed the trail that began with Mohamed Atta and Ayman Zawahiri and ended at Hosni Mubarak's doorstep. No great debate had materialized in the United States about the depth of Egypt's troubles, the rampant anti-Americanism in that land, the terrible bargain—$2 billion a year of aid to the regime of Mubarak—which bought for America the hatred of Egypt's middle class and the virulent enmity of its Islamists. It was in Mubarak's political prisons that countless Islamists had endured brutality and torture and had vowed revenge on the Egyptian ruler and on the foreign power that backed his regime.

In retrospect, it would be fair to say, Saddam Hussein's Iraq had drawn the short straw. Syria was a tyranny, but it flew under the radar. There was something timid and broken about the Syrian state: it was cruel at home, and in Lebanon, but it did not swagger with Saddam Hussein's abandon. It did not let stand the suspicion that it possessed deadly weapons. There was a caution built into the Syrian state, a knowledge of what the balance of power in the region (and beyond) could and couldn't tolerate. This caution had been the way of Hafiz al-Assad, perfected over three decades, and bequeathed to that shrewd man's son and political inheritor. This was the great telling difference between the despot in Syria and his nemesis in Iraq. Saddam, it turns out, had no weapons of mass destruction but strutted about as though he did. He ought to have known the weakness of his hand, but he played it as though he could defy Anglo-American power, fire at allied aircraft and get away with it. He would not step out of harm's way: even as a big expeditionary force was being assembled against him, he held on to the illusion that the American leader could still blink and avoid a showdown. The Iraqi ruler never understood the change that had come over America in the aftermath of September 11. A more cunning man would have ducked for cover. But this had never been Saddam Hussein's way. When the war against his regime came, some eighteen months after September 11, it had to it the inevitability of a chronicle foretold.

It was a wily and willful world that America was venturing into. A battle would have to be fought between an outsider with energy and zeal for reform and an old and cynical Arab world good at passing off defeats as victories, at hectoring outsiders, at dodging all responsibility for the ills of a political order where the rulers' tyranny is matched by the politics of a "street" choking on its own rage. A liberal foreign power had to bring with it to Iraq a belief that there was no Arab exceptionalism to the winds of political reform that had swept through other regions in recent years. The battle for Baghdad doubled up as a proxy battle, then, for a wider reform of the Arab world as a whole.

America had been bloodied on September 11, the Arab rulers reasoned; its righteous sense of violation had taken it to Afghanistan and Iraq. After its exertions in Iraq, after the American with the big gun discovered that the Iraqi exiles did not know their homeland, after a period of anarchy and American frustration with the ways of an unfamiliar land, the sun would rise again over the nothing new. There was no need to ride with America in broad daylight, and no tears were to be shed for Saddam Hussein. He had been unusually cruel and megalomaniacal; he had risen from poverty and dust to absolute power. His neighborhood was full of strongmen, but they could console themselves that they had lived within the limits of their world, that the culture of Saddam's regime with the ruler's countless statues—part Babylonian, part Stalinist—was not theirs. The Arab rulers could grasp the meaning of that proxy war for the Arab world playing out in Baghdad, while insisting they had tried their best to rein in American power and to warn the Iraqi adventurer against the errors of his ways. Foreigners have blown in and out of the Arab world. They have always arrived full of great expectations only to pack up and leave after their bids for dominion and their gospels of reform were thwarted. This new war, the Arab rulers hoped, would be true to an old pattern.

There is no marker, no exact turning point, that can with hindsight tell us when the war in Iraq turned into a campaign for the wider reform of the Arab world. It could be argued that Wilsonianism was built into this war: America had been brutalized on September 11, and a determination was born to root out Arab malignancies. Afghanistan had not provided a blow against Arab radicalism proportional to the American sense of loss and shock. Iraq was deemed a better target. The aversion to being drawn into the streets and alleyways of an Arab city—into the inner workings of the Arab world—gave way to a new reformism.

In one plausible line of reasoning, the Wilsonianism had come to the fore when the hunt for weapons of mass destruction had run aground. The war, and its sacrifices, had to be justified. As Saddam Hussein's vaunted war machine was shown to be full of rust and decay, as the dictator looked less like a modern-day Hitler and more like a Wizard of Oz behind a stage of illusions and make-believe, the case for the war appeared to shift. The satisfaction was to be sought not only in Iraq itself, but in neighboring Arab and Muslim lands. There was a truth that American officials hinted at but never explicitly laid out. The American imperial position in the two pillars of its influence—Saudi Arabia and Egypt—was reeling. The war in Iraq would provide something of an end run around these two regimes. The terrors of the Arab world—jihadists from Saudi Arabia and Egypt—had brought their furies to America, and a more ambitious war against Arab radicalism was the order of the day. America had lived with Arab authoritarianism, believing the choice was either Hosni Mubarak or Ayman Zawahiri and his breed of militants. America had not fared well with this choice: it had gotten both Mubarak and Zawahiri. Indeed, Ayman Zawahiri, that pitiless physician with absolutist convictions and an aristocratic Cairene background, had turned his wrath on America because he had been unable to topple the Mubarak regime. In a sudden shift, it had become good politics in America to advocate changing the ways of the Arabs.

For decades, the American choice in Arab-Islamic lands had been starkly posed: terrible rulers or worse oppositionists. The civil society in these Arabs lands had been truculent and anti-American, while the rulers seemed like eminently reasonable men, willing to strike bargains in the shadows. To be sure, these rulers were not democratic in the least. But it was easy to accept their authoritarianism as the cultural norm of the Arabs. Better Yasser Arafat than the Hamas movement, better the stern and unforgiving Hassan II of Morocco than his opponents, better the House of Saud than the ultra-Wahhabis in the realm. An accommodation could be struck with Mubarak and his court, whereas the Egyptian intellectual class seemed immune to reason. The kings and the pharaohs made peace treaties with Israel and stuck to them, while the professional syndicates and the lawyers and the journalists tilted against windmills and partook of the worst kind of antimodernism.

September 11 had, of course, cast the bargain with Arab authoritarianism in an entirely different light. Perhaps the clearest doctrinal statement of the democratizing ambitions of this Iraq venture are to be found in a speech that President Bush gave to the National Endowment for Democracy on November 6, 2003. The Iraq campaign had entered a difficult stretch; the hunt for weapons of mass destruction had proved futile. Saddam Hussein was still on the loose. The forum for this speech was chosen to highlight the message. This region, which had been left out of the most recent democratic wave of history, would no longer be given an exemption from democracy's push.

There was fervor in the speech, and belief. Indeed, there was a startling mea culpa for decades of American diplomacy. "Sixty years of Western nations excusing and accommodating the lack of freedom in the Middle East did nothing to make us safe—because in the long run, stability cannot be purchased at the expense of liberty. As long as the Middle East remains a place where freedom does not flourish, it will remain a place for stagnation, resentment, and violence for export. And with the spread of weapons that can bring catastrophic harm to our country, and to our friends, it would be reckless to accept the status quo." It would be hard for America to break this old bargain with Arab authoritarianism. But the reading of the region was on the mark. America's authoritarian friends were the source of this malady: they rode with America but brought down on it the wrath of the aggrieved and the disgruntled in their domains.

Iraq would provide the example of democracy's success: it would send the news "from Damascus to Tehran that freedom can be the future of every nation," President Bush asserted. Tehran and Damascus were easy targets: they were outside the American orbit of power. The regime in Tehran was openly at odds with America's purposes; the one in Damascus was a sterile tyranny that feigned anti-Americanism and was often stuck with its self-defeating poses. The American president was circling more difficult targets—the regimes in Riyadh and Cairo. To these rulers, George W. Bush would speak in code, and by allusion: "The Saudi government is taking the first step toward reform, including a plan for gradual introduction of elections. By giving the Saudi people a greater role in their own society, the Saudi government can demonstrate true leadership in the region. The great and proud nation of Egypt has shown the way toward peace in the Middle East and now should show the way toward democracy. . . . Champions of democracy in the region understand that democracy is not perfect, it is not the path to utopia, but it's the only path to national success and dignity."

This was a shot across the bow: these two regimes were deeply entrenched and good at resisting and thwarting the schemes of outsiders. A war had been fought—and was being fought—in Iraq. The Turkish state, with membership in NATO and a tight security relationship with Washington that reached back decades, had refused to accommodate the American war planners and had denied the use of its land and port facilities for this war. The earnestness of the Turks, the faith in the Pax Americana that had anchored their security policy (and their worldview) had given way before a strident anti-Americanism. The Kemalist elites who had long dominated the Turkish republic's life stepped out of the way: there was an Islamist government, and the Kemalists were keen to let it assume the burden of that historical decision. Democracy, by a vote in Parliament, had rendered a verdict against the American campaign in Iraq. The war had to be fought from Saudi Arabia, Kuwait, Qatar, and Jordan; the military supplies were being shipped through the Suez Canal. The authoritarian regimes in the Arab world had delivered, where Turkish democracy had been a disappointment to the American war planners, who had been ardent supporters of Turkey's strategic value and importance. It was not easy preaching the inevitability of democracy's triumph to the Arab holders of power. America was triumphant but still embattled and overextended, and Iraq was proving itself a treacherous terrain. The democratizing push had its ideological appeal. But the neighborhood was a hard place, and its rulers were possessed of a nose for the ways of foreign powers.

The ruler in Cairo had behind him nearly a quarter-century of political experience. The Cairenes spoke of his peasant cunning; he hailed from the countryside of Menouifiyah, in the delta. Those in the know said that the people of Menouifiyah have always been known for secrecy and shrewdness. An accidental heir to political power, he was now the longest-serving ruler of Egypt since the legendary Albanian soldier of fortune, Muhammad Ali, who was, for all practical purposes, the founder of modern Egypt in the first half of the nineteenth century. It would be hard to pressure Hosni Mubarak. The reforms were always a day away; besides, he was in the clear now, for nations that had lectured him on human rights were pitted in struggles of their own against the boys of terror. Washington and London knew better now, the old military ruler believed, and they would spare him their sermons about the way he fought terror and kept the order of his land.

Mubarak's writ ran on the banks of the Nile, and he had kept the peace of the place. Sure enough, a younger Cairene—a son of a respectable middle-class family, Mohamed Atta—had led the death pilots of September 11; more telling still, Ayman Zawahiri, the brilliant physician at the helm of Al Qaeda, hailed from the upper-class Cairo suburb of Maadi and was heir to an aristocratic pedigree. Moreover, Egyptians provided the backbone of the operational leadership of Al Qaeda, its deadliest practitioners of terror. If Al Qaeda's money came from the Arabian Peninsula, the Egyptians had brought to that movement their numbers, their military training in their country's reserves, the hardness bred into them by the torture many of them had suffered. But the regime still had room to maneuver. The crowds in Cairo and the university students taking to the streets may have been resolutely anti-American, but major joint exercises were held between the militaries of Egypt and the United States. And the Egyptian ruler could still call on the American president at his ranch, in Crawford, Texas, and could claim a privileged relationship with the United States. Countless younger Egyptians had taken to the road, and to subversion and terror. They could be found in London and Hamburg and Kandahar: the regime could dole out what bits of intelligence it was inclined to share. The claims of democracy could wait: Mubarak was good at hunkering down and waiting out powerful storms.

Nor would the Pax Americana have an easy time of it in the Arabian Peninsula. The Saudi realm may not have been hermetically sealed, but access to it depended on the will and good graces of the House of Saud. There was anti-Americanism among the populace, and that sentiment could be whipped up in defense of the regime and its prerogatives. There was the pride that this was Islam's birthplace and that outsiders could not presume to intervene in its affairs. Here too the promise of reform could be held out as something that the custodians of the realm had in mind all along. In the interim, the rulers could shelter behind nativism and authenticity and national independence. There was unrest in Arabia, but the rulers had assets to barter: the excess capacity of oil available to this kingdom, the understandable reluctance of Washington to tinker with the affairs of a realm it did not fully understand, the strategic cooperation in an Iraq war that the Saudi decision makers—publicly—disavowed. Even as the U.S.-Saudi relationship entered a time of discord, the Saudis, so we are told in Bob Woodward's *Plan of Attack,* could still press the Bush administration for a voice and a role in the kind of order that would emerge in Iraq.

Fate had been cruel in the way Saudi-American relations played out. An American war had been launched in Iraq, and the global oil markets had succumbed to new levels of anxiety. A windfall had come to Saudi Arabia as the price of oil rose to new highs. The Saudi budget would show a record surplus in the years 2003 and 2004, oil would reach a peak of fifty-five dollars a barrel, and the country would take in some $80 billion in oil revenues in 2003, and about $110 billion the following year. There was a real estate boom in the country and a stock market frenzy. Miraculously, it seemed, Arabia had shifted from the furies of Wahhabism to financial speculation. Arabia was not delivered from its troubles: there was still disaffection among the country's youth, and armed religious rebels in the underground challenged the rulers' assertions that all was well in the realm. But the oil windfall had bought time for the House of Saud; wealth had once again, as in the easier era of the 1970s, tranquilized the country. There had always been a mix—an alternation at times—of crass materialism and ideological zeal in Arabia. The fever of Wahhabism had momentarily subsided.

A trick had been played on the Americans. They were entangled in Iraq, while Arabia was in the midst of sudden boom. The Saudi purse strings could be loosened as the rulers played for time, walking a thin line between the new American scrutiny of their finances and their politics and the anti-Americanism and xenophobia of their people.

It was against this background that the Bush administration launched the diplomatic centerpiece of its democratic drive—a "Greater Middle East" initiative that would aim to support democracy and reform, all the way from Morocco to Pakistan. American officials were eager to present this effort as the brainchild of Arab reformers. There had been two United Nations Arab Human Development Reports, produced in 2002 and 2003, which had put some numbers on the maladies of the Arab world. The experts who had produced these documents were Arabs themselves. Their numbers were telling, but the retrogression they described was known to all Arabs who bothered to look at the world around them. The testimony of these experts would be cited as evidence that the Arabs themselves yearned for a fundamental change in their world. The numbers were to become mantras in their own right. (Those numbers were cited by President Bush in his National Endowment for Democracy speech; they would provide the backbone of a working paper that the American government prepared in support of its initiative.) The combined gross national product of twenty-two Arab states, it was revealed, was less than that of Spain. Approximately 40 percent of adult Arabs were illiterate; only 1.6 percent of the population had access to the Internet, a figure lower than in the states of sub-Saharan Africa. The entire Arab world translated fewer foreign books than Greece; women were virtually out of political power, and there was not a single Arab state that could be described as "fully free" by the criteria of Freedom House, which tracks civil and political liberties in the world.

The U.S. working paper, intended for a G-8 summit in the summer of 2004, had been leaked several months earlier. At the heart of this working paper lay the three great "deficits" of the modern Arab world: freedom, knowledge, and women's empowerment. The darkness of Arab politics, the inability and unwillingness of the rulers to keep their people—and the furies of their regimes—at home, had trumped the absolute logic of sovereignty. There was American interventionism in Arab affairs, to be sure. But the interventionism had been justified by the depth and danger of the new Islamism. An Arab world that could not keep its terrors, and its terrorists, at home could not claim full and absolute sovereignty.

The intentions behind this Greater Middle East initiative may have been noble, but men love the troubles they know, and there would be heavy resistance to it in Arab lands. The Arab rulers fell back on the prerogatives of sovereignty and independence; the intellectual classes offered their usual mix of anti-Americanism—shoot the messenger, ignore the message. The Greater Middle East was but an imperial project, it was said in Cairo and Damascus and Beirut, and in the Arab diaspora communities, and in the Saudi-owned media of the Arab world. A handful of brave men and women were willing to ride this initiative's coattails. They were even willing to use American power as a rod with which to spur the process of political reform. The Islamists appeared to be on the defensive, and the presence of a massive American force in the region had altered the calculations of rulers and oppositionists alike. In the Arabian Peninsula and the Persian Gulf, the Islamic "charities" and philanthropies ducked for cover, and the governments that had winked at the Islamists and given them running room were being pressed to make hard choices in this new war on radicalism. "The Americans are coming," the Islamists and their liberal opponents proclaimed. There was zeal among the Islamists, it is true. But they were also given to cold calculations of power. The Islamists worked within the limits of tolerance established by the regimes in the saddle. It was the better part of prudence to hunker down and wait for the ruling regimes to play their hand.

A space had opened for the would-be secular reformers among the Arab elite. They still did not have the upper hand: their dependence on this infusion of American power spoke volumes about their weakness at home. The hopes they came to invest in the fight for Iraq could be seen as evidence of the fragility of their position. To be sure, there was no consistency in the American attitude toward democratization and reform. At times, there was schizophrenia in the American policy: Wilsonianism brandished in the face of America's enemies (Syria and Iran) and realpolitik extended to old allies in Jordan, Egypt, and Saudi Arabia. But there can be no doubting the wider Arab agitation that came to surround the Iraq war. Nor could one miss the sudden sense of faith, among the embattled liberals in Cairo and the Arabian Peninsula and the Gulf, that American power was now arrayed on the side of reform.

In Egypt, a political sociologist and professor at the American University in Cairo, Saad Eddin Ibrahim, who had run afoul of the Mubarak regime and been sent to prison for fifteen months on spurious charges of corruption and of defaming the country's reputation abroad, saw in this moment the possibility of challenging the old entrenched interests in the Arab world. The bargain with authoritarianism, he too was to assert, had failed. "Few can now doubt that democracy, peace, and development are interlinked and must be sought together, especially in my part of the world." He surveyed the autocracies of the region with clarity. "In the Middle Ages there used to be something called the Silk Road, which was an overland route that ran from the Atlantic shores of Morocco to the Great Wall of China. It was a famous path steeped in lore and plied by picturesque caravans. . . . The romantic Silk Road of yesteryear has in our time become a kind of Despots' Alley or Tyrants' Row, with various sorts of unfree governments lying end-to-end on the map from Beijing right on through to North Africa." In this political activist's view, the Western powers had a choice to make: they could pursue genuine reform in Arab lands, distance themselves from the despots, or return to the region, time and again, on periodic armed interventions. Those interventions had, by his estimate, come once every seven years since 1958. The bargain with the dictators had offered false comfort and nothing more.

The Greater Middle East initiative died on the vine, it would be fair to say. The Bush administration had stepped back from it by the time the G-8 summit had come. The Europeans greeted the initiative with the attitude of realpolitik reserved for bold American initiatives that dare suggest that the ways of politics—and of "the East"—could yield to the foreigner's touch. There remained unresolved the question of Iraq and whether the American mission in that country could be the lever for overhauling the ways of the Arabs. Flipped on one end—its history, its temperament, the ferocious insurgency that would not die down—Iraq seemed the most forbidding place for a campaign of reform, the hardest soil. Yet every now and then, that country offered glimpses of hope that Iraqis may yet pull off a decent political world that works. There were days its sectarianism seemed like an affliction that would never go away. Then there were hints that the multiplicity of its communities could yet support a politics, and a culture, of pluralism.

Iraq had always had the thing and its opposite: the best part of the Arab world and its darkest. "We're like that," a noted Iraqi scientist said to me. "Iraq can never know the middle ground. It is either feast or famine, greatness or failure. It has been like this throughout our long history." I think of two corridors that predate the American mission in Iraq by decades: a Paris-Baghdad corridor that took Iraqi artists and sculptors to Paris, in the 1930s and 1940s, and fertilized a brilliant artistic tradition. Right alongside of it, there was a Berlin-Baghdad corridor. It brought to Iraq the ways and culture and hysteria of the Third Reich and inspired, if that is the word, a generation or two of political men raised to ideologies of absolutism and violence. What the American war planners thought they would find in Iraq is a subject of endless controversy. But the bet on Iraq was born of that broader frustration with the ways, and evasions, of other Arab lands.

Behold that defining scene of this war in Iraq: the moment the statue of Saddam was pulled down in Firdos Square on April 9, 2003. Recall that the Iraqi crowd had tried to pull down the statue but had been unable to do so. American marines then stepped in, and the statue was brought down with a cable attached to a tank-recovery vehicle. The head of the shattered statue was then dragged through the streets, to the joy of the crowd. There were old tales of resistance to the despot, Shia insurgents who had risen and been decimated a dozen years earlier. There were the exiles across the border in Iran, and they had a whole history of persecution they could recite. But it was America that had broken the back of the old order.

There was no single Iraq to begin with. The Shia had been set free but were sullen, the Sunnis had been overthrown, and no assurance could be given them that the new order boded well for them. There was no national political class that could step forth and concede that all had been lost, then work with the Western occupiers to put together a new public order. There was a precarious thin line here between liberation and occupation. After the day of liberation, Iraq and its liberators/occupiers would head into a twilight world. A shopkeeper of Baghdad quoted in the Saudi-owned Pan-Arab daily *Asharq Al-Awsat*, one Mahdi Mansour, provided the kind of verdict the Anglo-American force could hope for: "A just ruler from among the infidels," he said, "is better than a tyrannical ruler from among the Muslims." It was the classic bargain that harked back to the age of empire: good government versus self-government. The pride of nationalism had to be suspended if the new order was to stick. There had to be more Mahdi Mansours if the Americans were to succeed.

Saddam Hussein had held a country in fear and terror but had not bothered to defend it. Patriotism of an old and sober kind would have no trouble seeing the old dictatorship for the cruel fraud it was. But patriotism is no simple matter in a sectarian country with warring histories and identities. Years earlier, it had been claimed for Saddam Hussein by many of his admirers—and he had them aplenty in the Arab world and in the West as well—that he had created an Iraqi national identity, that at least he was a secular man who had put a lid on the country's sectarian and ethnic cauldron. We know better now. In distress, in the aftermath of the first Gulf War, the system of control had fallen back on clan rule and clan solidarity. A foreign power coming into Iraq happened on a country riven with sectarian troubles. There was nothing in the foreign power's gear or experience that could have prepared it for that kind of schism. Arabs calling the play from the sidelines would fault the Americans for their handling of their new military and political burden. But the Arabs themselves had been no better at understanding Iraq.

The dictator had effectively sealed off his country from the outside world. No Arabs had bothered to inquire into Iraq. It was some weeks after the fall of Baghdad to the American forces that Arabs began to take stock of the mass graves and of the brutality that the dictator had heaped on his country. But the appraisal was too little and too late. The dominant order in the Arab world had had nothing to say about the great crimes of the Saddam Hussein regime. The League of Arab States was an empty shell; this kind of blunt diplomatic instrument had never stood up to a dictator or called into question the brutalities of any Arab regime. It was enough for the Arab League to rail against Israel and to offer up the standard indictments of American policy. State terror in the Arab world was of no concern to that organization.

A year before the Americans had struck in Baghdad, the Iraqi regime had taken part in the annual meeting of the Arab League held in Beirut. One of the principal perpetrators of terror in Iraq, a close lieutenant of Saddam Hussein named Izzat Ibrahim, had represented his country. He had been well received, much to the dismay and the heartbreak of the Kuwaitis. The turmoil in the Palestinian territories, and the need for a common Arab strategy, was offered as the usual justification for passing in silence over the high crimes of the regime of Saddam Hussein. The Iraqis did not have to be unusually contrite about the calamity they had heaped on Kuwait. The de facto ruler of Saudi Arabia, Crown Prince Abdullah, had embraced Izzat Ibrahim, and a kind of traditional Arab *sulha* (reconciliation) was in the air. There was no Arab solution for Iraq's abnormality.

Who in the Arab world could sit in judgment of Iraq, at any rate? The Tikriti despot ruled with his two sons by his side, but it was common knowledge that the Egyptian ruler was busy at work leveling the political life of a country once proud of the vitality of its political tradition to prepare it for the ascendancy of one of his two sons, and that the other son had the run of the country's economic and business life. As for clan and sect rule: Iraq had it at the core of its political life, but so did Syria. For the rule of the Sunni Arabs in Iraq, substitute the rule of the Alawites in Syria, and Iraq becomes a normal polity in the Arab scheme of things. Had he held on to power, Saddam was destined to bequeath his rule to the younger of his two sons, but his Syrian nemesis, Hafiz al-Assad, had masterfully arranged the succession of his own son before his death.

The state treasury as a ruler's private purse: this was an Iraqi affliction, but Libyan as well. The "banking withdrawal" that Saddam Hussein's younger son, Qusay, made on the eve of the military campaign—more than one billion in dollars and euros, hauled away on trucks—was an extreme assertion of the ruler's claim to the public treasure. But it was true everywhere else in the Arab world that there was a lack of accountability and that the rulers had an unfettered claim on the public treasury. The master of the regime as an infallible man and the source of all wisdom: Saddam was but an extreme version of a wider Arab malady. He had not descended from the sky, Saddam Hussein. He was of a piece with the region's history. His peers could neither condemn nor overthrow him. He may have made a mockery of presidential elections when he won with 100 percent of the vote in a hastily scheduled election on the eve of the American military campaign against his regime. But was the presidential election any less a mockery in Egypt, where the military ruler, in 1999, prevailed with 93.75 percent of the vote?

There were uses for Saddam Hussein: he was a reminder to the populations of other Arab states that they had been spared the greater sorrows that had befallen the Iraqis. Political power may have been arbitrary in Aleppo, but it was surely much worse in Mosul; there may have been no representative life in the Peninsula, but the House of Saud was more merciful than Saddam Hussein.

Sectarianism too, the besetting sin of modern Arab political life, had made it easier for the Iraqi ruler to operate in the Arab councils of power and to be hailed by that fabled "Arab street." Saddam and his fellow Tikritis were of course Sunni Arabs, and for mainstream Sunni society outside Iraq, this was a matter of great importance. True enough, the Shia rebellion of the 1980s, the high-water mark of Ayatollah Khomeini's assault on the Arab-Muslim order of things, had passed. But no one wanted to see a replay of that era—the rise of the Shia in Lebanon, the troubles in the states of the Gulf between the Sunni rulers and their restless Shia communities, the veritable civil war over Islam itself that Ayatollah Khomeini had unleashed between the dominant Sunni order and its Shia stepchildren. The Tikriti political and military class could still draw on sectarian atavisms and loyalties. No effort had gone into healing that deep rift between Sunni and Shia Islam; the Arab world had not rid itself of its deadly atavisms.

Kuwait and Kuwaitis aside, the ruling stratum in the Arab world had an appreciable measure of tolerance for Tikriti rule. There was still a disinherited Shia majority in Bahrain, shut out of political power. And the Shia in Saudi Arabia were still denied a full sense of belonging in that realm. The Wahhabi creed had not made room for them, and the new radical Islamists had heightened the Shia sense of solitude

and disinheritance. A stagnant Arab world could have lived indefi-
nitely with a shackled Iraqi state. Political retrogression, rather like
misery, loves company. But the American fury and determination—in
particular the passion of an American president with an ambitious
view of the drastic reform to be brought to Arab shores—had swept
aside those old Arab restraints.

The Arab rulers could only worry and wonder: in Damascus, a
moribund regime with a new, untested leader at the helm would now
have Pax Americana on its eastern border. Was Syria next, and could
a regime with such dismal economic and political results to show for
itself withstand the pressure of a heady American push into the region?
In a different world, that master practitioner of stealth, Hafiz al-Assad,
had turned Lebanon into a satellite state of his regime. America had
winked at the Syrian conquest of Lebanon. That American acquiescence was the price paid, back in 1990–91, for the ride Syria took with
the American-led coalition against the regime of Saddam Hussein. For
Syria's ruler, it had been a lucrative ride. He had been amply rewarded
by the Arab oil states and by the Americans, without much exertion on
his part. Bashar al-Assad could not be sure that his father's luck would
be there for him. There were rumors and intimations from Washington that the sphere of influence in Lebanon could yet be challenged by
the Americans and that the pressure would mount for Syrian withdrawal from Lebanon.

Worries of a different kind played upon Egypt and Saudi Arabia.
Over the horizon loomed the prospect of Iraq as a new, favored base of
the Pax Americana in the Arab world. More secular and emancipated
than Saudi Arabia, much closer to the sea lanes of the Gulf and to the
vast oil reserves of the region than Egypt, a new Iraq held out great
attraction to the American imperium and its architects. The promise
of Iraq was that of a new beginning—a base of American influence free
of the toxic anti-Americanism at play in both Saudi Arabia and Egypt,
and of the social and religious mores that weighed so heavily on the
Saudi realm. In Iraq, American war planners and a powerful coalition
of defense and policy thinkers saw an opportunity to end the American dependence on the old pillars of the American presence, and to
construct a new American imperium in Araby.

A veritable Arab obsession had sprung up around Deputy Secretary
of Defense Paul Wolfowitz, the preeminent member of the neoconser-

vative camp. He was the perfect lightning rod: he was Jewish; his sister lived in Israel; he was intellectually ambitious; he put forth, and seemed serious about it, a view of a democratic Arab-Muslim world. He had a knowledge of East Asia and its economic recovery and regarded it as a model for the Muslim world to follow. He had served as ambassador to Indonesia, and in that country he had acquired an optimistic belief that political liberalism could be grafted onto Islamic culture. For years he had been interested in Turkey, and he looked with sympathy on what he saw to be the modernism at the heart of its political culture. On the face of it, all this should have endeared him to the Arab intellectual class, for he was free of the cultural determinism normally associated with conservative thought, a determinism that wrote off any serious possibility that political reform and liberty could survive on Arab-Islamic soil. But an Arab opinion given to dark speculations about America's intentions, and about what powerful outsiders held in store for the Arabs, saw in Wolfowitz and his allies in and out of government a "cabal" determined to draw a whole new geopolitical map for the Arab world.

Arab historiography had forever been fixated on the Sykes-Picot accord, which had drawn the boundaries of the modern Arab world in the course of the Great War. There were serious political men and women now, in Damascus, Cairo, and the Arabian Peninsula, convinced that a new colonial scheme was afoot. In this view, Baghdad would be detached from the rest of the Arab world; it would turn its back on pan-Arab priorities, provide the Pax Americana with a base in the Gulf, and perhaps arrive at a strategic accommodation with Israel. The celebrated Egyptian journalist Mohamed Heikal, who had been Gamal Abdel Nasser's alter ego and a powerful editor of the daily *Al-Ahram,* and who had retained a favored place in the public life of the Arab world as a link to a special era in the region's history, propagated this view with his customary skill. For all the political calamities of Nasserism, Heikal still had easy access to the region's papers and satellite channels. When he reigned over Arab journalism, he had had a gift for grand summations and had never let small facts stand in the way of his sweeping assertions; he would be true to this pattern once again. An "emperor from Texas" had risen, Heikal warned his Arab audience, and this war in Iraq was part of a larger imperial design. A cabal around George W. Bush was hell-bent on securing dominion over an Arab world that had lost its coherence and integrity; Iraq offered a "choice target" for this new American bid. This was the high priest of Arab nationalism, a man at odds with the Arab rulers, contemptuous of them and of their subordination to American power. But he had his unique authority, and his view of this Iraqi venture was a fair and good reflection of the thinking of the politically conscious among the Arabs. Heikal had had little to say about Saddam Hussein in the preceding years; his task was to explicate the creed of Arab nationalism.

There had always been a rivalry between Cairo and Baghdad. These were two poles of Arab culture and geography, two highly distinct expressions of the modern Arab experience. The two cities had clashed for primacy in the 1950s; they had competed a generation later when Iraq saw in Egypt's peace with Israel an opportunity for Baghdad to come into its own, under Saddam Hussein, as the home of a resurgent Arabism. An Iraq liberated by American means, and at peace with American power, was a new variation on that old theme. Cairo had cut a deal with the Pax Americana. Under the flamboyant Anwar el-Sadat, and then under a cautious successor who took American help but was keen to keep his distance from America's embrace, Cairo had worked out the terms of engagement with the American imperium: stealth official cooperation with America coexisted with anti-Americanism in the public square. The ruler and his security apparatus were America's partners, but the drumbeats of anti-Americanism in the ruler's official press never ceased. Over the course of a quarter-century, Hosni Mubarak had taken American treasure and American help but had been careful to show that he was his own man, that his purposes, on Palestine and Iraq and Libya, were not the same as those of the Pax Americana.

Egypt was an American dependency but the Sublime Porte—to use that old Ottoman analogy—was far away, and the ruler, the pasha on the scene, could govern by his own lights. The availability of Iraq as an American base, under leaders more willing to go the distance with America, was a challenge to all Mubarak had built. The American patrons could grow wiser about Arab affairs after time on the ground in Baghdad. The terrible secret of Egypt's retreat from modernism could be given to the Americans. This was why Mubarak emerged as the one leader on the scene who wished America ill on its venture into Iraq. He was a pessimist, and the American bid came loaded with a heavy dosage of can-do American optimism. Mubarak led a poor country that had drawn on American largesse for three decades and with no end in sight, while Iraq was potentially rich and, at some point in the future, more lucrative as an American base. Cairo had mastered the game of Israeli-Palestinian politics; this was its advantage in Washington, where it posed as a mediator of that conflict. This was a profitable trade, but also one burdened with troubles. The new leaders of Iraq seemed willing to make their own accommodation with Washington, free from the demands of the Palestinian problem.

Too old and weary to learn the rules of a new game, Mubarak fell back on what he knew best: he warned of the dangers of venturing into Iraq, he belittled the Iraqi exiles, and he foresaw the war in Iraq spawning a new generation of terrorists, an endless supply of bin Ladens, as he put it. The drama of the destruction of Saddam Hussein's regime was covered in an understated way by the Egyptian media. Contrast the subdued, almost resentful, way Egypt's newspapers covered the fall of Saddam Hussein's statue with the exuberant coverage given it by *Asharq Al-Awsat,* and the discomfort of Egypt and its ruler with what had happened in Baghdad is easy to see. Mubarak had become the vintage "Oriental despot." The country he ruled had to be immunized against the spectacle of revolts in other lands.

It was only days after the fall of Baghdad that Egypt and its vast intellectual-political class found their voice. The anarchy in the streets of Baghdad, and the looting, were the perfect message, just the right backdrop for an autocratic ruler's reminder of what befalls societies that slip into chaos. Iraq had not disappointed Hosni Mubarak, it was darkly said: its anarchy and its sectarian troubles should surely sober up those who would put it forward as a rival and an alternative to Cairo with its tradition of centralized rule. Mubarak governed alone, but he could deliver: he may have snuffed out any decent democratic alternative, but there was order on the banks of the Nile. This was not a brilliant hand to play, but such was Cairo's dilemma, and such were her stakes.

The Egyptian decision makers knew that all was not well in Egyptian-American relations. Egypt may have been spared some of the American fury directed against Saudi Arabia—the Egyptians were less interesting copy, American television and the print media did not pursue them with the same zeal with which the secretive kingdom was pursued—but Egypt's children were leading figures in the world of Islamic terror. The muzzled press in Egypt may have had nothing to say about Mohamed Atta, the lead hijacker who crashed into the North Tower on that brutal morning—to my knowledge, *Al-Ahram,* the official Egyptian daily, never once wrote of him—but Americans knew that something was terribly awry in that Egyptian-American relationship. Egyptian intelligence may have been helpful behind closed doors, but a son of one of Egypt's great urban families, the physician Ayman Zawahiri, had given Al Qaeda its organizational efficiency and its sense of merciless righteousness. Three decades of America's largesse had produced a terrible impasse with the Egyptians.

Cairo had enormous stakes in the play for Baghdad. Authoritarian rule—at once Cairo's bane and, in a turbulent region, her gift to Washington—had been good enough over the preceding quarter-century. Now this war in Iraq was wrapped up with the promise of democratic rule. Cairo did not want and needn't have worried about an Iraqi victory against American power. That kind of prestige for Saddam Hussein would not have worked in Cairo's favor. The hope lay in American disillusionment. After victory, that is, there would come the quagmire and the American discovery of Iraq's impossible ways. Hosni Mubarak would thus be given another reprieve.

Unlike Egypt, Saudi Arabia was not a recipient of American aid. But for the Saudis, as well, the new American bid in Iraq was fraught with all sorts of troubles. The Saudis were no fans of Saddam Hussein. Were a deed of God, or a palace coup, to blow him out of power, the Saudis would have been glad to be rid of him. But his removal by an American war was altogether different. The Saudis had hoped, and pressed, for a covert operation against Saddam Hussein: they believed that money and subversion could do the trick. War had been the American choice. Would the Americans call on Saudi Arabia to offer its facilities, and air space, as the command and control center for their air campaign, or would the new war be waged from Qatar, the plucky little challenger to Saudi Arabia, and from Kuwait? From the perspective of Saudi Arabia's cautious rulers, each course had its attendant risks. The first would force Saudi Arabia into an open display of fidelity to Pax Americana at a time when the world of the Peninsula was in the grip of a furious anti-Americanism. But a war in which Saudi Arabia's place in the American imperium in the Gulf would be usurped by smaller powers was a threat all its own.

Saudi Arabia was still reeling from the storm of September 11—the American scrutiny and the new assertiveness in Saudi Arabia itself, the angry denials of a Saudi population that their own young men had done those terrible deeds. A silent realm not given to faith in words had grown argumentative. The lay preachers and the religious scholars and the technocrats with American university degrees had picked up the Levantine passion for argument. What margin the rulers possessed was growing narrower by the day. Where the relationship with the United States had been a monopoly of the House of Saud, it was now in the public space: on the fax machines, and on the Web, and in the mosques, and on one of the great "infidel" inventions to which the Arabs had taken with a vengeance—the satellite channels.

Were these Saudis whom America had known and dealt with since the 1930s friends or foes? No public relations campaign could deliver the Saudis from the persistent inquiries into the nature of their society. Wahhabism, the creed of the realm, was to become the subject of endless analysis. There had never been a broad constituency in America for Saudi Arabia and its ways. A small segment of the American elite, in the business world, among former diplomats and intelligence operatives, had a Saudi bug of sorts. They savored the country's arcane ways, the trappings of its court life, the agility and subtlety of its rulers. The relationship between these two radically different countries had been sheltered from the rough-and-tumble of political life. That insularity had come to an end, and the doubts had accumulated as to whether a worthwhile relationship could still be maintained with a realm in the throes of a deadly anti-Americanism.

On the borders of the Saudi realm, the smaller states of the Gulf—Bahrain, Kuwait, Qatar—were eager to supplant the Saudi state and to offer their territories for an expanded American presence. For Saudi Arabia's custodians of power, Iraq presented a formidable new challenge. In public, the Saudi rulers put out the word that they opposed the war against the "brotherly" Iraqi people, that they believed Iraq's claims that it had no weapons of mass destruction. No shelter or sanctuary would be given American forces, they were quick to proclaim. They presented their opposition to the war as something normal and understandable, a choice that the bulk of Europe had opted for. But in the shadows, a different Saudi policy was at play. Saudi Arabia would do what was necessary only after President Bush had made an irreversible decision to go to war. When the time came, cruise missiles aimed at Iraq would be fired through Saudi air space; command and control facilities would be available for the American military, and so would an air base in the northern part of the country. Those who matter in Washington would know that Saudi Arabia had delivered, but the House of Saud could keep a discreet distance from the foreign power's war.

A young Lebanese volunteer, one Ihsan al-Khatib, twenty years of age, who had made it to Iraq through Syria, only to witness the great defeat of Saddam Hussein's army, gave expression to a wider Arab incomprehension. He had seen antiaircraft artillery and weapons everywhere, but the regime had fallen and had not fought. "No bird could fly over that city," he said of Saddam's capital, "and I still don't know how the city fell." The young man had answered the "call of jihad": he had gone to Iraq with a friend of his, both determined to "secure victory or be martyred." It had been a spontaneous decision, so eager were these two young men to fight the Americans and to take them on in an Arab land.

In Baghdad, the thing turned out to be a farce. The Iraqi authorities had taken their passports and sent the two men to southern Iraq, by the Iraq-Kuwait border. They and a dozen other Arab volunteers were placed under the command of a cleric: they were told that Republican Guard units were close by, and that their own mission was protecting the rear of these units. But a surprise lay in store: these fighters found themselves under fire from Iraqis who had risen to see the regime into its grave. "I had come to be martyred at the hands of the enemy, not to fall to the bullets of Iraqis," Ihsan al-Khatib said. He deserted his unit, made his way to Baghdad, got back his passport, and headed for home.

An Arab chronicle of the destruction of the Saddam Hussein regime would have to begin with the startling discrepancy between the joy of the great majority of the Iraqis, on that fateful day of April 9, and the utter despondency of wide swaths of the Arab world. There was something odd about the joy in Basra and Baghdad and the grief in Cairo and Ramallah. Despot in Iraq, and "anti-imperialist fighter" in Gaza and Ramallah: such were the great contradictions of Saddam's rule. To hear other Arabs, the Iraqis were not to be trusted with their own destiny, or with their own narration of what their life was like under Tikriti rule.

A measure of this dissonance between Iraqis welcoming a new dawn and Arabs despondent that Saddam Hussein had not given them their own Stalingrad, some new epic of resistance, could be attributed to the sectarianism of the culture: a Sunni Arab regime had been holding a country and had now lost it. While he ruled, the Iraqi dictator had welcomed Palestinian and Egyptian intellectuals; he had talked in grandiose terms about a big project and presented Iraq as the would-be Prussia of an Arab world that he would lead on a brand-new mission. There had been money and subsidies for Egyptian writers and Palestinian homicide bombers and Jordanian editors. There had been bravado for those who craved it: he was the "knight of Arabism" holding aloft a banner of resistance when all appeared lost and America had the run of the region. There had been, it is indisputably true, the acrid sectarianism of those in the Fertile Crescent and the Gulf for whom Shiism reeked of Persia and embodied an alien culture with its own mores and religious ritual.

Sectarianism, though, does not fully explain that wider Arab response to the campaign against Saddam Hussein. The new politics—martyrology, anti-Americanism—had its claims as well. How else can we account for the unexpected support for the Iraqi regime of Saddam Hussein given by elements of the Shia radical movement Hezbollah in Lebanon? By the strict call of the Shia faith, Saddam Hussein was pure evil. He had terrorized the Shia religious scholars and seminarians in his country; he had tortured and murdered hundreds of thousands of Iraqi Shiites and Kurds. Moreover, he had put forth a version of Arab history and identity and "race" that completely disinherited the Shia and put them beyond the pale. It should have been an easy call for a Shia movement like Hezbollah to rally to the cause of the Shia of Iraq. But politics trumped the faith. Hezbollah's anti-Americanism and, no doubt, the guidelines laid down for it by its financial patrons among the hardliners in Iran led it in the opposite direction.

Politics was in command, and the religious preachers were at one with the passions of the street. Consider the fatwas and pronouncements of two influential religious scholars: the Egyptian-born but Qatar-based Sheikh Yusuf al-Qaradawi and the preeminent jurist of the Shia of Lebanon, Ayatollah Muhammad Hussein Fadlallah. It was in the nature of things for Qaradawi (a man who must be reckoned the intellectual godfather of the Al-Jazeera satellite channel and perhaps the single most influential preacher in the world of politicized religion among the Sunnis of the Arab world) to condemn the American campaign in Iraq. He ruled that jihad against the American-led

Coalition was "a duty incumbent on every Muslim. . . . And if that duty is impossible for a particular Muslim to carry out, others should take up the obligation, until it covers the whole world of Islam." A "crusading" war had been waged against a Muslim country, and the faithful had to be rallied.

Qaradawi, working out of Qatar, was speaking to his base: he was an Egyptian; his roots were in the Muslim Brotherhood, his followers looked to him for this kind of guidance. He could not be outflanked within his own world. Even the quintessential establishment jurist Sheikh al-Azhar of Egypt, Muhammad Sayyid Tantawi, a functionary of the Egyptian state, had come forth with a standard fatwa in the same vein: "It is obligatory to stand with Iraq against any aggression, for resisting aggression against any Muslim country is incumbent on all Muslims. It is also impermissible to offer any assistance to the forces of aggression." American supplies for the war against Saddam Hussein were being transported through the Suez Canal: Sheikh Tantawi was a man of the Egyptian state, appointed by the ruler and answerable to him. But he had the running room to stake out the position he did. Qaradawi could do no less: the Muslim street, as far away as the communities in Western Europe and North America, looked to him, and his rulings would have to be consistent with the worldview of his followers.

Fadlallah, though, was a different breed of religious scholar. He answered to no national government; he was a Shia jurist from a noted clerical family that hailed from southern Lebanon; interestingly enough, he had been born and raised in the Iraqi holy city of Najaf. He had risen in the turmoil of Lebanon, in the fractured politics of Beirut. In the 1960s and early '70s, he had worked in northeastern Beirut, in an impoverished Armenian-Shia neighborhood, and he had been good at deciphering the ways of a polyglot city. He was a scholar of immense learning and political subtlety. He was historically aware; he knew the heartbreak and cruelty inflicted on the Shia seminarians in Iraq, and on the Shia as a whole, and he had written of Iraq with deep authority and intimacy.

Fadlallah had been close to countless clerics who had been struck down by the terror of the Baath regime. Yet days before the fall of Saddam's regime, he was denouncing the American plans for Iraq, stripping the American presence in that country of any legitimacy. The matter went beyond the fate of Saddam's regime, "which we all want to see destroyed," he said. It had to do with the future of the Arab nation and of generations to come. He had some words of advice to the Iraqis: "Don't listen to the promises of global hegemony, as it sings the praises of humanity and democracy, because plans are being prepared to occupy your country, dominate its resources in the name of lofty goals. The forces of hegemony only believe in democracy for their monopolies and all that entails by way of expropriating wealth and resources."

Fadlallah had always been interested in the realm of power; he had played a signal role in politicizing the Shia of Lebanon and in giving military power and combat a new kind of legitimacy. His influence had been felt in that turbulent history that had transformed Shiism and stripped it of its old quietism and its aversion to political activism. Proud of his learning, he was ambitious to give Arab Shiism—and himself—a base of influence independent of Iran's primacy in the Shia world. He would return to his old theme as he agitated against the American campaign in Iraq. There is no "absolute and eternal" power, and no "absolute and eternal" weakness, he said. The Americans are now ascendant, but they could be humbled and brought down if only the Muslims understood the logic of power and of sacrifice. Fadlallah was in Beirut, far away from the hell of Najaf and Karbala. He had no prescription for Iraqis eager to be rid of Saddam Hussein, no viable way out to offer them.

At its best, the Shia tradition, and its expositions, could be supple. Some of its great scholars, who had lived under tyrannical rulers, knew how to walk between raindrops, how to outwit brutal men who possessed worldly power. They had a tradition of *sukut* (silence) and a whole art by which the faithful around them interpreted their winks and nods, their periods of seclusion when they averted their gaze from things they abhorred but could not change. It was within that tradition that Iraq's preeminent Shia jurist, Ayatollah al-Sistani in Najaf, had worked when he called on the faithful "not to interrupt" the work and the progress of the Coalition forces when they swept into Iraq. Fadlallah could have honored that tradition as well. But he chose not to. He could have taken the foreign power's gift without hailing the giver. But the politics of his city, and the demands of the competition with other jurists and religious tribunes, got the better of him.

In an Arab culture that prides itself on the maxim "My brother and

I against my cousin, my cousin and I against the stranger," it was perhaps fated that the Iraqis would suffer—and celebrate—alone. Saddam's victims in Iraq were, in the main, Shia and Kurds, and Arab society could avert its gaze from their troubles. A member in good standing of the Palestinian elite, Adley Sadeq, a deputy minister of the Palestinian Authority and a onetime columnist, was, alas, all too typical of the political class in his world. Of Saddam, he would say, "The man was a thorn in the eyes of the imperialists. . . . We know that the man made mistakes, which are an inevitable part of the experience of great leaders who rule complex societies in dangerous geographic regions, during difficult times." The geography of the Arab world was being altered: a whole new Arab grief, that of Iraq's people, had to be acknowledged, but this man of Palestine was not ready for that change.

Palestine had always had primacy in the tale of Arab woes; a world accustomed to chronicling what sorrows had beset the Arab nation at the hands of strangers would have to turn inward to examine the self-inflicted wounds of the Arabs, the ways of a cruel political tradition. But the mass graves in Iraq would not stir or shame this political sensibility. Nearly three hundred thousand Iraqis had "disappeared" under the Baath dictatorship, but there were Arab devotees of Saddam who could pass over these great crimes in silence. A whole new political culture was needed if the Americans were to be seen as ushering in the dawn of a better order in Iraq. True, in Kuwait and elsewhere, there were men and women who knew the enormity of the terror Saddam Hussein had inflicted on his nation. But the age of genuine political accountability had not yet come to Arab lands. The time for bidding farewell to the pieties of Arab brotherhood had not yet arrived.

Cities beget legends, and the legend of Baghdad that presented itself to the pan-Arabists as American and British forces swept into Iraq was the fall of Baghdad to the Mongols in 1258. In a culture reliant on unexamined rote learning, even Arabs of the most meager historical awareness were given the bare outlines of that tale. Baghdad had been sacked in that year, and the event had become one of those great divides in Islamic history—the end of the Abbasid Caliphate, the passing of a high, urban pan-Islamic order, and the beginning of an age of decline and disorder. In the legend, the books in Baghdad's vast libraries were dumped in the Tigris, and thousands of the city's people were put to the sword. In the fevered imagination of Arab crowds at some remove from Baghdad, crowds chanting Saddam's name, those soldiers of the American-led Coalition were the new Mongols. History does not always instruct, and its analysis often goes astray. But this was the history available to the crowd.

There was no use reminding the street, and those who mold and shape it, that the Tikriti political order was no citadel of Arab culture and learning. The crowd works its will on history, and for the anti-American intellectual class, that historical parallel with the events of 1258 was good enough. The satellite channels—the new purveyors of fevered politics—were there to pick up and elaborate on the terror that the "new Mongols" had inflicted on Iraq. In the Arab commentaries, there was grief now that the Americans had brought lawlessness to the land where Hammurabi had issued the first proclamation of law in history. The Arabs had been living on their nerves, and the satellite channels had been feeding this restlessness. Over the course of some thirty months, from the outbreak of the "second intifada" in September 2000, through the terror attacks on America and the war against the Taliban regime, the world of the Arabs had been stripped of any sense of normalcy, and the culture as a whole had taken to this new addiction to fast-paced, inflammatory television.

In some quarters, satellite TV was hailed as the advent of "new media" and the coming of a time of awareness: Arabs would now hear truths denied them by the sycophantic media of the regimes. There was new freedom to be sure, but the staple of the new media was an incendiary mix of victimology and wrath. An Arab epic would have to be supplied in Iraq, and the satellite channels in Qatar and Dubai were there to provide it. There was that Iraqi peasant who allegedly brought down an Apache helicopter with an old hunting rifle: from Casablanca to nearby Amman, the man was a hero, and the signs were there, the partisans of Saddam believed, for a devastating American quagmire. There was "Baghdad Bob," the comical minister of information, Mohamed Said al-Sahhaf, foretelling a great Iraqi victory even as the American tanks were within shouting distance. The invaders, said Sahhaf, would commit suicide on the walls of Baghdad.

A world had changed and had not changed. Four decades earlier, there had been another braggart who owned the Arab airwaves of his time: an Egyptian broadcaster by the name of Ahmad Said. His medium was the radio, and he used it to inflame and feed popular passions. He too had filled the air with extravagant promises of victories that never came; he too had misled and bamboozled the Arabs of his time. In the Six-Day War of 1967, he and his guild in Cairo had told the Arabs of a great victory in the making, only to have them discover that the whole edifice of Nasserism had been undone.

A thoughtful Saudi commentator, Abdul Rahman al-Rashed, the editor-in-chief of the daily *Asharq Al-Awsat,* saw in the coverage of this war in Iraq a continuity with the old journalism. The new technologies and the satellite channels mimicked the journalism of the West, he wrote. But the content was the same diet of deception that had led the Arabs astray in the age of radical Arab nationalism. The new technology was put at the service of an old and stubborn refusal to face and name things as they are.

It is odd, this compact that a culture makes with false redeemers and pretenders. Arab society had been through it with Saddam Hussein before: a bare dozen years earlier, the man had promised the Arabs deliverance and victory, only to serve them another tale of defeat and heartbreak. "Angels of mercy," he had told his commanders, would come to the aid of Iraq's armies, and Iraq would frustrate and thwart the invaders. He had lost his air force—hence the angels of mercy providing a cover for his troops. His army was surrendering in droves; the bravado had been empty. The crowd that had been taken in by this new Saladin was not ready for the calamity that followed: the destruction of the pretender's army, his expulsion from Kuwait, the principality he had claimed as the "nineteenth province" of his dominion.

It would have been the better part of prudence not to believe the Iraqi regime's promises of a big, brilliant battle this time around. But popular cultures are what they are, and a regime that strutted with cruelty and machismo still held its devotees in thrall. When Basra fell, and its people went into the streets with evident joy, the Arab crowd wrote off this spectacle of celebration. It was a treasonous (read Shia) city, and the real resistance would yet be written in Baghdad. Myths die hard: it was only a handful of people, a hired mob at that, that had celebrated the coming of the Americans, it was asserted in Egypt and in the Palestinian towns and cities. But there was disappointment as well in the hero himself. When the full magnitude of the defeat was there to see, there were Palestinians who saw the military defects of a regime that had been easy to destroy. It was said that the town of Jenin had mounted a more formidable defense to an Israeli siege than had Saddam's capital. It was noted by the instant analysts that Baghdad's rulers had ignored the rudimentary rules of urban warfare, that no trenches had been dug around the city, and that the roads had not been mined. This military analysis only papered over the larger meaning of the regime's collapse.

The passion and anger of Egypt's response—fury at America, anger that Saddam had not given the epic resistance he had promised—must have been the working out of a trauma Egyptians knew and remembered all too well. There had been that cruel summer, thirty-odd years earlier, in 1967, when the Egyptian Army, and the legendary leader Gamal Abdel Nasser, had been defeated by a lightning Israeli victory. Then too, in a war that shattered the dreams of modern-day Arabs, the crowd had believed in the leader's magic, in the rockets and modern weapons of his army, only to be awakened to a devastating defeat. The battle for Baghdad was a reminder of the false promise of Arab power.

The street in Egypt had wanted a vicarious battle, and the crowd was not to have it. Egypt is an unhappy land; its spirit has been broken by its military ruler, its political life has been turned into a modern pharaoh's domain. The liberalism, the vibrant political tradition of an earlier age, the proud civic associations of parliamentarians, feminists—all had been overwhelmed by the ruler and his political-military apparatus. True, there had been a war between the regime and the Islamists that had raged through the 1980s until the mid-1990s. But that war had been settled; the regime had prevailed, and the middle classes had given grudging support to the ruler and his security apparatus as the lesser of two evils. Now all that remained was a political culture that externalized the popular anger and wrath, that forever dwelled on the great evils of American power.

The defining truth of Arab political life that was laid bare by the fall of Baghdad was the gap between the terror of the state at home and its weakness in dealing with the outside world. Oppressor at home, oppressed abroad; that is the way the Arabs are given to describing their postcolonial states. Egypt in 1967 had been about that weakness, and so had the fall of Saddam Hussein's Iraq. The trauma of the Six-Day War of 1967 was about the sudden collapse of Egypt's army, the failure of the ruler's magic. And that story line had played out the same way in Baghdad more than three decades later. This was the gap, and the duality, that the celebrated Arab writer Adonis explored in a piece of singular poise and depth. Adonis was writing from his own, independent vantage point: he had no use for the American invasion, and none for the regime of Saddam Hussein. "We must be ashamed," he wrote, "to see the American and British soldiers roaming the streets of Baghdad and Basra as liberators. We must be ashamed to see the Iraqis scrambling for bread and water as though they had not seen them before—they who lived in the land of bread and water. We must be ashamed for the theft and looting committed by some Iraqis in the name of need, or of greed, or because such is their profession and predilection. All of us must be ashamed for what has happened and is happening in Iraq. We must apologize to the great Arabic language for the name that has been given us—'the Arabs.' "

Adonis knew modern Arab politics: born in 1930, in the impoverished Syrian hinterland, he had known imprisonment in his country for political activism. This terrible experience, suffered in his early youth, had scarred him. He had given up on Syria after that and opted for the freedom of Beirut and the light hand of its political order. He had quit Lebanon in 1986, after a decade of civil war, and made a new life for himself in France. He was without illusions about the cruelty of authoritarian regimes or the perversities of Saddam Hussein. "But is not Saddam Hussein," he wrote, "responsible for all that has happened and is now unfolding in Iraq, from the beginning of his regime? Instead of giving his life to his people, he appropriated his people's life, and its wealth, as a private possession of his family. Since he claimed that he was the inspired and sole leader, the savior, why did he not tell his people that he could no longer bear their poverty, why did he not give them all opportunities for work? Why did he not say that he could no longer bear their illiteracy and educate all of them? Why did he not say that he could no longer bear their backwardness and inspire them with the dream of progress and modernity? Why did he not say that he could no longer bear their slavery and give them liberty? Instead, he knew only one expression: 'I am the sole leader and whoever defies me shall be beheaded, and he who submits shall be given bounty and largesse of every kind.' "

It is not enough, said Adonis, to reject foreign invaders; Arabs have to reject internal oppression as well. The lesson of Iraq was the emptiness of the police state. Iraq, the quintessential state of terror and police rule, should teach the other Arabs that there is no substitute for decent regimes that give their people self-respect, enable them to live with one another without charges of treason or accusations of religious deviation. Freedom was indivisible, observed Adonis, and the spectacle of Iraq revealed the unassailable truth that this nation, invaded from the outside, was already in captivity. "No self-respecting human being would defend a prison." The Iraqi ruler had annulled the culture of his country: the foreign invasion had found nothing of worth in the dictator's domain.

Can a new Iraq emerge out of this cruel time, and can it shed the burden of its history? Adonis was honest enough to acknowledge the weight of the image that he—and generations of Arabs—had inherited about Iraq. The past seems to repeat in Iraq, he wrote. The streets of Baghdad have always been littered with corpses; the image of that horrific regicide in 1958, when the young monarch, Faisal II, was gunned down with his entire family by military conspirators, is still "alive and present." In the name of noble-sounding goals—freedom, progress, patriotism, justice—Iraqis have shed blood indiscriminately. Pan-Arabists, Communists, Baathists had all taken part in that tragic history; no apologies had been made for that violence. Iraq had treated the Arab world to the spectacle of corpses dragged through the streets. The practice had a name, *sahl,* and it was, in the popular mind, associated with Iraq. The culture had coarsened; an Iraqi poet of the left, Adonis lamented, had once been proud to warn that the skulls of his faction's enemies would be used as ashtrays.

Can a culture steeped in that kind of pain and cruelty give birth to a pluralist-democratic era that "respects man and his rights and appreciates the attachment of the citizen to the soil of Iraq"? From afar, the Americans had come proclaiming that Iraq would be the showcase of a better Arab political order. This man of a progressive bent—anti-authoritarian, thoroughly secular, a believer in democratic culture—did not think that Iraq could bear the weight of such expectations. He warned Iraqis not to "march backwards into the sun." It was not enough, he wrote, for Iraqis to make a fetish of independence or to reiterate how devoted they were to the idea of national autonomy.

Twice exiled—from Syria, then from Lebanon—Adonis belonged to that class of Arabs who had become homeless. They could ruminate over Arab history, but neither they nor the Arabs still on the soil of their homelands had much to contribute to the struggle unfolding in Iraq. The history that mattered was being fought out, on the ground, between foreign soldiers and the remnants of a dying regime. In modern Arab life, war was a spectator sport. This standoff between foreign liberators and a native tyranny based on the call of the clan and the sect spoke in painful, stark terms of the terrible harvest of modern Arab history. A circle was closed in 2003. Some eight decades earlier, the fall of the Ottoman Empire had pulled, like a magnet, Pax Britannica into Iraq. Now Pax Americana had blown in; the postcolonial states of the Arab world had hatched a terrible new age of radicalism and cruelty. Soldiers from Kokomo, Indiana, and Burlington, Vermont, and Linden, New Jersey (I mention those towns, picked at random, from the grim announcements of the Department of Defense reporting the deaths of soldiers killed in the "Iraq theater of operations") were battling it out in Baghdad and Fallujah. These soldiers, and their counterparts from a handful of countries that participated in this war, had come to fight what should have been an Arab fight.

A righteous sense of violation over September 11 had taken America into the alleyways of Tikrit and Fallujah. The foreign power did not know the intimate details of Iraq. There was a leap of faith in the great expectations that accompanied the launching of this war. Perhaps it was American idealism at work; perhaps it was the understandable desire of the architects of this war to justify the costs in blood and treasure of an expedition deep into so tangled an Arab setting. But as the looters and the saboteurs were taking apart what little infrastructure the despot and his wars (and a decade of sanctions) had left in place, George W. Bush spoke of Iraq's promise. "The rise of Iraq as an example of democracy and prosperity is a massive and long-term undertaking," he was to observe in early July 2004. "And the restoration of that country is critical to the defeat of terror and radicalism throughout the Middle East." A new battle had opened between a foreign power bearing the promise of reform, and an old and stubborn Arab tradition that had seen the coming, and then the blowing over, of so many new bids to change it and to rid it of its ruinous habits.

A fortnight earlier, in Doha, Qatar, at Omar ibn al-Khattab Mosque, at fifteen or twenty minutes' remove from the headquarters of the U.S. Central Command, Sheikh Yusuf al-Qaradawi delivered a Friday sermon. The cleric's big theme of the day was the arrogance of the United States and the cruelty of the war America had waged against the Iraqi regime. "America was acting like a god on earth," Qaradawi told the faithful. It had willed Iraq's occupation, imposed on that country the law of the mighty. He was keen to state for the record that he had never uttered a word of praise for Saddam Hussein. But as befitting a man who came out of the religious learning of Al-Azhar University, who had memorized a good deal of the Quran at an early age and had assimilated huge chunks of traditional learning, the preacher gave his verdict on the American expedition into Iraq in the most predictable way: there was that old link to the sacking of Baghdad by the Mongols in 1258. Qaradawi gave the history its familiar and popular version: the Mongols had overwhelmed a great city. "The books were thrown into the Tigris until the river became black with their ink. There were days when it became red with blood, and there were days when it became black with ink." This history was not metaphor. To Qaradawi and his followers this was the truth of the history. "Blood flowed in the streets, in the houses, and above the roofs. Even in the drainpipes, rivers of blood flowed."

The history telescopes easily: for George W. Bush today, there had been the Mongol conqueror, Hülegü. "What is the difference between Bush and the Mongol king?" Qaradawi asked. And for those libraries that had been dumped in the Tigris, there are equivalent modern calamities. "This was also the fate of Baghdad in the twenty-first century; they allowed the looters to raid the museums, the libraries, and the universities. They showed us some of the people while they were looting, but they did not show us who opened the locked doors for them. This they did not film. This was organized looting, behind which stood international gangs." The preacher had conjured up a Baghdad of the imagination. In that city called up by rote learning and by accepted, unexamined history, the world is illuminated by knowledge and learning, and Baghdad's imagined past acquits the city of Saddam Hussein.

In his own life, Sheikh Qaradawi knew and lived by a different kind of truth. There was his access to Al-Jazeera and to a Web site of his views and fatwas propagated to followers everywhere both in Islamic lands and in *bilad al-kufr* (the lands of unbelief). Much of the preacher's craft could be the envy of the best of the televangelists in America; much of it, no doubt, was owed to the American example of modernized, televised religion. Three of his four daughters have PhDs in the modern sciences—physics, organic chemistry, and botany— from British universities. A fourth daughter completed her master's degree in history at the University of Texas. A son earned an advanced degree from the University of Central Florida in Orlando. The foreign reformers would have their work cut out for them. Qaradawi partook of the modern world but agitated against it. America's destiny and reach had taken it deep into Arab lands; the needs of the Arabs had brought them into a condition of resentful dependence on the United States. Between America and that resentful Arab world there would remain a great, deadly impasse.

This was a world that could whittle down, even devour a big American victory. It was a difficult, perhaps impossible landscape. There were countless escapes available to that Arab world. It could reject the message of reform by dwelling on the sins of the American messenger. It could call up the fury of the Israeli-Palestinian violence and use it as an alibi for yet more self-pity and rage. It could shout down its own would-be reformers, write them off as accomplices of a foreign power. It could throw up its defenses and wait for the United States to weary of its expedition.

A foreign power bearing reform, and dreaming of it, had its work cut out for it. In Baghdad and Basra, and in Mosul in the north, there were celebrations when Saddam's monstrous sons, Uday and Qusay, were killed in a firefight with American forces on July 22, 2003, and their corpses were displayed to an Iraqi public eager to know that there had been justice and retribution for what these men had done to the country. But next door in Amman, in a kingdom safely within the American and Western orbit, there were *majalis taziyah* (mourning assemblies) for Saddam's sons. They were "martyrs," it was said of the two men who had sown terror throughout the land. A culture that had seen so much bloodshed now feigned horror at the incivility of displaying the bodies of these two men. There was little that a foreign power could do to reach that impenetrable core of beliefs; there were no hearts and minds in Araby to be won for this American campaign and no way of convincing an appreciable body of opinion in the Arab world of the justness of this campaign. When the American occupation authority formed a "governing council" with a fair representation of Iraq's ethnic and sectarian diversity—thirteen Shia, five Kurds, five Sunni Arabs, one each from the Chaldean and Turkoman communities—the Arab states wanted nothing to do with this council, and this rejection was even stronger on the part of parliamentarians and intellectuals and civic associations.

In a world where tyranny and minority rule held sway, there were Arabs who with a straight face could say that this council lacked legitimacy because it was not a "representative" body, because strangers had imposed it on Iraq. Walking with strangers was impermissible, while tyranny of the Egyptian and Syrian variety was in the normal scheme of things. This was a truth so deeply entrenched in the Arab condition that no foreign power could alter or challenge it.

CHAPTER 3

In the Shadow of the Martyrs

Write something about Arab ungratefulness and hypocrisy," a man who hailed from the apex of one of the Arab states of the Persian Gulf wrote to me, in a note he sent as the cruel summer of 2003 was drawing to an end. The note was startling; the writer was no outsider to the Arab councils of power. A thoroughly decent and educated man, keen to see the Arab world shed its denials and retrogressions, he had welcomed the war against the regime of Saddam Hussein and seen in it the possibility of genuine change in Arab affairs. The liberation of Iraq had made a deep impression on him. He had been moved by the swiftness of America's victory, by these strangers who had come to prosecute a war so far away from home. He was without illusions about the terrible history of Iraq and its heavy burden, but the spectacle of the fall of Saddam's tyranny—the statues tumbling down, the crowds in the streets—had filled him with hope that Iraq's history could be remade, and that the Arabs would take this gift granted them by the Americans to come to terms with the harvest of their own history.

But the "Baghdad Spring" had been all too brief. Iraq was a hard land made weary and cynical by tyranny, its culture inaccessible to its liberators. There was joy to be sure, but the Anglo-American forces had been greeted by a measure of reserve and silence as well, as they made their way from the southern part of the country to the capital. A brutalized people were unable to take on good faith that the Americans had come to decapitate the regime this time around. A tragic history, it was soon told, sat uneasily on the encounter between Iraq and its foreign liberators. There was that memory of 1991, all but forgotten in America but retained by Iraqis, of their uprising against the regime, at America's urging. In the Kurdish hill country in the north, and in the southern Shia towns, fierce rebellions had broken out: an American president by the same name as the current one, promising

Iraq a new dawn of liberty, had called upon Iraqis to rebel and had then left them to fend for themselves. The rebellions had been put down without mercy; a population that had believed in the promises of the outsider had been betrayed.

There was no wishing away that history. It hovered over this venture into Iraq. It accounted for the mix of joy and caution with which the Shia of the country responded to the arrival of the Americans in their midst. An observer who knew the southern part of the country provided me with this sobering image, put it forth as a refrain: the Shia in the south were too broken, she said, to swat the flies off their faces, let alone to go out and cheer foreign troops whose intentions—and staying power—were at best a matter of conjecture.

In the scheme of things, the Shia stood to emerge as the prime beneficiaries of the new order. America had rid them of the Sunni ascendancy, given them a chance at normalcy. Still, the Shia held back. They were a majority of the population, it is true. But behind them lay long centuries of disinheritance and persecution. The habits of command were not yet theirs. The caution with which they received the American stewardship bore the mark of their unease with power. I had seen and chronicled that phenomenon among the Shia in Lebanon, my birthplace. There was a "Shia complex" in that country, and some among the Shia owned up to that sentiment. They were the stepchildren of the Arab world. They had to display their Arabism; they had to show themselves, and mainstream Sunni Muslims, that they were no "collaborators" of foreign powers. This explains the zeal and fury of the Shia militants on the Israeli-Lebanese border, their determination to show that they were fighting a large Arab fight.

In the turbulence that followed the dictator's fall, the Shia appeared uncertain about their ultimate political destination. There were those who fell back on the idea of clerical rule: the *hawza* (the religious institution and seminaries) should rule, they proclaimed. From the chaos, there emerged a young claimant, Sayyid Moqtada al-Sadr. It was this cleric, thought to be in his early thirties, who raised the banner of theocratic government. By the criteria of seniority and scholarly distinction, Moqtada al-Sadr was an upstart. But he was a son of Muhammad Sadiq al-Sadr, an ayatollah who had been assassinated (along with two of his children) by the Saddam regime in 1999. Moqtada had gone into hiding; he was to turn up after the fall of the dictatorship, looking for satisfaction and retribution. He had targets aplenty, beginning with the Baathists who had cut down his father and two of his siblings. But he had other enemies: ayatollahs and clerics who, by his light, had abandoned his father in his hour of need. His father had had a constituency among the newly urbanized of the Shia, "tribals" who had been drawn into the urban centers by the poverty of the countryside. The son had found that constituency in the slums of Baghdad. The young man's lineage gave him influence among the Shia poor: he hailed from one of the great clerical families of the Shia world. The Sadrs were sayyids; claiming descent from the Prophet Muhammad, they were for all practical purposes nobility among the Shia clerical establishment. They had played leading religious-political roles in Iran, Iraq, and Lebanon.

This young man of immoderate temperament was an heir to a great, distinguished history. Gertrude Bell, Oriental Secretary to the British high commissioner putting together a new Iraqi realm, had encountered this family of clerical luminaries. In her diary of March 14, 1920, she wrote of the difficulty of "getting into touch" with the Shia and with their clerics in particular: "There is a group of these worthies in Kadimain, the holy city, eight miles from Baghdad, bitterly pan-Islamic, anti-British . . . chief among them a family called Sadr possibly more distinguished for religious learning than any other family in the whole Shia world." Gertrude Bell was a woman of great determination. She visited one of these "worthies," the great scholar Hassan al-Sadr: a woman of free spirit, she refused to be veiled for the occasion. "I sat beside him on the carpet and after formal greetings he began to talk in the rolling periods of the learned man. . . . We talked of the Sadr family in all its branches, Persian, Syrian, and Mesopotamian; and then of books and collections of books." A few months later, a full-scale Shia rebellion erupted in which this scholar's son, Sayyid Muhammad, was a leading player, perhaps the most active of the nationalists.

In more recent times, two of the Sadrs had been "martyred" for the cause of the Shia and were iconic figures to their followers: Ayatollah Muhammad Baqir al-Sadr, who had been executed by the Iraqi regime in 1980, and a cousin of his, Imam Musa al-Sadr, who had led the Shia of Lebanon in the 1960s and 1970s, until his "disappearance" in Libya in 1978 while on a visit to that country's erratic leader. Both Sadrs, relatives of this young man, had been men of mild temperament and exquisite subtlety. Leadership had come to them in a "natural" way.

The hugely charismatic Sayyid Musa had come to Lebanon in 1959, from his birthplace in Iran, and over the course of a single decade had emerged as Shia Lebanon's most arresting public figure, straddling the boundaries of religion and politics, playing a seminal role in the rise of a community hitherto on the fringes of political power. He was beloved by the Christian communities; he had found a place for himself in the cultural and political life of Beirut. He gave popular talks in churches, went out of his way to underscore his ease with pluralism and cultural and personal dealings across religious lines. He was a modernist on women's rights. He had become a dazzling and beloved star of Beirut's media. In the summer of 1978, he traveled to Libya at the invitation of its military ruler. He "vanished" there, with two of his companions. The Libyan authorities insisted that he had left that country for Italy, but he had been a victim of foul play and was never heard from again. His disappearance in Libya had been a signal loss for Lebanon, coming as that country was sliding into a terrible civil war. For the Shia faithful who revered him, Musa al-Sadr's disappearance had unmistakable artistry. He became the "absent imam"; his fate recast him as a late-twentieth-century embodiment of the Twelfth Imam, who disappeared to the "eyes of ordinary men" but will return at the end of time to punish the wicked and fill the earth with justice.

Muhammad Baqir al-Sadr had been a more distinguished scholar than his Lebanese cousin and brother-in-law. But timing and history had picked him for grief as well. He had been heir to a great tradition: born in 1935, he was a child prodigy in philosophy and religious commentary. In the shadow of the Grand Ayatollah Muhsin al-Hakim, he had emerged as the most prominent and "modernized" leader of the clerical class. He may have been the twentieth century's most important Shia scholar. He had risen as a very young man with seminal works on Islamic philosophy and economics. In the staid world of the religious seminaries, he stood out with sustained serious books that provided an answer to the Marxist ideas then making inroads among the young Shia of the 1960s and 1970s. He had trod carefully, for by the late 1970s, the struggle between the Baath rulers and the Shia clerical class had taken a violent turn. Saddam Hussein had now risen to absolute and uncontested power. And the Iranian upheaval of 1978–79 had given the Sunni-Shia feud a new ferocity. Amid the Shia there was the exuberance of people awakening to new possibilities. For the Sunni Arabs—and for the Iraqi rulers in particular—it was a time of panic. Whether he willed it or not, Muhammad Baqir al-Sadr was now at the epicenter of a violent storm. He was dubbed "the Khomeini of Iraq," and this was nothing less than a death warrant in Saddam's tyranny.

Muhammad Baqir al-Sadr had done what he could to stay out of harm's way. With Khomeini at the helm of a theocratic state in Iran, he thought it prudent to cross to that country and take up residence in Qom. This was mid-1979, and the matter, of course, needed Khomeini's approval. The matter was taken up in a telling correspondence between the two sayyids and religious scholars. The exchange, reproduced by Chibli Mallat, an Arab authority on this material, catches a whole range of things: Sadr's sense of responsibility to his flock and guild right alongside his growing worries about the Tikriti regime, the newfound power of Khomeini in Iran, and the mercilessness that was always part of that man's character. The Baath rulers were closing in on Sadr. The word had been put out that Sadr might opt for asylum in Iran, and Khomeini took the initiative in writing to Sadr:

His eminence, Hujjat al-Islam and the Muslims, Sayyid Muhammad Baqir al-Sadr, with God's blessings. We have been informed that your eminence plans on leaving Iraq on account of the events there. I don't think that it is in the public interest for you to leave the holy city of Najaf, the center of Islamic learning. This is a source of considerable anxiety for me. May God remove your anxiety, and grant you His mercy and blessings.

Sadr's response came on June 1, 1979:

His Eminence Grand Ayatollah, the struggler-Imam, Sayyid Ruhollah Khomeini: I received your kind cable that embodies and expresses your fatherly and spiritual concern for the holy shrine of Najaf, which since your departure, is still living through the time of your great victories. I draw inspiration from your guidance, and I do feel the sense of responsibility for Najaf and its scholarly learning. . . . On this occasion I want to transmit to you the greetings of millions of Muslims and believers in our precious Iraq which has found a new light of Islamic guidance at your hands. . . . We ask God Almighty to grant us your long life, and peace and God's mercy be upon you.

This was no longer the exchange of two religious scholars. In his years in Najaf, Khomeini had not enjoyed primacy over Sadr; to be sure, he was three decades older, and there was the reverence due him by that factor of seniority alone. But Sadr was a star in the galaxy of Najaf, more at home in the modern world and in the modern fields of economics and Western philosophy. Now the world had altered. Khomeini was no longer an exile in Najaf but the ruler of a big country, with wealth and resources and territory to command. Exile in Iraq had been right and proper for Khomeini; he had done well by it. He had used it to write his religious and political tracts, and to wait out the Pahlavi regime. But Sadr was now being told to stay close to the fire—and potential harm—of the Baath Party. Stripped of the courtesy and the formalism, Khomeini was, for all practical purposes, denying Sadr asylum in Iran. Perhaps Khomeini hadn't foreseen the levels of violence the Baathist state would resort to under the unfettered leadership of Saddam Hussein. Perhaps he was being himself, the stern revolutionary for whom the end—the sacking of the Baathist regime—justified the means and the risks. Sadr would be offered no reprieve by the revolutionary in power across the border.

The manner of address between the two men, Chibli Mallat reminds us, was illuminating in its own right. Khomeini addressed Sadr as *Hujjat al-Islam,* a middling rank in the clerical world; Sadr, by contrast, was effusive: he had given Khomeini his due as a grand ayatollah; moreover, he had added the appellation of *imam* to take in the political primacy of Khomeini and his rise to new charismatic power. The sanctuary denied, Sadr was a marked man. Earlier in the year, the squads of the regime had tried to haul him off to prison, but they had been thwarted by his daring sister, Bint al-Huda, a poetess and scholar in her own right, who had summoned his followers from the Imam Ali shrine in Najaf by telling them that the "imam of the Iraqis" was in danger. The forces of the regime had backed off from the confrontation and had to settle for placing Sadr under house arrest. In the year, and the crisis, to come, the regime took no chances: both brother and sister were taken into captivity in Baghdad, where they were murdered. The Tikritis were not subtle: the execution of Bint al-Huda was, by the old culture's norms, out of bounds. No one was off-limits, the rulers announced, not even a woman of high birth and calling and a reputation for genuine piety.

Saints and martyrs always write and shape their own legends. In death, Muhammad Baqir al-Sadr was to be known as "the happy martyr." In the trying years that followed, the Shia said of this mild-mannered man that he had foreseen his own death and that he had told his disciples that he had made peace with his own destiny. They quoted and remembered his words: "I have chosen martyrdom, perhaps this is the last thing I will say to you." This was the "first Sadr," and his relative Muhammad Sadiq al-Sadr was to work in the shadow of this noble, and heavy, legacy.

Nothing about Ayatollah Muhammad Sadiq al-Sadr's life, or his murder, was to prove simple or straightforward. In the end, the regime had gunned him down, but before that there were rumors that he had had a period of *hudna,* a cease-fire of sorts, with the old despotism. In a time of fear and suspicion, some of the leading ayatollahs had opted for political quietism and withdrawal. Two or three years after the frightening execution of the first Sadr in 1980, leading members of the Hakim family fled to Iran. In 1992, after the death of the Grand Ayatollah Abolqassem al-Khoei, his family chose exile in London. The Baathist terror squads and their informers had the run of the Shia seminaries and holy cities. In Najaf, a consensus had emerged around Ali al-Sistani as the supreme *marja' al-taqlid* (source of imitation); born in the shrine city of Mashhad, across the border in Iran, in 1930, Sistani had settled in Najaf in 1952. He had done his best to ride out the terror visited on the Shia in the aftermath of the Gulf War in 1990–91.

It hadn't been easy; there had been an attempt on Sistani's life. But he had survived, and the Shia tradition itself, which gave a warrant to *taqiyya* (dissimulation) in places and times of danger, accepted his choice. Around him, other religious jurists were falling to assassins: in 1998 two grand ayatollahs, Murtada Burujirdi and Ali Gharawi, were struck down by killer squads of the regime. The Baathists were brazen by now. They had shrugged off the two assassinations, dismissed them as the deeds of rival ayatollahs and scholars within Najaf itself. Depending on the day, and the source of the rumor, the assassinations were passed off as the doings of Grand Ayatollah Sistani or of Muhammad Baqir al-Hakim or of Sadr himself. The audacity of the regime, and its ability to manufacture what truth it wanted, were a measure of the contempt the Tikritis had for their helpless subjects.

It was in this time of terror that Ayatollah Muhammad Sadiq al-Sadr rose to prominence. His pedigree was impeccable: born in 1943, he had been a student of the first Sadr, and of the Grand Ayatollah Khoei, the preeminent jurist of his time. He had also studied law with Ayatollah Khomeini; the latter, it should be recalled, had spent fifteen years in exile in Najaf. From both Muhammad Baqir al-Sadr and Ayatollah Khomeini, the second Sadr had imbibed a tradition of vigilance and an ethic of sacrifice. The written sources are not in agreement on his temperament and abilities. His admirers depict a prodigy of the religious sciences who immersed himself as well in nonreligious studies—psychology, the English language. His detractors describe him as a man of middling abilities, temperamental, given to wild swings of emotions, quick to get excited and then easily discouraged.

Typical of his guild, he ran afoul of the Baathists and was arrested twice in the early 1970s. There are reports that he was brutally tortured during his second imprisonment. Upon his release, in 1975, he took a turn toward mysticism and self-denial; indeed, so extreme was this phase of his life that his teacher, Muhammad Baqir al-Sadr, grew greatly concerned about his health and urged upon him a less severe regimen. By now the long night of Baathist despotism had begun to fall on Najaf. Saddam Hussein, hitherto second in command to President Ahmad Hassan al-Bakr, had started the consolidation of his own power. In 1977 the Shia religious procession from Najaf to Karbala, the annual commemoration of Imam Hussein's martyrdom, was banned. Shortly thereafter, the Iranian Revolution broke out—a herald of deliverance for the Shia, a time for the Baathist regime to hunker down at home and launch its war against the Iranian revolutionaries.

The Shia uprising in 1991 serves as the background of Muhammad Sadiq al-Sadr's activism and supplies the controversy that continues to swirl around him. One thing we know for sure, he was arrested for a third time in the aftermath of that uprising. The Shia world in Iraq was in the grip of an acute historical crisis. Grand Ayatollah Sistani's caution was an anchor for a traumatized community. But there were young people eager to fight back, and they were dissatisfied with Sistani's caution. For its part, the regime in Iraq was keener than it had ever been to separate Iraqi Shiism from its Iranian counterpart. A regime inflicting great terror on its own Shia population had taken to exalting the nobility and authenticity of "Arab Shiism," setting it apart from all that was Persian and "imported" and "alien" to it. Manhood, valor, the *asala* (authenticity) of tribal descent: all these presumably Arab attributes were now projected onto the Shia of Iraq, as a way of depicting them as a people apart from Persian "intrigue and treachery." In this time of uncertainty, Muhammad Sadiq al-Sadr appeared to have found his voice and themes. Unlike the Hakim family, who had fled to Iran, or the heirs of Grand Ayatollah Khoei running their foundation out of London, he was on the ground; unlike Sistani, he was of Iraqi birth, and willing to take on political issues.

If Sadr had been given a green light by the regime, if some subtle live-and-let-live had been agreed upon (as his enemies and rivals within the Shia world were convinced), the accommodation did not work. It must have taken courage, and a heavy dose of the fatalism that comes with high birth and with the clerical profession, for Muhammad Sadiq al-Sadr to begin an uneven and doomed battle with the regime. But there was an unmistakable streak of determination in him. He set out to organize a network of preachers and representatives throughout the country, and he found willing, immensely devoted disciples. The regime had banned Friday prayers and religious processions; Muhammad Sadiq al-Sadr defied this ban. He came out, as well, against holding prayers in the name of the ruler. He began putting in place a system of religious courts in direct competition with the regime's secular courts. The tribes were a special constituency of his: he seems to have gone a long way toward harmonizing their customary law and practice with codified religious law. His sermons and edicts became increasingly political. To a believer seeking his advice, he declared impermissible any dealings with Mujahidin al-Khalq—an Iranian opposition group allied with the regime of Saddam Hussein. In a play on words, he dubbed them *munafiqin* (hypocrites) as opposed to *mujahidin* (strugglers). The allegories in his sermons became increasingly transparent: there were endless references to tyrants and tyranny. He called on his followers to take up an explosive chant: "Yes, yes, to Islam. No, no to America. No, no, to the tyrant." He picked up issues of a decidedly political edge: the regime had close relationships with the Jordanian monarchy, and Sadr chose to brand the traffic between Jordan and Israel as a form of treason and a break with the faith.

A thorough (if admiring) biographer, Mukhtar al-Assadi, tells us that four days before his assassination, the ayatollah had received a telephone call from the dictator himself, commanding him not to lead Friday prayers. He had brushed aside the request, knowing the terrible consequences that lay in store. "I shall pray, I shall pray, I shall pray," he is reported to have answered. He was out to challenge the quiescence of other jurists. Sistani appears to have been one of his targets. In 1998, when grand ayatollahs Burujirdi and Gharawi were murdered, Sistani shut the outer door of his office to mourners and visitors and sat out the agitation that followed. Sadr castigated that behavior, branding it as silence and abdication of responsibility.

It was with Sistani, and the entire edifice of the quietist tradition in the clerical estate, in mind that Sadr came forth with a distinction between what he called the "speaking *hawza*" and the "silent *hawza.*" For that distinction he drew on the revered authority of the late Ayatollah Khomeini. The Iranian firebrand had been a stinging critic of jurists and clerics who sidle up to power and make accommodations with unjust rulers. He had beheld a particularly cruel fate, and a severe divine punishment, for those clerics who had done the rulers' bidding. Sadr fell back on Khomeini's worldview: the *ulama,* the men of the religious class, could not stay out of the line of fire. This was his rebuke to Sistani and to another rival in Najaf, Grand Ayatollah Muhammad Said al-Hakim.

The believers and their religious "sources of imitation" had been living on the expectation of justice, a day when the wicked are punished, and the world resumes its "normal" order and moral balance. But Tikriti rule (or Aflaqite rule, as the Shia pamphleteers and preachers called it, after the theorist of the Baath, Michel Aflaq) had defied the expectations of its demise. After three decades of Baathist rule, hope had begun to fade that deliverance was within reach. The rivalries within the clerical world had always been intense: rivalries over money, over followers, over bureaucratic turf. Tikriti rule had only deepened the antagonisms.

The fault lines within the Shia clerical establishment were laid bare in the aftermath of Sadr's assassination. A fierce enmity had separated Sadr from Ayatollah Muhammad Baqir al-Hakim. The latter, based in Iran, had turned up at a mourning assembly held in Qom in Sadr's memory, where all the bitterness between Hakim's exile organization and Sadr's people surfaced. The followers of Sadr protested Hakim's presence: Hakim had belittled Sadr when he was alive; Hakim had been one of those detractors who hinted that Sadr had been a collaborator of the Saddam regime. His presence at the mourning assembly was an affront. A riot broke out; Sadr's followers threw their shoes at

Hakim (a sign of extreme contempt and disrespect). The police escorted Hakim out of the assembly. Such were the wages of the Baath dictatorship. There were sacrifices by the Shia clergy, but in vain. There were expectations of deliverance, but twenty-five years of tyranny had tested the patience and will of the most resolute. There had been that brief moment in 1991 when fourteen of Iraq's eighteen provinces had erupted in rebellion against the ruler's tyranny. It had been a close call, but the tyrant had recovered, and tens of thousands had paid with their lives for taking on the regime.

Rumors and charges of treason and collaboration had become commonplace among the Shia seminarians in the 1990s. The terror was capricious and indiscriminate, as terror of this magnitude always is. Sadr himself, with a touch of resigned irony, said that there was no guarantee that those who spoke out would be punished and those who lapsed into silence would be spared. The life of the seminarians had been thoroughly taken apart by the rulers and their informers.

A conviction had spread that the security services had dispatched a large number of their own agents into the *hawza,* posing as students of the religious sciences, that they were helped by collaborationist teachers, while devoted students were studying in a clandestine fashion, in underground hideouts. In the eyes of Sadr's followers, Hakim had quit the field of battle for a sanctuary in Iran; it didn't help that Hakim's people had thwarted Sadr's attempt to open an office to represent him and conduct his affairs in Qom. Sadr had sent someone who should have been the perfect emissary both to Iran and to the Iraqis who had sought sanctuary in that country—a son of the revered Muhammad Baqir al-Sadr. But Hakim was on the ground in Iran and his opposition to Sadr had carried that day. Sadr was to be denied the footing in Iran that he had thought was his due.

An assessment as wise and sorrowful as the occasion called for was given Muhammad Sadiq al-Sadr by a peer of great standing: Ayatollah Muhammad Hussein Fadlallah, in Beirut. The latter was nearly a decade older and had known Sadr in their younger days in Najaf, before Fadlallah's return to his ancestral land in Lebanon. Fadlallah had the advantages of a freewheeling city; he had known Beirut's turmoil and civil war, but he knew he had lived as a free man, sheltered by Lebanon's pluralism and a vast Shia community that afforded him protection and great honor. Of Sadr, he spoke with genuine sympathy, in a eulogy he gave the day after Sadr's murder: "We feel a great loss and a great darkness, we ache for the sorrow of this Iraqi people that has been brutalized and tormented by its ruler, and by a cruel international order. It is a people that is subjected to hunger and expulsion and imprisonment and murder and what have you." He admonished those who would sit in judgment of Sadr. "This big and distinguished man was unjustly treated by the tyrant; don't add to the cruelty and injustice inflicted on him. The tyrant has liquidated him physically, don't assassinate him morally." It was permissible, said Fadlallah, and normal to take issue with a line of reasoning Sadr may have pursued, or a scholarly writ he may have issued, but "you can't speak ill of him, for he is an oppressed martyr who gave Islam quite a lot in his books, and who tried to revive Islam and its teachings under severe circumstances."

Fadlallah remembered a younger Sadr, "a pure, good youth, full of decency, using his early writings to take up issues that the religious society of Najaf at the time had not bothered to take up." A literary-political magazine, based in Najaf, and launched in 1960, had brought these two men together. Fadlallah had been in the inner circle of that magazine. And so had been Muhammad Baqir al-Sadr, and his sister, Bint al-Huda, who had tackled women's issues in its pages. Fadlallah was part of something special in Shia—and Najaf's—history. He summoned that revered past, placed Muhammad Sadiq al-Sadr in that time of struggle, in a "chain of martyrdom," that connected this Sadr to "the beloved first Sadr, his cousin Muhammad Baqir al-Sadr, may God have mercy on his soul. He studied under 'the happy martyr' who predicted for him great success and prominence in scholarship and research and religious reasoning. . . . He lived the pain of 'the happy martyr,' and the sorrow of that martyr's sister, Bint al-Huda. He lived the tragedy of Iraq, he entered prison and knew persecution. He then embarked on the work of a *marja'*, and it is unfair to call him the jurist of the regime, *marja' al-sulta*. . . . For me, I have never heard, nor was anything said or transmitted to me indirectly, that suggested his support for the rulers, politically or intellectually. Perhaps there may have been a temporary truce that he may have, with his reasoning and inference, judged to be legitimate in a society like Iraq, governed by one of the most tyrannical regimes. It is one thing to be outside Iraq commenting on things, quite another to be inside that big prison."

Fadlallah gave Sadr his due: he spoke of his reviving the Friday prayer, which the people of Iraq, crushed by tyranny, badly needed. He spoke of an escalating struggle between the regime and the jurist, of Sadr's calling on the rulers to release seminarians and prayer leaders they had thrown in prison. "For me this was the highest and purest form of speaking and spreading the word of truth. Perhaps the regime could no longer tolerate this kind of opposition to it, and saw in it a threat to its power. Oh dear ones, this man lived for Islam and died for Islam. We too have to work to preserve what remains of the *hawza* in Najaf, which the regime has all but crushed, and to defend the religious leaders who have been and remain in danger."

It fell to young Moqtada to take up the martyr's mantle and the martyr's cause. His oldest sibling, Mostapha, had been killed trying to cover his father's body with his own when their car came under fire in February 1999. Moqtada must have known hardship and fear after his father's death. One authoritative Iraqi source told me that Moqtada may have "worked with his hands" during those intervening four years between his father's murder and the fall of the Baathist regime. For Moqtada al-Sadr, released from fear and the underground by American power, the battle was now joined. There were accounts to settle: there was his father's sacrifice, and the death of two of his brothers. There had been ayatollahs who stayed out of harm's way in Iraq. And there were the exiles coming back to stake a claim to the power and the resources of Iraq—the Hakims returning from Iran, and Abdul Majid al-Khoei, son of Grand Ayatollah Khoei, who had been living in London. Muhammad Baqir al-Hakim had come back at the head of a militia, the Badr Brigade, armed and financed by Iran. Khoei was said to have arrived with a CIA contingent and a large American subsidy. The Baathists out of the way, a battle among the Shia was not far behind. Young Sadr had not risen as a scholar; he hadn't the patience and the skills. He had not pored over religious texts or pondered schools of jurisprudence. He had his name, his passion for revenge, and the young "Sadrists" in the poor Shia slums of Baghdad whose anger and unsettledness merged with and reflected his own.

Moqtada al-Sadr was to stake out a role for himself as an opponent of the American stewardship. If the older members of the establishment were willing to wink at the American presence, he was quick to assert that the senior jurists and the Governing Council that the Americans had selected were "collaborators" of foreign rule. A member of the Hakim family, a younger brother of Ayatollah Muhammad Baqir al-Hakim, had been appointed to the Governing Council;

young Moqtada had picked up his father's old feud with the Hakims. He could always turn out a mob; he talked of fielding an army of believers, *Jaysh al-Mahdi,* the army of the savior. But he was careful not to trigger full-scale American retaliation. His "army," he said, was a peaceful army. The four grand ayatollahs in the country had seniority, and precedence and scholarship, on their side; Moqtada had his rage and impatience with the clerical order. He wielded his father's old arsenal: the imperative of an Islamic government, clerical activism, the man of religion as a champion of the excluded and the dispossessed.

There was no restraint in Moqtada al-Sadr. He taunted Sistani about his Iranian origins and maintained that clerical leadership had to be exclusively Iraqi. (This was a new spin on things: the Sadrs themselves were perhaps of Iranian or Lebanese ancestry.) He held up his father's "martyrdom" and that of his beloved relative, Ayatollah Muhammad Baqir al-Sadr, as a rod over the heads of the four recognized grand ayatollahs in Najaf; these jurists had prospered, he asserted, because they had been quiescent during the years of dictatorship. He took pride in his old, frayed *abaya,* presenting the garment as a sign of his austerity and lack of interest in worldly wealth. He knew he lacked religious standing and seniority. He found an ally, an old jurist in Qom of Iraqi descent by the name of Sayyid Kazim Haeri. The older man, with the rank of an ayatollah, had left his native Iraq for Iran in 1976. He had opted for teaching and for keeping some distance from politics. The relationship between the old jurist and young Sadr on the scene in Iraq was a marriage of convenience. Sadr claimed Haeri as his religious guide and implied a division of roles with Haeri: religious authority for Haeri, political primacy for himself. The deference to Haeri was tactical, as the older jurist was at a safe remove in Iran. But even that cover was beyond this young man's volatile temperament. He was soon at odds with Haeri, insisting that the cleric's residence in Iran denied him a leadership role in Iraq.

Amid the anarchy and the new freedom, Moqtada al-Sadr was bound to find a role for himself. But a Shia community groping for a way out would not give itself over to this kind of radicalism. And a murder in Shiism's holiest shrine, the Imam Ali Mosque in Najaf, a day after the fall of Baghdad to American forces, showed the depths of the furies. Abdul Majid al-Khoei, fifty years of age, son of the late Grand Ayatollah Abolqassem al-Khoei, was killed by an angry mob of fellow Shiites. Khoei's father had been the highest religious authority in the Shia world from 1970 until his death in 1992. The son had been living in London, running a foundation named for his father. He was a practical, moderate man, but he had misjudged the mood in Najaf. By all accounts, Khoei had made a bid for control of Imam Ali's shrine. Nothing was simple here though; Khoei, with Anglo-American sponsorship, was seen as the choice of the foreign expeditionary forces to run the affairs of Najaf. More damning still, he had turned up at the shrine with a reviled Baathist who had been the keeper of the shrine under the old regime. He was stabbed and then shot to death in a place of sanctity during a melee incited by the Sadrists. The old tyranny had poisoned everything that had come in its way: the affairs of the Shia clerical class had been no exception to that rule.

A people so thoroughly brutalized, and made edgy by bloodshed, needed moral parameters in their lives. Men knew the cruel history of Iraq but still wanted the security of a sacred place off-limits to assassins and plotters. That was the shock of that murder: the place, the distinguished lineage of the victim. Imam Ali himself, the believers knew, had been struck down by an assassin in 661, and his caliphate had been brought to a violent end. People here were without illusions about the cruelty of political life. An innate caution about political life, and its bottomless betrayals, worked to the disadvantage of someone of Moqtada al-Sadr's temperament and reputation. In a brazen illustration of this young sayyid's radicalism, some six months after the fall of the regime of Saddam Hussein, on the eve of a holy day for the Shia and in defiance of the occupation authority, he declared his own "government." Few took his declaration seriously, and he was forced to "suspend" that government. There were older jurists in this land, and steadier and more cautious: the radicalism of Moqtada al-Sadr would still have to do battle with the traditional structure of authority in the Shia clerical world. Sadr had made the illegitimacy of the American presence his rallying cry, but the older members of the clerical class knew that the foreign presence would be needed for a "decent interval." There was enough skill and prudence in them to work with the foreign occupiers without being suffocated by them.

It was this kind of skill that Ayatollah Muhammad Baqir al-Hakim had in ample supply. His murder on Friday, August 29, 2003, took place on the grounds of the Imam Ali Mosque as well. The ayatollah had completed Friday prayers when a massive car bomb killed him, along with scores of his followers and other worshippers. As many as ninety-five people lost their lives in this attack. So deadly was the bombing, Ayatollah Hakim's corpse could not be found. Tragedy had been a steady companion of the Hakims—another of the great clerical families of the Shia world. Like Abdul Majid al-Khoei, who had been killed a few months earlier, Hakim was a son of a grand ayatollah, the supreme clerical guide of his time, Muhsin al-Hakim, who had died in 1970.

Like the younger Khoei, this man of sixty-four years had been killed in Iraq upon his return from a long exile. Hakim had been in Iran since 1980. He had come back on the heels of the American conquest, to stake a claim to the new order. Hakim had proved politically dexterous. He was a cleric, and a son of a grand ayatollah, but he put forth a "moderate" program: he refrained from calling for a clerical state. He gave the Americans the benefit of the doubt: he acknowledged their betrayal of the Shia and Kurdish rebellions in 1991 but accepted that their goals were different this time around, that they had come back a dozen years later to overthrow the regime they had spared. He had been granted Iranian patronage and sanctuary, but he had given a green light to his younger brother to work with the Americans, to take a seat on the Governing Council appointed by the American administrator of Iraq.

Perhaps the years in Iran had taught him the hazards of direct rule by a religious class. He wanted a place for himself and his guild, but no "sister republic" of the Iranian Revolution imposed in Iraq. "Iraq for the Iraqis" was one of his favorite mantras; it was his way of distancing his movement, and his aims, from Iran's clerical dictatorship. Moderation was in this man's temperament and family inheritance. His father had been a scholar of deep restraint. In 1969, a year before his death, the grand ayatollah had been pressed by his followers to issue a fatwa banning membership in the Baath. He had done it with some reluctance. (A decade earlier, he had issued a ruling banning membership in the Communist Party.) The violence to be visited on his descendants was a dark omen that the old order in Iraq, and its restraints, had yielded to a new age of terror.

Shia history is about lamentations: the virtuous are cut down, and the wicked beget worldly kingdoms of wealth and power. The history of the Sadrs and the Hakims embodies that theme; so does the triumph of the Tikritis, cruel tyrants who heaped sorrow on men better, milder, nobler than themselves. This story starts with the murder of the first of the twelve Shia imams, Ali ibn Abi Talib, for whom the Najaf shrine was named, the Prophet's cousin and son-in-law; he succeeded the Prophet, a quarter-century after the Prophet's death, and his murder, some five years into his reign, ushered in a Shia history of virtuous defeat. Two decades later, Ali's son was murdered as well. The iconic figure of the Shia faith, a son of the Prophet's daughter Fatima, Imam Hussein was defeated in Iraq by the troops of a cruel caliph of Damascus, the notorious Umayyad ruler Yazid, who loved his hounds and his pleasures. Hussein had been lured to Iraq from his home in the Hijaz, invited by the people of the city of Kufa to lead them in their rebellion against the rule of Damascus. He had been betrayed and let down by the Kufans; cut off from the waters of the Euphrates, he and seventy of his companions fought a doomed battle. He reminded the opposing forces of his noble lineage, that "the blood of the Prophet flowed in his veins," but to no avail. He was beheaded; his head and those of his companions were taken to the governor in Kufa, then to the ruler in Damascus. Virtue had not been rewarded.

The violent end of Muhammad Baqir al-Hakim was of a piece with this history. Hakim's killers got what they wanted: they removed from the political field a player possessed of moderation and enormous authority.

But the loss of Hakim notwithstanding, the idea of clerical rule remained the preference of a minority of the Shia. The Shia clerical institution is somewhat decentralized: the faithful choose their *marja' al-taqlid*, their "source of imitation," the cleric they defer to and to whom they make their financial contributions and owe their loyalty. In Iraq, it was the luck of the Shia that their grand *marja'* was a cleric of real caution and political skill, Grand Ayatollah Sistani, who wanted a "normal" political world. He rejected Khomeini's doctrine of *wilayat al-faqih*, the Guardianship of the Jurisprudent, and wanted nothing to do with theocratic rule. Reclusive and reticent (attributes of the great jurists), Sistani appeared to know Iraq for what it was. Feeling secure that the Shia demographic edge would grant his community its place in the new order, he pressed for a national census that would recognize and confirm the extent of the Shia majority. Beyond that, he was keen for the country to have the rudiments of representative rule: a constitution, elections, parliamentary life.

Sistani walked a thin line between the imperatives of the faith and the necessities on the ground. In early October 2003, he secluded himself, "in protest against the lawlessness in the land." It is a time-honored clerical practice: a period of solitude, *i'tikaf*, away from the public eye, and from the petitioners and the visitors. He then resumed his routine and issued an edict with a subtlety that bore the man's signature. It was permissible, he said, "to deal with the Coalition soldiers, to sell them goods and necessities." It was permissible, as well, for "the translators who work with them to lend them a hand, so long as the work is in harmony with the interests of the Muslims." On the other hand, the faithful were enjoined and authorized to query the foreign occupiers about their "length of stay" in Iraq, and to show them quiet disapproval. Amid the killings and ambushes of American troops and the terror attacks, this was a measure of civility worthy of the great jurists, who knew the follies of playing with fire. There were lesser clerics calling for armed insurrection; Sistani's gravity, and the care with which he measured and parsed his words, were his gift to a population unnerved by the anarchy and the chaos.

A supremely political man, Sistani knew how to make his adjustments. He had gained authority with the American occupiers; he would use it at critical turning points—to shape the political agenda and the nature of the political order sure to emerge in the aftermath of the American interlude. In late November 2003, after the Americans had put in place a plan for the transfer of power to Iraqi hands, the cleric issued a dissent of his own. Where the American plan called for indirect, caucus-style voting, Sistani wanted direct popular elections. There were "real gaps" in the American plan, he said, and the Iraqi people should be entitled to determine their own destiny at the ballot box. And in what must have been an indication of the struggles within the Shia community itself about the religious content desirable in political life, Sistani added that the new Iraqi polity should have a "more overtly Islamic character." As Sheikh Muhammad al-Haqqani, a senior cleric close to Sistani, put it to the American analyst Reuel Gerecht, "We want a non-Islamic state that is respectful of Islam." This was a far cry from an endorsement of clerical rule: it was, by all appearances, a measured call for a polity that would fall somewhere between full secularism and outright theocratic rule.

Whether political life would permit such fine distinctions in the new Iraq was an open question. Sistani was playing for time and groping for a political outcome that would give his community (and his clerical guild) a good measure of political power without triggering full-scale conflict with the other religious communities. The reticence was always there—part personal style, part the obligatory Shia distrust of political power born of centuries of disinheritance. He left the details of the electoral system to "specialists in such matters." What he was keen to uphold was the "legitimacy" and "representativeness" of the new regime. His Iranian origins were a baggage he could not shed. This fact of his biography and nationality did not trouble his followers, but his enemies were always conscious of it. When he opined that authority does not belong to the "exiles who came from the outside," one of those exiles, Saad Jabr, a son of a prime minister from the days of the monarchy and a Shia at that, answered that it was Sistani himself who was "an outsider, a foreigner who had come from Iran." Sistani's caution was bred in him by that fact of being an "outsider."

In the midst of this intra-Shia debate, an important outsider had turned up in Iraq: a religious scholar in his midforties, Sayyid Hussein Khomeini, a grandson of the late Ayatollah Khomeini. In an episode of supreme irony, this man of impeccable pedigree arrived in Najaf from Iran—to preach the virtues of secular rule. Iran, he told the Iraqis, was suffocating under the rule of clerical obscurantism. He described a reign of mediocrity and repression in his native land—the intelligence services loose in the holy city of Qom and its seminaries, the lack of channels of free expression. Despite his very special pedigree, he had not been allowed access to the media. There was nothing odd, he said, about his opposition to his grandfather's notion of clerical rule. The old man himself, "Imam Khomeini," had taken up the notion of *wilayat al-faqih* only late in his life, when he was in his fifties. The world changes, and men change with it: the notion of Islamic rule had played out in Iran and had failed.

Hussein Khomeini told of a letter he had sent to the "Supreme Guide of the Islamic Republic," Ayatollah Ali Khamenei, putting before that man the internal and external problems of the regime. He had described unsparingly the disaffection at home and Iran's isolation abroad. He called for a plebiscite that would ask the people of Iran to let it be known, in an open manner, whether they still wanted theocratic rule. Let the ballot decide, he had written to the clerical leader. If the theocracy failed at the ballot box, the men of religion "would go back to their homes, and change would come without bloodshed." The revolution, he had told its clerical leader, had been "hijacked," "stolen," and it was time to press for the separation of religion and politics.

A witness had thus come to Iraq from the very apex of the Iranian system. He congratulated the Iraqis on their new liberty. In an astonishing break with his grandfather's legacy, young Khomeini even spoke well of the Americans. The new liberty, he reminded Iraqis, was a gift of the Americans. There was nothing in Iran, he lamented, save sterility and misery. There was nothing to emulate in Iran: it was up to the Iraqis to build a better polity of their own. Hussein Khomeini was an unusual man: he would not take the bait before him when asked the obligatory question about Israel. The matter of Israel, he said, needn't concern Iranians and Iraqis. Reform, modernity, economic progress: these were the themes that mattered. It was important, he reiterated, that the principle of theocratic rule be turned back, that the harm it had done to Shiism be faced and acknowledged.

What poise the Shia could muster was badly needed; the Baghdad Spring was being scorched by a terrible summer. Over the course of several weeks came a succession of blows: a bombing of the Jordanian embassy, then a massive attack on the UN headquarters on August 19, which took a toll of twenty-two lives, including Sergio Vieira de Mello, a Brazilian career diplomat who headed the UN effort in Baghdad. Ten days later, there had been the murder of Ayatollah Hakim. The "remnants" of the Tikriti regime were in the midst of a rearguard attack against the American forces. Arabs had been there before: the car bomb was Beirut's weapon of choice in the 1980s; now it had come to Baghdad.

If the undoing of Beirut was any guide, there was little chance that anyone would ever know for sure the identity of the assailant who drove the cement mixer into the UN compound or the names of the plotters who arranged Ayatollah Hakim's murder. No one ever got to know for sure, it should be recalled, the name of that young boy who on the morning of October 23, 1983, drove a Mercedes truck loaded with TNT into the marine barracks in Beirut. What was known of that seminal event two decades earlier was the cruel aftermath: the death of 241 U.S. servicemen, the proud assertion that Lebanon would not be left to the forces of radicalism, then the scramble to pull America out of the hell of Lebanon. That country was left to the tender mercy of the Syrians. There were no discernible American interests in that city by the Mediterranean. America quit Beirut under Arab eyes, leaving the impression that it is easily discouraged, that a band of plotters could dissuade it from its larger goals.

Once again, the United States was at a crossroads in an Arab land. American staying power in Baghdad was obviously the target of these terror attacks. In Baghdad, truth be known, the United States had overthrown not only a man but a religious and ethnic sect, the Sunni Arabs, and this running guerrilla war was their response to their loss of hegemony. America's campaign had broken that minority's tenacious hold on the state: the oil of the country is in the southern (predominantly Shia) zone and in the Kurdish ancestral lands in the north. The Sunni Triangle lived off state terror, the whip as an instrument of enrichment. These "remnants" of the vanquished regime were fighting for what they had grown to see as their birthright: the state of terror and plunder that was Iraq under the Baathists.

It was no mystery that jihadists spoiling for a fight, or on the run and in search of a new mission and a new field of battle, would converge on Iraq to lend a hand to the remnants of the deposed regime. There were Americans to kill; there were piles of money for mercenaries with no rival opportunities in Yemen and Syria. It was difficult to ascertain the veracity of the reports, circulated in August 2003, that three thousand Saudis had "gone missing" and had found their way to Iraq. Most likely, the actual number of Saudi jihadists was much lower. The source of these reports was a London-based Saudi dissident with his own axe to grind. But the arrival of jihadists in Iraq was no great puzzle, for the distinction between secular terror and the terror of religiously based movements was always a distinction without a difference. It had always been a singular fight, two faces of the same terror. Nor was it a mystery that Syria and Iran hankered for America's defeat in Iraq. The power that had blown into Baghdad had come bearing the promise of a new order in the region. It had been an awesome victory, and woven into it were perhaps some extravagant hopes of reform. There would rise in Mesopotamia a state more democratic, more secular, no doubt more prosperous than much of the neighborhood around it. That state would be weaned from the false temptations of Arab radicalism. Without quite fully appreciating it, the Americans with their war had announced nothing less than the obsolescence of the ruling order in the neighboring lands.

For America's enemies, it was mightily important that the foreign power fail in Baghdad and be forced to pack up and leave. Who would wish the Americans well, strangers with mighty machines trumpeting new possibilities in lands made weary by cruelty and cynicism? There was menace in the demonstration effect of America's victory: an embattled breed of Arab and Iranian secularists and liberals were vicariously living off that nascent Iraqi promise. That promise had to be snuffed out if the entrenched systems of control were to survive. If a moderate brand of Shiism took hold in Iraq, on Shiism's holiest grounds and in its very cradle, there would have to be reverberations for the guardians of Iran's theocracy. It stood to reason that these wily, resourceful rulers would fight back. What America had brought along, loaded up with the military gear, was a threat that the clerical revolution that had triumphed in Iran a quarter-century earlier could be undone.

A battle broader than Iraq itself, then, was playing out in that country. There was no need for the United States to apologize to the other Arabs or to Iran's theocrats about its presence in Iraq and its aims for that country. The custodians of Arab power, and the vast majority of the political class in the Arab world, never saw or named the terrible cruelties of Iraq under Saddam Hussein. A political culture that averted its gaze from mass graves and worked itself into self-righteous hysteria over a foreign presence in an Arab country was a culture that had turned its back on political reason. There was a leap of faith, it had to be conceded, in the argument that a land as brutalized as Iraq would manage to find its way out of its cruel past and, in the process, give other Arabs proof that a modicum of liberty could flourish in their midst.

The terror of the snipers and the car bombs sought to drown the political question, trump it with issues of physical security. The aim was transparent: it was to frighten the Iraqi people and to turn them away from this new order and its possibilities. Where people huddle in fear, more lofty goals of liberty and participatory politics die. The analogy was not perfect, but that was in essence exactly what had unfolded two decades earlier in Beirut. A city that had once had big horizons became a place-name for banditry and ruin. The despots all around then pointed to that city as an example of what befalls those who would dream that there was something for Arab and Muslim peoples beyond the writ and the whip of the rulers.

CHAPTER 4

States of Mind:
The Liberators' Bewilderment

Iit's sinful how little we knew about Islam and Iraqi culture," said a young army captain and intelligence officer, Luke Calhoun, serving in Baghdad. There was bewilderment in the remark, and innocence. In the Iraq "theater of operations," Major General Stephen Speakes, a soft-spoken and thoughtful officer of the Third United States Army, told me about his interest in Islamic and Arab history. He wanted the men and women in his command to be literate about Iraq and the Arabs. He had brought a Muslim prayer leader to speak to his soldiers about the holy month of Ramadan and about wider Islamic matters. Americans were strangers in Iraq; no measure of literacy in Islamic history could have prepared the foreign rulers for the country that military power had delivered into their hands. The despot had disfigured the culture: there was nothing particularly "Islamic" about the place and the legacy on the ground. It was a huge criminal enterprise, the edifice that Baathism and the Tikriti clan spirit had created. Ideology, Sunni orthodoxy, Arab nationalism, tribalism, all plucked at will, were rearranged and put in the service of the master's cult and the master's terror. No "Orientalist" science could have prepared the American military and civilian administrators for the desolation, and the willfulness, they were to find in Iraq.

Patience was needed, and patience was in short supply in Iraq. A pent-up population that had cowered in fear for decades was now in a state of constant agitation. The television cameras and the print media were there, and a foreign power held back by its own liberal norms, and by the gaze of the world, was unable to cap the disorder.

Arab opinion had the images it needed: it conflated the disorder in the streets of Ramallah with that in the streets of Tikrit. The Arab world was being recolonized, the Arab intellectuals and the satellite channels proclaimed; the Americans had become colonial enforcers, and the Fedayeen Saddam of Tikrit had become soul mates of the "boys of the stones" in the West Bank and Gaza. America had waded deep into that sense of victimology at the heart of modern Arab life. The wrath of Sadr City was one type of unrest; the deadly riots of Tikrit and Fallujah were another. But all Iraqis, it appeared, were out in the streets giving voice to the muzzled screams suppressed during long years of tyrannical rule. America's enemies may not have been terribly sophisticated, but they had a basic view of things: the foreign power did not know Iraq and, if bled and harassed, was sure to pack up and leave. The insurgents aimed for the exhaustion of the foreign power.

The internal intelligence documents—both military and civilian—acknowledge the acute predicament of the Americans in this new, hazardous environment. From David Kay, head of the Iraq Survey Group, with some twelve hundred translators and linguists and aides scouring the country under his command: "It is hard to believe how little we understood." He described what followed the end of the military phase as a period of "our maximum ignorance." There were intelligence reports and paid informers, but "scores were being settled" by Iraqis with old grievances and schemes of their own. Coalition Provisional Authority leaked like a sieve, and the American soldiers and administrators were under no illusions about some of the Iraqis who had joined the American regency. The American intelligence records of the Iraq Survey Group contain a report about a local woman who had a CPA badge, lived in the CPA headquarters, and had been a mistress of five CPA officials "feeding information to the insurgents at the time she was living with a CPA official!"

The terror had of course made it virtually impossible for the foreign power to know the land and its people. The Green Zone was a place of isolation: the life of the country beyond was hard to decipher for those besieged in the American compound. "We went to Mars and they brought in Iraqis to meet us," said Leslie Gelb of his (and my) visit in the spring of 2005. He was speaking in jest, but there was a measure of truth in what he said. The food in the American compound was, for security reasons, brought in from outside Iraq; the bottled water came from Kuwait and Turkey; the staff who served us in the giant cafeteria were mainly Indians. In the trailers, the toilet paper came from the United Arab Emirates. Violence, and the understandable need to keep it at bay, had rendered the American compound a world unto itself.

Within this bubble, and in the regional offices of the American embassy, Americans of great talent yearned for a deeper contact with the people of Iraq. In Baghdad, one of the best of the young political officers, Jeffrey Beals, bridled under the limits and the confinement. He had mastered Arabic, and his feel for the ways of the Arab world was exquisite for someone just in his late twenties. He had not come to this work to hunker down in an American zone. He ached to break free, but the security considerations imposed tight limits. In Baghdad I met as well another political officer of real accomplishment, the gifted author and translator Peter Theroux. This man, perhaps a decade older than Beals, had made a significant contribution to the life of letters. He had translated from Arabic into English the great "oil novel," *Cities of Salt,* a multivolume work by the Saudi author Abdul-rahman Munif. It must have taken him years to pull off that deed, and he had rendered Munif's magnificent Arabic into a translation of equal beauty. The immersion in Munif's sprawling novel must have given him a genuine feel for the culture and the language of the Arabs. On his own, he had written a perceptive work of travel and commentary on Saudi Arabia. This expedition had pulled him into Iraq: he was doing his best to track the country, but it wasn't easy, and he knew enough about the Arabs to know the limitations of the knowledge available to the Americans.

Beyond expertise and knowledge, there was the frustration of an Iraqi population being denied access to people who meant them well, who had come here eager to serve. In a fortified compound in Kirkuk that housed the regional embassy office, I met two young Hispanics from Texas, Robby Gonzales and Mario Fernandez. It was Mario, the older of the two, a lawyer in his late thirties perhaps, a father of three children, who gave a summation that will stay with me about the sort of sentiments that were carried into Iraq by countless Americans. "I grew up in a small town in West Texas; public education sent me to college, then to law school, and to a career in the Department of Labor. I thought I should give something back in return; I thought these people in this country need and deserve a decent break; I thought I would give this a try." This was Kirkuk, Iraq's most "complicated" city, but Mario Fernandez and Robby Gonzales had a remarkable sense of serenity. Gonzales, twenty-eight years of age, ran this regional office with evident skill. He was just out of graduate school. As he kept track of the ethnicities of the city, there was no hint of paternalism in him. He savored the challenge, and he too wanted greater access to the life of Kirkuk. We were his guests, behind sandbags and barbed wire; Kirkuk's troubles lay at the edge of this compound. "Kirkuklis"—the local slang for the people of this city—were lucky to have this young man in their midst. He knew the communities of the city and the leaders as well as any outsider can grasp an alien world. But of course the troubles of Kirkuk were bigger than the best of his intentions, inaccessible to a stranger's touch.

First Lieutenant Seth Moulton, a young marine, twenty-six years old—he had the unusual background, for a marine, of a Harvard education and Ivy League liberal parents who had been antiwar protestors during the Vietnam War—spoke to me wistfully of his first tour of duty in the immediate aftermath of combat, when he served in the Shia town of Hilla. We were speaking in the Green Zone, in the headquarters of Lieutenant General Petraeus, and this was the summer of 2005, when freedom of movement for American soldiers had become a distant memory. He had savored his time in Hilla, and the opportunity to know its downtrodden people. They had been grateful for their liberty, and glad to have the Americans in their midst. He had found a television station, with an adequate transmitter. He had started his own television program, with his Iraqi translator, a young man his age. "Moulton and Mohammed" was the name of their program. It had been an easier time, he said, and a more meaningful one. He had learned a great deal among the people of Hilla. "I learned about the tremendous impact of what had taken place in 1991, the rebellions we had encouraged and then let down. We had underestimated the wounds of the Shia, and the extent of Sunni-Shia antagonism." Moulton's second deployment was drawing to a close. He was on his way home, to graduate school. The general security was better now, he observed, than it had been a year earlier. But the knowledge of Iraq's people, and the opportunity to move among them, were lost.

Lieutenant General Petraeus had on his staff at Camp Phoenix in the Green Zone a young army captain from Florida, Scott Handler. Thirty years of age but looking younger, Handler was eager to know the details of life beyond the Green Zone. He had been told that I had been to Najaf, and he wanted to know the ways of the Shia clerics and their culture. He was keen to know what I had seen of Sistani's life and home. He wanted greater knowledge about Iraq and its history. He had his duties in the American military compound; we talked of the large aims of the war. He neither offered, nor did I seek from him, some large judgment about the course and the justifications of this war. His curiosity about the country beyond the American compound was the thread that ran through our conversation. He had been told by those who had had earlier deployments that it had been easier to get around before the insurgency severely curtailed mobility. The curiosity he had brought with him could not be satisfied: the traffic between the Green Zone and the city was hazardous and bureaucratically cumbersome. The checkpoints in and out of the American compound were choice targets of the insurgents; the paperwork and the security requirements and the needed badges and passes discouraged all who would try to cross. I dreaded the experience whenever I had to do it. For a young American in uniform, this "Little America" behind barricades and concertina wire was cut off from the reality of Iraq. No wonder Scott Handler was as curious about Baghdad and Najaf as one would have been about some distant land.

The habits and skills of empire were not innate to the American temper, at any rate. The American occupation authorities appeared uncertain of what they truly wanted in Iraq. They handed their enemies some easy victories. They had appointed a Governing Council composed of men and women of standing, drawn from the principal communities of Iraq. (For all the carping about this Council, its Kurdish and Shia members were leaders possessed of genuine authority in their respective communities.) But no sooner had the American authorities created this Council than they set out to declare that no appreciable power could be turned over to such an "unelected" body. No one needed to undermine this American creation; the American stewards were doing a fair job of it themselves.

It took a grim tide for the American authorities to change course and to read the mood of the unhappy society they governed. The change came some seven months after the heady moment of the country's liberation. November had been a particularly cruel month, with mounting American casualties. And there were reports of the sort that American intelligence was prone to turn out: the liberating power, the pollsters had found out, had begun to lose the battle for Iraqi "hearts and minds." A "course correction" was announced: there would be a quicker transfer of authority; sovereignty would be turned over to the Iraqis. In return, a sovereign Iraqi government would ask the American forces to stay as guests of that government. There was no assurance that the bloody insurgency would be easier to deal with in the aftermath of the projected transfer of authority. It was hard to know whether the enmity would subside once the Iraqis were granted their "independence." It was safe to assume that those in the Sunni Triangle whose dominion had been undone by American power would remain unalterably opposed to the American presence and that they would dismiss a transitional government as mere quislings of foreign rule.

The former dictator was still on the loose. Indeed, days after the Americans had announced their change of heart on the transfer of sovereignty, an Arab television channel in Dubai, Al-Arabiya, broadcast an audiotape that appeared to be a genuine message from Saddam Hussein, calling for yet bloodier attacks on the Americans and the Iraqis working with them. Never known for his excessive religious devotion, Saddam Hussein spoke of the holy month of Ramadan as the herald of a blessed victory: "The wicked ones have led themselves to the trap that God willed for them. They thought they had come on a picnic to occupy Iraq, which shall remain resistant to their evil designs and to the hegemony of their armies. . . . He who is put forth by the armies of the foreigner in violation of the will of the free people of Iraq is akin to, and no better than, the foreigner. Resistance to those placed in power by foreign armies is a religious and national and human obligation." In vintage Saddam language familiar to Iraqis, whose lives he so thoroughly dominated, the old dictator foresaw for the Americans sure and bitter defeat and a disgraceful departure from Iraq.

Cool-headed analysts were apt to discount the influence of Saddam Hussein on the insurgency; the old despot was on the run, or hunkered down in some safe house or underground bunker. Saddam was only "a voice in the wilderness," the American administrator of Iraq, L. Paul Bremer III, said in response to the audiotape. But amid the disorder and the relentless insurgency, Saddam Hussein was no irrelevant phantom. There were still devoted followers of his willing to bet that they could outwait and outwit the foreign power. And the shadow of Saddam Hussein aside, there was still that deep chasm between the foreign power and the beneficiaries of the old regime.

A huge American reconstruction package had been promised Iraq, but Iraqis attached to the old order were in no mood to take the gift of reconstruction. On November 15, two American helicopters crashed over the northern city of Mosul, taking the lives of seventeen soldiers. A reporter who turned up at the scene the morning after found a gleeful crowd that had come to watch this spectacle of American heartbreak. The helicopters had collided over a private residence and a school nearby; there had been no Iraqi casualties. A legend took hold in this town that God had punished the Americans and spared the Iraqis. An unemployed young man, twenty years of age, said he felt like dancing and celebrating that morning, because "the Americans and the Jews" who were occupying his land had been punished. A day laborer did him one better: he had skipped his work and had come to the site of the crash at daybreak to savor this scene of American sorrow. No war blueprint, no "future of Iraq" survey conducted on the eve of the war could have anticipated what lay in store for a power that struck into Iraq with hopes that a decent reception awaited the liberators.

Against the background of troubles in Baghdad and the terror attacks in the Sunni Triangle, Mosul had been something of a showcase for the American presence. This is where David Petraeus was to make his name. He had worked out the terms of a decent administration in Mosul and its surroundings. He had permitted normal commerce across the Syria-Iraq border; his troops had turned from combat to a vast reconstruction effort—repair of schools and roads and public buildings. But no "separate peace" was safe in Iraq. Mosul had a terribly complicated history, and an ethnicity to match it. It had a Sunni Arab majority but a host of Kurdish and Christian communities as well. Kurds had always viewed Mosul as something of an "Arab rampart" in a region they claimed as their patrimony. Proximity to Syria had given Mosul's politics greater volatility still. No fewer than twenty-four thousand army officers hailed from Mosul, I was told by the Kurdish leader and former intelligence officer Dana Majid. There had been much bloodshed in Mosul's history, and in November this fragile peace that the Americans had secured appeared to crack. Indeed, for a grim moment, Mosul awakened raw and bitter memories of Mogadishu, where the corpses of marines had been dragged through the streets back in 1993. On November 23, two American soldiers became trapped in a Mosul traffic jam. They were shot in the head; then a crowd of young men dragged the soldiers from their car and tore off their watches and jackets and boots. Some early reports suggested that the throats of the two servicemen may have been slit. In other accounts, the soldiers were shot and then mutilated by a vengeful crowd that had beaten them with bricks.

The incident was a moment of reckoning, one of those episodes that illuminated and sharply marked the thin line between liberation and occupation, and the gap between the Americans and the Iraqis. It was not just that the assailants had struck at two American soldiers; more troubling still was the glee of those who had watched the brutal deed. Dexter Filkins of the *New York Times* filed from Mosul a sobering dispatch three days later. He walked into a fire station: a firefighter with a new uniform and an American salary ten times larger than his old salary had been under the dictatorial regime spoke with unadorned glee of the two soldiers' fate. "I was happy, everyone was happy. The Americans, yes, they do good things, but only to enhance their reputation. They are occupiers. We want them to leave."

The American authorities could console themselves that this was the sentiment of a fringe; they could roll out evidence of many things that worked on the ground. They could demonstrate, with charts and exact dates, the progress Iraq had made since the fall of the old regime. They could, as they were given to in the headquarters of the Coalition Provisional Authority in Baghdad, hand out comparisons between the speed of Iraq's recovery and the slower pace of Germany's rehabilitation in the aftermath of the Second World War. Over Paul Bremer's signature, a table of such "milestones" earnestly documented the magnitude of the American effort. It had taken three years to introduce a new currency in Germany; in Iraq the deed was done in seventy-five days. A cabinet had been seated in four months in Iraq, for Germany's fourteen months. An independent Iraqi central bank had been functioning two months into the new order; its German equivalent had taken a period of three years. The training of a new military in Iraq had been launched a mere three months into the new order, whereas a similar effort in Germany had taken a decade. Full sovereignty in Iraq was "pending," whereas Germany's sovereignty was restored after ten years, and no one had in mind a stewardship over Iraq of such length.

The numbers may have been accurate, but there was still terror in the streets of Baghdad, and there was still a bloody insurgency in the Sunni Triangle. And there was still that glee in Mosul. There had been hunger and deprivation in Germany in the period immediately following the war, but also obedience. A broken society had looked into the abyss and was ready for a break from that deadly history. Iraq presented an entirely different landscape: there were Sunnis determined to fight this new order; there were Shia who believed, rightly or wrongly, that their subjugation under the old tyranny offered them an absolution from the sins and the crimes of the deposed ruler, and that no excessive gratitude was owed the American liberators. The American leaders who had prosecuted this war had their work cut out for them.

The haunting image of those two soldiers, lying there in Mosul before an alien, hostile crowd, possessed its own power. The question posed by that image could not be brushed aside: can this distant power that blew into Mesopotamia emerge out of this venture with a genuine sense of conviction that something decent of itself could be left on Iraq's soil? On the morning of November 24, New York City's leading tabloid, the *Daily News,* carried a searing cover: one of the two American soldiers in the streets of Mosul, lying face up near the front wheels of his van, with a one-word headline describing the frenzied mood and the onlookers, "Bastards." No rendition of "progress on the ground" could offer Americans assurance that Iraq could yet redeem and vindicate these sacrifices. The promise of a decent, democratic Iraq "in the heart of the Middle East," as President Bush repeatedly put it, had to war with grim headlines and the steady bleeding in Iraq.

As the month of November came to a close, Secretary of Defense Donald Rumsfeld acknowledged the "contradiction" between the large achievements of the American stewardship and the constant bloodletting: "There is no question but that there are periodic incidents when people are being killed and wounded—we know that. We also know that schools are open, that the hospitals are open, the clinics are open; that people are engaged in economic activity throughout the country; and that the vast majority of the country is not in conflict." There was a duality to Iraq, achievements and heartbreak side by side.

Beyond the headlines of daily combat and losses, there was an ambivalence that ran through the very heart of this American interlude in Iraq. At times, the American administrators were imperial proconsuls keen to exercise the responsibility and power that came with this new burden. But they didn't know the country, and it was hard for them to navigate its deadly currents. The choices were not easy at any rate: hack away at the roots of the old regime with a vigorous de-Baathification program and face the wrath of the Sunnis who had been its backbone and beneficiaries; accommodate elements of the old order, work them into the new edifice, and be forced to traffic with a criminal political class and to trigger the enmity of those who had been victimized by the Saddam regime. Back and forth the American administrators oscillated. They opted for de-Baathification early on, then stepped back from it a year later, when the chaos within Iraq and the lobbying of the Arab states against de-Baathification brought about a reversal of the policy.

"Rifle in one hand, wrench in the other": this was the way then Major General Petraeus described his mission, and the mission of the 101st Airborne Division he commanded in Mosul. This was early February 2004, in the final days of the rotation and the "transfer of authority" to the Stryker Brigade that was relieving his forces. I had come to Mosul to catch a glimpse of the rotation, and of the man who had become something of a legend in the administering of this new Iraq. He had an important guest that day, Deputy Secretary of Defense Paul Wolfowitz, and Petraeus gave a briefing, replete with charts and a PowerPoint presentation of the work that his command had done. He spoke with obvious pride of this work: he spoke with some irony of the potholes his soldiers had repaired, of the cement factory they had gotten off the ground, of the well-drilling projects, of the donations of books to local libraries, of the local university they had reopened. He had given the people of Mosul a taste of something American through and through: the call-in show. He had done one himself, and the local politicians had begun to emulate him.

Petraeus had behind him assignments in Bosnia and Haiti. The work of reconstruction came with the mission, he believed. The needs of Mosul, and the large province of Nineveh that was his turf, were bottomless. There had been extensive looting, the stripping of practically all public assets. "If it wasn't guarded, it walked away," he said with resignation. The 101st Airborne Division had had to shift from combat to the work of reconstruction in record time. The officers and the enlisted men had been inventive and agile, and the pride of their commander in the work they had done was infectious. Mosul had named a street, he said with pride, for his division. There was little sentimentalism in Petraeus: the toughness and the knowingness broke through all the statistics of progress. He knew the Iraqis he governed: "The reward for a good deed done was a list of ten new requests." He was a believer in the power of money, its ability to pacify and absorb a good deal of the opposition of the Iraqis. "Money is ammunition, and if you have it, you don't need ammunition" was one of his favorite maxims.

Petraeus had launched his own "reconciliation" work: Baathists of the old regime had been given a chance to put the past behind them. The Petraeus flair was stamped on this process. There had been public assemblies where the Baathists "renounced" their old ways and their membership in the ranks of the discarded party. On one such occasion that he dubbed the "mother of all renunciations," some fifty-three hundred members of the Baath Party had recanted their old ways and been issued "certificates of renunciation." It hadn't been easy. Mosul was "Saddam country." It had supplied the old regime with hard-line Baathists and had been overrepresented in the officer corps of the army and the security services. There were skeptics in Mosul, he knew, who scoffed at this process and were convinced that men of the old order had conned the American occupiers. But it was important to move forward, he said. The country had had enough of recriminations and trouble.

Petraeus's time in Mosul was drawing to a close. (Months later, he would be back in Iraq with a promotion and the crucial task of training Iraqis for the defense of their own country, a massive undertaking meant to put in the field some 250,000 soldiers and border guards and police forces.) There was wistfulness in him: he had made his mark here. He noted, with nervous relief, that his command had gone six weeks without a single fatality. But he drew no consolation from that fact: the 101st Airborne had lost sixty of its people, he noted, and the video he presented on two huge screens at his headquarters paid tribute to those fallen soldiers. He had with him his designated successor, Brigadier General Carter Ham, of the Stryker Brigade. Petraeus had arranged for a tour of the police station and the municipality to introduce his successor to Mosul's leaders and to give Wolfowitz a sense of things in the city. A throng of reporters and security people trailed Petraeus and Wolfowitz: the streets were virtually empty; there were sharpshooters on the rooftops. Petraeus was leaving nothing to chance. This was Id al-Adha, a feast of sacrifice, an Iraqi handler told me, and the people of Mosul had gone on picnics or to their ancestral villages. I didn't quarrel with his spin; I only told him that I had grown up "not so far away," in an Arab city, where such feasts were vibrant, urban affairs. He gave up with a shrug of the shoulders and a hint of a smile.

The city center had been cleared for the Wolfowitz visit. Nearly four months earlier, there had been an attack on the Al Rasheed Hotel in Baghdad, where Wolfowitz had been staying. An American officer had been killed, and Wolfowitz himself had narrowly escaped injury or worse. The precautions in Mosul were in the nature of things. Indeed, as it happened, even as Wolfowitz and Petraeus and Ham were on their tour of Mosul, a Stryker vehicle of the kind the Petraeus party had taken to Mosul's central district was attacked by a rocket-propelled grenade on the other side of the city. The Stryker proved its worthiness that day. The slab armor on the vehicle had diffused the blast away from the Stryker's skin, and no one in the vehicle had been hurt. Power and vulnerability were there in this place and in this episode, side by side, as they are throughout this American experience in Iraq.

Petraeus had taken to "the East" and its ritual: he greeted his Iraqi interlocutors by kissing them on the cheeks in the traditional Arab way; he held hands with them, asked them to treat General Ham as a "brother," as they had treated him throughout his time among them. He said he will always be a "Mosulawi," and will remember his time among them as the best of times. In the police station and the municipality, pledges of fealty had been made to General Ham. Less flamboyant than his predecessor, Ham stayed in Petraeus's shadow: that day he was content to observe a virtuoso at work. The message that mattered was delivered: this "relief in place," in military language, should not be seen by the Iraqis as an American withdrawal.

If the American architects of this war had ever thought that they could confine their work to sacking the old regime, the accomplishments—and tasks—of the American presence in Mosul gave evidence of the cunning of such military expeditions and the unintended paths they take. On this day in Mosul, Petraeus had arranged for a ribbon-cutting ceremony on the outskirts of the city. A housing complex with a very American name, the Village of Hope, was to be turned over to eighteen Iraqi families, all in all 136 people ranging in age from seventy-one years to six months. Wolfowitz and Petraeus and a local official of Kurdish extraction were to turn over the certificates of ownership to the lucky families. The might of the American rulers was on display: a fleet of helicopters brought us to a clearing by the little village. Major Trey (Hugh) Cate, the division's public affairs officer, set to return to Fort Campbell, Kentucky, was oddly sentimental about this flight: it was his last helicopter flight over Mosul, he knew, and he spoke of his time in this place with genuine fondness.

There was something quaint and touching about the ceremony: two tents had been erected, and the families and the local artisans and laborers who had built this village sat in earnest anticipation. An effort had been made to heal this place and to acknowledge the multiplicity of Mosul's communities. Of the eighteen families, eight were Arab, six were Kurd, two were Turkoman, one was Chaldean and the other Assyrian. The violence in this place had been on a massive scale, and this little speck of a village was an attempt to provide a small solution and a contrast to what had played out under the old regime. A little handout prepared for the occasion gave the project's details. The soldiers of the 926th Engineer Group Headquarters had created the plans for the village; Bravo Company of the 52nd Engineers and the Oregon National Guard had begun the work, shortly after the fall of the old regime. Skilled Iraqi craftsmen had been brought into the project, and the Japanese had put some money into it as well. In the immense disorder, on the scale of Iraq's needs, this gift was small. But the occasion had a quiet joy and dignity. The families receiving these certificates were dressed in their best; the children trailing their elders to the podium to shake hands with Petraeus and Wolfowitz had the earnestness and the manners and shyness of the old ways of this culture. I was struck by the fact that all the women who came forth to the podium shook hands with the two Americans. It was a small but significant reminder that at heart this was a largely secular culture relatively free of the limitations imposed on women in stricter Islamic lands.

In the received wisdom of this war, Wolfowitz had been one of its "architects." (Indeed, several Iraqis he encountered on his tour of the country had used the very word to describe him and to thank him for the role he played in toppling the old regime.) For him, the ceremony at the Village of Hope was clearly a moment to savor. There has always been a dose of liberal redemptionism at the core of Wolfowitz's worldview. He has always held out the hope that after the war and the combat, there would come to Iraq a more decent political order. The Arab-Islamic world had always tugged at Wolfowitz; he had even made a stab at learning Arabic. In the early 1990s, during the Clinton interregnum, when he served as the dean of my school, he had asked me to locate for him an audiotape of the celebrated speech that Anwar el-Sadat had made to the Israeli parliament back in November 1977. He had been touched by the speech, by both the symbolism and the cadence of it. Two or three years later, I had been surprised to hear a funeral oration he had given for a Jordanian-born teacher delivered partly in Arabic. He had been studying and practicing Arabic with the Sadat tape. He had come to this war with a genuine belief that the wider Arab world was in desperate need of reform, and that Iraq offered the right setting for a campaign to rid the Arab world of its political and cultural malignancies.

The larger "complications" of Iraq were awaiting Wolfowitz on the next leg of his tour, in the city of Kirkuk. By common consent this is the place, a city of 800,000 people, where oil and ethnicity and the demographic "resettlement" schemes of the old regime came together. Kirkuk was the domain and specialty of Colonel William Mayville, commander of the 173rd Airborne Brigade. This brigade had secured the city in the opening phase of the campaign against the Saddam regime. Mayville, an officer in his early forties (West Point class of 1982), had come to master Kirkuk's ethnicities. America had not spawned the "native affairs" officers of older empires, but there was in Mayville something of that tradition. He had an air of restlessness. He loved his time here and was a superb briefer, and the details of Kirkuk were all at his fingertips. He had "broken bread" with the communities of this city: this was the language the notables used about him. He was unsentimental about the place yet respectful of its sensibilities. There was "dry kindling" aplenty in Kirkuk, he said, and he had done his best to make sure that no upheaval engulfed this place. He worked closely with Major General Raymond Odierno, commander of the Fourth Infantry Division, who oversaw the province of Anbar. He and Odierno were finishing their tour of duty; Wolfowitz had come to bid them farewell and to "show the flag" in the city.

For this occasion, Mayville was determined to give the deputy secretary of defense a flavor of Kirkuk's politics. He assembled a group of Kirkuk's leaders, the town's council, nine or ten people in all. The city's Kurdish mayor, Abdulrahman Mustafa, who doubles as provincial governor, was there, and so were men (and one Kurdish woman who was community head for city planning) drawn from the Turkoman and the Assyrian and the Sunni and Shia communities. A round-table discussion took place at the center of a small auditorium that had a smart, new look to it and must have been built or renovated after the fall of the old regime. An old Iraqi flag—one not bearing the words *Allahu akbar* (God is great) that Saddam had added to the flag in a sudden display of piety after the Gulf War of 1990–91—gave away the relative independence of this fragment of the country from the hold of the political order in Baghdad.

The mayor is an old political pro; I had seen him on a prior visit, three months earlier. He had been unstinting then in his praise for the American role in Iraq, and in Kirkuk in particular. He had talked of the "progress" made in Kirkuk, of its relative stability against the background of prophecies of its imminent descent into civil war. He was in his element now; in Wolfowitz he had an American "principal" with genuine power. He spoke of the new order with unbounded, and genuine, enthusiasm. He was not shy about asking for more American aid; he knew that the "supplemental" aid marked for Iraq would kick in before long, and he wanted Kirkuk's claims, and its needs, kept in mind. He acknowledged all the good work that General Odierno and Colonel Mayville had done in the province. They were "good and just men," he said, and they would be missed by all those who knew them. The worst had not happened in Kirkuk, and the place had defied the scenarios of its doom and descent into ethnic warfare.

Just when the session appeared headed for a display of harmony in the presence of a powerful man who had come from the distant imperial capital, a Sunni Arab notable, Sheikh Ghassan al-Assi, from one of the great tribes of the province, the Ubaydis, gave it a sudden jolt: "The oppressed have become the oppressors in Kirkuk," he said, "and democracy has become a whip in the hands of certain elements." He did not hesitate to name the beneficiaries of the new order—the Kurds. He spoke bitterly of the Kurdish militias administering their own brand of justice. He himself had been stopped and searched at a checkpoint by Kurdish militiamen. The rule of the Americans, for him, had been just a midwife for Kurdish dominion.

Sheikh Ghassan must have been in his early fifties. His checkered kaffiyeh and an elegant brown *abaya,* bordered with gold thread, over a Western suit, set him apart from the other participants in the meeting. He carried himself with genuine dignity. He fingered his worry beads as he spoke, without notes. He knew his brief and delivered it flawlessly and fluently. There was no excessive fawning in the presence of the stranger. Indeed, he had begun his remarks by saying that the "dear, distinguished guest" was owed a "word of truth" and an honest portrayal of things as they are. "Strangers," he said, from across the Iranian and Turkish borders, Kurds who had been forced out of Iraq by the old regime, were returning to Iraq, and Kirkuk's people were being "swamped" by those outsiders. The weapons of the old regime had been confiscated by the Kurdish militiamen, he added, and the "security situation" was not "healthy" in the tribal Arab areas. The place needed justice, he said, and the Americans had to disarm those militias.

Sheikh Ghassan had opened the floodgates. A subdued and thoughtful man, Saad Eddin Ameen, from the "Iraqi Turkoman Front," stepped into the debate. He felt "lonely," he said, on the town council, for he was the only Turkoman in its ranks. He echoed the Arab notable's complaints about Kurdish primacy, about Kurdish militiamen. He spoke of the historic rights of his community in this city and said that those rights were being breached. Liberty was good, he said, and he would still take the new order, but the "balance" among the communities was being challenged by the Kurds. He was clearly of the old order of Kirkuk. He spoke with the resignation of those who know that a certain order of hierarchy had been overturned.

Kirkuk's past had been "Turkish through and through," Hanna Batatu wrote in his book *The Old Social Classes and the Revolutionary Movements of Iraq.* Oil and the work opportunities of the oil industry had pulled Kurdish migrants and laborers into the city. In time, over the course of the 1950s, demography had tipped the balance in favor of the Kurds. Still, the Turkomans were of a higher social and economic status; they were the urban middle class, the creditors, the property owners. Then, into this witches' brew, Saddam Hussein threw his "Arabization" program. Arabs from other provinces in the country were dispatched to Kirkuk: they were called the "ten-thousand-dinar Arabs," for the housing and resettlement subsidy the Baath regime had given them.

American commanders had imposed the foreigner's justice in this contested place. But there was no assurance that the peace would hold if and when the American occupiers packed up and left. Indeed it fell to the Sunni Arab notable to say that the Americans could not leave at the present time, to prophesy bloodshed were they to do so. Away from the Sunni heartland, here his community was on the defensive and needed the foreigner's protection.

Wolfowitz told the assembled leaders that theirs was a "complicated" country, that it was all theirs and that they would bear responsibility for its social peace. The United States would not adjudicate housing claims, he let them know in no uncertain terms. He said that the resettlement of the Arabs in Kirkuk had not been the product of ethnic cleansing, as happened in the Balkans. All Iraqis, he said, had been victims of the old regime, including the Arabs who had been sent to Kirkuk by Baathist despotism. He offered them the assurance that Major General John Batiste, commander the First Infantry Division, set to replace Raymond Odierno, would be as committed to them as Odierno and Mayville had been. He knew Batiste well, he added; Batiste had been his military aide. They would find in him a good and wise partner. The place yearned for "imperial" benevolence, for the outsider's justice. In this setting, away from the prying eyes of their communities, these leaders were not shy to admit that they could not make a go of it without the benevolence, and the power, of the American military.

This command in Kirkuk, like Petraeus's in Mosul, had been pulled into civic and reconstruction work. The press packet, thick with projects accomplished and others in the planning stage, documented the work. There were monies for the repair of police stations and secondary and primary schools. One project was the renovation of a looted police building that was a "former secondary residence of Chemical Ali," the handout specified. There was a grant of $30,000 for the repair of a primary school in the "Kurdish sector of Kirkuk." The aim of the work was to provide a "better learning environment for the children of Kalafa." There were projects for traffic circles and security fences. And there was the obligatory PowerPoint presentation and a video narrating this division's work. "PowerPoint presentation versus Heart of Darkness," I scribbled in my notebook. The earnestness of this military, its desire to redeem and help, was on display everywhere. General Odierno, speaking of the fifty thousand jobs that had been created in the province covered by this command, exuded that American belief that radicalism and terror would be kept at bay once the economic needs were met.

It was hard to tell what of this earnestness would stick on the soil of

Iraq, for the needs of the country were bottomless. The American presence was at times a victim of its own success. Several months into the American stewardship, the gasoline lines had grown immensely frustrating: in this country of oil, that commodity had grown scarcer day by day, and the scarcity had become tangible proof of the inadequacy of the new order. But it was the new order that had made possible the import of some one million cars. The same was true of the shortage of electricity: liberation had released the pent-up demand of a population that had been denied the right to own television sets and satellite dishes, and the opportunity for the acquisition of consumer durables. Satellites dishes now sprouted everywhere, even in houses without rooftops. In wartime, over the course of three months, a whole new currency had been introduced: nine thousand tons of new paper currency had been brought into the markets, and thirteen thousand tons of the old currency had been withdrawn and hauled away. These achievements, substantial as they were, were warring against the willfulness inside Iraq and the daily American losses.

"Feed the stomach and embarrass the eye," an Iraqi man in his forties said to me as he tried to explain his antipathy to the Americans. Our chance encounter had taken place in the Water Palace of Uday Hussein, on the outskirts of Baghdad. I had gone into the palace, but the drabness and kitsch of it had driven me outdoors to catch the early morning sun. "This is an Iraqi proverb we hold dear here, and the Americans have not fed our stomachs." He had been an officer in the Iraqi army, and he was now on his own as a "minder" and a driver for foreigners doing business in Iraq. I told him that I knew the proverb, that we had something like it in my ancestral Lebanon. We circled one another; he wanted to know what part of Lebanon I hailed from. It was a way of asking about my religious and sectarian background. Offering him no help, I said that my family lived in West Beirut. Historically, West Beirut was home to the country's two principal urban communities: the Sunni and the Greek Orthodox. Then the Shia from the countryside, and from neighborhoods in the city's northeastern districts, had all but overrun that special part of Beirut and changed it beyond recognition. We had to talk across that uncertainty; he couldn't be sure of my religious identity.

I had made up my mind about him: the army affiliation, the attitude, the way he denigrated the leading Shia members in the Governing Council had all but clinched for me his own background. He was no doubt a Sunni. He dismissed Abdul Aziz al-Hakim, the Shia cleric who had inherited the mantle of leadership in the Supreme Council for the Islamic Revolution in Iraq after the assassination of his older brother, as a "simpleton" who had no place in politics. He heaped scorn on the secular Shia leader Ahmad Chalabi. He had given me what I needed to locate him on his country's religious and ethnic map. I had risen to his bait and told him that America had been unduly generous, that a vast subsidy had been allocated to Iraq, that a kind of boom had come to the place. He would have none of it: for him the "occupiers" had torn the peace of the country, and no one knew if it could be put together again. He spoke of the old order with nostalgia, contrasted it and its "prosperity" to the massive unemployment among his peers. He fell back on the "ignorance" of the Americans: they didn't know the place, and thus could not heal it.

The antagonism of this officer to the American project was understandable. From the security of the state, he had been thrown onto the vagaries of "the market." The social and psychic violation was very real in him. He had been a beneficiary of the old order, its child, and its verities had been taken away from him. But some weeks later, in a dispatch from the shrine city of Karbala, I read of an instance of anti-Americanism that was much harder to justify and to understand. A representative of Grand Ayatollah Ali al-Sistani in that city, Sheikh Abdul Mahdi Karbalai, had objected to a visit that Paul Bremer had made to the city. "He is an infidel and an occupier and he has no right to visit Karbala," this cleric opined. Karbalai no doubt knew what had befallen Najaf and Karbala, and the men of the religious class, under the old despotism. The debt owed America by Karbalai and his community was huge indeed. There was a real estate boom in Karbala itself. Four million "religious tourists" were expected to come to Karbala in the course of the year. There were new hotels under construction to accommodate the pilgrim traffic. Shia religious books, banned by the old regime, were everywhere.

All this was of course known by Karbalai. He lived by one code but spoke in an entirely different vein: it is a terrible affliction of modern Arab culture. A thoughtful Kurdish leader of the younger generation, Western-educated, deciphered for me this dualism, "this schizophrenia," as he called it. There was gratitude for the Americans, he said, but there was not enough honesty to admit it. False pride intruded, and fear of the judgment of one's peers and neighbors: this malady was endemic to this world, he reminded me. For him, senti-ments of the kind expressed by Karbalai were to be seen for what they were: mere dissimulation by people who knew truths they could not commit to print. (No one was spared here: Karbalai was assassinated some months later.)

The pride of Iraq was great, matched only by the severity of its wounds, and the extent of its needs. The country is too proud for its own good, Iraqis prone to introspection about their country readily admit. That pride made it harder to accept American tutelage. Public opinion polls must surely border on meaninglessness in a setting like Iraq—amid the insurgency and the violence—but one such poll taken by Oxford Research International, in February 2004, speaks to this defective pride. Some twenty-six hundred Iraqis, drawn from all the country's provinces, were queried about their attitudes toward the new order. One question was starkly put: Did the U.S.-led inva-sion "humiliate" or "liberate" Iraq? The verdict was a dead-even split: 41.2 percent thought of the war as a "humiliation" of Iraq, whereas 41.8 percent described the war as one of "liberation." (The remaining 17 percent had opted for the category of "difficult to say.")

Hamdi Hassan, the Baghdad bureau chief of the daily newspaper *Al-Adala,* told me about Iraqis' mixed expectations of American power: "They expected the standard of living of America to come to Iraq. They discovered that some things had gotten worse. Personal security is of course worse. Worst of all, the Iraqi citizen began to associate the scourge of terrorism with the presence of the Americans. To be fair, there are some who blame the insurgents, but this wrath against the Americans is a fact of life. There is widespread sentiment in favor of American withdrawal. But this sentiment is mixed with the fear of the unknown, and there is an unstated acceptance of the need for Amer-ican protection in this time of uncertainty."

A leading technocrat, Thamir al-Ghadban, a British-educated Shia in his early fifties, minister of oil in the interim government that the CPA put together, unintentionally gave away the expectations pro-jected onto the Americans. We were in the National Assembly when he asked me if I was in Iraq "to learn or to write?" I set my notes aside and told him I had come to put together a book. "What gift do you have in mind?" he said, after I gave this book's title. "Look outside, the terrible insurgency, the widespread insecurity, the lack of services, the heat." It was summer, and the heat outside forbidding. I had at moments thought that some Iraqis half expected that the Americans, with their magic, would dispose of the heat and the dust. This man of talent, and some impatience, had given voice to a feeling I had sensed but could not quite give credence to.

It was thus hard, if not impossible, for the American occupation authorities to divine the ways of Iraq. The country needed the American soldiers and administrators yet railed against them. An American commander in Kirkuk in northern Iraq, Colonel Lloyd "Milo" Miles, in a "warrior note" of March 17, 2004, wrote with candor to his soldiers about the country they had ventured into. They had been newly rotated into Iraq (from Hawaii, of all places), and he sought to speak to them of some of what they had witnessed. "I know that some of you are frustrated," he wrote, "frustrated that some of your fellow soldiers have been injured, frustrated that some of the same individuals that smile at you during the day are trying to kill you at night, and frustrated that the ethnic hatred seems so deep, the mission seems futile. Your emotions are understandable, and I would be lying if I told you I did not feel the same way sometimes. I want to remind you, however, that what you are doing is important. Do not focus on the long-term problems of Iraq or the historical animosity between different ethnic groups. I want you to focus on the good that you do every day. As a result of your presence, a hopeful people have been freed from tyranny and oppression; a nascent democracy is beginning to take root in towns and villages throughout the province; different ethnic and religious groups are able to celebrate and worship openly for the first time in several decades. A week does not go by without an Iraqi leader telling me that without you, the American soldier, there would be no hope in this land of tears."

The large "strategic picture of Iraq," this commander wrote to his soldiers, was no concern of theirs: what mattered was what they did as they went about their "daily missions." There were their tasks, and there was, he added, the very example of their own conduct in a society that desperately needed the power of a decent example.

A more senior military leader still, in the Iraq theater of operations, Major General Stephen Speakes, wrote a more personal note on March 19, 2004. He recounted the thrill of flying "low and fast" in a helicopter, at "150 knots per hour at about 50 feet of elevation." You see plenty of country up close that way, he said, in the main rural and open desert, with dense vegetation and population only near the

Tigris and the Euphrates. "But wherever you are so long as you are outside of Baghdad, I continue to see a sign that reminds me that all the sensationalism of the press terribly miscasts what is going on. As we fly overhead, we see townspeople walking in the street, farmers working fields by hand, and shepherds with their flocks out in the desert. About 70% of the time they take the time to straighten up, face us and wave. I will never forget the symbolism of the robed figures, statuesque in the desert, silently waving as we pass overhead. The memory of that gesture, made even as the sheep scatter and the rotor wash hits them, makes an impression. When I returned from my last trip I turned on my TV just in time to hear some talking head intone that Iraq was nearing civil war. Mentally, I contrasted the peaceful land I had just flown over with the TV declaration and dismissed it as so much nonsense."

The "mission" must simplify the soldier's life, give it measure and poise. A "warrior note" from Colonel Miles, dated April 29, 2004, expresses the simplicity of that code: "It is about loyalty and sacrifice and honor. It's about staying in the fight until the job is done. It's about taking care of each other, no matter what." In an accompanying note, Miles added that these principles are "well known to the soldier, and are as old as warfare itself." From the epicenter of troubles, from the Sunni Triangle, during a period of siege and fighting, a former student of mine, Colonel Jon Davis of the Marine Corps, wrote me an e-mail remarkable for its equanimity and its acceptance of the Iraqis. The note had in it the soldier's precision and restraint. He could not contemplate walking away from what was to be done. "The USMC just got here. We will fix and then return home. The Iraqis I have met—I like. [They] want the same stuff as all of us in the States. In the main they are Sunnis (some of whom are former communists). Obviously there are some bad folks out here stirring the pot—add to them a couple of urban areas with lots of unemployed youth. . . . Bad stuff but localized. Our Marine infantrymen are good young men. They are disciplined and they know what to do. They will make all of us proud. I, Sir, am immensely proud to be a small part of this lash-up and I am confident that we will be successful."

Reality shifted in Iraq. And the shift is caught in an e-mail by Major General Stephen Speakes, a military leader who had written more hopeful notes about the expedition. This time he was writing of the bloodletting in Fallujah, and the American losses in battle. It is an

Easter message, written on April 11. I include it at some length, both for the beauty of the prose and for the honesty of the voice:

Easter 2004 has been a time that I will probably remember. After several months of dry weather we had some light rain these past few days. The clouds and damp weather make the country seem sullen. That word conveys a part of the mood here. For this past week we have been in the business of separating out those who will continue on their path home and those who are being told to turn around and head back up to Iraq for a few more months. For all involved it's a hard time. The fact that it is Easter, a time usually associated with family and friends, makes the environment even more poignant. Lunch was a festive Easter meal. I sat down next to a stocky young guy in PT [physical training] gear seated by himself. He emerged from his focus on his lunch to greet me warmly. I learned he was an MP so I asked him what he was doing. He was one of the guys who was headed home until he was turned around literally days from flying. He was sad, as you would expect. I thought that he would be angry about being told that he was not going home. While he was saddened to know that he was not going home, I learned that he was really upset because of his frustration with Iraq and its people. He put it in terms that made far more sense than I could have expressed. He had been stationed near Baghdad escorting convoys. One time he had gone by a group of Iraqis and they were waving their AK-47s and shouting at his convoy when it passed. He had asked his interpreter what they were saying. The answer was "Yankee go home!" The MP's emotional response to me was, how dare they say this? After all we have had our country for only a few hundred years and look at what we have achieved. They had had their country since the times of the Bible and look at what they have achieved—they ought to want to listen to us and learn from us. He then went on to describe his frustration with the local police that he had worked with which had not inspired his confidence. What I saw in him was enormous commitment to the mission. His frustration was born of intense desire to do the job, he was not thinking of himself and the fact that he was going to spend several more months up in Iraq. He remained committed to make that miserable country safer and better and to make the livelihood of the people better. He wanted things to improve for the good people in the country and for the children, which remain everybody's hope when you see them because they clearly don't deserve the fate that they have endured. We worked the rest of the day ensuring that all the units that are being "remissioned" are being properly prepared for reentry into combat operations. Now it's late evening. When I go home I will turn on the Masters and be amazed with the beauty of the golf course, and the beautiful flowers and trees that surround the course. It just seems so strange to realize that something as beautiful as the Masters can go on at a time like this.

"There's no book out there that says, 'This is how you liberate a country,'" Marine Sergeant Major Gregory Leal observed in the aftermath of the combat in Iraq and the troubles that followed. There was little that was welcoming in Iraq. And there was, truth be known, little taste among Americans in that land for some new empire in the East. The nostalgia for golf, the mess halls that faithfully reproduced American cafeterias and their standard fare gave away the transient nature of this enterprise. In the tents and the mess halls, on the giant television screens, America was transmitted to these young men and women—NBA games, "reality" television, the chatter and noise of the talking heads on news programs. There had been no wholesale American acceptance of a mission in Iraq; no political-military class stood ready to claim an imperial mantle. A high American diplomat who had been rotated into Iraq, I was told, had asked an Iraqi professor the meaning of the word *hawza* (the Shia religious seminaries and clerical institutions). The Iraqi academic was taken aback. It was amazing, he told her, that America would dispatch a vast army into Iraq while the leaders of this expedition did not know the most basic realities of their new acquisition. Few Americans waxed poetic about the stark landscape of Iraq or the beauty of the hill country in the north. Behind the cement walls and the concertina wire, the Americans were embattled and apart, and their young soldiers were doing their best to survive the fury of the country.

In the Green Zone, in Baghdad, the administrators were more isolated still. Consider Gertrude Bell and her embrace of Iraq. "It's lovely out there. What shall I do here, I wonder," she said in London, on one of the home leaves she dreaded. Contrast her attitude with Paul Bremer's unease with Iraq and Iraqis. Nothing that the American proconsul had done prior to his Iraqi assignment had prepared him for the land and the people he would come to govern. It was known that he was eager to leave. He communicated no great enthusiasm for his mission. By the appearance of things, he was a fair administrator. But he gave every indication that he was marking time, that come June 30, and "freedom at midnight," he would leave the country without regrets and without looking back. (He would indeed leave two days earlier.)

It was no simple encounter—Iraq and the foreign soldiers who swept into it. There had been a massive breakdown in the country, a despotic tradition, the poison of sectarian hatred: there had been mass graves in the south, and the use of chemical weapons in Kurdistan. The evidence of neglect was everywhere: cities without sewers, schools without rudimentary equipment, scrawny children in tatters who turned up in the way of the cameras and the reporters when American forces struck into the country. There were barefoot recruits who deserted their army units and could be seen heading home to far destinations when the old regime fell. These soldiers on the open roads were a rebuke to all the empty claims of the "modern" and "powerful" country the Baathists had built.

The nationalist historiography had propagated the myth of Iraq's splendor and power, and its cultural radiance. There had once circulated in Arab literary life a maxim that maintained that Arabic books were written in Cairo, published in Beirut, and read in Baghdad. The truth of this proposition was beside the point: it was enough that Iraqis (and the Arab intelligentsia of nationalist disposition) believed it. The discourse of Iraq hid its reality. There was something in Iraq that resembled nineteenth-century Russia perhaps: a modern layer of immense accomplishment, a literary class of talent possessed of a genuine appreciation of high literary and artistic culture on top of a world steeped in backwardness and cruelty—and need. Everything about Iraq after the despotism cried out for help, but the fetish of national independence, and the idea of Iraq's gifts and talents, stood in the way of an easier accommodation with American power.

The legend of the unity of Iraq's Sunni and Shia communities was but a variation on the same theme. It is the norm in the country to speak of the high rates of intermarriage between the Sunnis and the Shia, and it is in the nature of things to say that those differences between the sects are exaggerated. "Sushi," they call themselves, these children of mixed Sunni-Shia marriages. They are everywhere; deep furrows run through the identity of many Iraqis. It had become routine to step forth, after the sectarian bombings and the sectarian troubles, to say that these antagonisms were alien to the spirit of Iraq. But the fault lines were deep: there were differences of temperament between these two communities. Samir Attallah, a Lebanese-born columnist and writer of long and distinguished experience, saw in Iraq the same denials that he had heard in his own birthplace when that country succumbed to sectarian and religious troubles a quarter-century earlier. Lebanon and the Lebanese had refused to believe that the hatred between Maronite and Sunni, Shia and Sunni, Maronite and Druze was innate to the place. The Lebanese too had been proud of their national tradition. There was an elite culture that drew on all the religious communities, and there were intermarriages across the sects and between Christians and Muslims. But slaughter had come to Lebanon, and the national identification cards that specified the religious sect of every Lebanese had been used at the checkpoints to sort out the victims in what became a long, dreadful descent into religious and sectarian warfare.

There had been mass killings in Lebanon, and the "cleansing" of entire towns that fell behind Muslim or Christian lines. Still, the myth of brotherhood across the communities persisted and the country refused to name and to acknowledge its troubles. The Lebanese journalist had seen his country's willfulness playing out in Iraq. The crowds that would come out with banners that read "Yes, yes to Islam, no, no, to occupation" were deluding themselves, hiding their divisions and warring aspirations in the drapery of false solidarity. To be sure, there were scholars and professionals and modern men and women free of the virus of sectarianism. But the truth of the feud was all around. Whose Islam would rule: that of Najaf or that of Fallujah? Whose Islam defined Iraq: that of the Shia shrine cities with their transnational links to the Shia communities beyond Iraq, or that of the Sunni Triangle, convinced that its Islam was Arab and true and uncontaminated by Persia and Persians?

The brutal sectarian truth at the heart of the insurgency that would bedevil the American occupation was simple. It was stated to me and to a group of American, French, and German colleagues back in October 2003 by a Western-educated Iraqi technocrat then working with the Coalition Provisional Authority. "We are building, and they are destroying. It is a race between us and them," he said. The insurgents had the easier time of it. This new order was hostage to their campaign of terror. There were "dead-enders" and jihadists in the ranks of the insurgents. But the insurgency had deeper roots than that,

and the insurgents fed off and worked with the anxieties of the Sunni
Arabs, and their stubborn belief that Iraq was rightly theirs. Sunni
Arabs had grown accustomed to dominion, took it as their birthright.
They believed—and they were right to do so—that they had been
bred and raised to power, that had it not been for the coming of the
Americans, the old order of primacy and power would have held and
the historical quiescence of the Shia would have continued.

Saleh Mutlak, a Sunni Arab and a soil scientist who had made his
fortune as an agricultural entrepreneur during the Saddam Hussein
years, and who had been expelled from the Baath Party for his streak
of independence, coldly explained to me in Baghdad that the Sunni
right to rule had been the natural order of things in Iraq: "We have the
heart," he said, "and the courage, and we know how to rule." He said
this as he thumped his heart with his fist. He offered this thought, and
in an animated way, as one offers a plain, incontestable truth. We were
in the big cafeteria in the Green Zone. A whole political history—the
way the Arabs of the Peninsula conquered Iraq in the seventh century,
the long war between the Sunni Ottoman state and the Shia Persian
state, which had played out on and near the soil of Iraq, the Pan-
Arabism that gave Sunni dominion its respectable cover—sat between
us as Mutlak explained the reasonableness of his claim to an ethnic and
sectarian dominion of a checkered land. No verdict that issued from
the ballot box and no political process that a foreign power had set in
motion could change this outlook overnight. Nothing in the history of
this man's country, nothing in the politics of the region around him
had taught him the ways of participatory politics, given him confidence that political life could be a benign realm of shared power.
Mutlak had a British education, was thus fluent in English, and knew
his way around the American enclave. Months after I had sat down
with him, he emerged as a de facto leader of a group of Sunni Arabs
who had been selected by the Americans for membership in the committee writing a new constitution. He had a diagnosis for the occupying power, and was not shy about proclaiming it: it had bet on the
wrong community—the Shia—and its stewardship of Iraq would
have been a more durable and a more successful affair had it entrusted
power to those Iraqis who had had it all along.

Perhaps it was too late in the annals of nations to pull off a foreign
dominion and have it accepted by a suspicious population with a difficult national history. Perhaps the world of Muslim Arabs was the

wrong setting for an experiment in benevolent alien rule. In the countdown that preceded the war, analogies had been made between the American interlude in Japan—the seven years between Japan's surrender in September 1945 and the restoration of its sovereignty in 1952—and the kind of challenge awaiting the Americans in a liberated Iraq. The American experience in Japan had been a singular tale of vindication; what was grafted onto Japan took and produced astounding results. A society poisoned by militarism and authoritarianism gave way to a democratic order. A country that militarists and demagogues had hijacked and disfigured turned its back on conquest and militarism. What the Americans found, MIT historian John Dower observes in his seminal book *Embracing Defeat: Japan in the Wake of World War II,* was a "populace sick of war, contemptuous of the militarists who had led them to disaster, and all but overwhelmed by the difficulties of their present circumstances in a ruined land. More than anything else, it turned out, the losers wished both to forget the past and to transcend it." The American occupiers had gone wholesale at the educational system and the civics textbooks, extirpating the old order and its culture.

No analogy is ever perfect though. Iraq was, of course, to write its own tale, and the American-Iraqi encounter was to be made of radically different material. There was no Hirohito here to surrender on his people's behalf. This was not an island nation easy to seal off from lands beyond; this was a frontier country with difficult neighbors who had their own schemes for Iraq, and their own stakes in the kind of outcome to emerge from the ruins of the old order. There may have been adversity in Iraq, but there was no hunger. Iraqis had not accepted their defeat, for that matter. For the Shia, the decapitated regime was not theirs, and its defeat was not "binding" on them. As for the Sunnis, they would turn away from the new order in sullen resentment and look to the insurgents to redeem their claims.

There was no wholesale embarrassment among the Sunni Arabs about the crimes and terrors of the old regime. To the extent that these terrors were acknowledged, they could be dismissed as the deeds of Saddam and the narrow clique around him—the despot and three or four dozen men in the highest ranks of the regime. But even that grudging concession was rarely made. Theirs was a cruel country, they believed, and the harsh rule had been the price paid for its stability. To rule Iraq, ran one of the popular maxims among Iraqis with no apologies to offer for the terror, you must have a stick in one hand and money in the other. Saddam had mastered that cruel but time-honored art, many Sunni Arabs were audacious enough to assert, and this raging anarchy was a vindication of the way the old order had functioned. This was not Japan, circa 1945, crushed by an over-whelming defeat and looking to reinvent itself. This was a Sunni Arab community with a memory of power, convinced perhaps that it was a campaign of terror away from the restoration of its old privileges.

There was oil in the ground, and the bounty of oil belonged to those who commanded political power. It had been so in Iraq, and it was still the case in the Arab oil lands around Iraq. The operatives of the old regime, the army and the police officers, and the larger Sunni community from which they were drawn in Mosul, Tikrit, Fallujah, and Ramadi were not about to learn new ways or new trades; they wanted nothing to do with the skills or the schemes of the American regency. When the American regime was new and sure of itself, there had been talk of remaking Iraq's economy, of opening it up to priva-tization and competition. For the untold thousands who had been beneficiaries and enforcers of the Baathist regime, these new schemes were nothing less than a violation of the order of the universe. Oil wealth beckoned, and the fact that these oil wells were in the main in the lands of the Shia and the Kurds gave this rejection of the new order by the Sunni Arabs added ferocity.

The American proconsuls were also different from those of 1945. They brought with them the doubts of a more modern world, its cul-tural relativism, its embarrassment with outright alien rule. In Japan, the viceroys had been openly paternalistic, sure of themselves and of their racial apartness from the conquered people. *Embracing Defeat* catches the high purpose of the Americans and their certainty, and the kind of America they carried with them into their mission: "The reforms that the victors introduced were unique to both moment and place. They reflected an agenda inspired by heavy doses of liberal New Deal attitudes, labor reformism, and Bill of Rights idealism of a sort that was being repudiated (or ignored) in the United States." It was not always pretty, that Americanism in Japan, or always sincere. "Democratization" often clashed with severe authoritarian rule. But Japan had taken the conqueror's justice and the conqueror's gift and his paternalism. Even the Communists, Dower notes, found it easy to describe the American forces as an "army of liberation." The Americans had drafted a new constitution for Japan; the Japanese took to it with fervor. In Dower's words, "No modern nation ever has rested on a more alien constitution—or a more unique wedding of monarchism, democratic idealism, and pacifism, and few, if any, alien documents have ever been as thoroughly internalized and vigorously defended as this national charter would come to be." Japan was lucky; pride had not intruded. And there weren't around Japan nearly two dozen nations partaking of Japan's language and culture and religion, taunting Japan about its acceptance of America's hegemony, as would be the case in Iraq six decades later. In Tokyo, the American regency had not blinked; there was a firmly held American belief that the conquered society had to be remade.

This kind of American certitude was not to be part of this new venture into Iraq. There had not been a full reckoning with the imperial burden that would come after the war. There was no national consensus in the United States for staying in Iraq, and for remaking that land. It was September 11, it must be acknowledged, that had given America's leaders a warrant for venturing into Iraq. Intuitively, and on trust, the public had accepted a link between the terrors of September 11 and the regime in Baghdad. The popular will that had underwritten the war against the Taliban had given a green light for a campaign against Saddam Hussein. But this kind of warrant can be easily withdrawn. Buyer's remorse soon stole upon this war. "Two years are an American eternity," the writer Leon Wieseltier observed on the second anniversary of September 11.

The terrors had not been forgotten, but the solidarity of grief, and the recognition of terrible dangers from distant lands, had given way. By then the war in Iraq had to stand on its own. A kind of normalcy had come to America, and the war in Iraq had become an affair of daily American casualties. "Major combat" had come to an end, and the bleeding had truly begun. There was enough presidential authority to hold the line, enough American patriotism and pride to preclude an open admission that the thing was a mistake or even a noble failure best abandoned in midstream. But there was no mistaking the disaffection with the war, the steady erosion of American popular support. And the faith in the architects and principals who prosecuted this war had begun to erode as well. They had not been "humble enough before the mystery of a foreign country," the novelist Nicholson Baker wrote of these leaders in *Checkpoint*, a short work of fiction published in the summer of 2004, which caught the mounting frustration with the Iraq war. The novel was hysterical in tone, its leading character a deranged loner railing against the "criminality" of the war and the illegitimacy of the leader who launched it. But there was shrewdness in that insight, and an eye for the cunning—and the surprises—of history.

Men and women are rarely, if ever, given the gift of foresight. There was no way of knowing whether the American leaders who prosecuted the war would have still chosen to do so had they known what lay ahead of them in Iraq. By the time of the first anniversary of the war, the consensus on it had come apart. Nearly six hundred soldiers had been lost, and a somber recognition had set in that the insurgents would always be there waging a campaign of attrition. No one expected the architects of this war to acknowledge their loss of faith in the war they had launched, but the certitude that surrounded the war had cracked.

With a marketer's exquisite sense of timing, it was on that first anniversary of the war that Richard A. Clarke, a senior counterterrorism official who had worked for four administrations, came out to offer his own account of a war foretold, a campaign of choice against Iraq that had been the Bush administration's strategy all along. The doubts about the war now had a credible witness from within the national security bureaucracy. True, some ten weeks earlier there had been another insider's account, by former Secretary of the Treasury Paul O'Neill, making the assertion that Iraq had been a veritable obsession of the administration of George W. Bush, and that plans for the war predated the terror attacks of September 11. O'Neill had made these charges in *The Price of Loyalty,* a book written by the political journalist Ron Suskind. The administration had ridden out that storm. Foreign policy had not been O'Neill's beat; he had been summarily—and gracelessly—dismissed from the cabinet, and it was easy to see his attack as a settlement of a highly personal account. Clarke offered a different kind of challenge. Terrorism was his beat, and he came forth, at the right time, to condemn the war against Iraq as a distraction from the campaign against terror.

There was no easy way around Clarke's assault on the premises of the war. As the country recalled the war's beginnings and worried about what was unfolding in Iraq, Clarke appeared to own the airwaves. On March 21, he appeared on CBS's *60 Minutes* to launch his book, *Against All Enemies*. A week later, he claimed the full duration of NBC's *Meet the Press*. In between there was a dramatic appearance before the 9/11 Commission, and his apology to the families of the victims of September 11. Try as they did to dismiss him as a disgruntled former official who had lost his bureaucratic turf, or a would-be profiteer hawking a book, the officials of the Bush administration had a crisis on their hands. What they depicted as a "war of necessity," Clarke described as a war of choice planned and prosecuted by an American leadership hell-bent on getting its way. In Clarke's words, "Iraq was portrayed as the most dangerous thing in national security. It was an idée fixe, a rigid belief, received wisdom, a decision already made and one that no fact or event could derail."

The "wrong war" had been fought, Clarke asserted: we had forgotten the war on terror, and the plotters of Al Qaeda, to invade and occupy an "oil-rich Arab country that posed no threat to us." There was a truth teller's certitude in Clarke's demeanor and message. The large analytical assertions he made were not particularly deep and were often off the mark. His assessment of anti-Americanism in the Islamic world as an animus that had been stirred up by the Iraq war was ahistorical and naïve in the extreme. Anti-Americanism in Arab and Muslim lands had not waited on the Iraq war. It had blown at will years before America had struck into Iraq. But what stuck was the narrower message Clarke delivered. The push for the war against Iraq, he claimed, had gathered force as early as September 12, 2001. Clarke recalled the meeting—at first denied, then confirmed—with President Bush in the Situation Room on that day. The president had been adamant in his instructions: he wanted everything gone over again. "See if Saddam did this. See if he is linked in any way." By his account, Clarke had wanted the emphasis to stay on Al Qaeda, but the president was not to be denied. "I know, I know, but . . . see if Saddam was involved. Just look. I want to know any shred . . ."

Two months earlier, David Kay, the chief weapons inspector, head of the Iraq Survey Group, had called it quits, leaving open the probability that Iraq had had no weapons of mass destruction to begin with. Kay had walked away from the hunt for the weapons on January 28, 2004, as he appeared before the Senate Armed Services Committee. "I don't think they existed," Kay declared. Now another insider was defecting. The Iraq venture was a case of bait and switch, Clarke would assert: the administration had taken the terrors of September 11 as a warrant for an unnecessary war. "I suspect that many of the heroic U.S. troops who risked their lives fighting in Iraq thought, because of misleading statements from the White House, that they are avenging 3,000 dead from September 11. What a horrible thing it was to give such a false impression to our people and our troops." In a highly polarized country taking stock of blood and treasure expended in Iraq, Clarke had found his audience with remarkable ease. For those who had opposed the war to begin with, and for those who were chastened by the bloodshed and the anarchy in Iraq and had concluded that the project had come to grief, Clarke supplied the needed ammunition.

Clarke did not agitate in a vacuum: his impact was of course enhanced by the truculence of the Iraqis. It would have been easier to defend the war had there been peace in Iraq's streets, had there been (beyond Kurdistan) communities and leaders eager to embrace the American presence. Where the Japanese had turned an American army of occupation into an "army of liberation" to enhance their own liberty, the Iraqis did the opposite. The Anglo-American liberators were turned into occupiers who had come to dispossess the Iraqis of their wealth. Perhaps it was the curse of oil, the suspicion that America had come to stay and to plunder Iraq's wealth. Then too, the Arab and Iranian spectators to the drama must have fed the Iraqis' eagerness to play a glamorous "anti-imperialist" role. Nature imitated art: the Arabs beyond Iraq's borders could offer Iraq no help in its hour of need. The American authorities had come through with a huge reconstruction package, nearly $20 billion in aid. It was the liberator's burden and bounty. But Iraq had become a big Arab story and the Arabic daily papers in London, and the satellite channels in Dubai and Qatar, had cast this encounter in Iraq as yet another duel between American "hegemony" and Arab resistance.

The Iraqis had to play the role assigned them by the Arab media; they couldn't disappoint their "brethren" in Arab lands. They could not accept the embrace of the Americans or the writ of the occupation authorities. Pride can be a terrible affliction, and the Iraqis appeared to have it in plentiful supply. Patience was needed, and a measure of gratitude for the work that the Americans were doing in Iraq. But gratitude was rarely expressed. As the American architects of the war were hard-pressed to justify it, and as the storm over its costs broke out

some six months after the liberation of Baghdad, the American civilian administrator, L. Paul Bremer III, spoke of what was being done
for Iraq—the forty thousand Iraqi police officers on the streets,
twenty-two million vaccinations, the renovation of fifteen hundred
schools, the new Internet connections, etc. He provided these details
in Iraq, but it was American opinion that was on Bremer's mind.
There were other markers down the road as the countdown for the
transfer of sovereignty to the Iraqis had begun. With one hundred days
left for him in Iraq, the proconsul was at it again, reciting at a public
ceremony all that had been accomplished under American stewardship: the security forces of Iraq had been augmented, twenty-five
hundred schools had been refurbished, eighteen thousand reconstruction projects had been launched, and there had been a thirty-fold
increase in health care spending. Unemployment had declined; the
value of the Iraqi dinar had risen 29 percent over the course of three
months. The statistics were real, but so were the scenes of mayhem.
What the dispatches and images from Iraq conveyed was a population
in a constant state of agitation. It was hard to imagine these people—
who shouted into the cameras, demanding instant solutions for age-
old problems—settling down to a routine peace, and hard to believe
that the American effort and sacrifices would stick to the soil of this
angry land.

The proconsul's celebration of progress proved tragically premature.
Less than a fortnight later, with ninety days to go before the transfer of
authority, the country erupted into open rebellion. Those precise figures of progress and accomplishment now had to battle with scenes of
horror. The gates of hell, as the Arabs would say, were flung wide open
in Fallujah on March 31, 2004. The grim events in Fallujah would
frame this war. Four American security contractors were ambushed
and killed; the bodies were desecrated. Americans and Iraqis now
stared into the abyss. Those frenzied mobs beating the corpses with
their shoes, those charred bodies hung from the girders of a bridge over
the Euphrates, those ten-year-old boys partaking of it all with such
cruel pride: a moment of genuine shame had come to Iraq. It took no
prompting for Iraqis to recall their own history. The desecration of the
dead was known to them. They had seen it, of course, during those
cruel days of July 1958, when the monarchy was overthrown. They
had seen it in Kirkuk and Mosul in 1959, and they had seen it in
1963, when the revolution of 1958 devoured its own and the strong-

man Abdul Kareem Qassem was killed, and his corpse and those of his companions were displayed on national television.

It was idle to say that Islam is particularly severe in its admonition against violations of the dead. Such scruples had no place in the moral calculus of that pitiless crowd. At any rate, the assailants deployed the faith on their side. A leaflet that claimed the deed opened with a verse from the Quran. " 'Those of you that act thus shall be rewarded with this world and with a grievous punishment on the day of Resurrection. Allah is watching over all your actions.' (2:85)." The verse had been chosen at random, it would appear. No care had gone into its selection. In the way of such leaflets and proclamations, the deed was claimed by the "Martyr Ahmad Yassin Brigade," named for the Palestinian cleric, the godfather of Hamas, who had been killed in an Israeli raid ten days earlier. There was no apology in the proclamation, no embarrassment over the desecration of the dead. The "angry masses" had done this "blind violence" to the dead out of their "great hatred for the Americans over their violation of the sanctity of homes and mosques, their imprisonment and torture of religious scholars and old men, their terrorizing of women and children." This had been a "gift that the people of Fallujah had presented to the people of Palestine and to the family of the martyred Sheikh Yassin."

The killers, and those who winked at them, knew the "rules of engagement" with the American forces in their midst. They struck in the knowledge that the rules and scruples of liberalism would hold, that there would be no mass internment, no collective reprisals. They knew that the satellite channels and the world media were there, that the lights were on, as it were. Their war was, by their reasoning, a righteous campaign to retrieve a lost dominion. They knew that the foreign power would threaten and then hold back and offer a cease-fire. The course of "major combat" had spared Fallujah, totally bypassed it. No victorious American tanks had rolled through the streets of Fallujah and Ramadi. Defeat had not been visited on Fallujah; the city had not been forced to acknowledge that its political regime had been overwhelmed. This reprieve played into the Fallujah insurgency, fed its sense of defiance. Defeat often acquits a population, forces on it an acceptance of a new order of things. Fallujah could press on in the conviction that the last had not been heard from the old hegemony.

Those who pulled off the murder of the American contractors had been both cruel and sly. The marines who had been newly rotated into Fallujah and the larger Anbar province around it had come in with a mission of "engaging" this town and this restive province. They had arrived without their heavy equipment and armor. In a sudden shift of strategy and tactics, they were now ordered to put down an insurgency. An officer in the Marine Corps spoke to me of this shift with some bitterness. "We were now ordered to wipe out the people we had been sent to engage." It had been hard to turn away from the cruelty of what had happened in Fallujah. Those behind the murders of the American contractors, and the ensuing barbarous spectacle, had gotten the fight they wanted. Engagement would have to wait for another day and another occasion.

Fallujah was predictable trouble. The surprise of this eruption came from the followers of Moqtada al-Sadr. Trouble in Kufa and Najaf and Karbala was a challenge from a community that was a beneficiary of this American presence. The militia of the young firebrand, the Mahdi Army, rose up to fight for its leader. On March 28, the Coalition had shut down his paper, and a day later his deputy, Mustafa Yaqoubi, was picked up on charges of complicity in the assassination of Sayyid Abdul Majid al-Khoei, back in April 2003.

Sadr seized his moment; he was now the repository of the wrath of the crowd. He appeared to own the alleyways of Sadr City in Baghdad. Freedom and anarchy were heady. "Terrorize your enemy," Sadr instructed his followers in a proclamation he issued on April 4 from Kufa. "Your enemy loves terror, disdains all people and all Arabs. I beg of you not to opt for demonstrations, for they are now useless, and we must choose other means of resistance. For me, I am with you, and my wish is to be with you until we are carried aloft to ample gardens. . . . Help me in any ways that would secure you God's blessings." He sought refuge in a mosque in Kufa, where Imam Ali had once worshipped and where he was struck down by an assassin in AD 661. In an attempt to summon up the memory of his father, he donned, as had his father before his murder, a white shroud—the shroud of death, and a message that he too was ready to be martyred for his followers. He then moved to Najaf, the stronghold of Grand Ayatollah Ali al-Sistani.

Where Sadr had once belittled Sistani as an outsider and an embodiment of passivity and political abdication, he now declared himself the "military wing" of the old jurist. (Sadr was borrowing a page from the book of Hamas in the Palestinian territories, where the operatives of that movement maintained that fictional distinction between their "political wing" and their "military wing." For months, the Coalition Provisional Authority had had an outstanding warrant for the arrest of Sadr but had not acted on it; there had been his role in the murder of Khoei, and there were also charges that he had been complicit in attacks on American soldiers. The Coalition's indulgence of Sadr had backfired, and the authorities now had on their hands a two-front war. A terrible week ensued: forty American soldiers were killed in the course of a violent week. There was fierce fighting in Sadr City, where eight American soldiers were killed. In the town of Kut, the Ukrainian troops withdrew, leaving the place to the Sadrists. By the time the month of April came to a close, 128 American soldiers had lost their lives.

CHAPTER 5

The Old Regime's Afterlife

It was a cruel irony that April 9, 2004, the first anniversary of the fall of Baghdad and the toppling of that statue of Saddam Hussein in Firdos Square, came amid such chaos. Weeks earlier, I had toured police stations and training outposts for the Iraqi Civil Defense Corps in Baghdad and Mosul. The police chiefs had spoken of their devotion to their work; their American trainers had praised them to the skies. Now when needed, the police and the civil defense units had melted away. They wouldn't fight the foreigner's war. They could not stand in the face of a righteous crowd. In Basra, Kufa, and Najaf, the police had stepped aside as the Sadrists overran police stations and municipal offices. No wonder: a handbill by the Mahdi Army of Sadr warned the Iraqi police and army and Civil Defense Corps that their blood was "forfeit" and "permissible" to shed if they cooperated with the "enemy occupiers."

Sadr's army of bandits and dispossessed young men had staked a claim to the spoils of anarchy. In his more grandiose moments, Sadr spoke of igniting a jihad against the Americans. The older jurists kept their distance from him. Even his acknowledged religious guide, Ayatollah Haeri in Qom, held aloof from the young pretender, questioned his right to summon the believers to a holy campaign, and opined that the young man did not have the religious learning needed to render binding judgments. When Sadr sought an audience with Ishaq Fayyadh (the Afghan-born cleric, one of the four grand ayatollahs of Najaf), he was rebuffed and told to get himself some religious learning. His own band of followers was of course indifferent to the fine points of jurisprudence. A thin line separated banditry from righteous belief and virtue. What the young boys of the Party of God did to Beirut a generation earlier was now replicated in Baghdad. The half-educated and the bewildered and the opportunistic found their way to Sadr's army. Belief, social advancement, the appreciation of what was there to be had came together in this movement. A Baghdadi man of commerce, Jassem Hussein, depicted the situation in his city with resigned clarity in mid-April: "In the past, we used to fear the secret police of Saddam; we were afraid to utter a word of criticism because his secret police were everywhere. Now these armed men do the same thing. They can come here and arrest me, and no one can stop them." From tyranny to anarchy: the Iraqi pendulum had not stopped in the middle.

In its eagerness to train and "stand up" an indigenous structure of security, the Coalition Provisional Authority had not been able to do adequate background checks on the new recruits and officers of the security forces. In a moment of genuine need and peril, the structure of security that the CPA had put in place gave way. The American authorities wanted to believe the very best about the forces they had trained. On the grounds of the CPA's headquarters in Baghdad, two months earlier, an army general who had spent years in Saudi Arabia training that country's national guard had praised the "professionalism" of the Iraqis and contrasted it with the tribalism and lax ways of the Saudi units. The work of standing up these Iraqi units boded well, he said, for the making of the new Iraq. But the Americans hadn't really known their Iraqi charges. One unit, the Thirty-sixth Battalion of the Iraqi Civil Defense Corps, had acquitted itself well in the fight for Fallujah. This unit comprised elements of the old anti-Saddam opposition—the Kurdish militias, the Supreme Council for the Islamic Revolution in Iraq, the Iraqi National Congress, and the Iraqi National Accord. But the Thirty-sixth was the exception: the CPA had opted for a "technocratic" approach that had opened the ranks of the new units to all comers.

Iraqis were given to legends about their own unity. This moment would spawn such illusions once again. In truth, the town of Fallujah had risen in rebellion because the new order promised the Shia a reprieve from the old Sunni ascendancy; now there were reports that the Shia were eager to come to the help of the people of Fallujah. Convoys of pickup trucks with signature black Shia flags could be seen hauling food to the people of that city. One Iraqi gave a foreign reporter a flavor of this new moment. "Sunni, Shia, that doesn't matter anymore. These are artificial distinctions. The people in Fallujah are starving. They are Iraqis and they need our help." The man was identified as Sabah Saddam, a thirty-two-year-old government worker who had taken the day off to drive one of the supply trucks. Five weeks later, it was time to return the favor. A convoy of nine trucks loaded with food and medical supplies was sent from Fallujah to Sadr's forces in Najaf and Kufa. A leader of this convoy, a Sunni cleric, said that "it was incumbent on all Muslims to defend our land and our honor." The Shia had been here before. For the entire previous year, they had lived in the shadow of the suspicion that they were collaborators of foreign rule. The Arab media beyond Iraq had written of them with derision. The domesticated media in Egypt and Saudi Arabia and Jordan, and the exile Arab press in London, never wearied of profiling the Arab "volunteers" who had been picked up in Iraq and turned over to the Americans by Shia "collaborators." The volunteers, upon their release, spoke in code. They reported being welcomed in the north and the center of the country—in Sunni lands—while the people in the south had been accomplices of the Americans, their translators and their aides.

A theory had taken hold in the Arab world that this Pax Americana aimed at using the Shia as a prop of the new American order. Now, in a familiar twist, the old legends of Arabism were given a new lease on life. Sadr was no longer a sayyid on the fringe of events but a man of the "Arab and Iraqi resistance." The very same pan-Arabists who had held the Shia all but responsible for the fall of the old despotism were now eager to take them in. Abdul Bari Atwan, a Palestinian publisher who puts out a radical paper in London, *Al-Quds Al-Arabi,* wrote in exaltation of the "resistance now uniting all Iraqis." He wrote with a sense of vindication, with the kind of gleeful abandon that has poisoned Arabic letters and thought in recent years: "We were always confident that the Iraqi people, with all its ethnicities and cultures, would resist the occupation, and would overcome the sectarian conspiracies that were hatched in the dark corridors of the Pentagon, and brought to Iraq via American tanks and helicopters." There was hope yet for the old orthodoxy: the old yarn could be spun yet again. The crowd had held aloft in Baghdad and Kufa portraits of Sadr and of the Palestinian Sheikh Ahmad Yassin, of the Hamas movement. Here was proof, in the crowd's euphoria, of Sunni-Shia unity.

This solidarity across the Sunni-Shia divide was fragile. On the walls of Baghdad the graffiti that appeared after the fall of Saddam Hussein told the real story of a deep Sunni-Shia antagonism: "Better a thousand Americans than one Tikriti." The gift of Fallujah's solidarity was

not destined to last. In early June, six Shia truckers driving into Fallujah were ambushed and killed. Worse still, their corpses were mutilated. The truckers had come with supplies for the Fallujah Brigade, a
military formation that the Americans had enlisted from former elements of the Republican Guard and the Baath Party. In the controversy that swirled around this incident in the days that followed, it
came to light that before their murder, the men had sought sanctuary
in the police station but had been turned over to "zealous men of religion," as the accounts of the incident had it. These clerics, it was
alleged, had then ordered the truckers' torture and murder and authorized the mutilation of their corpses and the confiscation of their property, including their clothes. The past had reared its head again; unity
had been a fleeting thing. Shia demonstrators turned up in Baghdad to
protest the murders, but no satisfaction was offered. The Association
of Muslim Scholars—a new clerical institution representing the Sunni
men of religion—said that no "convincing proof had been offered of
the complicity of the sons of Fallujah in the murder of these victims."

There was an easy way out of the responsibility for what had
befallen these six men. There were those who outright denied that the
grim deed had taken place: a campaign was afoot, they said, to smear
Fallujah's reputation, to depict it as a haven of terror. And from the distance of Cairo, there was a pundit or two who would write that the
episode was murky, that it was difficult to determine whether these
men had been killed because they were Shia or because they had been
working with the Americans. But the sectarianism was always there,
always an ambush or a quarrel away.

Now and then, as is the way of great, painful truths, the claims of
modernity and patriotic brotherhood are brushed aside, and the
wounds of historical enmities exposed for what they are. Thus it was
in November 2004, when Fallujah had finally been stormed by American forces: the governor of the Shia holy city of Karbala, Saad Safouk
al-Massoudi, permitted himself an open expression of satisfaction at
Fallujah's suffering. The American assault, he said, had been a "punishment from God" for the role Fallujah's people had played in crushing
the Shia uprising in Najaf and Karbala, back in 1991. The grim
images of dogs devouring corpses in the streets of Fallujah were a
replay, he said, of similar scenes that had occurred in Karbala a generation earlier. The life was raw here, and the suffering bottomless. Fallujah's people had ridden the dictator's chariot, had been his enforcers.

Men and women are not angels: it stood to reason that some would feel satisfaction in the fall of a city favored by the tyranny.

For their part, though, the true believers in the Arab world beyond Iraq needed the legend of Fallujah, and they were particularly eager to bring together the causes of Iraq and Palestine. In truth, Palestine had been indifferent to Iraq: it was enough that the dictator had given money to the homicide bombers, that he had written off his own deeds of aggression by linking them to Palestine and to the grievances of the Palestinians. After all, even his conquest of Kuwait, in 1990, had been justified and sanctioned on the Arab street when it was "linked" to the Israeli occupation of the West Bank and Gaza. And the great crimes of his regime had been forgiven and overlooked in the name of putting together a center of Arab power that would, in time, challenge Israel's military edge. Now the two causes, so the purveyors of the pan-Arab orthodoxy insisted, were one and the same.

The old pan-Arab orthodoxy had been on the sidelines; the liberation of Iraq, and the capture of the despot, had thrown it on the defensive. Now a raft had been extended to it by Fallujah. One of the pan-Arab journalists in London (the exiles are most fierce; the radicalism grows with the distance from home, and with the years), a columnist for the Saudi-owned *Al-Hayat,* merged Fallujah and Palestine. "Rafah (Gaza) = Fallujah," he wrote. "Armed American helicopters over Iraqi streets. . . . Demonstrations in the streets against Israel (and America) in Palestine, demonstrations in the streets against America (and Israel) in Iraq. . . . Israeli policy in the hands of Likud and the extremists, American policy in the hands of Likudniks and extremists from among the neoconservatives. . . . Collaborators and traitors from among the Palestinians working with Israel, collaborators and traitors from among the Iraqis working with the American occupation." The darkness of this view, and its extremism, were a mirror of that Arab street and its indifference to reason. It did not matter that this change was made from the safety of London: the radicalism had a warrant to pronounce on the Arab condition, to throw in the air charges of treason and collaboration. Pragmatism had remained the embattled creed of but a few.

If there was hope that the old Arab obsession with Israel, that deadliest of all Arab alibis, would "vacate" this Arab land, which had its own burdens to carry, there were indications that the old legacy would hold on. There were steady charges that the Kurds had made room in their territory for Israeli intelligence operatives and businessmen. There were dark rumors that Iraqi Jews, banished from their country in the early 1950s, were plotting their return and buying up property in Baghdad. There were charges made with no small measure of zeal and conviction that the Americans would force on this new Iraq reconciliation and a peace treaty with Israel. The "Arabness" of Iraq was at stake. It did not matter that there were Kurds and Turkomans for whom this Arabness was an alien form of domination. Nor was it forthrightly faced that this Arabness had been, to the Shia, one long nightmare. Israel was on the sidelines of this big struggle. But it had to be brought into the fight.

An aged Iraqi artist and writer residing in London, Rifat Chederchi, ran into this old Israel obsession. In late April of 2004, he completed a design for a new Iraqi flag. He had been given the assignment to come up with a "forward looking" flag that was "inclusive" and true to Iraq's realities. Gone was the color green, said to be the Prophet Muhammad's favorite, and the red, white, and black colors of the old Iraqi flag (the colors of Arab revolutionary flags) and the inscription of *Allahu akbar* (God is great) added to the flag by Saddam Hussein. Chederchi had come back with a simple design: the blue crescent of Islam on a white field and three stripes. Two stripes were blue, representing the Euphrates and the Tigris rivers, and the third was yellow, the color of Kurdistan.

The new flag, pretty and dignified, was an affront to old-style Arab nationalists determined to hold their ground. The flag's inspiration, they said, came from the blue-and-white color scheme of the Israeli flag. Looking past the crescent that adorned it, they insisted that it lacked Islamic symbolism as well. The flag designer, a man of seventy-seven, had been away from the hell of Iraq too long. He harked back to a different Iraq. He descended from one of Baghdad's oldest, most respected families. His grandfather had been mayor of the city in Ottoman times. His father, Kamel, a lawyer-journalist driven by a spirit of reformism, had been one of the most beloved and incorruptible figures in Iraqi politics under the monarchy. "I didn't think about Israel. Political opinions don't concern me. I approached the design from a graphic point of view." The Governing Council that had commissioned the flag bent to the wind: it darkened the blue stripes and said that the flag was temporary and that a future sovereign government would come up with its own flag.

Chederchi faced the storm with equanimity. In an interview he gave in mid-June to an Arab daily, he went to the heart of the matter. The controversy around the flag, he said, was an opportunity for those who had not been able to defend the old despotism to strike back and to reassert a hegemony they had lost. The attack on the new flag was a way that those who had once held aloft the banners of "the inspired leader" or the "sole leader, God keep him," could return to the political arena. A battle was being waged in Iraq between a "dark ideology" from the past and "a new vision of pluralism and justice." Never in the history of Iraq, he added with a sense of subdued realism, has any ruling order accepted the claims and realities of pluralism, and the diversity of the country. Power has always been singular, a monopoly of those who claimed it at the time. It was not for him, he said, to decide whether the flag should be adopted or not. The artist was a man of candor; yes, he said, he had wanted to move away from the old red, green, and black colors of Egypt, Syria, and the former Iraqi regime. There was a difference, said Chederchi, between religion and culture, and those who had built and carried forth Arab-Islamic civilization in Iraq had been "Arabs and Kurds and Persians and Turks and Christians and Jews and Turkomans, and others. What we are after today is a flag that symbolizes this multiplicity and this pluralism. Even the crescent, for me, is more a cultural symbol than a religious one." The matter of Israel, and Israel's design of its flag, he added once again, and with defiance, did not concern him in the least; flags resemble each other, and no particular nation held a copyright over artistic and design matters.

Chederchi had the integrity of his art. His enemies partook of a different worldview. For them the old Israel obsession could not be abandoned; it was handy once again. Palestine was Iraq now, Iraq was Palestine. It had happened in Lebanon before, in the 1970s and '80s. In that country, the Shia of the southern hinterland had endured Palestinian power, the rise in their midst of a Palestinian state within a state. The Palestinian gunmen and pamphleteers had had the run of that part of that country. Arab nationalists in distant lands had hailed that Palestinian sanctuary; Arab oil wealth had paid for it. The Shia relief in 1982, when Israel swept into Lebanon and shattered that dominion, was to the Arab nationalists proof that the Shia stepchildren were treasonous. Then a Shia militant movement, Hezbollah, rose to challenge Israel. Its homicide bombers, its politics of "virtue and terror" acquitted the Lebanese Shia in Arab eyes.

Iraq was a variation on that old theme. The worries of the Arab nationalists in Nablus and Cairo, and in the exile communities of Europe and North America, that Iraq would find a new political vocation, away from the pieties of Arab nationalism and from the pull of the old Palestinian cause, were momentarily laid to rest. The Shia were no longer collaborators of foreign rule, or proxies of the Persian state to the east. Those who had once hailed Saddam as the faithful son of the "Arab nation" were now adopting as their own the former victims of the Saddam regime. Moqtada al-Sadr was now a hero in the Egyptian press, and there were Palestinians speaking well of him.

By mid-April, in an act of transparent willfulness, radical pan-Arabists were referring to the young pretender as "Imam Moqtada al-Sadr." The title had a special sanctity, and precious few had claimed it or had it bestowed on them by their followers. There had been Musa al-Sadr in Lebanon, in the 1970s. And of course there had been the special case of Ayatollah Khomeini. Now a young man without religious credentials had been given this rare designation by politically mischievous types who had no religious standing. But politics trumped religion, for this was the crowd that gave Osama bin Laden the religious title of "Sheikh," when that man too claimed no religious training of any kind. Those earnest Americans in the Green Zone in Baghdad could only be outsiders to this tangled history.

Whether a foreign sword—however swift and however mighty—could cut through this Gordian knot of Arab history was an open proposition. The radical Arab nationalists were what they were and could not change. The written, published word in Arabic letters had long since lost the ability to name and describe the world as it was, an effect of the long history of Arab political and cultural decline: the very connection between the (written) word and the world had been severed. In the privacy of their homes, countless Arabs named and described things with brutal candor, saw through the evasions and the bravado. There were thus many who could see through this false gift of Fallujah's resistance and heroism. A brilliant and wealthy merchant from the Persian Gulf whom I have known for many years—a man who suffers no fools—wrote a note to me, in this vein, on April 13, about Fallujah and Moqtada al-Sadr:

> I'm not at all disheartened with what is happening in Iraq in Fallu-
> jah and with Al-Sadr. This was a long day coming.

The US should have taken care of al-Sadr and his killers six months ago when they compiled enough evidence of his involvement with the murder of al-Khoei. As time passed he was more emboldened with the lack of response and started to exert his will with the help of Iran and his killers. Do not believe what you hear about the support that the media thinks he has. It is all false. I believe that his time has come and it will be soon. Fallujah and the rest is not new. They lost and they think they can win with the help of their Arab brothers who are not happy with their diminished status and are fighting desperately to retain their power which they have enjoyed for the last 80 years. The looting, killing & the mutilations are not something new. These might be new for the West but they are not new in Iraq or the third world for that matter. The only difference is that it is played on TV for the American audience. It is very sad to see all of these people that have come to help being killed by those whom they have come to liberate. But remember this is not all of Iraq and these are not all of the Iraqis. I have not yet seen any Iraqi that wants the Americans to leave. They complain about their security, which is true since the US is not acting as a policeman and there does not seem to be anyone who is doing this.

The biggest problem in the Middle East is that George Bush opened a can of worms and all of a sudden everybody realized that there is no such thing as the Arab world or Moslem world for that matter. With one sweep he cleared the deck and exposed everyone to the false world they have been living in. A fact that they do not want to recognize and do not want to face. They are scared of the future and fighting to preserve the false world they have been living in. Their dream is to make the US fail.

"Iraq as a dictatorship had great power to destabilize the Middle East. Iraq as a democracy will have a great power to inspire the Middle East," George Bush declared to the United Nations General Assembly in a speech that he delivered on September 23, 2003. The president who had willed, and waged, this war had come to defend it before a skeptical audience. For Iraq, this was a closing of a circle. "When we have made Mesopotamia a model state, there is not an Arab of Syria and Palestine who wouldn't want to be part of it," Gertrude Bell said in 1921 of the new Iraqi state she and fellow "colonial hands" had created. She had been "king-maker" and had helped install Faisal ibn Hussein, the Hashemite prince, as the first king of Iraq. She had high hopes for him as well. "Before I die I look to see Faisal ruling from the Persian frontier to the Mediterranean." Something about this state had always recommended it as a "model" for those who wanted to rehabilitate and remake the political world of the Arabs. The promise of Iraq was always—as the desert Arabs would say—a day's camel ride away. There had been a time, during Britain's primacy in that country in the 1940s and 1950s, when Britain saw in Iraq the possibility of redeeming its presence in Arab lands. A British cabinet paper of 1948 expressed those hopes: the "energetic development" of Iraq would silence the "troublemakers" and enable Iraq to become "a great food-producing country for the Middle East, which is at present a net importer of cereals." This would be Britain's showcase, and her answer to the nationalist agitators in Iraq and beyond. The intentions may have been sincere, but Britain's rule, and the weight of its influence, were highly conservative. British administrators had worked through tribal sheikhs and through an Ottomanist group of officers and bureaucrats who had come to this new domain with the Hashemite dynasty that Britain had imposed in 1921. No great effort had gone into grafting British political ways onto this new acquisition.

Strangers to this turbulent country, the Hashemites affected British manners. Of the strongman of the dynasty in the mid-1940s, the regent Abdulillah, a British counselor and Orientalist wrote that the prince had "a great admiration for and liking for British methods and persons. His cars, his aircraft, his clothes, his hunters, his fox-hounds, even his swans, are British, and so are many of his closest friends." The world beyond, and beneath, this court was an altogether different matter. Britain wanted, and secured, hegemony on the cheap, a veiled protectorate. This was an area vital to the defense of India, and a land possessed of oil reserves. Those interests secured, Britain was content to let well enough alone.

British hegemony put off but could not resist the rise of new social classes and the onset of radical politics. It was against this background of growing radicalization within Iraq that the British came to believe that Iraqi oil and agriculture might transform the country and thus justify their position in the region as a whole. Those hopes came to naught. What the historian Majid Khadduri described as a race between revolution and development was settled in favor of revolutionary upheaval. Iraq would not be Britain's showcase, or proof of its benevolence. The regicide and revolution of 1958, by younger and disaffected elements within the army, capped a long period of turmoil. Nothing much was left on the soil of Iraq of Britain's good intentions.

It was those terrible events of the summer of 1958, more than anything else, that shaped the image of Iraq, and gave modern-day Arabs (and Iraqis themselves, no doubt) a sense of Iraq's terrors. Arabs of my generation, who came into political awareness in the late 1950s, were given the tale of two revolutions as emblematic statements on the character and temperament of the lands where these revolts played out. First came the peaceful "Free Officers" revolt in Egypt, in the summer of 1952, and then the bloody upheaval, six summers later, that destroyed the Hashemite monarchy in Iraq. In the Egyptian tale, King Farouk had set sail from his palace in Alexandria to a twenty-one-gun salute, bound for Naples aboard the royal yacht. The titular head of the coup, General Mohamed Neguib, had kissed the monarch's hand and apologized to him. There was no need to kill the king. "History will condemn him to death," the principal coup maker, Colonel Gamal Abdel Nasser, assured his colleagues.

It was a wholly different story in Baghdad, on the morning of July 14, 1958. The mutineers from the armed forces had broken into the royal palace. The boy king, Faisal II, a harmless young man, twenty-three years of age, and his grandmother and a devoted aunt, along with all the other members of the royal household, were assembled in the courtyard and gunned down. The body of the king's uncle, the former regent, was thrown to the mob and dragged through the streets. A pillar of the regime, Nuri al-Said, a soldier-politician who headed the court faction, a ceaseless intriguer who had been at the center of political life since the inception of this monarchy, had made a run for it, disguised as a woman. But he was caught the next day and killed. The crowd wanted still more vengeance. His body was disinterred, strung up, then burnt.

I remember the summer of 1958 well. A boy of Beirut, a couple of months short of thirteen, I possessed the politics of my generation, and my time and my city. In my small world, we were "Nasserites," and we felt no grief for what had happened in Iraq. There were two young Hashemite monarchs, Faisal in Iraq and Hussein in Jordan, in their early twenties, and those of us who partook of Arab nationalism had no use for either ruler. There had been photos of both young kings, in the press, and in the homes of some Lebanese of an older political sensibility who thought well of the Hashemites. Faisal had not had a chance to govern or to come into his own. I still remember the photograph of his coronation: a young man of eighteen, slight and small, with his uncle and former regent beside him. The terrors awaiting Iraq after his murder would in time make many yearn for the benign ways of these Hashemites. But in the summer of 1958, sorrow for the Hashemites would have been the unforgiven response of a "reactionary" breed.

Modern Iraq bore a fatal brand. Those three provinces of the Ottoman empire that had been forced into this most peculiar of states were three distinctly different worlds: in the north, Mosul's ties and commerce were with Turkey and Syria, whereas Baghdad and the Shia shrine cities of Najaf and Karbala on the Euphrates were oriented toward Persia, and Basra looked to the Gulf and to the commerce with India. The Hashemites saw deliverance in the spread of education. But in truth the educational system was to contribute to the rise of ideological politics.

In the late 1930s and 1940s, a virulent form of Arab nationalism, a terrible simplification of Iraq's many identities, wrecked the political order. Oil and official terror gave this ideology its deadly power. The Sunni-based political and military elite who had dominated the state since its inception fell back on Arab nationalism to overcome their minority status within Iraq itself. The state in Iraq was forever at war with the society, and the country remained, to the ruling Sunnis, an inheritance due them as Arabism's favored children.

It was out of this flawed political tradition that Saddam Hussein, a small thug from the town of Tikrit, in the Sunni Arab zone by the Tigris, would emerge. By the time he stepped forth to tame his country, the culture of the land had been taken apart and disfigured. The town of Saddam's birth, for example, had lived off the making of *kalaks*, rafts of inflated goatskins. The steamships had broken the *kalak* industry, so the Tikritis found their way into police work and the military academies. Here they found a new, lucrative endeavor: state terror.

It had taken a big American war to shatter that dominion. The foreign soldiers pulling down Saddam's statues, chasing his killer squads into their hideouts in the Sunni Triangle, had stepped into a schism as old as Islam itself. Those soldiers had come looking for "weapons of mass destruction": those would prove elusive. What was there, and so easy to find, was the riddle of Iraq itself. Was this a single national state that the Americans had conquered? There was no chance that young American soldiers and their officers could take in all this terrible "anthropology," and this sectarianism. Arabs themselves had been choking on that history; in Iraq, that history was particularly deadly. It had been from garrisons in that land that the Arabs had over-whelmed the more settled civilization of Persia. In more contemporary history, it was there that Arab nationalism slipped from the grasp of bright intellectuals formed at Cambridge and the Sorbonne, and became the weapon of angry young men, displaced peasants who came into their own in the 1950s and demolished everything that stood in their way—property and wealth, accumulated culture, the old habits of ethnic and religious accommodation that had once been the hallmark of proud Arab and Muslim cities.

There was no crash course that could give some newly minted lieutenant from the United States Military Academy at West Point wis-dom enough to understand the deadly hate that separates a man from Fallujah from his counterpart in Najaf or in the Shia slums of Bagh-dad. No military sword could cut through that rancid history. The sol-diers in the field, in the way of young men and women facing an alien world, distinguished between *"hajjis"* and *"sadikis"*: the former desig-nated enemies, while the latter, deriving from the Arabic word of *sadik* (friend), described friendly Iraqis. No power so proud of its own modernism, and so free of the hold of the past as America is, could even comprehend the furies of Iraq's atavistic loyalties.

A veritable army of translators was supposed to make up for this deficiency of knowledge. Iraqis were of course pressed into this endeavor, but there were Lebanese and Egyptians and Palestinians and Jordanians as well. In this environment, the translators became pow-ers in their own right. They were of uneven quality, these interpreters and mediators between the American authorities and the Iraqis. Many acted by the book, but others were in it for what could be gotten by the way of kickbacks from would-be recruits to the army and the police, from businessmen and contractors in search of opportunities. Nor did all these interpreters think well of this expedition or of the power that waged this war. Hardship wages provided an opportunity to pay down bills or to save for a rainy day. In the Green Zone, I always did my best to avoid an Arab-American translator of virulent anti-American sentiments. He was there working with the Iraqi media, but the American project in that country was not to his liking. He was not given to restraint, and he was always in search of an audience. In him, the Arab street had an envoy in Baghdad.

"One's natural desire to share the life and experience here is diminished by a tendency to internalize what is happening," Major General Stephen Speakes wrote in a message of April 23. "We now measure life in terms of before and after Good Friday, April 9th," he was to add in an e-mail two days later, "on that day we collectively realized that times have changed and that we have a more intense and complex mission to take on." The second message referred to a memorial service Speakes had attended for a reserve officer from Bowling Green, Kentucky, Lieutenant Robert Henderson. Henderson had been a trucker, and the supply convoys between Kuwait and Iraq had grown deadly. On Saturday, April 17, within a few hours of the Kuwaiti border, Henderson's convoy had been ambushed, and the lieutenant had been killed. Speakes would preserve that sorrowful occasion with his lyrical prose and his eye for both the physical world and the awe of the moment. The service had been held in "Truckville," a tent city, "typical of the places that soldiers live in while they are in Kuwait. Acres of dull green tents, framed with gray gravel around each tent covering brown earthen sand. . . . [In] so many ways these places look like how a medieval army must have encamped, as you see the peaked tops of the tents against the desert sky broken only by the state flags of the residents of the camp." Like their "Civil War ancestors," these reservists (as most of the truckers were), "take their state origins and pride with them."

The faces at this ceremony were of "country America," Speakes wrote. Henderson had been married for thirteen months, and his wife was pregnant, due in two months. From the chaplain speaking of Henderson, and the men who came forward to recall him, Speakes could make out the simple good life of a young man who had worked for Lowe's and had aspired to be a manager for them, who loved the men in his platoon and insisted on being part of the convoys. "As you looked forward to the silent memorial for Lt. Henderson with the boots, dog tag and dirty helmet, your eyes were immediately drawn to the 8 x 11 picture of Lt. Henderson. A young, fresh-faced, blue-eyed, 31-year-old good-looking young man dressed in a simple T-shirt leaning over a chair looking at you—he came to life instantly. Just a great young man, you could feel it." No wonder Speakes's mood had darkened. Six months earlier, I had seen him in Kuwait. It had been a more

optimistic time for this undertaking. I had told him of the pride
back home in the victory in Iraq. A thoughtful man of measured
temperament, perhaps even some shyness, he had been prescient. He
was indulgent of the exuberance of a civilian booster; he had talked of
the joy of his soldiers who had gone back home on short leaves to genuine affection from strangers. But he had enough wisdom to know
that the mood at home could change. He had only hoped that the
men and women of the military would be spared the backlash and the
disaffection that followed the experience in Vietnam. The sorrows of
the bloody month of April, only little more than a year after the
heady—and easy—conquest of Baghdad, brought back memories of
that conversation. That military leader had had in him a premonition
of war's uncertain fortunes.

I had seen those tent cities that General Speakes described. I had
flown into Iraq from bases in Kuwait. The view I had of these bases
was what the outsider could see—the tents, the calling centers, the
doughnut and sandwich shops, the mess halls, the blue mail boxes
evoking home. Flying into and returning from Iraq, I had seen these
places at dawn or dusk. Their isolation in an immense desert spoke to
me of the might, and then the solitude, of the distant power that had
pitched its tents in this forbidding, alien landscape. Kuwait City lay at
some remove: these tent cities were a world unto themselves. The foreign power that stood sentry there had very little traffic with the
society it protected. Its presence was unobtrusive; Kuwaitis were grateful to have the protection, and grateful as well for its light touch in
their world.

Speakes had written of faces drawn from "country America." I had
seen these overwhelmingly young men and women jogging in the cool
of dawn, the crews going about their assignments; I had been the
recipient of small, thoughtful deeds of kindness—the indulgent young
crewmen aboard the C-130 who were always ready to strap my seat
belt on for me, for I could never get the hang of it on my own; the
patient soldiers who answered the personal queries of someone clearly
eager to make a connection with them; the flight crews tolerating my
presence in the cockpit of their planes. I shall always retain the memory of young Jamie Jones, of West Virginia, in Baghdad, "just turned
nineteen, six days ago, sir." He was the driver of a military bus for a
small group of journalists and academics who had come to visit Iraq;
I had pressed for a connection to him, and one presented itself: his

mother was a public school teacher, as was my wife. He told me that
his father had just completed his tour of duty in Iraq and was in
Kuwait on his way home. "It will be a relief to my mother to have one
of us back," he said. He beheld his work with the wonder and openness and earnestness of youth and of his country upbringing. He was
keeping a journal, he said. He had been given a rare experience, he
said, and he aimed to preserve it. "How many eighteen-year-olds
have seen what I have seen?" he said. He told me of plans for college
after service in the military. He told me of his love of reading. I had
carried with me to Iraq a copy of Graham Greene's *The Quiet American.* I had always loved a passage in it about American innocence
roaming the world like a leper without a bell, meaning no harm. I gave
him my copy, and told the boy of eighteen that he would find something of this war in Greene's fiction. He had been brought up well; he
took a stranger's gift, this marked, yellowed-out book, and promised
he would read it in his "downtime."

In the headquarters of the CPA, I intruded on the quiet break of a
young soldier. Amid the tumult, the comings and goings of soldiers
and CPA civilians, he had found a dimly lit corner, and there he sat
alone. He was a strikingly handsome young boy, and there was about
him an air of serenity. His solitude in that quiet corner was affecting.
I was on my first trip to Iraq, and my eagerness got the better of me.
I made my way to him. I could only force what little could be forced
between perfect strangers. I asked him how long he had been in Iraq;
he told me that he had put in six months already. What was he up to
these days? I queried, with no small measure of clumsiness. "Mostly
trying not to get shot at, sir," he said. He was twenty and from St.
Louis, Missouri. Yes, his parents missed him, but he had his work and
his tour of duty in Iraq. My graces left me. I wished him well, and a
safe return home, but never managed to ask for his name. In the
months that followed, I was to find myself intermittently going
through the names of the soldiers killed in Iraq, released by the
Department of Defense. The names, the ages of the soldiers, the
hometowns of the fallen: every name calls forth grief of its own. That
boy in the Baghdad palace, from St. Louis, was never far from my
mind as I read through the rolls of the fallen.

A war of choice or of necessity? An American imperium in Arab and
Islamic lands forced on a reluctant America by terrors inflicted on it on
a clear September morning in 2001, or a stark imperial choice by a

great power convinced of its vocation in the world and cast into a dominant role in an Arab-Islamic world coming apart at the seams? Either way, those American truths, and those American interests, were being borne by young soldiers like Jamie Jones and his unnamed fellow soldier from St. Louis. Driving through the streets of Kirkuk, with those young men in their swivel seats atop their Humvees, and taking in that watchful world of Iraqis on the streets or on their balconies, I could never banish the consciousness of the "outsiderness" of the foreign power. You can stand up Iraqi police and civil defense units, you can refurbish schools and paint over the graffiti of the old regime, you can pull down the dictator's statues and reopen universities, teach the Iraqis PowerPoint presentations, and build an amusement park in Kirkuk "to provide a safe, fun play area for Iraqi children" (I quote here from the press packet of the 173rd Airborne Brigade), but you will always be an outsider. The American military personnel had made earnest attempts to accommodate the ways of the culture. The soldiers were told to receive and drink the coffee and tea offered them by Iraqis with the right hand and never with the left, because the left hand is considered unclean. They obeyed this injunction, and more. But this was not a place that bared its secrets to outsiders or truly took them in.

America had blasted its way into this place; then Iraq exerted its will on the mighty foreign power. After the speed of the invasion, the American effort had to yield to the grinding ways of Iraq. I was given this metaphor of this war one day as I was riding in an official convoy to the National Assembly. There were six or seven Land Cruisers with tinted windows, and a jeep preceded this convoy with a bullhorn clearing the traffic in our way. The convoy drove over the dividers in the road, bobbed and weaved its way through the traffic. Then this traffic came to a checkpoint, a circle onto which other cars were converging. The traffic ground to a standstill, and the bodyguards now grew nervous and attentive. This convoy was now at the mercy of the elements, prey to any would-be assailant.

A young Iraqi businessman, with years of Western education and experience behind him, explained to me how Iraq had outwitted and thwarted its American liberators. He had begun this tutorial by showing me the body armor he had bought for his guards on the black market. He had bought thirty jackets at seventy dollars each, the body armor that the American authorities had given the Iraqi soldiers and police. One jacket had scribbled on the inside the name Mike Lamb and the location of South Tikrit. This is Iraq, he said, and the Americans will never crack its code. "The Americans are overlords, and the Iraqis tell them what they want to hear. Those in on the take could not care less what happened to this whole enterprise. To those who fell into things, the Americans are cash cows." He described one exile who had come back with the American war as "Wolfowitz's stallion." The "stallion" had not stayed long; he had made his bid for power, then returned to Detroit.

The Americans, this young man said, were in fact subsidizing the insurgency. Vast logistical bases had been set up in Anbar province and in the rest of the Sunni Triangle. One of the largest bases, the Anaconda, was in Balad, a Sunni Arab stronghold. These bases were essential to the prosecution of this war: the armed forces had to be provisioned, and supplies were coming in from Kuwait and Turkey. These bases required protection, and tribal brokers and middlemen had stepped into the breach. There were good/bad guys and bad/bad guys, he said, an exquisite Mafia-like system of extortion. The good/bad guys worked with the Americans, obtained the contracts, then they paid protection money to the bad/bad guys, who were the backbone of the insurgency. "The Americans are nurturing their enemy. . . . For logistics and big contracts, you need heavy capital outlays, and skills, and the men of the old regime had these skills. They turned up at the doorstep of the Americans, and the latter had to cut them into the spoils, knowing full well how the extortion racket worked. The Americans reward their enemies: they give a loyal Shia tribe a quota of police recruits, and they balance that with a quota of equal size to a Sunni tribe deep into the insurgency. On paper, this is perfectly understandable, but the consequences feed into the virulent insurgency now engulfing the country."

A great effort had gone into training Iraqi forces; the American commanders had given it their best. But these recruits were easy targets of the terror, and at the end of the day, they returned from their bases and training academies into the fractured reality of their country. I had repeatedly gone on excursions to the new training facilities. The recruits seemed eager to me, to the untrained eye predominantly young men anxious to serve, glad for the training and for the fellowship with the Americans who were teaching them the ways of combat. On an outing with the defense minister, Saadoun Dulaimi, I watched the recruits of a SWAT team in a remote campsite, donning their masks, breaking into a dance, chanting "woe to terrorism today," waving their assault rifles in the air. They were thrilled to have the defense minister in their midst; they were happy to see the American commander, General Petraeus, whom they knew from previous visits. When they spoke to the defense minister, they spoke of their country with devotion and pledged that they would honor the mission entrusted them. No one could predict what these troops would do in a crunch, if they could withstand the terror, or the call of their religious sects and communities.

For America, the surprise was that it had expected to sweep into Iraq and encounter Iraqis seared by the dictator's brutalities and glad for their deliverance. Those it found, but Americans encountered Arabs in Iraq, people given to all those defects that had frustrated American power and intentions in Egypt, in Arabia, and among the Palestinians. That journey into the "heart of the Middle East," as President Bush described the expedition into Iraq time and again, turned out to be a venture into all the malignancies of Arab politics. Despotism, sectarianism, antimodernism, willful refusal to name things for what they are: they were there in plentiful supply in Iraq. A great power that had had its fill with the anti-Americanism and unreason of the Arabs suddenly found itself yet again in the thicket of that Arab mix of victimology and wrath. Those Iraqi Shia who followed Moqtada al-Sadr, calling themselves *al Sadriyyun,* the Sadrists, and thanked God and not the Americans for Iraq's liberation, offered their own variation on Egypt's refusal to acknowledge three decades of American aid.

America had previously encountered and battled radical Shiism in Iran and Lebanon. It had been a heartbreaking experience: radical mullahs, young foot soldiers of terror, the exaltation of martyrdom. The Sadrists were a throwback to that earlier war of the 1980s. They were a minority, but they were in the streets, and they had been helped by the vacuum created by the murder of Ayatollah Muhammad Baqir al-Hakim, and the relative silence (enigmatic at times) of Grand Ayatollah Sistani. The American campaign into Iraq had not sought to be the midwife of a Shia theocracy. But the opponents of the war in America itself, and within the Arab world, held up the specter of a Shia state as a rebuke to this war. There were even doubts about the reticent old man himself, Grand Ayatollah Sistani. He had kept his distance from the Americans; he would never meet with Paul Bremer. Perhaps the old jurist himself was no "moderate," the critics could claim. Could it be that the idea of an Islamic state was his real program after all? A Pandora's box had been opened: those Iraqis who genuinely believed that the American forces had infrared goggles that enabled them to see through women's garments were but an echo of the dark anti-Americanism and the tales told about America in other Arab and Muslim lands. Outlandish tales had been told by the Egyptians about America's deeds. Now similar tales were afloat in Iraq.

There were even shades of Palestine and the Palestinians in this new American dominion; there were Iraqis in that Sunni Triangle who cast themselves as Palestinians and assigned the Americans the role of an Israeli occupying force. The Arabic satellite channels needed no extensive commentary: the footage from the Sunni Triangle with young boys throwing stones at the American soldiers was a framing of this new encounter in the familiar images of Gaza and the West Bank. There had been hopes that a new Iraq, sobered and hardened by the knowledge that Saddam Hussein had so favored the Palestinians as he brutalized his own people, would put Palestine and the Palestinians at a distance, and these hopes had been tempered by the impasse between Iraqis and Americans. Even Sadr City, the Shia stronghold in Baghdad, displayed Palestinian banners and graffiti. There was willful defiance in the act, and some insincerity no doubt. But the foreign power was being placed at arm's length.

In the American scheme of things, the defining image of Arab lands in the days that followed September 11 had been the scenes of scapegoating on the loose in Arab cities, the abdication of responsibility, and the wrath of the crowd toward all things American. All this Iraq seemed to possess with abandon. What had been seen as an escape from the Arab condition, a new land that would present an alternative to the wider Arab malady, was itself given to all the defects of Arab politics.

On the face of it, there had been no excessive religious zeal in Iraq, but here it was, on demand, called up by the competition between the Sunni and the Shia Arabs. Where the Baath Party had once served as the container of Sunni power, and Arab nationalism as its respectable cover, religion now reared its head among the Sunnis, and the *ulama* and the preachers and the prayer leaders of the mosques stepped forth to fill the political void in their communities. If the seminaries and the *hawza* in Najaf had their claims, the religious class in Ramadi and Tikrit and in the Sunni quarters of Baghdad would have theirs as well. No sooner had the old regime come apart than a new clerical body, the Association of Muslim Scholars, made its appearance. The power once secured through secular means would now be defended by religious stridency: what the ideologues and *mukhabarat* (security services) once upheld now fell to the Sunni religious class. It had been an easy, perhaps inevitable transformation: this was a frontier country between Arabia and Persia, its Sunni and Shia loyalties burdened with deep historical and ethnic antagonisms.

The history of Iraq had been worked on, willfully arranged and rewritten. An "invented" identity had taken root in Iraq; its historiography had become nothing but a vehicle for the dominion of a minority of Sunni Arabs. "The Americans have brought us the *Ajam*," a member of the Sunni elite said of the new order. *Ajam* meant the Persians, the non-Arabs, but what the man had in mind was the new political power of the Iraqi Shia. In truth, no "Persians" had come to power: the Shia of Iraq were Arabs through and through. But such was the American burden, and such were the hard truths of Iraq. Some members of the Shia clerical estate in the seminaries of Najaf hailed from the Shia communities of other lands. This elite was always a transnational group drawn to the scholarly-clerical vocation. There was of course Ali al-Sistani, who was born in Iran, in the city of Mashhad; there was another grand ayatollah, Ishaq Fayyadh, of Afghan background. There was a grand ayatollah of Pakistani origins. But Shiism was a phenomenon of Iraq itself, deeply entrenched there centuries before it crossed to Iran, brought to that land by the Safavid rulers as a state religion in the opening years of the sixteenth century.

Shiism had originated in an Arab religious-political dispute over succession to the Prophet Muhammad long before the converted Persians took to it. The feuds of Shiism had been fought in the Hijaz, Damascus, and Iraq—within the Arab tribes, and along those quintessentially Arab issues of *nasab* (lineage) and blood and rightful inheritance. Persia may have made the iconic figure Imam Hussein, the Prophet's grandson, its hero and the exemplary figure of martyrdom and disinheritance, but we should remember that he was a man of the Hijaz, Arabic his only language, the Persian realm terra incognita to him. He had died in southern Iraq in the year 680, on the plains of Karbala, lured there by the invitation of Arab tribesmen who had offered him allegiance to lead them in their struggle against a rival center of power, the Umayyad rulers in Damascus.

Those who Persianized the Shia had to work their will on history and work backward in time, distorting the history into a convenient tool. The great seminaries and the sacred places of Shiism were in Iraq—in Najaf, Karbala, Kadhimiyyah, and Samarra. The Shia of Iraq, Arab tribesmen by origin, had been converted to the Shia sect over the course of the eighteenth and nineteenth centuries. Commerce had brought them into the market towns of Najaf and Karbala, and it was in those towns that Shia clerics instructed the tribesmen in the doctrine and ritual of the faith. It had not been a matter of religious zeal. The (Sunni) Ottoman rulers who governed from the urban centers had not bothered with the countryside; the Arab tribes of southern Iraq that had taken up Shiism did so in their transition from nomadic ways to settled agriculture.

The sacred geography of Shiism, it is true, had brought to Iraq Shia religious scholars and seminarians from India, Persia, Lebanon. Thanks to geographic proximity, the Persian component had been particularly strong: Persians had used the shrine cities of Iraq as sanctuary, a way of checking the power of their own country's rulers in the ceaseless tug-of-war between rulers and religious scholars. But in overwhelming numbers, the adherents of Shiism were drawn from Arab tribesmen. Arab nationalism, which came to Iraq with the Hashemite rulers and the officers and ideologues who rode their coattails, covered up Sunni dominion with a secular garb. As Iran was nearby—larger and more powerful than Iraq—it became convenient for the ruling stratum of Iraq to disenfranchise its own Shia majority, to claim that they were Persians or a fifth column of the Persian state.

Nothing less than a grand historical fraud had been pulled off in the making of modern Iraq. The Arabism that came to Iraq in the 1920s, and was to hold until the destruction of the Saddam regime, had imposed its will on a diverse country. In a startling display of official mendacity, an estimated three hundred or so ex-Ottoman officers and bureaucrats who had been at home in the multinational bureaucracy and army of the old empire underwent a sudden conversion to Arabism. In the course of the First World War, this political-military elite bet on the Hashemites and their Arab Revolt. They rode with Prince Faisal to his short-lived kingdom in Damascus. Evicted by the French in 1920, they came into Iraq with the new, alien monarchy. To this new domain, which they never quite accepted (they forever yearned for Damascus and for a bigger, pan-Arab state), they brought the zeal of the convert. This harsh Arab state would serve their grandiose ambitions. There were Jews and Assyrians and Kurds and Shia in this new polity, groups the ex-Ottoman officers and bureaucrats were determined to subjugate. In the face of tribes and tribal norms and old arrangements of power, the new elite was convinced of its right to rule, to herd this backward realm into the age of the centralized state. There was property, and the newcomers—in the main, men of lower- and middle-class backgrounds, sons of minor civil servants of the Ottoman bureaucracy—were eager to claim it for themselves.

This political class, with its ideological zeal, knew no shred of restraint. Take the Jews of Baghdad: they had been in the country since the Babylonian Captivity, two and a half millennia of settled history. In three short decades, this new order would dispossess and denationalize them, banishing them from Iraq. That great son of modern Baghdad's Jewry, the political philosopher and historian Elie Kedourie (1926–92), who rose to great academic and intellectual prominence in British life, has given us a memorable account of the cruelty of Iraq's new rulers. The Jews had been faithful to Iraq. The Book of Jeremiah had enjoined them to pray for the peace of Babylon, "for in the peace thereof shall ye have peace." There was an injunction in that tradition to accept the world as it was, to all but forget Jerusalem and the promise of Zion, to render unto the Babylonian rulers obedience and loyalty. From the Book of Jeremiah again: "Therefore harken not yet to your prophets, nor to your diviners, nor to your dreamers, nor to your enchanters, nor to your sorcerers, which speak unto you, saying, ye shall not serve the King of Babylon, for they prophesy a lie unto you."

Through changes of regimes and sovereigns, this old arrangement had held, and "the empires under whom the Jews of Babylon successively lived," Professor Kedourie writes, "took it for granted that the communities subject to them would worship their own gods, and practice the rites peculiar to them." This system had been good enough for the pre-Islamic Persian rulers and for thirteen centuries of Islamic rule and for that brief interlude of British primacy. But the new pan-Arab state was wholly different. And in the astounding span of some eighteen months, in 1950–51, the Jewish presence in Iraq was brought to an end, consigned to official oblivion.

In the making of this new Iraq, education and pedagogy played a ruinous role. The future was foreshadowed by the work of the most influential figure of this new Arabism. The educational bureaucrat who left an indelible mark on his time, and on decades to come, was the ex-Ottomanist Sati al-Husri (1882–1968). Born in Aleppo, educated at the Mulkiye Mektebi, the school in Istanbul that trained the Ottoman empire's bureaucratic elite, Husri was a creature of the Ottoman state. His first language was Ottoman Turkish, his second was French, and Arabic had come to him in middle age.

A child of a minor civil servant, Husri had moved in and out of different parts of this sprawling empire. He himself had served in the Balkans. Now, in one of those moments when a world gives way, and marginal men are thrown on their own resources to make new lives and worlds for themselves, Husri became a militant believer in Arabism. He was appointed director general of the Iraqi Ministry of Education in 1921. Elie Kedourie describes Husri well when he labels him the "recruiting-sergeant of the pan-Arab ideology." The Germanic ideas of nationalism, of Herder and Fichte, exercised a powerful hold on this man's intellect. The nation he wanted was to become one large barracks: compulsory education tethered to compulsory military service. In the late 1930s, this man sang the praises of Nazi ideology and discipline. In Kedourie's words again, Husri combined the "cold centralizing passion of the Ottoman bureaucracy with a rigid and humorless pan-Arabism."

The curriculum this stranger imposed on his new country exalted the Arabs and Arab history: it had no place for minorities or old traditions. The role of the Persians in Islamic history was deliberately belittled. (In a pathetic attempt to Arabize himself, he gave himself, in the Arab fashion, the name Abu Khaldun Sati al-Husri, after his eldest son.) Husri bore the Shia, and their schools in Najaf, a cold, deadly animus. They were, for him, full of superstition and of the spirit of Persia. The bigotry—and irony—of this Ottomanist's lording Arabism over his new compatriots was best caught in a standoff the educational bureaucrat had with a Najaf-born poet, Muhammad Mahdi al-Jawahiri, who would go on to become the acknowledged national poet of Iraq in the twentieth century. Jawahiri was blessed by the literary gods; he had an exquisite way with the Arabic language and its poetic tradition. Born with the twentieth century (he lived practically the entire length of the century, dying in exile, in Damascus in

1997), Jawahiri rose to national fame at an early age. In 1927, he sought employment as a secondary school teacher, but his appointment was blocked by Husri; the latter insisted that Jawahiri was a Persian. He asked the poet for proof of citizenship.

The Jawahiris had behind them centuries of settled life in Najaf, and the poet was proud of the "pure Arab" ways of Najaf—the legacy of Bedouin Arabian tribes that had descended on it for trade and provisions and there "left some of their temperament and their stories and their poetry." He was proud, in that quintessentially Bedouin-Arab way, of the "five centuries of blood and pure Arab descent" that he claimed as his rightful inheritance. One could not find, he said, among the scholars of Najaf anyone who had not mastered the oral traditions of the Bedouins, their poems, their distinctive way with the Arabic language. The "citizenship" of the modern state was new to this young inheritor of this long history, and to Iraq as a whole. The poet was in the midst of a particularly prolific and creative period of his life. His poetry was rendering his country's mood and yearnings. But the ex-Ottoman official had the power of the state; he denied Jawahiri the appointment he sought. A consolation prize, an appointment as an elementary school teacher, was offered the great poet, courtesy of admirers who had lobbied for him, when the affair had become a scandal of the realm. Jawahiri turned it down.

Years later, in a two-volume memoir written when the poet was in his mideighties and living next door in Syria, he still bristled with injured pride as he recalled the incident. He grieved for what had befallen him—and what had befallen Iraq as a whole. The impasse between the ex-Ottoman official and the young poet who had grown up at the edge of the great Arabian desert in the end was broken by the Hashemite monarch, Faisal I. The mild-mannered ruler, an heir to the cosmopolitan ways of the Hijaz of his birth, and to the worldliness of Istanbul, where he had spent his early youth on the Bosporus, was forever walking a thin line between the British and the new realm he was bequeathed, and between the different communities of this checkered realm. Faisal took the young poet into his court, gave him a variety of literary-journalistic assignments. But Husri's ideology would poison the life of the country. For two crucial decades, 1921 to 1941, this ex-Ottomanist had the run of a new country and access to an educational system he was determined to dominate. He was in and out of governmental posts; after the ministry of education, he served as dean of the law college, then director of antiquities. There were no second thoughts in this man's mind. He distrusted all of Iraq's minorities, the Shia all the more because of the proximity of Persia, and because he saw them—rightly—as the repository of another conception of Iraq. There were inheritors of Husri—cruder and more vulgar—who worked their will on the history of this land. By whip and terror, and an invented history, a frontier country of many faiths and traditions was given a new, belligerent identity.

This invented history took on a life of its own. But in truth, before the Tikriti rulers terrorized the Shia religious establishment and shattered its autonomy, a healthy measure of competition was always the norm between the Shia seminaries of Iraq and those of Iran. Few Iraqi Shiites were eager to cede their own world to Iran's rulers. As the majority population of Iraq, they have a vested interest in its independence and statehood. Over three decades, they endured the Saddam regime's brutality, yet they fought its war against Iran in 1980–88. No fidelity to Iraq, though, could rid them of that Persian shadow. An American order that put the Shia beyond the terror of their recent history in Iraq was inevitably cast as a foreign dominion hacking away at a larger Arab truth.

A political order that made room for the grand ayatollahs in Najaf had to accommodate the Sunni religious scholars. In early December 2003, with the debate under way about the transfer of sovereignty from the Coalition Provisional Authority to Iraqi hands, the Sunni Association of Muslim Scholars weighed in as a counter to the weight of the Kurds and the Shia. There was talk of Iraqi squads and military units working side by side with the American Special Forces in hunting down the insurgents: the Sunni religious scholars warned against that strategy, saw in it the threat of "the Lebanonization of Iraq"—the spread of rival militias, the descent into sectarian violence. "It was a grave error," they noted in a declaration of December 7, "to ignore a large community of Muslims and to consider them enemies as the forces of occupation have done. . . . The resort to sectarian and ethnic choices is a deed of the occupiers, along the lines of divide and conquer, and is totally illegitimate." After decades of acquiescence, after the fall of a political order that had given their sect nothing less than political and cultural hegemony, these men were now petitioners on behalf of a community thrown on the defensive.

It stood to reason that the interests of the Sunnis would be dressed in "Islamic," rather than sectarian, garb. The "strangers" who by the accounts of witnesses from Tikrit and Fallujah had begun to converge on the Sunni Triangle, those jihadists who crossed from Syria or Saudi Arabia or Jordan, came into a fragment of Iraq eager to accommodate them. They were Sunni Islamists: the Americans they had come to do battle against had given the Shia and the Kurds new political possibilities. It was easy to pass off the defense of the Sunnis of Iraq as a defense of Islam itself. A bomb outside the Imam Ali shrine in Najaf doubled as a blow against American power, and against what the more fanatical among the jihadists saw as a monument to "polytheism" and heresy.

In the face of this sectarianism, there was a convenient way of telling history: a way that took in modernism and papered over the deep antagonisms of the sects and ethnicities. In this convenient history, the Sunnis and Shia are both children of Islam, and the Kurds and the Arabs are brothers, and Iraq is the patrimony of all its communities. But there was no denying the three separate and competing histories in the newly liberated country. A member of Iraq's political elite, National Security Adviser Mowafak al-Rubaie, born to a Shia father and a Sunni mother, a neurologist and a man who had suffered imprisonment and torture under the Baath dictatorship, gave a fair summation of the three (principal) ethnic and sectarian communities, and the worldviews they brought into the new struggle over the country. It was "unrealistic," he said, "to expect the Kurds to abandon the gains they made over the preceding thirteen years. They live in the shadow of fear of what happened to them under the old government in Baghdad. Among them, this fear has become obsessive: the gains they have made will not be turned over to a central government whose direction they can't foresee. They have a government on the ground; they need only codify it, give it laws and legitimacy. Big concessions will have to be given them and everyone is afraid and no one can guarantee these concessions."

Rubaie then took up both halves, as it were, of his own identity— the different forces at play among the Sunnis and the Shia: "The Sunnis are afraid of the demographic weight and ascendancy of the Shia, while the latter are worried that the old tyranny could still make a comeback. Everyone is afraid, but fear doesn't build a country. Fear only forces people to fall back on themselves and to hunker down in their trenches."

This "ecumenical" way of Rubaie did not have the run of Iraq's streets. Iraq had its own heavy legacy of sectarianism, but there was let loose on it now the deadly animus of younger jihadists drawn from other Arab lands. These pitiless men, from Jordan and Syria and Saudi Arabia and Yemen, had come to do battle against the Americans, it is true. But they brought with them a hatred of all things and people Shia. The jihadists were literal-minded and totalitarian. Those Shia shrines in Najaf and Karbala, those Shia rituals reeking of Persia and Persians: they were, to these jihadists, the proofs of idolatry. And there was the conviction of the jihadists that the Shia had opened the gates of the city, as it were, for the American invaders. Everything in Iraq had come together to embody the jihadists' apocalyptic view of history. Muslims would lose their way, and the "seceders" within the world of Islam would ride with the infidels. There was that view of history given by the fall of Baghdad to the Mongols in 1258. Hülegü's armies had turned up at the gates of the city, and Ibn al-Alqami, a Shia minister, had done the Mongols' bidding. He had acquiesced, so the history of that event insisted, in the conquest and defilement that would befall the seat of the caliphate. Arabic books had been burned and dumped in the Tigris, a variant of this legend had it, but Persian books had been spared, and Islam's people, the *umma*, had paid for the treason within the walls.

The new jihadists once again distorted history. In February 2004, a courier was intercepted in Iraq: he was taking a message to the two preeminent leaders of Al Qaeda, Osama bin Laden and Ayman al-Zawahiri. It was a plea for help, and a depiction of the situation on the ground by a jihadist who would come to considerable fame in the months to come, a Jordanian in his late thirties called Abu Musab al-Zarqawi. (Zarqawi's real name is Ahmad Fadil al-Khalayleh: the nom de guerre was owed to Zarqa, the town of his birth, east of Amman.) The letter was remarkable for its brutal candor: the jihadist was pleading for help from the "battlefields of Iraq." He had victories and accomplishments to report, "martyrdom operations" he had overseen, prepared, and planned throughout the country. "Praise be to Allah, I have completed 25 of these operations, some of them against the Shia and their leaders, the Americans and their military, and the coalition forces." But he was at work in a difficult land, a "political mosaic" of races and ethnicities. The Americans were there, but there were "apostates within," there were Shia and Kurds scheming with the

Americans, and there were the Sunnis of the land, like "orphans at the dining tables of the wicked," lost and divided among themselves. It was at knife's edge in Iraq, Zarqawi wrote: the infidels were taking heavy losses, but the Shia heretics, "cowardly and deceitful," were "the real danger," "the enemies of God" killing "the people of Islam in the name of law and in the name of order." The *mujahidin* were giving it their best in this land full of treachery: "There is no doubt that our field of movement is shrinking and the grip around the *mujahidin* is tightening. . . . The country of Iraq has no mountains in which to seek refuge, or forests in which to hide. Our presence is apparent and our movement out in the open. Eyes are everywhere. The enemy is before us and the sea is behind us." The alternatives were stark: ignite a war in this country or "pack our bags and look for another field of battle as has been the sad case in other tales of jihad because our enemy grows stronger by the day." There was a tone of resignation in this plea for help: "People follow the religion of kings," the Jordanian opined. "Their hearts may be with you, but their swords are with the powers." This is why a sectarian war against the Shia *"rafida"* (refusers of Islam) was the way out for the holy warriors.

Zarqawi had been on the road. As a drifter who could not come to terms with his life in Jordan, he epitomized this new breed of Islamist warriors. Like others of his generation among the "Afghan Arabs," he had made his way to Afghanistan in the late 1980s, when he was about twenty years old, and had returned to Jordan in 1991. Back home, the man had been unable to find work that would sustain him; a video store he opened in his town had failed. He had taken to radical ways and had run afoul of the authorities. During seven years of imprisonment, he had emerged as the prison bully and enforcer. Released in 1999, he had returned to the lands of Pakistan and Afghanistan. He had hit his stride in the city of Herat, in western Afghanistan, becoming a leader of his own band of jihadists. In December 2001, he had fled Afghanistan and made his way to Iraq. According to the available evidence, Zarqawi was in Iraq when the Americans sacked the regime of Saddam Hussein.

In his letter, Zarqawi had no use for the Kurds: they had "opened their land to the Jews, they have provided them with a base, and with a Trojan horse for their plans." The "voice of Islam was faint among them," and those calling people to the right path were "few and weak, afraid that the vultures would carry them away." The true enemies, though, were the Shia. "We have many rounds, attacks, and black nights with the Shia, and we can't hesitate and delay the moment of reckoning. Their menace is looming, and this is a fact that we should not fear, because they are the most cowardly people God has created. Killing their leaders will weaken them and with the death of the head, the whole group dies. They are not like the Sunnis. If you knew the fear in the souls of the Sunnis you would weep in sadness. How many of the mosques have they turned to *husayniyas* [Shia houses of religious mourning and observance]? How many brothers have they killed? How many sisters have been raped at the hands of this treacherous, idolatrous lot?"

The modernist conceit that those old sectarian feuds would die out was a hope against hope. Zarqawi was an outsider, to be sure. But in Iraq he was to find fertile, receptive soil. The sectarianism of the Fertile Crescent, the tight truths that men upheld and clung to, had immense power. History never decapitated or bypassed those stubborn feuds; it only gave them added ammunition, new relevance.

There was an idea of Arabism (really covert Sunni Islam) that had written off the "compact communities" of the Shia and the Alawites and the Druze as collaborators of foreign rule and "secessionists" from pan-Arab nationalism. History was cruel. Two "great revolts" became the stuff of legend in the annals of the Fertile Crescent: the 1920 revolt in Iraq against the British, and an anti-French rebellion that broke out in Syria in 1925. Both were ferocious upheavals that tested the will and the resources of the two mandatory powers. The first was instigated by the *mujtahids* (religious scholars) of Najaf and waged by the Shia tribes of the lower Euphrates. Out of religious scruples, the *mujtahids* had come out against the legitimacy of "infidel" rule; they had called their followers to arms. The second had been a revolt of Druze highlanders in the southeastern hinterland of Syria. Communalism and a fierce streak of independence among the mountain Druze had fed that upheaval. In both revolts, the "nationalist" towns had remained quiescent or had played second fiddle to the rebellious countryside.

In Iraq, the Sunnis had emerged with the best of possible worlds: the British mandatory authorities had given them political primacy in the newly constituted kingdom, and the Sunnis went on to spin a legend of their devotion to the pan-Arab idea. The historian Elie Kedourie aptly described the monarchy as an Anglo-Sunni regime.

The Shia and their clerical tribunes had gambled and lost. That revolt had been, in Kedourie's words, their "last throw of the dice." Britain would take no chances in the aftermath of that upheaval. The British had seen Shia fury and wanted no repeat of it. Above all, they wanted to sever the ties between Mesopotamia and the turbulent politics of Iran. British rule would work with, and through, the Sunni urban elite and with the military officers and ideologues who had come into Iraq with the Hashemite dynasty. The men of the new political class at the helm of this most artificial of states fell back on a cruel and simple idea of Arabism to compensate for their estrangement from the country and the communities they governed.

The idea of Arabism was thus both false and cruel. A generation of former Ottomanists, in the barracks and the academies of an old multinational empire, coming into a new exclusive ideology of nationalism and using it as a veritable deed to the land and to political inheritance, wrecked the political life of Iraq. The nationalism here had to be strident. Indeed it was destined for greater cruelty as it was transmitted down the social and economic order to military officers and displaced peasants armed only with their resentments and their will to rule and to hoard what was there to be had of state wealth. By the time Arabism and all the ideological pretenses made their way down from the old Ottomanist class to the generation of Saddam Hussein and his lieutenants, Arab nationalism Iraqi-style had hatched a monstrous new world.

Set Saddam Hussein aside, and take the cruelest of his lieutenants, his onetime minister of the interior, then vice president Izzat Ibrahim al-Duri. For this man, born in 1942, the world had a brutal simplicity: before political power, Duri was a street vendor of ice, as was his father before him. He had meager schooling: in an Arab society keen on lineage and given to hierarchy, Izzat Ibrahim al-Duri came from the ranks of the despised. It was only the politics of the Baath Party, and the turbulence of Iraq and the destruction of time-honored privilege and culture, that had carried him past his old circumstances. The Baath Party had been formed by two Sorbonne-educated Syrian intellectuals, Michel Aflaq, a Greek Orthodox, and Salah al-Din Bitar, a Sunni Muslim. The two men had been born in the same quarter in Damascus, two years apart, but had met at the Sorbonne in 1929, where they imbibed the same ideas (European socialism) and books and culture. It must have been a time of hope: Aflaq was nineteen,

Bitar seventeen, both away from home and its restrictions. They stayed in Paris until 1934. A decade later, they launched the Baath.

The two young men of the Sorbonne were to come into great power. Their party was to attract legions of young people in Syria, Iraq, Lebanon, and Jordan, and among the Palestinians. What Bitar and Aflaq offered was an amorphous mix of secular nationalism and a doctrine of radical, redistributive economics. Their program was not precise, nor did it have to be. It was enough that the young and the half-educated and the newly urbanized found in it a way out of poverty and parochialism and the hold of the elders. Aflaq, the more literary of the two founders, remained the party's theorist; Bitar became prime minister in a Baath-led government in Syria in the early 1960s.

But Syria and Iraq, the two domains where the party had its greatest success, were to work their ways on those lofty ideals conceived in the Quartier Latin. Unsentimental younger men, ambitious men drawn from the military and the political underground, took the creation of Aflaq and Bitar and turned it into an altogether different endeavor. Patricide was visited on the Baath founders as they were overwhelmed by a more pitiless breed. Bitar eventually quit Syria for Paris, but the operatives of the Hafiz al-Assad regime trailed him to France and gunned him down in 1980. Aflaq knew a different fate. He was "imported" to Iraq from self-imposed exile in South America and turned into a museum piece, an old witness to be brought out now and then to give testimonies to the genius of Saddam Hussein and his singular gifts. By then, Saddam himself had become the "theorist" of the Baath, its Trotsky. He had had little schooling, but despotism dispensed with that requirement. He had outgrown Aflaq. The latter lived until 1989 to see the cruel fate that overtook his and Bitar's creation.

From Aflaq to the ice vendor: the edifice of modern Iraq had been taken apart. Izzat Ibrahim and his likes showed their enemies no mercy. They couldn't grieve for the subtlety of the old world and its graces: they had not been shown the mercies and restraints of the old order. As the Americans were hunting him down around his old hometown, and as rumors circulated that the man was directing the anti-American insurgency, the old ice vendor was playing out his destiny. A foreign invader had taken away by force the power he had accumulated through conspiracy and terror. As late as 2002, the man had attended an Arab summit in Beirut: he had been full of swagger and confidence. He had been embraced and welcomed into the fold by the Arab leaders assembled there. There had been that reconciliation with the Saudis, and much was made of the warm embrace between him and Saudi Arabia's crown prince. He had been unrepentant at the summit: he offered no apologies to the Kuwaiti delegation, derided that country's foreign minister, and dismissed him as a "monkey." No internal opposition in his own country, he knew, could shake off the hold of his clique on political power. And no neighbors could or would threaten the Tikriti-Sunni system of control. This American war was the only challenge that Izzat Ibrahim and his apparatus of terror could not ward off.

It was the fashion among progressive Arabs to say that those old sectarian schisms were over with, that a newer political world had emerged out of the modernisms and the new ideological movements. No such thing had happened: in Syria, Iraq, and Lebanon, the ideological movements were only containers for darker, deeper sectarian attachments. Indeed, more recent history had only sharpened the old sectarian differences. There had never been a reconciliation between the Sunnis and the Shia anywhere in the lands of Islam; peace had not come between the Alawites and the Sunnis in Syria, nor had an accommodation been reached between the Sunnis and the Shia in Iraq. Scratch the progressive veneer, and the old feuds, the warring histories, were there.

A Palestinian-born scholar, the late Hanna Batatu, whose book, *The Old Social Classes and the Revolutionary Movements of Iraq* (1978) is the most ambitious and monumental study of Iraq attempted in any language, documented the steady descent of the Baath down the socioeconomic ladder and deeper into sectarianism. Batatu was an encyclopedic scholar, a Marxist historian with a passion for the socioeconomic details and life histories of the ideologues and officers he studied. We are indebted to him for an unsparing account of how the Baath became a vehicle for Sunni-Tikriti dominion. There had been two Baath regimes—one that came to power in 1963 and was then overthrown by the end of the same year, and a second regime, that of Saddam Hussein and his ilk, that seized power once again in 1968.

These were practically two different Baath parties, it seemed. The first had the characteristic, Batatu notes, of a "genuine partnership between the Sunni and Shia pan-Arab youth." It was different five years later: the role of the Sunnis had "risen sharply, while that of the Shi'is had decisively declined." Under the first Baath regime, the Shia indeed had something of a preponderance at the command level: of the top positions in the party, they had 53 percent, while the Sunnis had 38 percent and the Kurds 8 percent. The comparable figures for the command positions for the post-1968 regime were approximately 85 percent for the Sunni Arabs, 6 percent for the Shia, and 7.5 percent for the Kurds. Whatever progressive hopes had been grafted onto the Baath were devoured by three decades of plunder and cruelty and sectarian animus.

The road to perdition had been paved with both noble and cruel intentions, with the yearnings of two generations of political men for both reform and absolute power. A measure of patriotism, no doubt, was poured into the quest that carried the young men of the Baath on their volatile ride to power—and ruin. In Iraq (and in Syria), it is easy to see the mix of ambition and resentment and unbridled lust for socioeconomic and political revenge against the old order that gave the Baath "revolutions" their pitilessness. A whirlwind carried those officers and ideologues along: it would take them where it would. It would land them in prison or in exile, or at the end of a hangman's rope, or at the commanding heights of political power. These men had no mercy; none had been shown them. They had lived with the contempt of the upper classes and they would now pay them back in the coin of cruelty.

In a memoir of extraordinary power, titled *The Baath* and published in Beirut in 1969, one of the leading figures of the Baath of his generation, a Syrian by the name of Sami al-Jundi, who played and lost at the game of politics and was lucky to find a safe haven in North Africa, wrote of the Baath's early hopes and of the betrayal that overtook those bright beginnings. "We were strangers from our society, rebels against all the old values." Jundi came from an immensely literate and talented family, and he recalled his zeal and that of his fellows; for them there was no personal life; politics was everything: "A lesson that we would teach young students, a new member of the party to recruit, a talk with the peasants in a distant village . . ." Jundi's peers were sure that they had broken the hold of the old world and its tribal attachments, only to discover greater "backwardness" and "tribalism" in their own midst: "We thought we were the great beginning only to end up as informers, torturers, murderers." Alawite rule in Syria,

Tikriti rule in Iraq, the spectacle of the revered theorist of the Baath, the young man of the Sorbonne, Michel Aflaq, dubbed *al-ustadh* (the teacher), reduced to an old broken figure at the court of Saddam Hussein—this wasn't quite the bargain the early Baathists had made. In Syria, Hafiz al-Assad emptied the party of all grand claims and filled it with the power of the military and the security services and the Alawite brigade commanders; in Iraq, a grotesque cult of personality, and the cruelty and greed of the class around the ruler, turned the country into one large prison and a system of outright plunder and appropriation.

Nothing could check the greed of the ruling stratum; nothing stood in their way: the Shia holy cities had historically possessed a fair measure of autonomy, but the ruling clique broke it with a systematic campaign of terror and assassinations. The seminaries of Najaf that could once boast of thousands of students—seven thousand, according to the reliable estimates of the early 1970s—were decimated. An elite culture that had taken in Sunnis and Shia and Kurds and Chaldeans alike was taken apart by the terror. In place of all that, a small number of clans around Saddam Hussein, closed off from the rest of the country by intermarriage and inbreeding, came into full possession of the place.

Learning, culture, higher education: they were cast aside by a violent breed of men and their families. Oil and oil income powered this primitivism. Older regimes in Iraq may have been narrowly based, they may have lacked parliamentary and democratic mechanisms and protections, but they all had the checks and balances of traditional arrangements, and the rulers had to pay heed to the tribes or the seminarians in Najaf or the Kurdish chieftains, or to the power of private capital and property. Even Ahmad Hassan al-Bakr, Saddam's patron and immediate predecessor, a fellow Tikriti nearly a quarter-century older than Saddam, had known restraint and caution. Bakr had gone to the military academy (something Saddam pined for and was denied); he was the son of a landed notable; he had known the push and pull of political life in a country that had not yet been bent to the will of a despot. When Saddam forced Bakr from the presidency in 1979, the links with the old game of Iraqi politics were severed.

A glimpse of the world before the despotism, and of the early beginnings of the Baath, came my way not long after Saddam had willed his way to absolute power. One of those young Baathists chronicled and depicted by Sami al-Jundi, a cultured and tragic figure by the name of Taleb Shabib, had been lucky to escape the purges and the executions that befell so many in Iraq (and Syria) and had made a home for himself in New York City. A mutual Egyptian friend brought us together, and we saw each other on a frequent but irregular basis. When I knew him in the early 1980s, the bottle was his steady companion. I did not know all that had gone into his political odyssey, but he had lived a full and turbulent life. At twenty-eight, he had been one of the principal leaders of the Baath Party when it came to power in 1963. He had served as foreign minister of that Baath regime, which lasted less than a year. He had made a comeback with the second Baath coup in 1968. It was a partial comeback; a "harder" wing of the Baath had by then claimed the power of the state. He served as his country's ambassador to Bonn, Ankara, London, and the United Nations. By 1979, when Saddam's moment had arrived, Shabib was a figure of the past.

Born in 1935, Shabib was a Shia who came from landed gentry; by training, he was an engineer educated at the University of London. He spoke with the elegance of his class and background. He could have walked out of the pages of fiction—a political exile who never made peace with his new surroundings, and who carried within him the memories and details of the old country. Shabib had been one of the bright stars in the Baath. In 1963, in Damascus, he was in attendance as a "sympathizer" of the Baath was sworn in as a full member: the new recruit was a young thug from Tikrit by the name of Saddam Hussein, twenty-two years of age. The Tikriti had been on the fringe of a failed attempt on the life of the strongman of Iraq, General Abdul Kareem Qassem. He had been added to the "hit team" because another would-be assassin had taken ill at the last minute. By the time I knew him, two decades of purges and bloodletting had done their work: Shabib had his memories, and Saddam had risen to absolute power. Shabib died in 1998. Thoughts of him came to me now and then after his country's liberation. The despotism had fallen, but it was too late for Shabib and countless peers of his who had once thought that the old order would yield to a better political world.

In the aftermath of the fall of the regime of Saddam Hussein, I learned that there was something of a biography of Shabib, a long book on Iraq in the 1960s based on interviews with him. I tracked it down: it was a way of knowing and honoring a life, and of understanding how these early hopes for reform and change had begotten a monstrous world. The book was *Iraq: February 8, 1963*, by Ali Karim Said; the title referred to the date of the first Baath coup. From this work, put together by an attentive and devoted friend of Shabib, I could finally stitch together the man's life.

Shabib had started out his political journey as a young Communist; he was in his late teens when he joined that party. He was hardly unique in the choice he made. There had been a vibrant Communist Party in the holy city of Najaf, and even sons of religious scholars gravitated toward it. It was, indisputably, the main ideological challenger to the monarchy and its politics. Two or three years later, Shabib had walked away from the Communists and opted for the Baath. This was at the high-water mark of Arab nationalism, and the worldview of this intensely political and adventurous young man was shaped by his years of schooling in London. He was in London when the Suez War broke out in 1956; he was "secretary general" of the Arab Students' Union.

It was a tumultuous time, and no young Arab student in British universities was left untouched by that seminal moment in imperial and Arab history. As an Iraqi, Shabib was particularly engaged. Britain upheld the ruling order in his country, and it was public knowledge that the Hashemite dynasty and the political class around it thought the Suez campaign should end with the destruction of Gamal Abdel Nasser and his military regime. Shabib was passionately committed to Egypt's cause; he had met one of Nasser's principal colleagues and was proud of having been given that chance. He was to take his passion for Arab nationalism back to Baghdad in 1958, and to retain a lifelong reverence for Gamal Abdel Nasser.

He returned home, of course, when an old world—the Hashemite monarchy, the British primacy in Iraq, the rule of the old merchants and bureaucrats—was swept away in a frenzy of violence and extravagant hopes. He partook of his generation's expectation that a new, emancipated world would be brought forth. An Iraqi poet revered by this young generation, Abdul al-Wahhab al-Bayati, gave voice to this sense of pending deliverance:

> The sun rises in my city
> The bells ring out for the heroes.
> Awake, my beloved.
> We are free.

It did not take long for the new order of "free officers" and ideologues to drown in its own blood. The two leading "free officers" who
pulled off the revolt of 1958, Abdul Salam Aref and Abdul Kareem
Qassem, clashed, and Qassem ended with supreme power, the sole
leader of an erratic revolution that cast about for direction. As Communists and Arab nationalists and Baathists battled for primacy,
Qassem drew closer to the Communists. There had been violent outbreaks in Kirkuk and Mosul in 1959 as Qassem struggled to hold his
own against the appeals of Arab nationalism and a steady Egyptian
campaign against his rule. An ascetic and enigmatic man who came
from a background as checkered as Iraq itself—he had a Sunni Arab
father and a Kurdish-Shia mother—Qassem was an "Iraqist," and
this put him at odds with the Baath and the pan-Arabists.

Young Taleb Shabib had a gift for this kind of political contest. He
would become one of the principal organizers and leaders of the
Baath Party. Qassem was a dictator, but the totalitarianism that would
suffocate the political life of the country had not yet arrived. Shabib
and a handful of fellow Baathists in the army and the party had
ample room to plot. It was the Baath that had made an attempt on
Qassem's life in 1959. The decision to go through with the assassination had been by a vote of the "Baath Command" in Iraq. Five people
had deliberated, and three votes had carried the day. Shabib had been
one of the two dissenters, but once the decision was made, he gave it
his utmost support. "Once made," he observed with the discipline and
odd legalism of underground parties, "the decision acquired legitimacy,
and we were bound to work towards its fulfillment."

Qassem suffered a minor injury, and an anti-Baathist purge followed. There was a measure of forgiveness, though, in Qassem. Some
of the participants in the plot were spared; the Baath would use the
next four years to put together a more ambitious bid for power.
Shabib, though only in his midtwenties, would become one of the
leaders of his party. In the parlance of the time and the place, he was
a member of the Command of the Baath Party in the Iraqi Region:
this was to set it apart from the "Syrian Region," and to reflect the
hubris of the Baath as a pan-Arab party in Syria, Jordan, and Lebanon
as well. His fearlessness and optimism gave him the chance to meet
and work with the man who was then seen as the great theorist of the
party and its intellectual godfather, the Syrian Michel Aflaq. He was
one of seven or eight astoundingly young men, in their twenties and
thirties, who set out to attain political power for their party.

In an odd twist, the civilians in this group had the upper hand, and the military officers played second fiddle to them. This order must have reflected the ascendancy of the text and of the idea—and the underground cell—over the military formations. Three civilian workers and ideologues were dominant, and Shabib was one of them. On the fringe of this group, there was a military officer a good generation older, Ahmad Hassan al-Bakr. Cunning and suspicious, Bakr's placid and unthreatening demeanor concealed a capacity for intrigue and deviousness. (Bakr would rise to power, and would carry with him to the top his fellow Tikriti and enforcer, Saddam Hussein.)

The chance to do away with the regime came the way of these conspirators in February 1963. Two young men of this inner circle were at the center of this revolt: Shabib himself, and a fellow Shia and party worker by the name of Hazem Jawad, like Shabib himself twenty-eight years of age. This breed of young political men bobbed back and forth between the world and superstitions of their elders and newer ideas and temptations given them by the spirit of the era. Shabib tells us that the group of conspirators drank whiskey before they pulled off their deed, but that Hazem Jawad's mother lifted up a copy of the Quran and that the young plotters walked underneath it and received the old woman's blessing as they headed off on their venture.

The conspirators had been fair planners, and they had been lucky. They secured control of the radio station: this was what the Arabs called the era of the "Military Communiqué Number One," when people in Syria, Egypt, Iraq, and Libya woke up to the radio broadcasts announcing the sacking of incumbent regimes and the coming to power of men promising a new dawn. Even before the ruler had fallen, Shabib and his companions told the nation that "that enemy of the people Abdul Kareem Qassem" who betrayed the "glorious revolution" of July 14, 1958, had been overthrown. Qassem offered feeble resistance. He was loath to trigger a bloodbath; he refused to arm Communist irregulars who were willing to resist this coup d'état. He surrendered and was brought to the radio station to face the plotters. He pleaded with them. He bargained for political exile. Four years earlier, he had spared the life of his rival Abdul Salam Aref; he invoked that precedent in his plea for mercy. But Aref, who had been brought into the current coup as an elder statesman, had no nobility in him and no mercy. He brushed aside Qassem's pleas and his talk of the "bread and salt" they had shared together. Aref had something entirely different on his mind: he pulled out of his pocket a small Quran and told Qassem to swear by it and admit that it was he, Aref, who had been the guiding force behind the July Revolution of 1958 against the monarchy.

Qassem kept his last shred of dignity. He refused to bow to Aref's will. That seizure of power in 1958 was his pride, and that of his entire generation. The matter was sealed and Qassem was executed. It was important to scare off the Communists and the inhabitants of the slums of Baghdad who had taken to Qassem. The ghastly images of his corpse, and the corpses of several of his companions, were broadcast over Iraqi television. Five years earlier, it had been the turn of the Hashemites and of Nuri Pasha al-Said. Now the revolution had devoured its own.

There had been no trial of Qassem, Shabib concedes. A discussion, a *hiwar,* had sufficed. Shabib's memoirs are curiously devoid of guilt over Qassem's fate. He gives Qassem his due: he says he was "a patriot who looked after the interests of the poor," but that he was a dictator who monopolized power and ruled with emergency decrees. "Before he was brought to the radio station and executed, I only met him once, for I had no official position that would give me access to him. I viewed him as an enemy who had deviated from the pan-Arab line and who had led astray the July Revolution." No sorrow had come, no acknowledgment that blood would call forth more violence.

It was Shabib's partner in that seizure of power, Hazem Jawad, who would come to this guilt and this awareness. In an interview conducted in February 2004 with the pan-Arab daily *Al-Hayat,* Jawad, now an exile in London, looked back with sorrow on the harvest of that time: "I wish to God we had spared the blood of all, Nuri al-Said and Qassem and the royal family and the rest of them." Did the Baath fail? he was asked. It was all a failure, he said, not just the Baath but the entire "revolutionary-nationalist tradition of the last forty years." The end, some big union of Arab states, had been used to justify the means, and the effort had all collapsed in tyranny and plunder.

The young revolutionaries who had seized power in 1963 would not have it for long. Before the year drew to a close, Aref, a titular figure within this regime, turned on the Baath, with help from Egypt, and claimed power in the name of pan-Arab nationalism. He was of a mind to execute Shabib and Hazem Jawad. It was only the intervention of Nasser, and his offer of a Cairo asylum for them, that saved their lives. Aref governed badly and died in a mysterious airplane accident in 1966. His brother then governed for two years until the Baath struck back in 1968. The second Baath regime was dominated by a harder clique: Ahmad Hassan al-Bakr and Saddam Hussein, and the rest of the Tikriti lot. There was work for Taleb Shabib—foreign embassies, a stint in New York as a representative to the United Nations. But the bloodletting had given birth to a different Iraq. By the late 1970s, Saddam had consolidated his hold on power; the protection afforded Shabib by President Bakr had eroded as Bakr's own fortunes had declined. Shabib took no chances; he quit the country in 1977 after being informed that Saddam thought that he was an "American agent." The man I got to know in New York belonged to an irretrievable time. It had not been pretty, the politics of that period. But Iraqis could still keep count, back then, of the numbers of those who had fallen to spasms of political violence. Iraq had not yet reached the time of mass violence and mass graves.

As far as I know, Shabib never saw Baghdad and the Middle Euphrates—his birthplace—again; in the final years of his life, he may have gone to Kurdistan, which Anglo-American power sheltered against Saddam Hussein, but it was not his part of the country. The sorrow of Iraq clung to him; like so many exiles, he lived on the rumors of coups and revolts that never came. In 1991, after the first American war against Saddam Hussein, there had been a period of hope and a mistaken belief that the despotism of Saddam Hussein had had its day. The former Communist and Baathist was even invited to Saudi Arabia in an attempt to put together an alternative to the rule of Saddam Hussein. The conservative Gulf states, now awakened to the threat of their former enforcer in Baghdad, wanted Saddam replaced. But Shabib had a life of political experience behind him, and his travels to Syria and Saudi Arabia were the dutiful errands of a man who knew the odds. This intensely gregarious man died alone, in a London flat. His son found him two or three days later, when he came to look in on him. Little did the two young men of the Sorbonne, who founded the Baath, and little did the generation of Taleb Shabib, who came after the founders, know of all that would pass in the name of what they had created and let loose during those more innocent times.

CHAPTER 6

The False History

It was the luck of the imperial draw that America had come into so tangled a dominion as this Iraqi polity. Seven decades earlier, in early 1933, shortly before his death, King Faisal I, the Hashemite prince who had been brought to Iraq and imposed by British power, penned some thoughts about the realm he had governed for more than a decade. He was disappointed in the country. He found a people "devoid of any patriotic idea, imbued with religious traditions and absurdities, connected by no common tie, giving ear to evil, prone to anarchy, and perpetually ready to rise against any government whatever. Out of these masses we want to fashion a people we would train, educate and refine." It was hard going, and Faisal died a frustrated man.

In the intervening decades, Iraq was the thing and its opposite: a realm of culture and learning right alongside great brutality and sorrow. A country of genuine pluralism, enjoying a culture that had traffic with Iran, Turkey, Syria, and the Arabian Peninsula and the inheritance of four decades of British tutelage, nevertheless treated the Arab world to a cruel idea of Arabism, racial identity, and merciless clan rule. This duality was there awaiting the American liberators. The insurgents could not win, but they had the sympathy of large numbers of Sunni Arabs. The seeming "unreason" of their war of attrition was but an expression of an unwillingness to let go of a country that had been fully, and exclusively, theirs.

In the face of this terrible, stubborn history, the American strategy rested on the hope that the logic of force and of inducements would prevail. "With a heavy dose of fear and violence, and a lot of money for projects, I think we can convince these people that we are here to help them," said Lieutenant Colonel Nathan Sassaman, a battalion commander whose soldiers were stationed in a difficult town in western Iraq. This was early December 2003, and the preceding month had been hellish for the American forces: eighty-one soldiers had fallen to hostile fire, and in Abu Hishma, a town of seven thousand people in the Sunni Triangle, Sassaman had lost one of his soldiers to a guerrilla attack on a Bradley armed personnel carrier. The town had been encased with razor wire: good intentions had not been enough. The war of liberation had become, in this unhappy and bitter zone of Iraq, a counterinsurgency, and the commanders had to acknowledge the enmity between the occupying power and these difficult towns. (Sassaman himself, a star officer, tripped up in this war and crossed a line. On January 3, 2004, his men forced two Iraqis into the Tigris. One of the two men survived, but controversy swirled over the fate of the other. Sassaman was tried and received a reprimand for impeding the army's investigation of that incident. He retired a disillusioned man, his fate a reminder of this war's, and this insurgency's, moral hazards.)

Terror and tribal loyalties came together in these towns; jihadists from Yemen and Saudi Arabia and Syria and Jordan found sanctuary and a friendly population. We don't know for sure whether the deposed dictator planned in advance for this insurgency. But the country was one huge munitions dump, and money had been stashed away in this Baathist/Sunni stronghold in the Anbar province in preparation for a rainy day. For the American commanders, the priorities had been established by the realities on the ground: hunt down the dictator, root out the insurgency, get into the terrorist "cycle of finances," seize or purchase the deadly missiles. The battle for hearts and minds would have to wait. Payments of up to three thousand dollars were being offered in this zone for the killing of an American soldier and five hundred dollars for any attack on American forces. A large number of Baathist military and security operatives had returned to these towns and villages from other provinces of Iraq that they had governed and terrorized under the old regime.

Major General Raymond T. Odierno, the commander who oversaw this zone, a big swath that ran from the northern oil town of Kirkuk to the Iranian border in the east, knew the magnitude of his challenge. In December, he was able to report that the attacks on his soldiers had dropped to six a day from twenty-two a day a month earlier. A child of Rockaway, New Jersey, a graduate of West Point, a physically imposing man who had played football at the military academy (he was a linebacker), Odierno was on Saddam Hussein's tribal and sectarian turf. His mission alternated between counterinsurgency and reconstruction. In published interviews and in a long briefing in Kirkuk that I had been party to in late October, he showed a steady concern for the social and ethnic details of his region and its extended familial and tribal loyalties. "The tribal and family connections are binding, and it's very tough to get inside them. But one day we will." The writers elaborating on how Americans had "botched" the occupation would perhaps have written in an entirely different vein had they better understood the enormity of the burden that the Anglo-American coalition had found in Iraq.

For Odierno and his command, diligence paid off on December 13: after eight frustrating months of pursuing leads good and bad, Odierno's soldiers found Saddam Hussein at the bottom of an eight-foot "spider hole" on the outskirts of Tikrit. "He was just caught like a rat," Odierno said of his captive. The dictator was found on the grounds of a run-down farmhouse by the Tigris. He had closed a circle: his legend had been born there, in 1959, when as a young hit man of the Baath party, he had been part of an assassination attempt on General Abdul Kareem Qassem. He had hidden in this farm country, his mythmakers said, then swum across the Tigris and made it to safety in Syria. This time he hadn't gone so far, for he was a creature of his village and district. He couldn't have hidden in Basra or Kirkuk. The country beyond Tikrit and that fabled Sunni Triangle was, to him, an alien, hostile land. Odierno's forces captured Saddam, but the commander resisted a face-to-face encounter with his captive. I was curious about his reticence: some ten weeks later, I had the chance to ask this officer—by all accounts a soldier's soldier, and by all appearances a man of few words and no particular eagerness to please or charm—why he had passed up the opportunity for an encounter with the dictator. Odierno gave the question a moment's pause: "I did not want to say something to him that I would later regret," he said. He would say no more. The task had been done, and he would leave the commentary and the triumphalism to others. (This war would give Odierno both exhilaration and heartbreak. Eight months after the capture of Saddam Hussein, on August 21, Lieutenant Anthony Odierno, the general's son, was severely wounded in action in Baghdad, and his left arm was amputated.)

We owe the late political philosopher Hannah Arendt one of the central insights of our time: the banality of evil. Arendt returned with that verdict after covering the trial of Adolf Eichmann in

Jerusalem in 1961. The deeds of Eichmann and the Nazi regime were monstrous. But then there was the man in the glass booth whom Arendt saw and described: "medium-sized, slender, middle-aged, with receding hair, ill-fitting teeth, and nearsighted eyes, who throughout the trial keeps craning his scraggy neck toward the bench, and who desperately and for the most part successfully maintains his self-control despite the nervous tic to which his mouth must have become subject long before this trial started." There is a swindle, a disappointment to great evil. It never quite lives up to our expectations. The image of Saddam Hussein in captivity was true to Arendt's theme. The haggard, disoriented man at the bottom of the "spider hole" was the very same man who had inflicted unspeakable sorrow on his people, and on the peoples of two neighboring lands. The discovery of the smallness of the men behind the most terrible of deeds is always an affront: if Eichmann was only a clerk, Saddam was only a thug.

The former dictator on the run had become a rebuke to American power, proof of its inability to penetrate an alien, seemingly inaccessible place. America had awed the region with its machines and high-tech wizardry; its enemies fell back on the consolation that the strangers were destined to lose their way in Iraqi cities and towns. Save for a minority of Arabs who cast their fate with the United States in this campaign (I think of Kuwait and Qatar) the Americans were in truth alone in an Arab world that wished them ill in this campaign. The mighty Americans had gotten their comeuppance, their enemies and false friends alike were happy to proclaim. The rebellion of the insurgents had bought time, and additional yarn, for Arab delusions; the disappearance of the dictator had fed the idea that the Pax Americana had blundered into a place destined to thwart its power.

November had been a particularly grim month: American Chinooks and Black Hawks were being shot out of the skies over Tikrit and Fallujah and Mosul. There were rumors that America's leaders had begun to scramble for a way out of the country. The capture of the dictator was a badly needed victory. America's troubles were not over, not by a long shot. But the message was received in Iraq, and in Arab lands beyond. The man who had strutted around the region, who for all practical purposes dominated Arab politics for nearly a generation, surrendered without a fight. Legends die hard. The crowd is, of course, what it is, and its capacity for self-delusion is bottomless. In the hours that followed the dictator's capture, and in the shadow of that image of him meekly undergoing his medical examination, the legend spread, in Amman and Cairo and Gaza, and as far away as the Muslim suburbs of France, that it was all a trick, that the man had been drugged, and his capture had all been an American hoax.

The very same Arabs who had averted their gaze from the despot's mass graves were now quick to take offense that the dictator had been exposed to such public humiliation. The Middle East is home to the quintessential "shame culture," and this spectacle had taken from that crowd a cherished legend. For every Cairene and every Palestinian, and for every intellectual in Amman, who was second-guessing the way the American captors "processed" the dictator and displayed his surrender, there were other Arabs who saw into the tyrant's legend and his legacy. Outside the Sunni Triangle, celebratory gunfire in the streets of Iraq was the testimony of a people eager to be done with a political legacy of radicalism and terror.

Pity the admirers of Saddam Hussein—in the Sunni Triangle in Iraq, among the Palestinians and the Egyptians, among the Arabs to whom Saddam had peddled a legend of heroism. He had told them he was a reincarnation of the twelfth-century Muslim warrior Saladin, who had defended his world and his faith against the Crusades, and whose chivalry had earned the respect of the Franks. (Saddam could not grasp the irony of his appropriation of the cult of Saladin, who was of Kurdish ancestry.) Saddam had exalted "martyrdom," speaking of it over and over again. Yet the Arab crowd that had stayed with him, through thick and thin, had to watch as the man with a pistol and two AK-47 rifles gave up without firing a shot. Nearly five months earlier, it should be recalled, in the town of Mosul, Saddam's two sons and a fourteen-year-old grandson were killed in a firefight with American soldiers. Trapped, they had fought back. But Saddam was of a different breed: he was homicidal rather than suicidal. Not for him was the cult of "martyrdom"; he peddled it but would not partake of it. No sooner had Saddam been caught than one of the leaders of Hamas expressed his deep disappointment that the Iraqi despot had not fought back.

In those unsettled lands of the Arab-Islamic world, preachers and plotters tell about America all sorts of unflattering tales. The tales wend their way through Beirut and Mogadishu and other places of American heartbreak and abdication. It was different this time around. The capture played out under Arab and Muslim (to say nothing of French and German) eyes. The matter of Saddam Hussein was seen to its rightful end.

Iraq had tested the resolve of its American occupiers. No weapons of mass destruction had been found. There was some gratitude in Iraq, but not enough. What America encountered was a country wrecked and poisoned by a dictatorship perhaps unique in its brutality in the post–World War II world. Sectarianism, undemocratic habits, and impatience were rife. But the abject surrender of a tyrant who had mocked America's will and staying power, and whose very political survival had stood as proof of American irresolution a dozen years earlier, was a statement to the Arab street and others watching this war in the Arab world that a price was paid by a leader who had flouted every norm of international order.

The great drama of the dictator's capture was of course heady. Surely, there were grounds for hope that Saddam's fate would be a cautionary tale for the crowds in Fallujah and Tikrit and Ramadi, and perhaps for jihadists pondering a passage to Iraq. The dictator's myth had been shattered: it was not lost on those watching this spectacle that the man who knew no English had learned, by rote, enough of it to introduce himself to his captors and to say that he was willing to "negotiate." But the commanders and the intelligence operatives in the field knew that an insurgency gathering momentum would go on without him. As early as three days after Saddam Hussein's capture, a report from the Defense Intelligence Agency drew sober conclusions about a broader security challenge in Iraq: "Saddam's capture will have little impact on foreign terrorist operational planning in Iraq. Sunni extremist groups are fighting against the US-led coalition, not to restore the Hussein regime to power. Saddam's capture will have little impact on their motivation and operational capability."

To the extent that a vast and varied Arab world could be read with reasonable accuracy, it seemed that a decent minority of Arabs stepped forward to bury the dictator's legacy, to brand him a false savior, a pretender who had promised the Arabs an age of chivalry and power only to hand them a steady flow of calamities. Ahmad Rabie, a noted Kuwaiti liberal, writing in the London-based pan-Arab daily *Asharq Al-Awsat,* gave the legacy of Saddam and Saddamism an apt summation, the farewell of a man who lived in close proximity to the dictator's domain. "Countless mothers will light candles and celebrate the tyrant's capture—mothers in all the cities of Iraq, in all the villages of

Iran, in all the streets and quarters of Kuwait, everywhere the tyrant's cruelty was felt, and where his power translated into mass graves and mass terror." Throughout its history, Arab-Muslim society had had its fling with despots and had been led astray. From that historical torment, there has been born an ability—after the denials, and the angry assertions that all had been well and that the false heroes had been faithful sons of that Arab nation—to see tyrants and pretenders for what they are.

Bashar al-Assad, the Syrian ruler, may have insisted that what happened in Iraq was of no concern to him or his regime. But he knew better. His people grew emboldened by the changes in Iraq. True, no popular revolution swept the Syrian Baath out of power. But political life in Syria began to stir. By early March, there were reports of protests and sit-ins in Damascus. Then the Syrian Kurds mounted a challenge of their own to the Baathist rulers. In mid-March 2004, riots broke out in several towns adjacent to the Iraqi and Turkish borders. The troubles began in the northeastern town of Qameshli, then spread to Aleppo. In Qameshli, the rioters knocked off the head of a statue of the late dictator Hafiz al-Assad. In the nearby town of Malkiya, two plaster busts, of Assad father and son, that adorned a local cultural center were decapitated and the building was torched. A young shopkeeper spoke to a foreign reporter, in his own way, of the contagious ways of liberty. "We want democracy like the others. The whole world is like one big ball now, nothing can be hidden from us." Before the troubles subsided, scores were killed, and hundreds of Kurds had been arrested.

The political silence at the heart of Syrian politics had been challenged. Ever since the early 1980s, and the terrible bloodletting in the city of Hama, in 1982, when the regime subdued with unspeakable brutality a town that had been a stronghold of the Sunni bourgeoisie and of the Muslim Brotherhood, Syrian politics had been a quiescent affair. The regime had won; a grudging acceptance of it had settled in. In 2000, dynastic succession from Hafiz al-Assad to his son had taken place without the hint of a challenge. Now this "liberty"—dangerous and violent, it is true—across Syria's eastern border was full of meaning for Syria's own Baathist rulers.

A daring filmmaker, Omar Amiralaya, probed the Syrian system's red lines with a documentary with the working title *Fifteen Reasons Why I Hate the Baath*. He had another one in the works, *A Flood in*

Baath Country, for a European arts channel. He made no secret as to the source of his inspiration. The collapse of the despotism in Iraq had given him his courage, he said. "When you see one of the two Baath parties broken, collapsing, you can only hope that it will be the turn of the Syrian Baath next. . . . I think the image, the sense of terror, has evaporated." An old, stagnant regime that had robbed the country of any sense of vibrancy or life was being questioned. This place had of course known endless disappointments, and the custodians of political power were no doubt merciless and desperate enough to prevail in a test of arms against the daring filmmaker and men and women who shared his hopes. But Syrians had looked across the border and had seen it all. The culture of statues and obedience, and official plunder and terror, was theirs as well. The rulers in Damascus, heirs of a moribund political tradition, could warn of the "defilement" that befell Iraq at the hands of the "foreign occupiers." But there was enough wisdom in Aleppo and Damascus for people to know that the "foreign occupiers" were destined to pack up and leave, while the homegrown tyrants would hold on to power and bequeath their dominions to their progeny.

The Syrian regime could only be itself. It responded with staged demonstrations by a few obliging Kurds, who were sent into the streets to chant, "God, Syria, and Bashar only." The troubles, the rulers proclaimed, had been staged by American agents who had thrown money around in an attempt to destabilize the regime. No greater sophistication was available to these rulers: they lived and worked in a spider hole of their own. Still, these hopes of change swirled around this war. In a wonderful and poignant turn of phrase, a Syrian of Armenian ethnicity described the war in Iraq to a foreign reporter as a "stone thrown into the pond." He placed his hopes in that struggle at play in Iraq: "I believe democracy in Iraq must succeed," he added. He was not alone, that man eager to see his world give way to a better one.

The despots could not be sure of the determination of Pax Americana to have its way in the region. The frustration of American power in Baghdad and Fallujah and Tikrit gave them hope that they themselves might yet be spared. But their sense of mastery had cracked. Was it pure coincidence that only days after Saddam's capture, the Libyan strongman Muammar Qaddafi threw his country wide open to international inspectors and owned up to an extensive program for the development of chemical and biological weapons? Qaddafi was at the helm of a smaller, more vulnerable country than Iraq. For a generation, he had been beyond the pale, a veritable outlaw in the world of nations. But there was method to his seeming madness. He had enough cunning to know that the world had grown more dangerous for rogues in the aftermath of September 11, 2001. He had seen the sacking of the Taliban; closer to home, he had seen the man once dubbed *saif al-Arab* (the sword of the Arabs) come out of the bottom of a hole, hands up, to a humiliating surrender.

As erratic as ever, the Libyan strongman now came forth as an advocate of ridding the region of weapons of mass destruction. It was of course hard to judge the arsenal of weapons Qaddafi had at his disposal. A "rogue operation" conducted by the father of Pakistan's nuclear weapons program, Abdul Qader Khan, had been supplying the Libyans with banned weapons and technologies. It was perhaps safe to assume that Qaddafi himself (like Saddam before him) had no real mastery or knowledge of modern weapons, no full sense of what he was buying with his oil money. But Saddam's fate was no doubt a factor in the calculations of the Libyan strongman. He knew it was time to plea-bargain his way out of trouble. He knew that George Bush and Tony Blair needed political ammunition and proof that the Iraq war had been a success, and that its dividends were on display in Libya. Qaddafi was duly and promptly rewarded with reconciliation with the United States and a visit to Libya by Tony Blair on March 25, 2004. Bedouin kitsch had always been part of the Libyan dictator's style. He pitched a tent on the outskirts of Tripoli and turned up in one of his countless costumes for the occasion with Blair. If surrender it must be, it had to be done in style.

What the dictators give, the dictators take away: Qaddafi too had once been full of bluster and bravado. To be sure, the Arabs had tired of him. But he had had his moment as the self-anointed successor to Gamal Abdel Nasser, and the hope of the "masses" looking for a redeemer. It was now time to call off the pretense. Those once deluded by Qaddafi would know the familiar taste of disappointment. Ghassan Charbel, a columnist for the daily *Al-Hayat,* and a man who by and large marches to the beat of the Arab Street, gave that episode an intelligent and thoughtful assessment in a column titled "That Day and That Tent." With Saddam in mind, the journalist described the episode as the "mother of all surprises." The "wheel of time" had turned, Charbel wrote. It was farewell to the age of revolutionary utterances; it had become dangerous and costly to set Western interests on fire. The era of explosives and hijackings had drawn to a close. "It had become quite expensive to take on the West. If you were to stay now outside this new international order you are sure to grow old in your isolation, stranded alone with your old weapons, your dying economy, your primitive universities. Time has changed: he who used to cause fear is now himself afraid, he who used to threaten is now threatened, and he who used to spread instability now has to offer concessions to secure his own stability." The spider hole on the outskirts of Tikrit, and the tent in Tripoli: the Arab crowd that had followed the despots, and knew no way around them, was being treated to a reckoning with the harvest of modern Arab politics.

The capture of Saddam, like the war itself, was still a foreigner's gift. This was a truth that stalked the American effort in Iraq and the determination to fight a wider Arab battle on Iraqi soil. Saddam Hussein was an upstart, it is true. The squalor he was found amid was in truth that of his modest, wretched beginnings. But he had not descended from the sky; he had emerged out of the Arab world's sins of omission and commission. He had plucked powerful weapons from within his culture's dreams and deadly utopias. Anti-Westernism, a virulent hatred of Persia and Persians, the promise of torching Israel with chemical weapons, the promise of nuclear weapons that would avenge the humiliations inflicted on the Arabs in modern history: all those had been Saddam's arsenal. No one in the region had drawn limits for him. No "velvet revolution" within Iraq itself blew him out of power, no Arab cavalry had ridden to the rescue of Iraq's population. It was an American war that disposed of this man.

Saddam Hussein, it is true, was alone in that spider hole amid the litter of a run-down farmhouse. But he had been a creature of the Arab order of power; it is not so difficult to see that a different destiny could have been had by that dazed man flushed out of his hiding place by the soldiers of Task Force 121. He had once been the beloved son of that fabled Arab nation, the "knight of Arabism" marked by destiny to crush the "fire-worshipping Persians" in the east, and to lay to waste the Jewish state by the Mediterranean. The knight has stumbled, but those deadly dreams are not abandoned.

"We should have said 'No' to Saddam, as we said 'No' to Khomeini," an Arab analyst, Ghassan al-Imam, wrote in the pages of *Asharq*

Al-Awsat in the aftermath of the dictator's surrender. It was easy now to see through the despotism and its fraud. But Saddam Hussein's ascendancy in the Arab councils of power was a headier run than the columnist made it out to be. Among Arabs, it was easy to walk away from Khomeini's "gifts" and Khomeini's campaign. To be sure, he had turned up, as the 1970s drew to a close, offering a gospel of redemption and a furious revolt. He had risen during a time of distress and expectations, when oil wealth had unsettled the old social order. He had been sure that his was a pan-Islamic rebellion. But Khomeini was a Persian; his interlude in Najaf had been forced on him by Pahlavi rule. He had gone back to his country, a turbaned shah in all but name. Arab society in the Fertile Crescent, and in the Gulf, had insisted on the Persianness of Khomeini. It was the Shia underclass in Lebanon, and the Shia merchants shut out of political power in the Gulf, who had rallied to him. They had done it out of pride and need, and a sense of deliverance. Legions of Khomeini's Arab followers had bet on Pan-Arabism only to be disappointed; they had knocked at the gates of Sunni-Arab society, but were always excluded. The turbaned revolutionary from Qom had offered them the promise of a return to the sources of their own Shia tradition.

Some Sunni Islamists in the Arab world had taken to Khomeini. They had admired his unbending will; more important, they had admired his worldly success, for he had expelled a monarch from power, while the Arab officers and kings had put down with ease whatever challenges arose to their power. But this minority of Arabs aside, the drama of Ayatollah Khomeini had played out across the Arab-Persian, and the Sunni-Shia, divide. This was where Saddam Hussein was at his best. For all his cruelty and clumsiness, he appeared to read the Arab world unerringly. Bravado was needed; he supplied it. He conjured up the mythical borders of a single Arab nation and presented himself as the defender of the "eastern gate" of the Arab world. There had always been an Arab unease with Persia and Persians, a temperamental difference between these two peoples of Islam. Saddam found that unease and turned it into a force of racial and cultural animus. If Egypt had bolted out of Arab affairs, in the late 1970s, rescued from the captivity of Arab politics by Anwar el-Sadat, the Tikriti upstart put forth his regime as an alternative to the power and primacy of Cairo in Arab affairs.

The Arab literati were looking for a hero and a patron; Saddam offered himself to their imagination. Filmmakers, writers, and journalists for hire made their way to Baghdad. This city was, for perhaps a decade, the place where Arab hopes and delusions found a measure of fulfillment. The man terrorizing Najaf and its seminarians was generous to a fault with Jordanian editors and Egyptian publicists and Palestinian expositors of his legend. I know a brilliant Egyptian filmmaker, born in the mid-1920s, at a time of genuine enlightenment in his homeland, who accepted a commission from Saddam Hussein and produced a film about the dictator's life and his cult. The filmmaker practically walks out of the pages of Lawrence Durrell's *Alexandria Quartet:* the reference is apt, for he was born and raised in that city. He speaks English, French, and Arabic with equal ease and fluency. Yet in the 1980s he went to Iraq and produced a big work of crude propaganda and hero worship. One of the two sons-in-law of the despot, playing young Saddam, reenacted the centerpiece of his legend—the botched attempt, in 1959, on the life of General Abdul Kareem Qassem.

The film made, the director had come back to his Egyptian homeland. The commission was his nest egg. But in the 1990s, the filmmaker came to a genuine sense of disappointment in himself, and in his craft, for having made the film. In his world, the man was unique: he, at least, had the decency of his second thoughts. In the wider intellectual and political world of the Arabs, the dictator operated with the warrant granted him by popular consent and approval. He drew on a kind of awe at his abilities and at his spirit of defiance. He had prided himself on his ability to bob back and forth between what he called *tarheeb* (terrorizing) and *targheeb* (inducements, the offering of rewards). His apologists loved the cadence and the cunning of it all: if dictatorship is a pact between a crowd and a pretender, this pact Saddam made with the crowds in Amman and Ramallah and in Cairo had a force all its own.

Arab culture in the 1980s—Saddam's moment in the sun—couldn't have stood up to Saddam Hussein. He had run away with its very desires. He had taken onto himself all its yearnings and defects. And even on the morning of August 2, 1990, when he pulled off an astounding deed of betrayal by invading Kuwait, the crowd couldn't—wouldn't—break faith with him. He had sacked a wealthy emirate, and the crowd wanted done with kings and emirs. Some bold new destiny awaited the Arabs, and this man with his confident strut was its embodiment. He held out the promise that there would be a sharing out of the loot, that around the corner lay a big Arab project that would vindicate the conquest of the small principality he had sacked. The crowd, and the street, loved the rhythmic chant, *"Ya Saddam ya habeeb, bi al kimawi udrub tel abeeb."* "Oh Saddam oh beloved, with the chemical hit Tel Aviv." Nothing deeper was needed, no program of political repair, no project of economic rescue. The street feasted on the odd mix of Tikriti tribalism and racial solidarity married to the latest of lethal weapons.

Grant the Tikriti his due: effortlessly, he intuited the needs of the crowd, and its appetite—the things it thrilled to, the things it could sanction or even fail to notice. He had struck at the Kurds, but in the Arab reckoning, the Kurds were outsiders, a mountain people, on the fringes of Arab life. He had brutalized the Shia, but they were schismatics; they reeked of Persia and things Persian. In Kuwait, Saddam had stumbled, it is true. He had broken the pact with the order of power in the Arab world. He had been taken into the fold as gendarme of this Arab order, its defender against the "Persian hordes" of the east and the Shia "sectarians" within Arab lands. He had been forgiven his violent means; those had been written off as personal predilection best ignored, or the ways of his cruel frontier country. If the crowd had begun to walk away from Saddam Hussein, toward the end of his political career, the explanation was to be found in his two devastating defeats in the face of American forces, a decade or so apart. But there had been no tears for his victims, no rejection of his autocracy and terror.

A Saudi author and academic, Khalid bin Saaban, at King Abdulaziz University, in Jeddah, came close to the truth after Saddam's capture. It was inappropriate, he observed, for Arabs to gloat over Saddam's captivity or to think of his fate as something out of the ordinary in Arab life. Saddam was an "embodiment of the Arab malady," he wrote: the veritable ownership of the state, the cult of personality, the absence of political institutions that would take politics beyond the writ and the power of the ruler. It was natural, bin Saaban observed, for George W. Bush to play *mufti* (judge and arbiter), to dispose of Arab and Muslim affairs, for this right had been granted him by "our inability to face ourselves and to reform our condition." The ride with despotism had issued in political failure and ruin. The man who climbed out of the spider hole had "shamed" (the word turned up over

and over again in the Arab commentaries on the surrender of Saddam
Hussein) an entire political culture that had given rise and sustenance to him.

It was odd, this belated sense of shame. It took the dictator on his
own terms. The broken bargain with *rujula* (machismo, manhood)
was what troubled those now bewailing what the despot did to himself, and what the Americans did to him after his capture. In truth, the
despot had supplied his world with annals of shame aplenty. He had
shamed those who chanted his name, or wrote poetry for him, or did
business with him, long before he had emerged from his spider hole.
He had given material for moral embarrassment the full length of his
political career. There had been his cruel execution of the brilliant
jurist Muhammad Baqir al-Sadr and his refined sister in 1980. There
had been that willful and terrible war he launched against Iran, later
that same year, in the name of a racialist Arabism, and in a deliberate
attempt to position himself as a valiant defender of the Sunni-Arab
order of power. Those likely to be shamed ought to have felt a dread of
the man and of the genocidal campaign he had unleashed against the
Kurds in the late 1980s. And there was shame to spare, on that
summer morning in August 1990, when Saddam sent his army
into Kuwait and announced that a principality with two centuries of
independent political existence behind it was now a province of his
dominion.

Those given to shame ought to have heard the screams of Saddam's
victims, in southern Iraq, and in the Shia holy cities, in 1991, when
the dictator rebounded from his military defeat at the hands of an
American-led coalition and sent his cousin, "Chemical Ali," to put
down a Shia insurgency without qualms and without mercy. The
tanks that had driven into the shrine cities of Najaf and Karbala carried banners that read "No More Shia After Today." The barbarous
cruelty had been easy to forgive; the abject surrender a dozen years
later was what hurt.

After the fall of Baghdad in April, and before Saddam's capture, one of
the most venerable and brilliant of the Arab journalistic elite, Ghassan
Tueni, a publisher of Lebanon's preeminent daily, *An-Nahar,* wrote a
book of commentary on what had played out in Baghdad, titled
Hiwar ma' al-Istibdad (Dialogue with Tyranny). In that collection of his
columns, Tueni came forth with an autopsy of what Saddam, and Sad-

damism, represented for the Arabs. Born in 1926, to wealth and privilege and responsibility (his father had been publisher of the paper), a
Greek Orthodox by religious background, at home in French and
American and Arabic culture and letters, Tueni has behind him a
career of unrivaled distinction as a parliamentarian, a diplomat, an
author of exquisite style and talent. (I still recall the joy I felt, as a
young man in my late teens, reading his sparkling editorials.) To this
autopsy, he came, as ever, with his signature turn of phrase and his
ability to see and name things.

In these meditations on tyranny, Tueni's literary device was an
imaginary dialogue with Saddam Hussein's statue in Tikrit. A journalist turns up by the statue to ask about the "mother of all battles" that
never came, and about the war for Baghdad that never materialized.
Standing before the statue, the journalist wonders why none of
Saddam's vaunted doubles—legend had it that he had ten of them—
had volunteered for a great battle worthy of the ruler's epic. "Where is
your Stalingrad, oh great hero? Where is your Leningrad which
endured a 3-year siege, and where hunger led its people to eat the
corpses of the dead? What of you?" The journalist knew he was speaking to history, that he was in Tikrit, the birthplace of Saladin, the city
that only the great Tamerlane had been able to subdue, and that Saddam had transformed into a cesspool of tyranny and domination.
"The mother of all battles. . . . If only you had spared us using this
label for a 'victory' over the Persians that American weapons had
made possible for you. You threatened America with the fate of the
Mongols faltering at the walls of Baghdad, but the Americans took
Baghdad, sweeping past the walls that were only a figment of your
imagination."

The journalist spoke to the statue of the looting and of the looters
picking apart what was left of the country's schools and hospitals and
other infrastructure. "They looted and tore through their country, for
you had raised them on a diet of greed that bordered on madness.
They were raised to this greed for they had seen you build your
palaces on the ruins of their shacks, they had seen your wealth alongside their deprivation. Your two sons adorned their palaces with the
most precious objects, their garages with the most elegant of cars,
while the looters had to satisfy themselves with petty theft that they
hauled off on their donkey carts: here a mattress, there a refrigerator,
or a set of tires."

The journalist spoke as a man possessed. "Saddam, do you know that the most damaging scene that broke the hearts of those who witnessed it was that of the American soldiers making their way in the alleyways of your prisons, displaying before a watchful world images of the tunnels of these prisons, so that free people everywhere would take to hating the Arabs." It was getting dark. An eerie silence had descended on the place. There were faint echoes of chants that the journalist could not make out, mixed with echoes of heavy bombardment. The journalist was eager to leave; then the statue called out to him, and the statue spoke: "Tell the Arabs to destroy all the statues that commemorate the rulers while they are still alive and in power. Tell them to remove the pictures of the rulers from the palaces and the streets and the government offices. Tell them that it is only the statues that are built after a ruler's death that will guarantee immortality."

If Tueni had to conjure up Saddam's ghost, four Iraqi leaders, members of the Governing Council, were given the unusual gift of a visit with the tyrant himself after his capture. Curiosity led them to the dictator's cell. But no illumination was to be offered these men; no second thoughts would be expressed by the tyrant. There was no depth in him that could even begin to speak to the depth of terror he had unleashed when he was the master and veritable owner of a whole large country. "The world is crazy," one of the visitors, Mowafak al-Rubaie, observed after he had had his encounter with the former ruler. "I was in his torture chamber in 1979, and now he was sitting there, powerless in front of me without anybody stopping me from doing anything to him. Just imagine, we were arguing, and he was using very foul language." There was a disarming honesty about Rubaie; he admitted that he had been reluctant to leave the dictator's cell, that his colleagues had left him behind for a minute or two. He had taunted the dictator about his meek surrender, so at odds with the legend of the noble Arab that he had presented of himself when he was in power. "May God curse you, Saddam Hussein, in this world and on Judgment Day" were Rubaie's parting words.

In that meeting, the former dictator revealed the hurt he must have nursed all along: an obsession with social class and pedigree. He had come from the most modest and impoverished of Iraq's social strata. But he had asked two of his four visitors, Ahmad Chalabi and Adnan Pachachi, to stay behind because they were "sons of good families," while dismissing the other two, Rubaie and Adel Abdul Mahdi, as "children of the streets." The dictator had "ennobled" himself; political power had raised him into the ranks of the classes he had envied and resented as he fought his way out of poverty and social marginality.

For the Americans in Iraq, the capture of Saddam Hussein was a milestone. The insurgency was not put down, but the American commanders and their civilian counterparts could be forgiven their moment of jubilation and perhaps the thought that jihadists pondering a passage to Tikrit or Fallujah across the Saudi or Syrian or Jordanian borders would have taken notice of the despot's surrender. What wealth the despot had stashed away in his hideouts was anyone's guess. For yet another moment, Americans and a majority of Iraq's people had an occasion for common joy. There were paper American flags on the streets of Baghdad, it was duly reported. Americans were beyond innocence this time, but while it lasted, the sense of deliverance from the despot recalled that buoyant, brilliant day months earlier when the dictator's statue in Firdos Square had been taken down in what seemed like a genuine coming together of Iraqis glad for their liberty and Americans thrilled to have provided it.

The large questions about Iraq's unity as a nation-state were still there the morning after. The evasions and the denials of sectarianism were still there, that debilitating insistence that sectarianism was alien to the land and an import brought to it by the foreign occupiers. The Sunni Arabs had yet to acknowledge the abnormality of what had passed for the familiar order of things under the despotism. But there were cracks even in the epicenter of Tikrit. As that Sunni stronghold hailed the anti-American insurgency, an undercurrent of pragmatism could be discerned in Saddam's birthplace. It was a pragmatism born of fear that Sunni maximalism may leave the Shia as the principal beneficiaries of the American interlude in Iraq. Raw power played its part. In the first year after the fall of the regime, the Fourth Infantry Division was headquartered in Tikrit, then the First Infantry Division had relieved it, and the town came to a realistic sense of the balance of forces on the ground.

Though no wholesale break with the Baathist legacy had swept Tikrit, there could be seen, in that town, the beginning of a separation from that legacy. A month after the dictator's surrender, an Arab reporter for *Al-Hayat*, Halim al-Aarji, found in Tikrit those second

thoughts and the desire to be rid of the stigma of that association with
Saddam Hussein. A man of eighty years took the reporter by the
hand and pointed to the Tigris nearby. "Saddam Hussein deprived us
of the joy of the river and its banks. He took from us the places of our
fathers and forefathers to build palaces which have now become
fortresses of the occupiers." A younger and more educated man split
the difference with the new order of things. Tikrit, he told the reporter,
was a city proud of its history, aware of its responsibilities. This was
why, the man added, it dealt with the anti-American insurgency with
"some caution and reserve: it neither condemned the attacks against
the Americans nor sanctioned them. None of its prayer and mosque
leaders called for jihad against the occupier. Had they done so, they
would have drowned the occupier in a sea of blood." The truth of that
account was open to debate, but behind it could be discerned a measure of pragmatism.

A well-known "man of religion," Sheikh Abdul Qadir Munir, on
the outskirts of Tikrit, gave the same reporter a variation on that
theme. "The Americans," he said, "had fallen into a great error. They
insist on equating us here with Saddam Hussein. We have been trying
to explain to them that the men of religion here have not authorized
armed struggle or declared the jihad. Had we done so, no American
would have been able to stay in Tikrit. . . . We believe that the time has
not come for legitimate armed resistance, because the Americans have
declared that they will be leaving before long."

This was the dictator's base of power, and then his hideout, but the
man had fallen, and revisionism had reared its head. It was not just the
Tigris he had taken away from them. There were assertions and complaints now that he had been cavalier with the town, that he had taken
Tikrit and its people for granted, that everything had been subjugated
to his will. Hypocrisy is the tribute vice pays to virtue. If this was the
way out of the culture of terror, this hypocrisy had its uses.

Tolerance would not be so easy to find, though; a Sunni mosque in
Baghdad that the dictator had named the Mother of the Drums
Mosque had been given a new name after the fall of the despotism. It
was named the Ibn Taymiyyah Mosque, for the zealous religious
scholar of Damascus, Ahmad Ibn Taymiyyah (1263–1328). Ibn
Taymiyyah was no ordinary jurist: he was severe and vigilant; he
hated the Shia; he abhorred the Sufi tradition in Islam; he had a
jaundiced view of philosophy and philosophers. His zealous and stern

view of the faith had long endeared him to the diehards. A people in search of reconciliation would have picked a different ancestor. Here, the faith had remained a weapon, sharpened for very worldly purposes. Now the Ibn Taymiyyah Mosque had become a center of Sunni political militancy. It sits on the deadly road to the airport, and in the way of places that acquire a reputation, it gives a sense of unease to a passerby approaching it. I drove by once in the company of two young Shia men, and a decided nervousness came over them as they surveyed the mosque and the neighborhood around it.

The changes that had overtaken Islam in the world beyond Iraq had found their way to that country as well. In Arab-Islamic lands, and in the Islamic diasporas in Europe, the faith had become portable. The preachers had found their way to the satellite television channels and had become media celebrities in their own right. This phenomenon came to Tikrit and Fallujah as well, and to Baghdad and Kufa. A writer for *Asharq Al-Awsat,* Tariq al-Homayed, caught the damage done by this new radicalized use of the faith. "The Friday prayer leaders," he observed, "have become political leaders who speak to the television cameras rather than men of religion who speak to the worshippers." The preachers in Fallujah—like their Shia counterpart, the leader of the Mahdi Army, Moqtada al-Sadr—had disfigured and bent the faith to their will and to their needs.

The fact that Iraq had been at heart a secular society was now of little practical consequence. Religion here had formerly yielded to tribalism; religious parties had historically been weaker in their pull than the secular political parties of the left and the pan-Arabists. But now the faith had been summoned. The preachers and prayer leaders had stepped forth to fill the void left by the collapse of despotism and by the inability of the foreign power to master the ways of the country. "Iraq was held together by the army before. Now it's held together by the mosques," a self-described secular Sunni academic at Baghdad University, Wamid Nadhmi, said of the new landscape. "For the first time in thirty years, I went to a mosque the other day because I needed a guard for our street and the only way to organize this was through the mosque."

The clerics were happy to oblige. This was the road to power that Hamas had taken in the Palestinian territories and Hezbollah in the Shia slums of Beirut. And the religion that came was cut to the fury, and the combat, of the moment. In Fallujah, amid the siege and the fighting, a Sunni cleric, Ali al-Juburi, gave an Arab reporter a sense of this new faith: "America is a handmaiden of Israel, a creation of the minds of Jewish rabbis. Warring against America is a duty incumbent on every Muslim man and woman." This town prided itself on the lore of tribal solidarity and the blood feud and the "unforgiving life that pleases the friend and the death that smites the enemy." The religion that sprouted here was but a response to the demise of the old Sunni, pan-Arabist regime. Fallujah was known as *madinat al-masajid,* the city of mosques. It was home to more than eighty mosques, and a whole new political—and military—role was to be given them.

A price would be paid for this terrible use of religion. The vigilantes murdering and mutilating American contractors and fighting American soldiers were to exact their tribute from Fallujah. They would come to be known by the honored name of *mujahidin Fallujah,* and with the honor and deference came a reign of virtue and bigotry. Masked men turned up in the center of the town and applied the whip in public to vendors of wine and liquor and pornographic videos. The rule of the sharia had come to Fallujah, they announced. In the back of a pickup truck, on one occasion, four "guilty" men were slowly driven through the town. The men were blindfolded, naked from the waist up. A young man of Fallujah, in his midtwenties, gave the deed his blessing. "This is the duty of the *mujahidin,* they are our example," he said. Yet another gave vigilante rule its real warrant. "The *mujahidin* liberated the city from the Americans, and it is their right to protect its reputation." The standoff in Fallujah, and the grim cruelties visited on the four American contractors, were the vigilantes' means of ascent and power.

Nothing escaped the zealots' attention: beyond the ban on liquor and pornographic material, they had decreed that pharmacies should refrain from selling medication that had any banned substances. There was method to this zeal, the vigilantes proclaimed. Virtue was indivisible: any person who would run afoul of the sharia was subject to the temptations held out by the Americans, liable to betray the faith and the folk. The vigilantes were unapologetic: they had no use for courts or elaborate procedure. Suspicion of backsliding was enough, and suspicion was everywhere. Who would stand up to a band that had strung up four Americans on a bridge nearby?

Occasionally, a voice could be heard breaking through the bravado, the voice of someone knowing that the armed men and the fiery sermons would beget nothing save the familiar ruin and retrogression. From Fallujah itself, a man of the Sunni religious class, Sheikh Muhammad al-Hamdani, allowed himself a dissenting thought: "Words are useless. We are suffering here, and the world is indifferent. We have no choice but to reach an accord with the Americans. We are an occupied people, and the occupier has a big war machine." The man had done the prudent thing; he had read the balance of material power and delivered a reading of the world as it was. He was the exception that proved the rule. This is not a culture that has ever been kind to those who tried to tell it verdicts it did not want to acknowledge. "They live like this, they will die like this, and their sons will do so after them," a wise and shrewd character in the Lebanese novelist Amin Maalouf's brilliant work of allegory on the Arab condition, *Leo Africanus,* says of the Muslim exiles of Granada in the year 1500. They are people living on the hope that they shall recover their fabled city once again: "Perhaps one day it may be necessary to teach them to look unflinchingly at their defeat, to explain to them that in order to get on one's feet again one must first admit that one is down on the ground. Perhaps someone will have to tell them the truth one day. But I myself do not have the courage to do so."

That passage in Maalouf's searing fiction captures the sentiments of a worldly old man of Granada, explaining to his nephew why he could not bear telling the Granadans who had taken to the road after the loss of their domain to the Castilians that their defeat and dispersion were final, and that no Muslim sovereign would take them back to their lost homeland. "You will ask me, why I should have told all those people the opposite of the truth. You see, Hasan, all these men still have, hung up on their walls, the key to their homes in Granada. Every day they look at it, and looking at it they sigh and pray. Every day their joys, their habits and a certain pride come back to their memory. . . . The only reason for their existence is the thought that soon, thanks to the Great Sultan or to Providence, they will find their house once again, with the color of its stones, the smell of its garden, the water of its fountain, all intact, unaltered, just as it has been in their dreams." Few Arabs have dared challenge those deadly dreams of their own people. The Arabs have been living in a "false world," as a man of the business elite wrote to me in mid-April 2004. He could have added that it was both false and powerful at the same time, that reality often faltered as its bearers attempted to breach those walls of denial and illusion. That lone man urging caution in Fallujah was not about to alter age-old ways.

In his Friday sermon of April 9, 2004, in the midst of Fallujah's troubles, the imam of the Grand Mosque of Mecca, Sheikh Saud al-Shraim, took up the events in Iraq. This was no ordinary preacher; his pulpit had unparalleled prestige. Nor was he a freelancer: the imam of the Grand Mosque stays within the parameters of the political and cultural order of his homeland. The mosque is close to the apex of the religious establishment, and the prayer leader here trims his sails to the preferences of the dynasty. There was something odd, "strange to the mind," the preacher said, playing out in Iraq. "Is it reasonable that the murder of four people is an unforgivable crime while the murder of an entire people is a small matter?" The cleric was of course referring to the four American civilian contractors ambushed and mutilated in Fallujah. Of these four people, and of the desecration of their corpses, the cleric would say no more in that sermon: he had come to speak of Iraq's troubles, and he had come with a broader agenda aimed at the Pax Americana and its message of reforming the Arab world. This was the perfect occasion for the Saudi religious elite to ward off the foreign power and to question its campaign on behalf of cultural and religious reform in Arab lands.

"What liberty do they want to bring to 'wounded Iraq' and to the 'dispossessed Palestine'? What happiness do they announce from the mouths of cannons, and what life do they advocate which is only based on corpses and murder and destruction, and the demolition of houses of worship?" the cleric asked. He wanted to "awaken" the Muslims to the dangers stalking them. "The infidels, people of oppression, may claim that they are a people of reform, the bearers of liberty, when in truth they are a people of destruction, in pursuit of their own interests."

It was known to this cleric, and to his audience, that "reform" had become the banner of this American war, a successor idea, perhaps, to the hunt for weapons of mass destruction. Faithful to the ruling dynasty, and to the Wahhabi creed of the realm, this cleric knew that his country had been on the defensive since September 11, that its teachings and its basic view of "the other," and the workings of its "charities," had been under intense scrutiny. With Fallujah, and the disorder of Iraq in the background, the preacher would go right at the messenger of reform. America couldn't proclaim the cause of reform and come bearing it to Islamic lands, he sermonized. "Where are these rights? Where is this liberty they preach?"

The Wahhabi preacher was no doubt relieved that the subject of the day was not the curriculum in Saudi schools, or the radical preachers stretching Wahhabism to the breaking point, railing against the infidels defiling the world. Fallujah had been kind: its battle came in the nick of time. Two years earlier, it had been the town of Jenin in the West Bank, and its siege by Israeli forces. That crisis too had come when needed. The Arabs, and the Saudi state in particular, were under the gaze of the world over the terrors of September 11. Jenin had once brimmed with pride that it was the home of a large number of homicide bombers. *Madinat al-shuhada,* the city of martyrs, it came to call itself. In 2002 the Israelis had laid siege to the town, and the battle of Jenin became an opportunity to return to the familiar pattern of Arab victimology and wrath. Fallujah had picked up where Jenin had left off. It was another pretext for keeping the advocates of reform at bay.

At considerable cultural remove from Mecca and the custodians of its Wahhabi orthodoxy, in the worldly city of Beirut, the Shia jurist Ayatollah Muhammad Hussein Fadlallah had spoken of Iraq a few days earlier. He offered a subtle view of the country, its transition from "the tyrant" to "the occupier." He of course had no use for the deposed Tikriti dictator. Few rulers and tyrants in history, he said, matched Saddam Hussein in both his cruelty and obtuseness. He had terrorized his people; he had attacked the Islamic Revolution in Iran and invaded Kuwait. With that invasion he had given "legitimacy to the American presence in the Gulf." He had sold himself, and his services, to the devil, and had filled the good earth of Iraq with mass graves and indiscriminate terror. Now that tyrant was gone, his reign demolished by the power that had been his patron. Iraqis were free, Fadlallah conceded, to form their own civic associations, to express themselves in their media, to shape a different country.

It was America that had made possible this liberty, and this man of the Shia world, who aspired to a place of great prominence among the Shia Arabs, was smart and shrewd enough to recognize this fact. There dances between his lines a tacit admission that this big change in the fortunes of Arab Shiism was owed to the Americans. Sunni and Tikriti dominion, he observes, had been shattered, but the occupying power that "destroyed the state has been unable to run the country and unwilling to give Iraqis the power and authority to guarantee their own security." What credit the occupying power had earned, she had now squandered, by continuing to insist on her own vision of Iraq, in the face of deeply felt Iraqi aspirations. It was clear, said Fadlallah, that America was bent on imposing a "secular state in Iraq disconnected from Islam in practically all aspects of public life. This is why the Americans have taken to the Kurdish model, and why they want Kurdistan's way applied throughout Iraq as though the Kurds live in a state separate from the Iraqi people." For this cleric, the foreign power had done its work but had overstayed its welcome, and the new Iraq would have to be built by its own people.

From the Wahhabi preacher, fury that the "infidel power" was having the run of the region, remaking Iraq (read: overthrowing the Sunni ascendancy) and speaking of more profound changes to be unleashed on the culture of the region; from the Shia beneficiary of this foreign power's new campaign, ambivalence at best, and grudging acceptance. This region has always been good at outwitting—and outwaiting—outsiders. For centuries, its ramparts may have been woefully inadequate and its people unable to ward off foreign armies, but its alleyways have always been bewildering to strangers from afar. Perhaps all cultures elude, and outwit, foreign intruders, sending them on false trails. But this Arab-Muslim civilization is particularly good at it. It was one thing to be opposed and second-guessed by the Wahhabi preachers and the Fallujah insurgents; the truculence of the Shia was altogether something different.

It wasn't just the inaccessibility of language that kept the American stewards at bay here. There was a more profound inaccessibility, which manifested itself in this Iraqi case: the outside power did not and could not really know the place. What the CPA knew about Iraq, and about Najaf and Fallujah, was spotty at best. The military commanders in the field were better positioned, closer to the ground, but the wellsprings of the culture were virtually impossible to reach. And the steady refusal of the Shia to come out, openly and without equivocation, in support of this American project had been one of the great surprises of this expedition into Iraq. There may or may not have been an explicit Shia strategy built into this war, but it had been the expectation that the country's Shia majority would take to the new order. The inevitable debate about "losing the Shia" had been gathering force; the fight with Sadr's militia brought it into the open.

If the dominant order in the Arab world had been worried that this Pax Americana in Iraq would find anchor among the Shia, those fears were allayed by the time the first American year in Iraq had come to a close. Despite what the bigot and terrorist Abu Musab al-Zarqawi, the confederate of Al Qaeda, had believed to be in the works, and despite the same worries among the political classes in Saudi Arabia, Egypt, and Jordan, there would be no Shia Trojan horse for the Pax Americana.

In the Saudi state, there had always lurked the fear that the eastern province, with its oil deposits, would be severed from the realm, that the Shia concentrated in that fragment of Arabia would rebel, and that the Najdi heartland of the Arabian Peninsula (the cradle of the Wahhabi creed and the geographic base of the Saudi state) would then be left to fend for itself. The fear was unnatural, but it was always there, and it made the rounds in the prelude to the Iraq war. In July 2002 a Rand Corporation foreign policy analyst of French birth, Laurent Murawiec, had provoked a small storm when he turned up before a blue-ribbon panel, the Defense Advisory Board, then headed by Richard Perle, and described Saudi Arabia as the "kernel of evil." The Saudis, he said, had been present at every level in the chain of global terror—the financing, the ideology, the execution. Murawiec had suggested that perhaps the Arabian Peninsula could be "de-Saudized," that the eastern province could be detached from the kingdom. He had done so in an off-the-record meeting, but the proceedings had leaked. In Washington, the briefing could be dismissed as the work of an analyst with a dark view of the Saudi state. But in an Arab world at once attentive to America's "chatter" and unable to really comprehend the ways of American political life, the briefing was proof that an American scheme for the region was afoot. In this scheme, the Shia of Iraq and of the eastern province in Arabia itself and the other Gulf states would break with the Arab world and opt for American patronage. The fact that the Defense Advisory Board was headed by Richard Perle, and answered to Donald Rumsfeld and Paul Wolfowitz, was the proof needed of the danger of this scheme.

For all the fury of the antagonism between America and the Iranian theocratic regime, the thought that America would turn its back on the Arabs and enlist Iran and its Arab Shia tributaries in a new order in the region was an unexamined idea in the Arab political imagination. The Iraq war revived that old, dark view of Shia intentions and of their willingness to break with the Arab world. A year into the new American occupation, that convergence of interests between the Pax Americana and the Shia had not materialized.

There was no shortage of explanations for the alienation of the Shia from American power. In one interpretation, it had been idle for America to try to win over the Shia because the well had been poisoned by the American "abandonment" of them back in 1991. In other words, the liberating power had come a generation too late: it had come after a particularly cruel decade had heaped on the Shia great devastation and sorrow. There was no faith in the foreign power that had called for an insurrection only to walk away from the rebels. There was no certainty that the outcome would be different this time around, and that those who flocked to America's banners would not be betrayed yet again. This was a population with a long, bitter history. The suspicion and the fear ran deep in them.

In yet another interpretation, America had "lost" this community of Iraq by refusing to opt right away for direct elections that would have allowed the weight of Shia numbers to prevail in the new polity. In this view, this was when the Grand Ayatollah had opted to distance himself from American power. The Kurds had cut their own deal with America, and the Sunnis were bound to be sheltered and protected by the weight of the Arab states beyond Iraq, Sistani no doubt believed. The Shia could come out empty-handed in this new Iraq: it had happened to them before, and there was no guarantee that this new American order would differ from the old, familiar history. The fear of a Shia theocracy that had stayed America's hand during Desert Storm still stalked this encounter between America and the Iraqi Shia. True, the attacks of September 11, 2001, had been waged by Sunni Islamists, and America had learned in a particularly grim way that the fears of Shia radicalism spawned by its experience in Iran and Lebanon had to be balanced by a new awareness of terrible dangers from Islamist movements in Sunni Arab lands. But the Shia stepchildren could be forgiven their own view of the workings of history. Pax Americana was still tied to the ruling orders in Saudi Arabia, Egypt, Jordan, and the Arab states of the Persian Gulf.

It was known to these Shia of Iraq that decades of diplomatic and commercial traffic with the imperial power had given the Saudis a special kind of access to Washington. The Shia politicians and clerics needed no expertise in American politics to know of the weight of

Saudi Arabia in the American councils of power. There were countless American authors chronicling the intimacy of the "House of Saud" and the "House of Bush." There were reports by journalists in the know that the ambassador of Saudi Arabia in Washington knew the intimate secrets and workings of the American system. There was Washington's legendary journalist, Bob Woodward, in his first draft of history, his hugely publicized book *Plan of Attack,* reporting that the Saudi ambassador, Prince Bandar bin Sultan, had been informed of the imminence of the war against Saddam Hussein two days before the American secretary of state had been let in on the decision. On the very day of the launching of the war, March 19, 2003, the Saudi ambassador had been summoned to the West Wing by National Security Adviser Condoleezza Rice and told that the attack was hours away. That kind of access could not be matched by anyone in Iraq.

Egypt too had worked out the terms of its own relationship with the Americans. That state may have been impoverished and burdened, but its ruler knew the ropes, and its influence in Israeli-Palestinian matters gave it a good deal of diplomatic leverage. Egypt took America's coin but ran afoul of America's purposes. Its intellectual class and media ran a steady campaign against the Pax Americana, while its ruler presented himself as a reliable ally. There were no Shia assets remotely comparable to the weight of the established Arab order of power. A whole political and cultural and military edifice had favored the Sunni Arabs: there were "the Arabists" in the imperial capital, and the world-view that informed generations of American officials who dealt with the Arab world. They had imbibed truths given them by a historiography fashioned by Sunni Arab nationalists and their Christian Arab partners in the Levant and the Fertile Crescent. That historiography had given pride of place to the Palestinian question; it had looked past—and through—the minority communities in the Arab world. It had paid no heed to the terrors of Iraq, for there too, under Saddam Hussein, that historiography had reigned. It was symbolized in the union of the Sunni despot and his Christian foreign minister, Tariq Aziz, who took the tyrant's deeds and prettified them on Western shores, and in the Arab circles of power.

The Shia of Iraq could not remake themselves overnight. The habits of command and power, the ways of order, were alien to them. Their leaders, like their Shia counterparts elsewhere in the Arab world, were outsiders. In Iraq, under the Baath, the Shia of any talent were in exile or in prison; then there were the clerics in the shrine towns and the seminaries ducking the tyrant's fury. Moqtada al-Sadr was what he was—a young avenger given a rare chance, by an American invasion, to settle his accounts with the world. The historical skills of the clerics were defective; their knowledge of the outside world was the kind of knowledge given to men in a cocoon.

Perhaps this impasse between America and the Shia was inevitable all along. The Israeli experience with the Shia of Lebanon, in the aftermath of Israel's Lebanon war of 1982, was a forerunner of what awaited the Americans in Iraq. The analogy is not perfect in every way, but that war in Lebanon was for the Shia of that country a war of deliverance. Israel had swept into Lebanon, it should be recalled, in the summer of 1982, to put an end to the Palestinian sanctuary. The people of southern Lebanon's towns and villages, who had endured Palestinian anarchy and bravado over the preceding decade, received the Israelis with rice and flowers. Israel had for all practical purposes been the midwife of a Shia resurgence in Lebanon: it had defeated and banished the Palestinians, doing for the Shia what they had not been able to do for themselves.

But wars of liberation have a short shelf life, it turns out. The liberated have a way of forgetting the old tyranny and of wanting the new alien rulers to pack up and leave. The Shia now wanted Israel out of their land. On the coattails of the Israelis, local (principally Christian) militias had stepped forth to claim new power for themselves. No Shia political movements of any standing or independence would embrace Israel in broad daylight. A year or so after the rice and flowers, the peace between Israel and the Shia had broken down. Trouble erupted on a particularly symbolic day: October 16, 1983, the day of Ashura, the tenth of the Muslim month of Muharram, commemorating the martyrdom of Imam Hussein. An armed Israeli convoy had coincidentally turned up in the southern Shia town of Nabatiyya on that day and had tried to make its way through the mourners and flagellants. Two people were killed, several wounded.

The die was cast. The next day, the highest Shia cleric in the land issued a fatwa calling for "civil obedience" and "resistance to occupation in the south." Dealing with Israel, he said, was "absolutely impermissible." Every generation, this cleric exhorted, has its own great battle, makes its own choice: the believer can "soar and sacrifice," or he can "submit and betray." It didn't take long before the suicide bombers

and the "martyrs" turned up. On November 4, a suicide driver struck
the Israeli headquarters in the coastal city of Tyre. He was a young
man, it was reported, around twenty years of age. It was a calamitous
day for the Israelis: sixty people were killed, including twenty-nine
Israeli soldiers and security personnel. Israel responded by closing a
bridge that connected the southern hinterland to Beirut. Clinton
Bailey, a thoughtful Israeli academic (and a remarkably sympathetic
scholar on the Bedouins of Negev and Sinai) who served as a liaison
officer in southern Lebanon, summed up the impact: "The basis of the
southern economy collapsed. It was this event that finally smashed the
last friendly sentiments toward Israel." A relentless war had erupted
between the Shia and the Israeli forces. In 1984 alone, there were more
than nine hundred attacks against Israeli soldiers in southern Lebanon.
The brigades of Hezbollah were not far behind. Israel held on in the
ancestral land of the Shia but was embattled. In the year 2000 a brave
soldier and political leader, Ehud Barak, liquidated that venture and
walked away from Lebanon and the security zone Israel had established in southern Lebanon.

The specificity and distinctiveness of Iraq notwithstanding,
Lebanon was a cautionary tale about the short shelf life of wars of liberation, and about the ability and the willingness of the Shia Arabs to
cut their own deal with "the stranger." It is the stepchild's burden and
handicap, this lack of historical self-confidence and the need, rather
like that of Caesar's wife, to be above suspicion. The Shia of Lebanon
had displayed that timidity in their traffic with Israel, and the Shia of
Iraq showed it as well. In the Arabian Peninsula, the House of Saud
had happily made its accommodation with American power in the
mid-1940s; Egypt had made its own separate peace with Israel and the
Pax Americana three decades later. Even Yasser Arafat had concluded
the peace of Oslo in 1993, and for a few years at least, was able and
willing to defend it. The "schismatics"—the Alawite rulers of Syria,
and the Shia of Lebanon and Iraq—were not possessed of the self-
confidence needed for grand historical breaks with established ways
and pieties.

It could not have been harder, the coming of age of the Iraqi Shia, their
assumption of political power and responsibility. The Shia political
temperament had always swung from quietism to rebellion; in Iraq,
those wild swings of political emotions were the "normal" responses of

a community long repressed and denied but now awakening to its own power. Sadr was a young upstart, but he had noble lineage; Sistani was authoritative but too subtle for the young and for the dispossessed, and the secularist leaders had not yet come into their own.

Where the Kurds had clarity—in their heart of hearts they desired independence but were willing to settle for the safer course of autonomy—and the Sunnis had their furious fight for their lost dominion, the Shia were truly in the wind. They were played upon by all sorts of political tendencies. There were those who genuinely believed that they had come into a new role as the inheritors and defenders of Iraq's statehood and independence—against the Turks to the north, against the Iranians, against the other Arabs. For this current, the choice was bound to be secular nationalism in order to keep the borders—and the communities—of Iraq whole and intact. There were others given to the claims of historical revenge, and to fanciful ideas that the country as a whole could be won and a theocratic regime put in place. There were optimists who were willing to let their weight and their power assert themselves in the normal push and pull of political life. And there were those whose opinions were informed by that brooding Shia view of history, that the faithful are always undone by the wicked and the worldly.

This was still a country, we are reminded by one of its sophisticated sociologists, Ibrahim al-Haidari, where the Shia had to resort to tricks to hide their sectarian identity, to select first names for their children that could pass them off as Sunni Muslims, or to conceal the town of their birth if it was too blatantly Shia. A well-off Shia businessman of Baghdad, Isam al-Assadi, told me that he had been made to pay a heavy fine, fifty thousand dollars, by Uday Hussein, for having given his seven children Shia names. The Shia were still the children of Karbala and its great drama of virtuous defeat. Sure, they were armed and empowered, and in the streets, but the historical confidence had not yet come. By the objective measures of material power and demography, the Shia had arrived. A young and shrewd man of the Hashemite dynasty of Jordan—his family of course had a deep and tragic knowledge of Iraq—observed to me that the future of Iraq now depended on the Shia, and on their ability to show "magnanimity" to the other communities of the country. They had won, he said, and in victory, magnanimity. It was easy for this man of genuine tolerance, an heir to power and pedigree, to make this call. But the Shia temper in Iraq was made of more volatile—and fragile—material.

Iraqi history had not been kind to the Shia. Politically disinherited, they had drifted into commerce and the marketplace. In the 1950s, they had filled the void left by the banishment and expulsion of the Jewish community, which had had a huge role in the economic life and commerce of Baghdad. But that shelter had been taken away from them as well: the chambers of commerce of Baghdad and Basra had been forcibly removed from their control. The state had subordinated the economy, and the state had become for all practical purposes a Sunni monopoly. The two sects, the Sunnis and the Shia, were marked: they were, in the words of one of Iraq's own, the writer Hassan al-Alawi, the "sect of the rulers," and the "sect of the ruled." The political order of the Arab world beyond and around Iraq reinforced that sense of Shia anxiety. There were worries that that order would pass onto gullible Westerners fears of Shia primacy within Iraq. Foreign diplomacy threatened to rob the Shia of their gains in the name of "balance of power" considerations and of regional stability.

This was not just a dark view of history held by a people long shut out of power. It was the truth of their history. Consider this scene, drawn from the furious diplomacy and intrigue that led to the creation of Iraq in 1921: Gertrude Bell, Britain's "Oriental Secretary" and would-be maker of this realm, had come calling on the *naqib* of Baghdad, Abdul Rahman al-Gailani. (*Naqib* meant the head of the notables and religious guild.) He was a revered figure, the undisputed religious leader of the Sunnis in Baghdad, with a family mosque and shrine near his home; his ancestors had been ascendant in the religious life of Baghdad for centuries. The most renowned of his ancestors had been a holy man and a founder of his own Sufi order, Abdul Qader al-Gailani, who had lived a long, exemplary life (1064–1166). The shrine honoring him had been built in the thirteenth century. The British were now casting about for a king, and an heir to this legacy had to be consulted: Gailani would either be king or kingmaker. To his British visitor, the old man had a simple, private message: stay in Baghdad, ignore the naysayers and the nationalists. "Most of those who spoke against you are men without name or honor. But I tell you to beware of the Shiahs. I have no animosity against the Shia. . . . But turn your eyes on the pages of history and you will see that the salient characteristic of the Shiahs is their volatility. Did they not murder Musa bin Ali whom they now worship as a God? Idolatry and mutability are combined in them. Place no reliance on them."

This was from a man who had claimed that he was no enemy of the

Shia, that they loved and respected him. The *naqib* had pushed against an open door. Bell and her colleagues in the British colonial bureaucracy had turned away from the Shia. We will have to wait for future chronicles of this Iraq war (we won't have Bell's literacy, of course, but the raw material will do) to know with some depth and detail the campaign the Arab rulers waged with this new imperial power against traffic with the Shia. The Saudis, the Egyptians, and the Jordanians made no secret of their dread of an Iraq ruled by the Shia. The fear of Iran was the standard alibi—and no doubt partly sincere and justified. But the age-old struggle within the Arab world between the Sunni rulers and the Shia communities was playing out as well. Here is a hint that the status of the Shia in the Arab world had not changed. It comes from Paul Bremer's account of his regency in Iraq. It is early in Bremer's tenure, June 4, 2003, and Bremer is meeting with President Bush at an American air base in Qatar. The political leader wants to know from his man on the scene if this American project will work. "Will they be able to run a free country?" the president asked. "Some of the Sunni leaders in the region doubt it. They say, 'All Shia are liars.' What's your impression?" A whole history had passed between the time of Gertrude Bell and that of George W. Bush, but the new imperial power was being fed what the old one had been told. And this message had been given the American president by leaders steeped in the politics of intrigue and dissimulation, men who have never told their people—or foreign powers—simple truths about the doings in their domains. "Well, I don't agree," said Bremer, to his credit. "I've already met a number of honest, moderate Shia and I'm confident we can deal with them."

It was not lost on the Shia that the Arab campaign against Ahmad Chalabi had made much of his return to his country on the "back of an American tank" (he had actually been given an American military airlift) while conveniently looking away from the similar return from exile of the Sunni Arab nationalist Adnan Pachachi. Pachachi had been a figure of the 1960s, a foreign minister of that era. In exile, he had made his home in the United Arab Emirates. He knew the princes and the rulers of the Arab states of the Gulf and partook of their outlook. His claim to power, and to restoration, was taken as something inevitable and legitimate. He was a man of the old order; he hailed from a Sunni family of Baghdad merchants who had made their way to politics under the monarchy and had spawned state ministers, parliamentary deputies, two prime ministers. In other Arab lands, there was nothing threatening about him: he offered the reassuring prospect of Sunni primacy but without the violence and cruelty of the Tikritis.

Pachachi had been a beneficiary of America's war in Iraq, but no one on the Arab satellite channels, or in the Arabic media in London, described him as a "favorite of the Pentagon" or a "carpetbagger" or an instrument of American power. He flew under the radar: those who knew him or purported to speak for him had let the word out that this was an Arab nationalist of a familiar, respectable mold, that he was a man to keep his distance from Israel and Israelis, that he would not be unduly solicitous of America's larger purposes in the war. Chalabi was, of course, seen and depicted in a dramatically different manner. The campaign against the man doubled as a statement about his sect as well.

The Arab sense of belonging, and of outsiderness, is unusually sharp. The Shia hadn't been granted the right to their political primacy within Iraq. A big change in the Fertile Crescent was afoot. In the 1970s, it had taken brute force, an intermittent civil war between the Sunnis and the Alawites in Syria, and the skills of Hafiz al-Assad, to bring about the Alawite conquest of military power in Damascus. The Syrian (Sunni) bourgeoisie had waged its own struggle against the regime, but the military rulers had triumphed. A decade later, it had been Beirut's turn: that city had to make way for the Shia underclass who had flooded and remade the city, and challenged the Sunni merchant notables who had been Beirut's mainstay. Now the fight for Baghdad was of a piece with this history. This was an epochal change in the ordering of Arab society, nothing less than the rise of Arab Islam's stepchildren from obscurity and acquiescence. Power had shifted in three great cities, and this had happened over the course of three or four decades.

The new possibilities for the Shia, and their traditional fears of what the world held in store for them, were both laid bare when the Bush administration appeared eager to shed Iraq's burden, and to turn for help to the United Nations. This change began in the opening months of 2004 and was given added impetus by the American losses in April. An administration that had had no use for the United Nations now appeared to be "dumping stocks" and turning to the international body it had both spurned and ridiculed. An envoy was found, Lakhdar Brahimi, an Algerian diplomat of pan-Arab outlook and orientation.

He had been foreign minister of his country, a member in good standing of its political class, and a functionary of the League of Arab States. It stood to reason (American reason of course, uninformed as to the terrible complications of Arab life) that Brahimi was "an Arab" and was thus better prepared to understand Iraq's realities than Paul Bremer. But nothing in Brahimi's political experience had given him sympathy for Iraq's Shia—or Kurds, for that matter. Brahimi hailed from the same political class that had wrecked the Arab world. He partook of the ways of that class: populism, anti-Americanism, anti-Zionism. Coming to heal Iraq, he brought his ideological baggage with him. He opined that Israel and its policies were the "poison" of the region. There was a bitter fight between the insurgents in Fallujah and the marines; Brahimi described that fight as the "collective punishment" of an entire city. He described Paul Bremer as the "dictator of Iraq" and spoke of the Governing Council as an illegitimate, unelected body. The man was an Algerian who had spent a lifetime with the authoritarians of the Arab world; his scruples about unelected governments were odd, to say the least.

More problematic still, Brahimi had come forth with a "technocratic" scheme for an interim Iraqi government that would sideline key players within the Iraqi Governing Council. He seemed to go out of his way to pick a fight with, and to single out, Ahmad Chalabi as a political figure he was determined to marginalize. The technocratic scheme—a government of apolitical experts—was a thinly veiled attack on the gains that the Shia and the Kurds had made after the fall of the Baathist-Tikriti edifice.

The Shia leaders saw through Brahimi's scheme. A history of disinheritance had given them the knowledge they needed to recognize those who bear them ill will. Gone was their old timidity: they would strike back at Brahimi's proposals. The Pax Americana may have been eager to unload its imperial burden, but the Shia would not oblige. On the fifth of May, twenty-four of the leading political figures in the country, drawn from the Iraqi National Congress, and the Daawa and Hezbollah parties (both of them Islamist Shia parties), and the Faili Kurds (the Kurds are principally Sunnis; the Failis are the minority Shia sect among the Kurds) took apart the Brahimi proposal in a public declaration. The political transition, they noted, ought to be a product of a "serious dialogue among the political and religious forces of Iraq." The United Nations envoy had sought to "bypass the Iraqi reality and to leave out those political forces." There was no "neutrality" in those proposals; they merely "perpetuated the failed policies of the past" which had denied Iraqis the chance to make their own history. Moreover, these proposals, the signatories asserted, "opened the door for the return to power of men of the old regime, which is completely unacceptable, and which would guarantee instability and force many among our people to take up, on their own, the defense of Iraq's future."

No surprise, Chalabi was among the signatories, and so was a widely respected ally of his, the religious scholar Sayyid Muhammad Bahr al-Ulum, himself a member of the Governing Council and a descendant of one of the noted clerical families in the land. A leader of the Marsh Arabs, from the south, Abdul Karim al-Mohammedawi, a man who had suffered six years of imprisonment under Saddam Hussein, had attached his name to the statement as well: this was no political exile with years in London behind him. The transition scheme of Brahimi had run into serious opposition. The United Nations was ensnared in a scandal of its own, the oil-for-food program it had administered and the allegations that the program had involved systematic kickbacks and bribes. There was no great faith in that organization among Iraqis who had been opponents of the old regime. Nor was there any faith in Brahimi himself.

Brahimi had served in the League of Arab States, and that organization had looked away from the terrors of the Iraqi regime of Saddam Hussein. He made his home in Paris, and the traffic of his political life had not been with the Shia opponents of the Baath, or with the Kurds. He was a creature of official Arab life. On the evidence of it, he had no great fondness for American power, nor did he view this new Iraqi order with any enthusiasm. An assignment had come his way, and the way of the secretary-general of the United Nations, Kofi Annan. The "technocracy" he proposed was an escape from the politics of Iraq, but these political inheritors were in no mood to step out of the way. The place of the Shia in the new order in Baghdad was at the heart of this controversy.

And those Shia possibilities were being contested in the streets, among the Shia themselves as well. Those men and women signing petitions and playing the conventional political game still had the brigades of Moqtada al-Sadr to contend with. There was no frontal battle with Sadr. The clerical and political establishment had given him rope and time. He had brought the economic life of Najaf and Karbala to a standstill. The hierarchy—religious and political, not to mention the merchants and shopkeepers—had eyed the Mahdi Army with suspicion. The people of Najaf were not eager to have a major battle with the American forces fought out in their city. Four weeks into the crisis between the Mahdi Army and the American authorities, the clerical establishment was done with hints and subtlety. In a Friday sermon of May 7, one of Najaf's most noted prayer leaders, Sheikh Sadr al-Din Qabanji, known for his close ties to Grand Ayatollah Sistani, called on Sadr's militants to quit the city: "Listen to the advice of the *ulama,* come let us together find another way. Go back to your homes and towns and defend those places, and banish the occupiers and the Baathists alike." This was delivered from Shiism's holiest pulpit, the Imam Ali Mosque. And it had a forthright assertion of Najaf's own prerogative against the Sadrists who had come into Najaf from the slums of Baghdad. "The Najafis are the ones to bear the responsibility for Najaf's defense."

Qabanji's sermon, it was known, had the blessing of Sistani and bore his distinct mark and caution. The Mahdi Army was a movement of the dispossessed; order and hierarchy and property, and the rule of the elders and the tribal notables arrayed around the senior jurists, now sought to contest the ways of the street. Sadr and his lieutenants had grown increasingly radical and unsettled. In the city of Basra, on the very same day that Sheikh Qabanji had taken on the Sadrists, a representative of Moqtada al-Sadr, Sheikh Abdul Sattar Bahadali, speaking to three thousand worshippers, with his assault rifle next to him, offered a reward of a hundred thousand Iraqi dinars (seventy dollars) to any believer who would capture a British female soldier; he said that that soldier could then be kept as a concubine of her captor. There was no need for the clerical hierarchy to speak of the dangers posed by the Sadrists. The latter were doing a fair job of it themselves. Anti-Americanism, an animus toward the Anglo-American coalition, was one thing, but the keeping of "concubines" and slave women was a wholly different matter, a clear pathology on display.

There was no subtlety here: this was a direct appeal by Sadr and his inner circle to the yearnings of the young and to their notions of hegemony and war booty. This primitivism, it so happened, came on the very day that an audiotape of Osama bin Laden turned up offering "ten thousand grams of gold" to anyone who would kill Paul Bremer or the Algerian-born United Nations envoy to Iraq, Lakhdar Brahimi, and "one thousand grams of gold" to anyone who would kill a civilian or a soldier from Japan or Italy. The air was filled with talk of "infidels" and "apostasy" and "Crusaders" and "slave women" and "grams of gold." Sistani's gift remained the assurance given a people caught in the throes of great upheaval that their tradition was there for them as a safe harbor, that amid the troubles there remained political limits and reason. Men can't live on their nerves, and Sadr had nothing to offer save ceaseless agitation. Tyranny had wrecked the country; now anarchy offered ruin in its own way.

And there was cunning and method to the violence: Shia moderation appeared to be a target of political murders of brutal efficiency and clear intent. In the preceding year, there had been the assassinations of Abdul Majid al-Khoei, of Ayatollah Muhammad Baqir al-Hakim, and of Aqila al-Hashimi, a diplomat, who was one of three women on the Governing Council. On May 17 the terror struck again. There was no randomness here: the target was Ezzedine Salim, a Shia man of letters who held the rotating presidency of the Iraqi Governing Council. Salim, sixty-one years of age, was killed by a suicide bomber at a checkpoint on the perimeter of the CPA headquarters. The assailants were the terror brigades of Abu Musab al-Zarqawi, hacking away at "collaborators" and "heretics" and "apostates." Salim was not the big political-religious player that Ayatollah Hakim had been, but his life's work, and his political message, were unmistakably an inheritance of moderation and decency.

Salim, educated in Najaf in the early 1960s, had come from Basra, and his literary-religious output had the flavor of that port city. There was a Basra tradition of poetry and letters shaped both by Shiism and by the openness of a port city touched by Iranian and Indian currents and the ways of sea trade. Salim, as we learn from a fond eulogy of him by the Kurdish author and journalist Sami Shoursh, had started out in the Shia underground movement, the Daawa Party, said to have been launched by the great figure of Iraqi Shiism of recent years, the "first martyr," the jurist and writer Ayatollah Muhammad Baqir al-Sadr. Salim paid for this affiliation: he was imprisoned for four years, from 1974 to 1978. Upon his release, he had made his way to Kuwait, and in that city-state, he was to give voice to his disillusionment with radical politics. He took to a life of writing. He produced a steady output of religious and philosophical books of rigor and sophistication. He quit Kuwait in the early 1980s for Iran. By all accounts, this passage to Iran had not been a happy choice. Kuwait was then in the shadow of Saddam Hussein, and the Sunni-Shia division within it had grown unusually acrimonious.

Salim did not find ease in Iran: he was on the move, with long excursions to Syria and Lebanon. He had no taste for the Iranian theocrats, and was much distressed by the cavalier, patronizing way they treated Iraqi exiles. In his Iranian sojourn, he had formed a deep personal and political tie to Ayatollah Muhammad Baqir al-Hakim of the Supreme Council for the Islamic Revolution in Iraq. It is said that he encouraged Hakim to reach out to the Americans—no small undertaking for a Shia cleric with an Iranian sanctuary.

In Iran, Salim had seen the wages of theocratic rule; he came back to Iraq eager to work for the cause of a pluralist society. He accepted membership on the Governing Council, where he was a consistently liberal and secularist voice. He cast his vote on behalf of women's rights and was unfailingly sympathetic to the Kurds and their aspirations. He knew that his traumatized country had to be governed with mercy and care, so he advocated giving the Sunnis the psychological assurance they needed in the new order. He urged subtlety in the pursuit of de-Baathification. For him, the roots of the Baath ideology had to be struck down, but the old Baathists were to be treated humanely and granted the possibility of rehabilitation. There was nothing in this man of Moqtada al-Sadr's radicalism, or of the zealotry of Iran's hard-liners. But he was a Shia, and he was on the Governing Council, and so an ideal target for Zarqawi's campaign of terror.

Iraq's American regency was reeling: displays of utter helplessness in the face of terror alternated with empty assertions of hegemony. Three days after the murder of Salim, American and Iraqi forces in Baghdad ransacked the headquarters of the Governing Council member Ahmad Chalabi and raided his house, stormed into his bedroom. The raid had been at the behest of the Iraqi judiciary, it was claimed, and the police had come to arrest members of Chalabi's entourage involved in "kidnapping, torture, embezzlement and the theft of government property." This was a stunning reversal of fortune. In the way of such facile descriptions, Chalabi had been the "Pentagon's favorite Arab." The journalists loved this cliché, and it acquired the status of truth. He had enjoyed access to the highest reaches of the Bush administration. Four months before this public American break with him, he had been in the gallery, seated just behind the first lady, as President Bush delivered his State of the Union speech. The coalition that had launched the war had begun to come apart.

Chalabi had been running afoul of his erstwhile American allies and backers. He had always been at odds, at any rate, with the Central Intelligence Agency and the Department of State. And there had been personal enmity between him and Paul Bremer. On February 19, he was quoted in a *Daily Telegraph* article with words that startled even his most fervent backers. He dismissed the charges that he had provided the Americans with faulty intelligence: "We are heroes in error. As far as we're concerned we've been entirely successful. That tyrant Saddam is gone and the Americans are in Baghdad. What was said before is not important. The Bush Administration is looking for a scapegoat. We're ready to fall on our sword if he [Bush] wants." Those remarks had come at a time when the Bush administration was on the defensive about the course of the Iraq war. At the Department of Defense, the hawks were reeling. For them, Chalabi was now beyond the pale. I was given a small view of his changed status on a trip to Iraq I made for *U.S. News and World Report* with Deputy Secretary of Defense Paul Wolfowitz during that period. Chalabi was off-limits then, the campaign to marginalize him in full swing. Wolfowitz met with a good number of Iraqi leaders, and Chalabi, a presumed ally of the deputy secretary of defense, was given the cold shoulder. (*Wall Street Journal* editorial writer Rob Pollack offers a similar experience of his own, when, traveling with Wolfowitz in June 2004, he had to "break away" from Wolfowitz's military delegation to visit with Ahmad Chalabi.)

But there were more ruptures to come. There had been a disagreement over de-Baathification: the Bush administration was now eager to rehabilitate elements of the old regime. Chalabi, who had been a stalwart of the de-Baathification effort, would not step out of the way. The change in policy, he said, was akin to putting the Nazis back in charge in postwar Germany. Then there had been that quarrel, with and over the UN envoy Lakhdar Brahimi. It was a casting director's dream, that encounter of Brahimi and Chalabi. The latter had been the driving force behind an inquiry into the UN-administered oil-for-food program and the allegations of bribes and kickbacks leveled at it. With access to machinery of the Governing Council, he had helped launch an inquiry into that program, and had come into possession of records documenting a pattern of abuse and corruption. The Iraqi polity that the Algerian envoy proposed to hatch was anathema to everything Chalabi had in mind. But Brahimi was now carrying water for the Americans, and Chalabi had crossed one red line too many. He had ridden with the great foreign power and had broken with it.

Chalabi and his former American patrons had now reached the breaking point. There were charges that Chalabi aides may have passed intelligence secrets to Iran. These charges were odd: Iran was next door, and a factor in the political life of Iraq. Over the course of the preceding decade, Chalabi had been in and out of Iran, a fact that had been open knowledge in Washington. Moreover, in the run-up to the war, a Shia exile group of considerable weight, the Supreme Council for the Islamic Revolution in Iraq, and its Badr Brigade, based in Iran and supported by that theocratic government, had been pulled into the American diplomacy, and a leader of this group, a member of the Hakim family, had been appointed to the Governing Council. Mutual disillusionment had come. In Washington there was disarray, and a scramble to evade and shift responsibility for the course—and the mounting costs—of the war. In Baghdad, the first phase of the American interlude was drawing to a close.

Chalabi had seen and assimilated this shift, and made his adjustments. He wanted a transfer of sovereignty to the Iraqis. "The relation between sovereignty and power is not unidirectional" was the way he put it to National Security Advisor Condoleezza Rice. He challenged the director of Central Intelligence, George Tenet, to prove that he had given American intelligence to the Iranians. He had seen no classified American documents, he said; he had had discussions of a "general nature" with the American officials once said to be his patrons and defenders, Vice President Dick Cheney and Secretary of Defense Donald Rumsfeld. He further broke with the American regency on the matter of Moqtada al-Sadr. "How many lives would it take to serve an arrest warrant?" he had asked Paul Bremer. He thought that the Sadrists had to be pulled into the political process. If Chalabi had allies at the Pentagon, those officials were now fighting for their political lives, overwhelmed by the Abu Ghraib prison scandals, which had erupted a fortnight or so before the raid on Chalabi's home. Nor could the assertion, made in Baghdad by the CPA, that the American regent, Paul Bremer, had nothing to do with this raid be given credence. It was easy to see through the pretense. The judge on the Iraqi

Criminal Court who ordered this raid had been a protégé and an appointee of Paul Bremer. A deed of this kind, like all important decisions in Baghdad, could have only been undertaken at the behest of the American regency. Iraq was six weeks away from the transfer of authority. Names were being picked—perhaps they were already picked—to administer the new Iraq, and to enable the Bush administration to claim that sovereignty had been granted the Iraqis, that a seminal goal of the American regency had been accomplished. It had become timely, and urgent, to silence Chalabi, and to remove him from the circle of claimants to the transitional régime. In the battle for bureaucratic turf, Chalabi had lost out to the Central Intelligence Agency's protégé, Iyad Allawi. The larger context of this raid was spelled out by an experienced foreign affairs columnist who had known Chalabi for more than three decades, the *Washington Post*'s Jim Hoagland: "The idea that this raid had nothing to do with Chalabi's bitter opposition to US policy will be seen as laughable by Iraqis and other Arabs. They know the long American record of supporting or accepting national kleptocracies in Egypt, Jordan, Saudi Arabia and elsewhere. Iraq is not Vietnam, but Baghdad is turning into a latter-day Saigon—a place where intelligence agents and prison guards are laws unto themselves and take revenge on uppity locals while senior Americans help or look the other way."

In his political fight, Chalabi was more or less alone. He would have to fight within Iraq, for in the Arab world beyond Iraq, the knives were out for him. He was an uppity man from a sect not yet given the right to defiance. In the Arab circles beyond Iraq, it was important that Chalabi's bid for power, and for a place in his country, be thwarted. This was a Shia who knew his way around the modern world. The mathematician and former banker was devoid of the reticence of his community. He had had the social capital of his class and his wealthy family, he had had the best of American education at MIT and the University of Chicago, earning a PhD in mathematics from the latter institution. In exile, he remained unbent, free of that self-pity that invariably trailed the Shia like a permanent shadow.

Chalabi was totally at odds with the pieties of Arab nationalism and Pan-Arabism. He was a child of the old order of Iraq, a scion of one of the ancient régime's aristocratic-merchant families. On the eve of the revolution of 1958, the Chalabis were perhaps Iraq's single wealthiest family. They were landholders and grain merchants and owned a modern large-scale agricultural estate south of Baghdad; they were the local representatives of a British concern which all but dominated the barley trade and the export of packed dates. Ahmad's father, Abdul Hadi, had a net worth of some nine million dinars when the price of a decent Baghdad home was in the neighborhood of five hundred dinars. And the Chalabi wealth was not new. Their roots in business and public life ran deep. They had enjoyed excellent relations with the Ottoman government and with the Hashemite monarchy. All told, the Chalabis had had seventeen ministerial appointments under the monarchy. They were pillars of the old order. Ahmad's grandfather, Abdul Hussein, had been minister in eight of Iraq's cabinets between the coming of the monarchy in 1921 and his death in 1939. As minister of education, he had been keen to educate the Shia and had sent a large number of their gifted people on foreign educational missions. As for Ahmad Chalabi's father, he had served as minister of public works and vice president of the senate. Born in 1944, Ahmad Chalabi had thus known the grace of old Iraq and seen its demolition. Away from his native land, he had known success, but he had never relinquished the idea that the Baathist regime would one day be overturned.

After the destruction of the monarchy in 1958, Chalabi's family had made a home of sorts in Lebanon. There he had married into the apex of the Shia world. His wife was a daughter of Adel Osseiran, one of the leading figures in modern Lebanese politics, perhaps Shia Lebanon's most enlightened politician in decades. Osseiran had been, at one time or another, Speaker of the parliament (the highest office in the land open to a Shia) and minister in countless cabinets. The Osseirans were one of the great notable families of the southern Shia world of Lebanon. They had learning, property, and pedigree. (By a twist of fate, Chalabi's rival, Iyad Allawi, was descended from the Osseirans on his mother's side.) A son-in-law of Adel Osseiran was no stranger in Lebanon, nor an ordinary exile; he would have had access to the political life of the country. He would have been given a sense of place and of belonging. Chalabi taught mathematics at the American University of Beirut, but politics was his avocation. I first met him in Amman in 1983. He was a young banker, and Saddam was perhaps the preeminent figure in Arab politics. But Chalabi spoke with astounding confidence of the weakness of the "Sunni Pact" of Arab states and spoke of a day when the dominant order in the Arab world would crack. He had lived to see the fulfillment of his dreams. Two decades later, he was back in his birthplace, on his father's old estate.

The exile making the rounds in Washington, courting American legislators, was no stranger to the corridors of power. He had helped sell America on toppling the tyrant. Implicitly and explicitly, before his troubles, Chalabi had held out to the Pax Americana the promise of a new base of power in Iraq, and a new regional alignment. He gave the custodians of power and the opinion makers in the Arab world plenty to worry about. He was restless and bold; he had made his peace with American power; he knew the civilian leadership at the Pentagon and the policy intellectuals at the American Enterprise Institute, and he felt at home with them. He had never bonded with the officials of the League of Arab States, nor been given a hearing in the Arab councils of power. Chalabi was without illusions about Pan-Arabism and saw it for the cynical ideology that it was in Iraq. He had made no secret of his worldview. In the new Iraq, he foresaw an American military presence and the promise of normalcy with Israel. In the new Iraqi order, Chalabi and his allies in Baghdad made clear that there would be no subsidies for the homicide bombers in the Palestinian territories, and that there would be a serious departure from the Pan-Arabism of the Tikriti rulers.

The American break with Chalabi was greeted with glee by the political classes in Amman, Cairo, and Riyadh. Where Chalabi had once been attacked as an American puppet, he was now branded as an American reject and a castaway of the empire. (The speed with which the same pundits shifted their line of attack was of a piece with the broader willfulness of the Arab intellectual-political class.) Ironically, in a region where political power is always used as an instrument of enrichment, Chalabi's Arab detractors had a weapon at the ready: a Jordanian military tribunal's verdict against him dating back to 1989. He had been chairman of a family concern, Petra Bank. That bank had failed, and charges of embezzlement and diversion of funds had been made against Chalabi. He had fled the country, and a state security court had tried him in absentia and sentenced him to a prison term of twenty-two years. The man had insisted on his innocence. Saddam Hussein's shadow then had hung over Jordan. Saddam was a patron of that country's business and journalistic and political elite, a hero of its refugee camps and swank districts alike; Chalabi was in the way.

Two years after Chalabi's departure from Jordan, it should be recalled, that country's monarch had broken with his allies in the West, and with his fellow monarchs and princes in the Arabian Peninsula and the Persian Gulf, and sided with Saddam Hussein in the great crisis over Iraq's invasion of Kuwait. The collapse of Petra Bank was not a straightforward business endeavor. The inner details of the affair were the exclusive domain of the two rulers—Jordan's monarch and Saddam Hussein. The Jordanian ruler, by temperament a man of mercy and of caution, had split the difference. He had banished Chalabi from his realm but had not given him over to the savagery of Saddam Hussein. Four Jordanian warrants for Chalabi's arrest, forwarded to Interpol, had been turned back. The secrecy of the proceedings, and the fact that they had been the product of a military tribunal, were cited as reasons by Interpol. But the legalisms were beside the point. Chalabi was not a political man of the conventional Arab mold. No sooner had the Americans struck at him in Baghdad than the Jordanians were at it again, pressing for his extradition. There were real limits to what loners could do on their own in the politics of the Arab world. Chalabi swam against the current of Arab politics.

Falling out with the Bush administration, Ahmad Chalabi found his way to Grand Ayatollah Sistani. The American-educated mathematician had always had deep interest in Shia history and sources. He had known the great Muhammad Baqir al-Sadr. His own grandfather had been buried inside the shrine of Imam Ali in Najaf—no small honor in the Shia world. His parents had died in London, in 1988–89, and he had brought his mother's remains from a Shia shrine in Damascus, where she had been buried, to Baghdad. His detractors had depicted him as marginal, but his ties to Iraq's Shia clerics were remarkably strong. The old jurist needed secular allies, political players who knew their way around the game of politics but would still give Najaf and the Shia clerical institution their place in the political world. Chalabi stepped into that role. There wasn't here some sudden transformation from secular to religious politics; a quintessentially secular man, Chalabi had always had in him an awareness of Arab Shiism's political disinheritance. He was a Shia in the way secular Jews could be devoted Zionists and culturally and psychologically Jewish. This was no huge leap for him; the politics of the country were a violent, uncertain whirlwind, and the American protectorate had shown itself to be capricious in its choices.

Several months after he was written off as a figure of the past,

Chalabi was back at the center of political life, having played a major role in the cobbling together of a powerful coalition, the United Iraqi Alliance—an assemblage of Shia-led political parties that contested the national elections of January 2005. He did not leave the country as his CIA detractors said he would. No one here—among the Shia and the Kurds, to be more precise—held it against him that he had helped pull America into Iraq. No one bothered with the feud between Chalabi and the Central Intelligence Agency. If a native son who knew the *franjis* (the Westerners) had been able to bring them from worlds away to sack an entrenched tyranny, his own culture would make room for him. After all, the mighty Americans themselves, with all their technologies and listening devices and satellite images, had asserted that Saddam Hussein's possession of deadly weapons was an indisputable fact—a "slam dunk," in the memorable words of George Tenet, the director of the Central Intelligence Agency. As it happens, a high-level presidential panel on American intelligence, the Robb-Silberman Commission, had issued a report to the president of the United States, *The Commission on the Intelligence Capabilities of the United States Regarding Weapons of Mass Destruction* (March 31, 2005) that had sustained Chalabi's case that his organization, the Iraqi National Congress, had had no significant role in providing the intelligence that led up to the war. "In fact, overall, CIA's post-war investigations revealed that INC-related sources had a minimal impact on pre-war assessments," the report concluded. There had been one notorious Iraqi defector with the memorable name Curveball, who had fed American intelligence fabricated information about Iraq's weapons; Curveball had been almost universally depicted as an operative of the Iraqi National Congress. And that matter too the Robb-Silberman panel had laid to rest. "Despite speculation that Curveball had been encouraged to lie by the Iraqi National Congress (INC), the CIA's post-war investigations were unable to uncover any evidence that the INC or any other organization was directing Curveball to feed misleading information to the intelligence community." Curveball had been on his own, an operative in search of permanent asylum in the United States, and American intelligence had taken him into a witness protection program, and then "recalled" all of his intelligence tips.

Chalabi's characteristic audacity had not deserted him during that time of adversity. He offered no apologies for his political choices. He berated the ministers of the interim government for moving about the country in American military helicopters; he broke a big story about the shipping out of the country to Lebanon of $300 million in cash by Allawi's defense minister. He lived in the Red Zone, in Baghdad, beyond the protection of the Americans, and insisted on doing so to demonstrate the peace he had made with the life of Iraq. He had his own security detail, all Iraqis. In early January, as Iraq was bracing for its national elections, he made a short visit to Iran. He came, he told the Arab press, with a straightforward message to Iran's rulers. He made it clear that "Iraqis did not want their soil to become a battle-ground between Iran and the United States." He reiterated to the Ira-nians that Iraqis looked forward to the establishment of a "democratic, federal Iraq that differed from the Islamic Republic in Iran." Further-more, he told the Iranians that the Iraqis he represented did not seek an "immediate withdrawal" of the American forces from Iraq, but instead favored a phased withdrawal that would be linked to the training of Iraqi forces. He was at peace, he added, with the role of Najaf and of the Shia religious institution in the country's politics. It was well known, he said, that Ayatollah Sistani did not embrace Khomeini's notion of *wilayat al-faqih* (the Guardianship of the Jurisprudent) and that Sistani accepted the pluralism of Iraq and sought social peace among its different communities. He had faith in Iraq's future as a "big, serious country" and saw its rise to promi-nence in Arab life as an inevitable outcome. He kept the door open for the Sunni Arabs, and did not want them confined to an area of "gravel and sand" in western Iraq. Chalabi was a "doer" and that part of him appealed to the Sunni Arabs, who would find their way to him after his rupture with the Americans. He had not waited on the Americans; they would catch up with him when he emerged as deputy prime minister; there would be congratulatory calls from Richard Cheney and Condoleezza Rice. The American regency would find its way to him.

The road to elections and to democracy, so it seemed, was going through Najaf and the Shia clerical institution. Sistani had decreed that voting was a "religious obligation," and Chalabi and worldly politicians of his bent were running the political space that the revered jurist had opened up for them. The United Iraqi Alliance had the dis-tinct advantage of Sistani's blessing. A quarter-century earlier, right across the border in Iran, secularists and liberals had accepted Ayatol-lah Khomeini's claim that the cleric would sack the monarchy and then head to Qom and leave power to those who knew the ways of modernity. We know it didn't come out that way, and that Khomeini's revolution demolished the liberals and swept them aside. There had been Westernized disciples of Khomeini given to illusions about the old cleric. They were to pay dearly for the hopes they had entertained: they either were physically liquidated or ended up in exile. For Iraq, Chalabi and the Shia secularists were holding out a different future: there would be an honored place for Najaf and its scholars and seminarians in an essentially secular republic.

This was the best Shia secularism could do. The weight of tradition and of religion would be used to build a tolerable political order. It remained to be seen whether this nascent Shia secular outlook could play and win in a culture where the custodians of religion had so dominant a role. There was liberalism here, but it was fragile; there always hovered over this political landscape the risk that the clerics—and the crowd that believed in their moral authority—would prevail in a test of political wills. For the secular politicians, and for the exiles attempting to secure a foothold in an environment they did not fully know or master, this was the bargain this political moment offered them; this was the best they could do—seek cover in the shadow of clerical authority.

History had realigned things. In the 1920s it had been the Shia clerics who turned their backs on the new Iraqi state, declared impermissible traffic with the British occupation authorities, and summoned the tribes in the Middle Euphrates for a jihad against the "infidels" and their presence in Iraq. The faith and its rituals and passions were thrown into a huge challenge to British rule. The revolt of 1920 had backfired, and the Shia were left with the hollow consolations of a tale of noble defeat. Now it was the Sunni community, its religious scholars, and its provinces that were in rebellion against the Americans. A clerical aide of Grand Ayatollah Sistani, Sadr al-Din Qabanji, permitted himself an unsentimental reading of what had happened in 1920 and its meaning for today's struggle. "This time," he said, "we must take our place in the institutions of the state, for we have been on the margins of political life for a long time, all the more so in the aftermath of the revolt of 1920." Politically, this was veritable heresy, for much Shia ink, and much Shia poetry, had glorified that desperate revolt. Martyrology and noble defeat had had their day; there was eagerness now among the Shia to have a crack at political power.

They would leave it to the Sunni Triangle this time to go up against a mighty foreign army.

No one could be sure what the Shia would do with this new gift of political power. No one could offer the ironclad guarantee that a Shia-led political order would withstand a theocratic temptation. There was ambiguity here aplenty, and there was the precedent of Iran, where the religious had devoured the political realm. Now and then, Iraq's Shia jurists gave reasons for concern. Only days after Iraq's voters had gone to the polls to select their National Assembly, there came a demand from the Shia religious institution in Najaf, from the clerics arrayed around Grand Ayatollah Sistani, calling on the country's political leaders to enshrine Islam "as the sole source of legislation, and to reject any legal provisions that violate the maxims of Islam." This demand was presented as a political given, "not subject to any compromise." Further, the religious authorities warned against "changing the face of Iraq and separating religion from politics, for that way forward is full of danger, and that is unacceptable to all religious scholars and authorities."

The legal basis of political power was one problem that concerned the jurists; public decorum was another. In this statement from Najaf's custodians, the jurists were keen to remind the government of the danger of "provoking Muslim sentiments by recruiting women into the armed forces and publishing their pictures with their foreign instructors in the magazines and the newspapers, for this would damage the credibility of a government in desperate need today of popular support."

Much had been made of the secular basis of public life in Iraq. But this was not Sweden, or France, and a place for Islam in the political and cultural realm was inevitable. When the Shia jurists pronounced on legal and political matters, their central concerns tended to be the traditional concerns of their guild: personal law, matters of inheritance, marriage and divorce. The political realm could accommodate those concerns. When it was finally crafted, the constitution's language had shifted: Islam was now *a* main source, not *the* main source of legislation. And truth be told, the insertion of the clause "Islam is a main source of legislation" was not novel or unique to Iraq. Even the secular powers in Syria and Egypt had let this clause stand in their constitutions, and it had not constrained the powers of the state or tied the hands of the rulers. Iraq was thus fated to live, then, with a religious component in its public life. In Iraq's constitution, the clause "No law that contradicts Islamic principles shall be issued" is immediately followed by an equally stark declaration: "No law that contradicts democratic principles shall be issued." The jurists in Najaf were not recasting the life of the land. Their pronouncements gave hints of recognition of Iraq's complications: there would be no banning of liquor, for one, but care would have to be exercised in its consumption in the public space.

The Shia sense of disinheritance had to yield to the new responsibility of power. That historical and psychological transition would not be easy. What the Shia jurists would bring to this change was unknowable. Najaf and its scholars had never ruled. For these scholars, power was within reach. No longer would there be a knock at the door at dawn, and terror squads in the Shia seminaries. No revered figure from their ranks would be executed by the rulers, as the great jurist Muhammad Baqir al-Sadr had been by the Tikriti tyranny. The scholars would be free to read and write; there would come their way respect and reverence. In the best of outcomes, the life of Najaf would revive, and the *talaba*, religious students from the Shia world, would converge on it as they had in better times. They would repair it and give it the care it deserved. There was Shia wealth—in the Gulf, in Lebanon, and in South Asia. It could come to Najaf's help. But the scholars would have to draw their own line on the temptations of politics. And they would have to know their country as it is—the things it could bear and the things it couldn't.

Humam Hamoudi was not a scholar of Najaf; he was the cleric who headed the constitutional drafting committee. He belonged to the Supreme Council of the Islamic Revolution in Iraq. Curiosity about the Shia clerical estate led me to him yet again. He was then, in the summer of 2005, in the midst of the seesaw effort to write the country's constitutional document. But I sought from him a personal narrative, the sources of his outlook. He was a man of striking good looks and possessed of an easy manner. I could not quite pin it down, but there was something unclerical about him. He wore a white turban—he was not of the sayyid class; he did not hail from the families claiming descent from the Prophet—and the clerical attire. But the worldliness and the ever-present smile, and the absence of pedantic talk were distinctly modern, the ways of an accessible man. His biography confirmed what I had seen. He was born in 1952, in one of

Baghdad's most affluent and cosmopolitan suburbs, East Karrada. He belonged to the apex of the merchant class; his grandfather had been head of Baghdad's chamber of commerce, and his father had continued in the family business. "The East Karrada of my youth had more churches than mosques," he recalled. "In my family we had extensive foreign contacts, and there was a large number of Western wives in the extended family." His father had encouraged a culture of learning and books in a home with twelve children—seven brothers and five sisters. "No veiling had been enforced on my sisters; they were free to pursue higher education and the arts. My father did not force me to pray but rewarded me when I did. He was a reader of books; he liked the subject of Muslim paradise more than he did the subject of hell and punishment. I would read books to my father, and this was my earliest source of awareness. My reading was eclectic. I was not biased either for or against religious books. I studied scientific subjects at school, did well in science, but my bent was for the humanities. I settled on studying psychology."

It was in the late 1960s, when Humam would have been in his late teens, that this graced existence came under pressure. The Sunni Arab ideologues and officers were on the move. They were children of western Iraq, lower-middle-class boys with ambitions, and with resentments of the upper order and of the Shia merchants who were still holding their own in the marketplace. "In the name of nationalization and the command economy, they began to encroach on our economic domains. We would come to greater awareness of mounting pressures on the Shia. I became politicized during this period, and oddly my father did not mind; he did not warn me against the dangers of political involvement. I flirted with the Muslim Brotherhood, but it was not for me. I then met the first martyr, Muhammad Baqir al-Sadr, and he touched my life, really changed its direction. It was only a matter of time before I got into political trouble. In 1975 I was arrested, and I was to stay in prison for three years. I suffered my share of humiliation and torture. But I met many like-minded people in prison. My political education is probably owed to that time in prison. When I was released, there was quiescence and complacency in the country. My peers had done well, married, acquired property. Even relatives turned me down when I proposed to their daughters, for I was trouble. My political troubles did not end, and a second warrant was issued for my arrest. I was determined to avoid prison at any cost. I thought of fleeing to Syria, but that plan did not work. I then fled to

Iran. My older brother was an engineer and a turbaned religious scholar at the same time; he was married to the daughter of Sayyid Muhammad Baqir al-Hakim. I joined Hakim's circle of supporters and came to believe in him. I then enrolled in *al-hawza al-Iraqiyya* (the Iraqi religious school) in Qom. My teacher was one of the students of the blessed Muhammad Baqir al-Sadr. I donned the turban in 1984. In my boyhood, I would never have dreamt of doing such a thing. I had thought that the life of clerics was not active enough, that they sat around and discussed arcane subjects, and now here I am."

The political whirlwind had brought Hamoudi to the National Assembly. He was aware that he was a Shia turbaned man, that his Kurdish and Sunni colleagues were perhaps unsettled by his role in the constitutional drafting committee. "I like to think that I am a fair-minded man. I like to think that the people who have worked with me now mind me less than they did before. As a boy, I loved the image of the two rivers, the Tigris and the Euphrates, coming together at Shatt al-Arab to form a single source of life. After all these political years, I hold on to this image. When Sayyid Muhammad Baqir al-Hakim was murdered in the summer of 2003, I thought that Iraq was orphaned, I thought the Shia were lost. Then I came to know Sayyid Ali Sistani, and I was hopeful yet again, for I was deeply touched by his love of his community and by his moderation. The Shia had always been divided, and in the national elections Sistani united them. At first I did not want to head the constitutional drafting committee because I knew people would see my turban and judge me unfit for the task. But in time, I grew hopeful that the work itself will be my message."

Hamoudi gave me this outline of his life with the skill of a story-teller. He told it with confidence; there were no shadows in it. He had a brother, a physician, who lived in Columbus, Ohio, and a sister, a physician as well, who lived in Indiana. He had thrown in this piece of family history when I asked him about the American presence in Iraq. "Before the war, I took part in a video conference with Vice President Cheney. I told the Americans that they would be welcomed in Iraq, but that they should not try to make the Iraqis feel marginal in the work of liberation. Despite the mistakes the Americans made in this country, none of this would have been possible without them. One day they will understand the Shia better. One day they will release themselves of the burden of what the Arab regimes tell them about the Shia."

We were talking at the Al Rasheed Hotel, in the Green Zone,

across the street from the convention center that housed the National Assembly. It was time for him to return to the endless bargaining over the constitution. I walked with him, past the Georgian troops. He chuckled when I told him that I had in mind a quick piece of journalism with the working title, "Lawmaking in Iraq: From Hammurabi to Hamoudi." In the delegates' lounge, his arrival caused a stir. There were greetings from friends and queries about the work of his committee. His smile never left him. A handsome, stylish middle-aged woman, with a light scarf and a pantsuit, Samia Muhammad, a member of the Assembly, pressed Hamoudi about a matter of interest to her. She was a Faili (Shia) Kurd, and the Failis, a community with a deep mercantile and urban tradition in Baghdad, had not a single representative on the seventy-odd-member constitutional drafting committee. They had slipped between the cracks; the Kurds had not claimed them, nor had the Shia. He acknowledged her point. That cause would have to wait as this new country was being called forth. I could not see this man bringing religious bigotry to Iraq. But beyond the Assembly's gates, and the Georgian troops—and Hamoudi's goodwill—the country's identity and the division of its spoils were still up for grabs.

CHAPTER 7

After Innocence

On May 18, 2004, in the shock of the aftermath of Abu Ghraib's revelations, the young Jordanian monarch, Abdullah II, stepped forth to endorse the age-old Arab recipe for the mayhem in Iraq's streets—a man on horseback, an Iraqi "with a military background who has an experience of being a tough guy who could hold Iraq together for the next year." It was safe now to speak in such terms: the old order in the Arab world had been given a reprieve. The Pax Americana was mired in a prison scandal in Iraq; the Abu Ghraib prison abuses had begun to overwhelm the Iraq war. And the chaos in Iraq had made authoritarian rule once again the safe bet in Arab life. Jordan's monarch, a young ruler in the orbit of American power, was sensitive to Washington's ways. He had "bought stock" in the Iraq war; unlike his late father, Hussein ibn Talal, who had ridden with Saddam Hussein a dozen years earlier, King Abdullah had bet on American power in this new war in Iraq. He had let the crowd in Amman know that this was royal prerogative and state policy.

By way of Arab rulers, Abdullah II was a fairly benign monarch; he had talked of "reform," and he knew that this American war had made political and cultural reform in the Arab world one of its principal goals. The return to the "tough guy" recipe was no accident: authoritarianism had grown respectable, once again, and the great foreign power that had brought reform along with its military gear was less sure of itself. A fortnight earlier, the images of torture from Abu Ghraib had been made public. Abdullah II had traveled to Washington, and he had received an apology from President Bush for the treatment of Iraqi prisoners at Abu Ghraib. It was odd, that apology—the Jordanian ruler being paid in Iraqi coin. The apology was due Iraq's own people, but it had been forwarded Jordan's way. If the Pax Americana had struck into Iraq and hoped that it would release Iraqis from the captivity of pan-Arab politics, the foreign liberator was now consigning Iraq yet again to the Arab states around it.

In King Abdullah's words, it had been an error to disband the Iraqi military, for salvation lay in that very same Iraqi army. "There were a lot of heroes; there are strong community leaders who are products of the Iran-Iraq war. They are national heroes that do appeal to the Iraqi street." King Abdullah had reprised his father's role. Jordan, the quintessential buffer state, lived off the shifts in regional alignments, and the dividends that came with its strategic choices. In the 1980s, it had been pulled into the economic and political orbit of Saddam Hussein. Perhaps out of a mix of conviction and necessity, King Hussein had become the point man in the struggle against the theocratic revolution in Iran. Now his son, Abdullah II, had picked up the old banner. Abdullah may not have harbored religious phobias about the Shia, but he had thrown the weight of his state behind Sunni restoration. The Palestinians had come into their own, the resourceful Egyptians had become the Arab "brokers" of Israeli-Palestinian matters, and the young monarch was in search of a new strategic role for his country; he was to find it in Iraq. There were four hundred thousand Iraqi exiles in Jordan; there were ties of commerce and kinship between Iraqi and Jordanian tribes. A lucrative contraband trade in Iraqi oil that operated from the early 1990s until the fall of Saddam's regime in 2003 had been nothing short of a windfall for the Jordanian economy. The devastating report by the Volcker Commission, *Independent Inquiry into the United Nations Oil-for-Food Programme,* would establish beyond doubt that Jordan was the financial epicenter of a smuggling operation that helped keep Saddam's regime afloat. Jordan was no innocent bystander in this fight. Abdullah openly lobbied for a kinder and gentler version of the old order in Iraq. He had standing in Washington, and he would trade on it. And in one of those exquisitely Arab twists, his half brother, Prince Ali ibn Hussein, had just announced his engagement to the daughter of the UN envoy, the Algerian diplomat Lakhdar Brahimi. Grant Iraq's Shia their sense of outsiderness: the representations from Amman would not be on their behalf. King Abdullah's military "heroes" and "tough guys" were not their heroes—or their kinsmen.

What decent drapery covered the Jordanian monarch's sentiments was to be removed several months later. In early December, King Abdullah had come out with a more explicitly sectarian message. He was worried, he let it be known, about the rise of a "crescent" of Shia movements or governments all the way from Iran to Iraq, Syria, and

Lebanon. The subtlety had been pushed aside, and the great foreign power was being frightened by the Shia bogeyman yet again. It was as though the terrors inflicted on America by Sunni Islamists on September 11 had never happened, as though Osama bin Laden and the jihadists (and a Jordanian fanatic by the name of Zarqawi) did not exist. It was Zarqawi who was spreading death and barbarism in the streets of Iraq. The young ruler's view was really a scarecrow. The truth of the Arab world was being simplified and distorted in the extreme. There was no Shia population in Syria, to begin with; the Jordanian had chosen to lump together the Alawite minority of Syria with the Shia in neighboring lands. Nor had the Shia of Lebanon come into dominion of a diverse country where power remained a pluralistic affair shared by the Christian Maronites, the Sunnis, the Shia, and the Druze. True, Iraq's Shia had been liberated from a terrifying oppresion. But they were not a monolithic force, and there had always been deep wells of anticlericalism among them. There was no "Shia International" in the works, no plot to overturn the Arab political order.

The Hashemite monarch affected the hipness of the elite American prep schools and the ways of modernity. He had been educated at Deerfield Academy; he and his wife were fixtures on the international circuit of conferences and weddings and the gatherings of the glitterati. Arab culture needed a way out of its atavisms, but this monarch was indeed offering a soft version of the anti-Shia animus that a subject of his, Abu Musab al-Zarqawi, was preaching on the Internet and in these dark videotapes that had become Zarqawi's art form. He was no bigot, Jordan's ruler, but he opened the door to bigotry, lent it his authority. He had brought to the doorstep of a foreign power an old Arab schism. American soldiers were not fighting and dying in Iraq for the sectarian privileges—and phobias—of the Arab elite, but Jordan's ruler could do no better than reach into an old bag of tricks. More damning still, where the great struggle in Iraq needed a healer's art, he had injected into it the old, uncompromising sectarianism. Abdullah II played a peculiar game: he warned of Shia dangers, but then made representations in the councils of American foreign policy, and in the bowels of the national security bureaucracy, that as a Hashemite he had a special link to the Shia of Iraq and could thus serve as a "bridge" to that community. That contradiction would, in time, be understood by his American interlocutors.

The Jordanian ruler's remarks about the "Shia crescent" would not go away. There was antagonism between Jordan and Iraq's Shia, and it was no use pretending that Jordan was neutral in the Iraq struggle. True, Iraqi police units were being trained in Jordan, for the impoverished Hashemite realm was keen to secure a share of the Pax Americana's largesse. But the well was poisoned in Jordan: the Islamists and the pan-Arabists and the tribalists in the country had been die-hard supporters of Saddam Hussein. It had been in Jordan, it should be recalled, back in 1990–91, where all the currents of political revisionism, the envy of the poorer Arab lands toward the oil states, the bitter sense that history has dealt the Arabs a terrible hand, seemed to converge.

It was in that country, more than in any other in the Arab world, that the Iraqi dictator was both an avenger and a would-be redeemer. He had *rujula* (manhood), he had money to throw around, and he held out the promise that the oil dynasties would be brought down. It had been that radicalism that had forced King Hussein to stay a step ahead of the crowd, breaking with the Arab states of the Peninsula and the Gulf and the United States to side with Iraq. Jordan's strategic choice had shifted this time around. Abdullah II had cast his lot with American power, but the street had different loyalties. There were Jordanian poets writing verse in Saddam's praise; there were intellectuals and journalists who gloated over Iraq's troubles. There was a strong Islamist current in Jordan—both domesticated types, the Muslim Brotherhood, and "harder" jihadists. On the eve of the American campaign in Iraq, a group of religious scholars, the Conference of the Ulama of the Sharia (an offshoot of the Muslim Brotherhood), issued a fatwa banning any assistance to the Americans, such as "opening airports and harbors to them, providing their planes and vehicles with fuel, offering them intelligence for their war against Muslims." It was impermissible, the fatwa added, "to sell the American aggressor a piece of bread or to offer him a drink of water."

The monarchy had provided what services and staging facilities the American war planners required. But the entire American project in Iraq—the deposing of Saddam Hussein, the rise in Iraq of Jordan's nemesis, the politician Ahmad Chalabi, the very empowerment of the Shia—was anathema to the Jordanian political class. Instinctively, there was fear in Jordan that the Shia would take Iraq and its commerce and weight eastward toward Iran, leaving Jordan in the shadow of a mighty and wealthy Israel to its west. Saddam Hussein's two daughters had secured asylum in Amman, and they were unrepentant. So had countless operatives of the deposed regime. They came with the money they had plundered, and with a determination to restore their lost hegemony. The Lawyers' Syndicate in Jordan brimmed with enthusiasm for Saddam Hussein, and there were volunteers aplenty who were ready to join the dictator's legal defense and the defense of his principal lieutenants. But there was a darker truth still to this difficult relationship between Jordan and Iraq. Jordanians were overrepresented in the ranks of the jihadists who made their way to Iraq to do battle against the Americans—and against the Shia as well. It was not just Abu Musab al-Zarqawi: there were less celebrated practitioners of terror, Jordanians who took it upon themselves to wage "holy war" in Iraq against the Americans and against the Shia "apostates."

It was this darker truth about the play of things in Jordan that was brought out into the open by a terrible deed of terror that took place in the town of Hilla on February 28, 2005—to that time the bloodiest single deed of terror of the war and the insurgency. A Jordanian of respectable middle-class background, Raad Mansur al-Banna, thirty-two years of age, a lawyer, drove a car packed with explosives into a crowd of ordinary Iraqis, in the Shia town of Hilla, killing more than 130 people. As Iraq was reeling under the impact of this brutal act, a Jordanian newspaper, *Al Ghad,* broke the story that a "martyr's wedding" had been held for Banna in his family home in the town of Salt. Martyrs' weddings are joyous affairs, festive occasions that celebrate those who fell for Islam on their way to paradise.

The obituary notice for this terrorist had celebrated this deed, and Iraqi Shia who had had their fill with such deeds of brutality held a large demonstration in front of the Jordanian embassy in Baghdad. The flag of Jordan was defaced, and there were denunciations of the Jordanian authorities and their monarch issued by the leading Shia clerics in Iraq. Well into this struggle in Iraq, it was fair to say that Jordan became the Arab regime most resented by ordinary Iraqis. Jordan had edged out Syria, which had fed the flames of Iraq as well. The Jordanian authorities were duly embarrassed by the Banna episode. The reporter who broke the story for *Al Ghad* was picked up by Jordanian intelligence for "spreading rumors" and besmirching the reputation of Jordan. There were righteous statements about all that Jordan had done for Iraq and Iraqis; there were the obligatory assertions that

Jordan was a land of religious tolerance, that the Hashemites, descendants of the Prophet Muhammad, were devoted to Islam's "moderation" and to the unity of all the believers, Sunni and Shia alike. The asylum granted Saddam Hussein's daughters was passed off as a deed of decency extended to a family that had come into adversity. The family of Raad al-Banna had its say as well. Their son had fallen in Iraq, they conceded, but he had gone there to do war against the Americans. In a pattern all-too-depressingly familiar, the jihadist was depicted as a good and normal man who would never do such a thing. In the family telling, Raad al-Banna was a man at ease with the world: he had lived in southern California; he loved Harley-Davidson motorcycles and cowboy hats. There had been no intimations of the path he would take to Hilla: he had told his family that he was leaving for Saudi Arabia in search of employment when he made the journey to Iraq.

But the tale of this "normal" man was of course more tangled than that. The town of Salt, Jordan's second most important political center after Amman, has a powerful current of Islamism. The town was proud, it came to be known, of its thirty "martyrs" who had fallen in Iraq. This was a town possessed of a tribal culture, and the jihadists had made inroads there, competed with the authority of the tribal leaders for the allegiance of the young. The jihadists had certitude on their side. They saw their struggle with the tribal elders as a modern reenactment of the struggle of the Prophet Muhammad with his own Meccan tribe, the Quraysh. The Prophet had quit his native city for Medina, and had returned triumphant to erect an Islamic polity. The jihadists in Salt—and the larger society that gave them its warrant and sly approval—were not about to issue an apology to the Shia of Iraq. Jordan put on display the schizophrenic nature of those Arab societies arrayed on the side of the United States. The Jordanians took America's coin, and the rulers negotiated their way between their American obligations and deadlier currents at play in their country. There were knowledgeable reports that Jordanian intelligence had known jihadists under surveillance, and had a live-and-let-live agreement with them: operations within Jordan itself were impermissible, but the passage to Iraq was a matter that the authorities were willing to tolerate.

Where the family of the man who had brought death to Hilla had dissimulated on his behalf, there was another Jordanian family, that of a young man who had gone to Iraq and come back with light chest wounds, one Ziad Horani, which was willing to state the matter in blunt, unadorned terms. "He hates the Shi'ites," the mother of this young warrior said of her son, who was awaiting trial on charges of taking part in an underground radical cell. He was still, though, a beloved, tender son. "He has a heart of milk, a baby's heart; he's a well-brought-up boy." Countless Arabs had been robbed of an ability to see and name things as they are, and this woman was no exception. The faith—militant, full of bigotry—acquitted her and her son as well. The "good boy" could still hate and want to kill the Shiites.

This mother could be forgiven the fact that she could not see into that contradiction. An animus toward the Shia had gripped Jordan; it was tethered to reflexive anti-Americanism. The moderate pro-American regime, and the virulently anti-American population: the combination had become familiar by now in Arab political life. To the embarrassment of their rulers, young Jordanians took pride in their compatriot Abu Musab al-Zarqawi. He had the right enemies, his admirers were honest enough to admit: the Jews, "the Crusaders," and the *rafida,* the heretics—the last being a label for the Shia. So much of Jordan's life—the gap between rich and poor, the split between the "natives" of Jordan and the Palestinians—lay beyond scrutiny and beyond discussion. The rage was displaced, shifted onto Iraq and its Shia majority, and onto the Americans who had empowered the Shia.

The newness of the American project in Iraq had been tarnished, and the foreign power had begun to scale down its expectations of what it could pull off in Iraq. The old order in the Arab world had shown its resilience and recuperative power. The prison scandal at Abu Ghraib may have been a "body blow"—the term is Donald Rumsfeld's—to the American war planners, but it was nothing short of a deed of deliverance to the custodians of power, and to the political orthodoxy, of the Arab states around Iraq. The foreign power had stumbled; its failures and shortcomings at Abu Ghraib and the fury of the insurgency in the months that followed had thrown it on the defensive. There were Arabs now, in the shadow of Abu Ghraib, walking away from any historical responsibility for the terrors of September 11, and the death pilots and the ruin they had brought onto American soil. These terrors were now folded into the course of things, traded as in a Middle Eastern bazaar, for the depravities at Abu Ghraib. In a world where all sin, no one can judge. The logic was willful, but it floated over a region remarkable for its failure to accept responsibility for the deeds of its own.

Abu Ghraib gave the anti-Americanism of the Arab world a target, and an outlet. Men and women in Amman and Jeddah and Cairo who had looked away from the terrors of Iraq under the Baath were now seized with outrage over Abu Ghraib. The outrage had worked, and contrition settled upon the architects of the Bush foreign policy. There had been that apology to the Jordanian monarch; there had been an interview, given by President Bush, to Ibrahim Nafie, the editor in chief of the Egyptian daily *Al-Ahram*, where more contrition was offered. The Egyptian was not really a working journalist; he was the caretaker of an organ of the regime. There was obtuseness in the way American officials were reading their crisis. This Egyptian daily, *Al-Ahram*, established in the 1870s by two gifted Christian Lebanese brothers who had sought sanctuary in Egypt and freedom from the limits of the Ottoman order in Greater Syria, had atrophied. Few in Egypt itself were reading it, let alone in Baghdad and Basra. Nafie himself, as was the case with the overwhelming majority of his columnists, could be counted upon for a steady output of abuse aimed at American power.

It would have been the prudent and proper thing for the American president to grant an interview to the editors and representatives of a budding Iraqi publication. Iraqis were the ones who were owed the apology over Abu Ghraib; it was their trust that had been violated. Besides, it had been the practice of the CPA to celebrate the vibrancy of the new journalism in Iraq and its openness. But the wider Arab campaign had worked; the confidence had cracked in Washington, and the interview with *Al-Ahram* was of a piece with this moment of panic and confusion.

There had been a running controversy between the American embassy in Cairo and the Egyptian authorities over the tone and content of the Egyptian media. The newspapers in Cairo had grown increasingly strident. Their animus toward Israel, and toward America, had crossed the bounds of reason; they offered little by way of analysis or of reliable reporting. They peddled conspiracy theories and little else. The regime had winked at all that hatred and let it rage—the safety valve for a people proud of their history but now denied a participatory culture. This concession to *Al-Ahram* had shifted the terms of the argument over Cairo's ways and its culture. No surprise, *Al-*

Ahram, long released from the rigors of serious journalism and given to a culture of sycophancy toward the man at the helm of political power, trumpeted the interview with President Bush as evidence of American solicitude of Egypt.

Pan-Arabism may have begun to lose its hold over the practices of the Arabs, but it was alive and well in Washington. Once again, the Arabs were treated as an undifferentiated whole, a world intact and bound by common political interests. The intellectual edifice of "the Arabists" at the Central Intelligence Agency and the State Department had not collapsed; its deference to the Sunni Arab orthodoxy still animated a good deal of America's Middle Eastern policy. The neocons had no monopoly on America's view of the Arabs. It was in the midst of this crisis triggered by Abu Ghraib that the Bush administration, which had endorsed Israeli prime minister Ariel Sharon's plan for withdrawal from Gaza, suddenly distanced itself from that plan. A tacit decision had been made. The fortunes of America in Iraq would be redeemed in Arab lands; the Palestinians would be paid in Iraqi coin. These concessions would not release America from its troubles. Indeed, these retreats were seen for what they were—the concessions of a great, foreign power now unsure of itself.

"I sent American troops to Iraq to make its people free, not to make them American," President Bush observed in a speech he made at the Army War College on May 24, 2004. The transfer of authority was five weeks away, and the defense of the war had become a domestic imperative. But that statement was now—painfully—beside the point. If there had been plans to remake Iraq, they had long yielded to more limited expectations. No big American project was at play. Politically, the American interlude in Iraq was drawing to a close, a man of the Iraqi political class had said to me days earlier. True, there would remain a huge American military force. But Iraqis of all stripes had begun to stake a claim to the new order and to prepare for life after the Americans. Deference to the American regency was a thing of the past. Even that American creation, the Governing Council, mounted its own open rebellion a week after the American president had sought to defend the war and to sketch his vision for the transfer of sovereignty to an interim Iraqi government.

The rebellion erupted over a choice for the interim presidency of Iraq. The American regent, and the UN envoy, had been set to choose the eighty-one-year-old Adnan Pachachi for what was billed as a ceremonial post. The Governing Council had balked and had preempted the Americans and their new United Nations ally, opting for a younger man from their own ranks, the forty-six-year-old Sheikh Ghazi al-Yawar. Pachachi was an unreconstructed Arab nationalist; he hailed from a prominent Sunni family of Baghdad. He had been foreign minister in the early 1960s, and his years in exile had been spent in the United Arab Emirates. It was an open secret that he was not favored by the Shia, and that he returned their distrust. The rejection of Pachachi had been a rejection of Bremer's writ. Two members of the Governing Council had fallen to assassins; a third had just lost her eighteen-year-old son in an attack on her convoy. The members of this body were in no mood for tutelage but were keen to demonstrate their independence from the foreign power that had given them their place but never allowed them the exercise of any genuine power. If Pachachi was a throwback to the past, Yawar embodied a more inclusive sense of Iraq's checkered identity.

In their fashion, the Iraqis had come to see their history as passage from the rule of the tyrant to the rule of the foreigners. The American occupation authority had moved into the ruler's palaces and the ruler's prisons—out of logistical necessity, of course—but that shift in their world acquitted the Iraqi people, absolved them of the burden of their own history, left them on the sidelines as foreign soldiers and technicians and pollsters and advocates and monitors of "civil society" programs took control of that country. In a familiar twist, in that speech to the Army War College of May 24, President Bush had proposed—with the approval of a sovereign Iraqi government, of course—the demolition of the Abu Ghraib prison. He acknowledged the terrible symbolism of Abu Ghraib—for Iraqis, now for the American stewardship. "Under Saddam Hussein, prisons like Abu Ghraib were symbols of death and torture. That same prison became a symbol of disgraceful conduct by a few American troops who dishonored our country and disregarded our values."

The Iraqis hadn't stormed their own Bastille: American bulldozers would demolish it for them. Iraq's shame would be cleansed—and America's as well. No surprise, many Iraqis saw through this American pledge and were quick to reject it. This was another episode, were it to come to pass, where Iraqis would remain spectators to their own history. Within days of President Bush's remarks, a group of Iraqi intellectuals asserted a claim to their own history and to the terrible monuments of the old regime. "The Iraqi people," they observed in a statement made public on June 1, "have suffered systematic violations of the rights of man. We want to express our belief that so much of what the former Baathist regime built, particularly the prisons and the palaces and the other buildings used for repression, must be preserved as monuments of memory and history."

Days later, a man who had spent eight years in Abu Ghraib under the Saddam regime, Abdul Hadi al-Hakim, sent an open letter to the leaders of the "new Iraq." He wanted the prison kept intact. He wanted it standing there as a monument and a reminder of the degradation and the terror. "It is my hope," he wrote, "that we and the rest of the Iraqi people are not deprived of our natural right to remember and to learn and to ask for mercy for the dead." The American judgment was being rebuffed, but that way—paradoxically—lay America's vindication, and the possibility of a measure of success in Iraq. In the age and in the legends of colonialism, having incurred a prison sentence on the eve of independence was often a requirement of power in the new states. The Pax Americana was served by this Iraqi mutiny on the eve of the transfer of sovereignty. Resistance was one way Iraqis could reclaim their own political life. They could keep their prisons or they could demolish them. The display of independence from American power was their way into a new political life.

"We're due some luck," Major General Stephen Speakes wrote to me in an e-mail in late May. This military leader had ridden the roller coaster of the war and had caught and chronicled both its accomplishments and its heartbreak. The note came during a difficult run for this war, but the general was prescient. The luck came in the most paradoxical of ways—in the "rebellion" of the Governing Council, and in its choice of a new president. On that very same day, the country's designated prime minister, Iyad Allawi, a Shia secularist given to secrecy and to strong ties to "reformed" Baathists and former operatives who had broken with the old regime, acknowledged a debt of gratitude owed to the American-led Coalition and its soldiers. He condemned the terror attacks on Coalition forces, praised those who "sacrificed the blood of their sons" on behalf of Iraq. The American stewardship was still loaded with troubles. But on the eve of the transfer of "sovereignty"—circumscribed to be sure, limited by the presence of a vast foreign force—Iraqis were now willing to claim their own political life. They could thank the foreign soldiers for services rendered and then ask them to stay. They could turn down the American choice for president and put up a candidate of their own.

There was no harm in this new display of independence. The Iraqis had refused to go into receivership; Lakhdar Brahimi had arrived in Iraq to trumpets and drums. On June 3, his mission ended. Brahimi "left Iraq forever," his spokesman announced. The statement was made in Arabic, by an Egyptian-born aide. And in Arabic the statement gave away better than any translation could render the envoy's helplessness. He was leaving Iraq *"ila al abadd,"* never to return. He hadn't promised a "government of angels," said the envoy's spokesman. What he had come up with was all that he could hope for: this was what was possible. For all its limitations, the interim government was a fair reflection of Iraq. There was something of the old "confessional" arrangement of power familiar to those who knew Lebanon, where power was apportioned among the religious communities. There was a similar balance in this new Iraq, the Sunni president checked by the Shia prime minister and the Shia and Kurdish vice presidents. All in all, three dozen appointments had been made with anxious regard for sectarian representativeness—sixteen Shia, ten Sunnis, eight Kurds, a Turkoman, a Christian. There were former Baathists and former political prisoners in the cabinet, a Shia Islamist or two, a former Communist. Several portfolios were given to old, rehabilitated Baathists: the ministries of defense, interior, higher education, commerce, and municipal affairs.

There was mirrored in this cabinet the burden of Iraq's history under the Baath—the different places of exile and of education where those leaders had waited and hoped: engineering degrees from Germany and Liverpool, a PhD in animal husbandry from Iowa State, a PhD in information technology from the University of Southern California, a doctorate from the Sorbonne in political geography. The Kurds had behind them European places of exile; some of the Shia had returned after years in Iran. The prospects for these men and women were uncertain; the purveyors of terror were still on the loose. But an observer looking at this list, and these life histories, could be forgiven the thought that there was more political life in this group than could be seen in the ruling circles of Saudi Arabia, Egypt, and Syria. The war had not hatched a democratic state. But the effort had not been in vain.

Beyond the prison of the old despotism, the Iraqis were face-to-face with the hazards and uncertainties—and promise—of freedom. The interim prime minister had been an old "asset" of the Central Intelligence Agency; he had been recruited in 1992 to balance the reliance on Ahmad Chalabi. (Allawi and Chalabi, distant relatives, had both been educated at the same Jesuit prep school in Baghdad, the elite Baghdad College High School, the country's leading academy from its beginnings the early 1930s until the Baath seizure of power in 1968.) There were reports that Allawi had been a "thuggish" operative of the Baath regime. A medical schoolmate of his, Dr. Haifa al-Azawi, recalled that he was given to terrorizing the medical students with a gun that he had carried on his belt. Allawi could never shake off the charges that he had been at one with the ways of the Baath. There were snide references to him as "Saddam Lite" and charges that his conversion to the cause of "democracy" had been the opportunism of a man in search of power. If Shiism in this place had to come to terms with power and to find that middle ground between quietism and martyrology, this political man, a fifty-eight-year-old neurologist with a checkered background, was an embodiment of this new lesson to his Shia kinsmen. There was something oddly liberating and healthy about Allawi owning up to his long relationship with American intelligence. He had been "in contact" with fifteen "regional and international intelligence agencies." He was not "embarrassed or ashamed"; he had done it for the liberation of Iraq. Power could betray and could compromise and isn't always practiced by people with clean hands. The "sect of the ruled" and the persecuted now had one of their own in the inner sanctum of power.

The education of the Shia was under way. From darkness and fear, they had stepped forth into a blinding light. They could make Iraq, or they could break it. It was no longer enough for the Shia to narrate a history of persecution. There would be no further need to lament that other Arabs—and Westerners who fell for their view of things—attributed to the Shia of Iraq that burdensome "Persian connection." The Iraqi Shia were now free to bid for a normal political life of their own. There was a good deal of unintended irony to the charge made by a Sunni prayer leader at the Abu Hanifa Mosque in Baghdad, in a Friday sermon on June 11, that Allawi was an "agent" of American intelligence. The preacher had come to incite against the interim government and to call on the officers of the former regime to answer the call of "honor" and duty. But there was a reversal of roles here, a break with history. The man in power was a Shiite, the preacher lamenting the state of things a Sunni. The Shia rise to political power in Iraq had just begun.

If Allawi worked outside the confines of his religious sect, there were many other Shia leaders coming into their own, learning the ways of politics. Disputations had always riddled Shia history: the Shia had the temperament of an oppositional people long in the underground. Sons of Najaf's religious scholars had taken the lead in the founding of Iraq's Communist Party; Baathism had once pulled in some of the best and brightest of the Shia youth. There were immense differences among the Shia. And their leaders seemed to be aware of the unease of Iraq's other communities about Shia clerics' making their way to political power. There would be no "turbans" in the inner sanctums of administrative power, Shia leaders repeatedly promised. There were clerics, of course, active in the Shia political parties, and there was the overarching presence and influence of the old jurist Grand Ayatollah Ali al-Sistani. This was a delicate balancing act for the Shia: shedding old subjugation for new power while providing assurances that they would respect the division of political power and the rights of the other communities.

All this had to be done against the background of a steady campaign of terror aimed at the Shia. It was their mosques and their religious assemblies and their weddings and their neighborhoods that had been the targets of a sustained campaign; it was their leaders and their clerics whom the insurgents struck down. Men are not angels: Shia restraint in the face of this terror derived from the belief that power shall come the way of the Shia by virtue of their numbers. There would of course be no convincing those in Iraq—and beyond—who continued to distrust the Shia and to see their ultimate project as the creation of a sister republic of the Iranian theocratic regime. This restraint, it was said, was only tactical. Come political power, the true intentions of the Shia would be revealed. The classic Sunni view of the Shia—passed down through the centuries—was that of a people given to secrecy and dissimulation, to a deep, undisclosed history. This view had not altered and was now out and about.

It was not just Abu Musab al-Zarqawi hurling abuse and unadorned hatred at the Shia. There were men and women of the written word, and of politics—perfectly respectable types—who were not embarrassed to give voice to crude anti-Shia arguments. I shall take one example, that of Ghassan al-Imam, a columnist born in Syria, I believe, in the pages of the respectable London-based daily *Asharq Al-Awsat*. There is nothing unusual about this man of opinion and punditry; his writings are a fair reflection of mainstream Arab opinion—that mixture of Sunni culture and Pan-Arabism. With Iraq braced for its elections for a National Assembly—and Zarqawi's terror brigades and the insurgents doing all they could to drown these elections in violence—Ghassan al-Imam came forth with a bitter indictment of these elections and of their potential Shia beneficiaries. These were strange elections, he said, rigged for the Shia. "The principles are gone, the candidates are in hiding, and the turbans are everywhere. The leaders of the Shia slate have promised that they will not call upon Iran's help, that they will not establish a theocratic government in the image of Iran. An old man of religion [Sistani], isolated in a small room, with no knowledge of this age, who refuses to meet anyone except his retainers and his candidates for office and his subordinates, still claims that he does not interfere in political life, even though he accepts that elections be held under the protection of a foreign occupier. So steeped is this man in dissimulation, *taqiyya*, he has postponed revenge against suicide operations until his sect acquires an electoral legitimacy, and its official sticks and power, with which the Sunnis will be disciplined as 'outlaws'."

Ghassan al-Imam could see, then, through the hidden ways and the cunning of Sistani; the journalist was writing as a man who knew about Shia ways. He was coming forth to warn his Sunni brethren of Shia cunning. That "Shia crescent," he added, that the Jordanian monarch had warned against, was on the verge on becoming a "full moon" extending from the Tigris of Iraq to the land of Lebanon.

There were signs that the Sunni-Shia schism in the Arab world had been reignited by Iraq's new troubles. The dispute had been ferocious in the early 1980s, with the eruption of Ayatollah Khomeini's revolution and its impact on the Shia Arabs in Iraq itself, in Lebanon, and in the states of the Gulf. That struggle had subsided a decade later, when Saddam Hussein, the self-appointed gendarme of the Sunni-Arab order of power, sacked the principality of Kuwait, breaking faith with its rulers and its Arab nationalists. There had been a coming together then of Kuwait's Sunni and Shia citizens alike, and there had been the sobering impact of a subtle Iranian policy that let that great intra-Arab feud play itself out. Iraq now called up once again the dor-

mant tension between the Sunni and Shia Arabs. This was not quite
the civil war within and over Islam that had erupted in the 1980s, but
the fragile peace had begun to crack; in a time of distress, the old suspicions had reemerged.

It was odd that this concern with Shiism's radicalism would be
asserted in the face of all that had played out in the aftermath of September 11—the terrors of Al Qaeda, the fierceness of the ultra-
Wahhabis, the virulence of the Sunni Islamist movements the world
over. A memory of the Iranian Revolution's terrors and of the radicalism of its Arab Shia tributaries in Lebanon was no doubt a factor in
the persistence of this unease with Shiism. But the larger story was the
fight between a Sunni order of privilege and a new Shia bid for a place
in a pivotal Arab country loaded with oil and other resources. An old
edifice of material—and moral—power was being overturned. This
revolution couldn't be pretty, and the Shia could provide little assurance to those who had accepted the old ways in Iraq as the proper
order of things.

There was little that was specifically Shia about interim prime minister Allawi, but even this former Baathist's rise to power was repug-
nant to those who would deny the Shia their emancipation from the
old tyranny. In an audiotape released on June 23, Abu Musab al-Zarqawi beheld for Allawi the fate that had overtaken Ezzedine Salim, the
president of the Governing Council who had been assassinated five
weeks earlier. "We have prepared for you a vicious poison and a sharp
sword. We have prepared for you a full cup of death. We will not relent
and we will not rest until we have you drink of that cup as we did with
Ezzedine Salim." The Americans had made much of the transfer of
authority to Allawi and his cabinet, but for Zarqawi the war against
"the apostate" was no less legitimate than the war against the infidel.
"We do not wage our jihad in order to replace the Western tyrant with
an Arab tyrant. We fight to make God's word supreme, and anyone
who stands in the way of our struggle is our enemy, a target of our
swords. . . . Just as the American Muslim is our brother, an Arab
apostate is our hated enemy." God's will, Zarqawi warned, was sure to
befall Allawi and his "band of collaborators, symbols of evil, and a people of hypocrisy." Power had come to this Shia man of politics with a
checkered background. But it had not yet been secured and defended.

Where the Shia could place their faith in the weight of their numbers, the Kurds were, at best, ambivalent about this new political

order. They had done well by this new freedom, but their unease with Arab rule had remained. They would participate in the political life of a Baghdad-based government so long as the Shia refrained from pushing for theocratic rule and the Sunni Arabs recognized that a pan-Arab national state was a thing of the past. The two preeminent leaders of the Kurds, Massoud Barzani and Jalal Talabani, were men of considerable political skill. Their people had put behind them the fratricide that had bedeviled Kurdish history, and an era of autonomy under Anglo-American protection had given the Kurds the experience of self-rule. The two Kurdish leaders had been bitter enemies, with warring turfs. Barzani, a tribal chief through and through, had never forgiven or accepted the rise of the more urbane and more charismatic Talabani. Now as the American protectors were keen to cobble together this new interim arrangement and to highlight the return to Iraqi self-rule, the two Kurdish leaders set out in a letter to President Bush—made public on the eighth of June—their worries about the place of their people in the new Iraq. This letter carried a message of Kurdish loyalty to the Pax Americana but also the threat of "walking away" from the Baghdad-based polity. It was carefully crafted—the profession of loyalty to the great power, and the lament that the Kurds were being taken for granted as the Americans were conciliating the Shia and the Sunni Arabs.

The immediate pretext for the letter had been the decision communicated to the Kurds by President Bush's special envoy to Iraq, Robert Blackwill, that no ethnic Kurd would be considered for the posts of president and prime minister. Most likely, the Kurds were at peace with this particular decision. But a marker was being set, and the Kurds were determined to specify the limits of their acquiescence in the new order of power. The Kurds were not about to go quietly into a new Arab-dominated state. "We consider the people of Kurdistan the most loyal friends of the United States. A year ago our fighters fought side by side with American forces for the liberation of Iraq," the two leaders wrote. There has been peace in Kurdistan and no American soldiers have been killed in areas under the regional government of Kurdistan, the American president was told. "The people of Kurdistan continue to embrace America's lofty values, and to welcome American soldiers and to offer unlimited support toward Iraq's liberation." The destiny of the Kurds, the two men added, was irrevocably tied to the fortunes of America in Iraq. "If the forces of freedom prevail in the other parts of Iraq, we know that our alliance with the United States was important to that victory. We also know that this alliance will turn us into a target for revenge should the new order fail."

The Kurds were done with "second-class citizenship," Barzani and Talabani asserted. Ceremonial posts had been granted them under former regimes in Iraq, and the Kurds wanted no return to the ways of the past. In the reckoning of these two men, Iraq was composed of two principal nationalities, Kurdish and Arab, and the Arabs had better accommodate themselves to Kurdish aspirations. An impasse had been reached between the Kurds and the Shia over an important provision in the interim Iraqi constitution adopted earlier in the year, and in Kurdish eyes, American power had shown excessive deference to the Shia. The provision stipulated that a permanent constitution would require a majority vote of the Iraqi people unless rejected by two-thirds of the vote in three of the country's eighteen provinces. That provision had been written solely for the protection of the Kurds; they constituted a majority in three of the provinces. In the name of "democracy" and "majority rule," the Shia leaders had said that that provision would not be allowed to stand. This issue lay at the heart of the joint appeal by the Kurdish leaders, although there were also the usual demands for "equity and just distribution" of the oil income of Kurdistan, the thorny issue of Kirkuk once again rearing its head, and a demand that the "Arabization" and forced settlement of Arabs in Kirkuk be rescinded.

The Kurds were not about to take up arms against American power. There was secularism in Kurdistan, and pro-Americanism aplenty. The Kurds wanted it known that, unlike the Arabs in the rest of Iraq—and unlike their historical enemies in Turkey—they had been willing to cast their fate with American power. Great Western powers had come and gone in this region, and those who rode with them had known patronage and abandonment in equal measure. The Kurds had known their share of history's capriciousness and betrayal; foreign powers had repeatedly left them at the altar. Promises of autonomy and independence had been made to them and betrayed time and again. Winston Churchill, back in 1921, had held out to them the promise of independence and had asserted that the "Kurds are not to be put under Arabs if they do not wish to be," but that promise had yielded to the imperative of creating an Arab government in Baghdad. The Kurds were "needed" by the new Hashemite ruler as a balance to the influence and power of the Shia. The notion that had engaged some of Britain's soldiers and statesmen of building up an independent Kurdistan as a buffer between Turks and Arabs was abandoned. The view took hold that the Kurds were not a "nation." "No Kurd repines over his lost empire. The Kurdish national songs do not tell of the palmy days when Kurdistan was really Kurdistan," one of Britain's most influential colonial hands, Sir Mark Sykes, opined. His conclusion, and views in a similar vein, carried the day. Britain's abandonment of the Kurds was dressed up in this convenient "anthropology" of national communities, in which some peoples were developed enough for nationalism and others unworthy of it.

Richard Nixon and Henry Kissinger, as well as the shah of Iran, had toyed with the Iraqi Kurds half a century later, encouraging their rebellion against the Baath regime, while having no intention of seeing that rebellion come to any fulfillment. The aim had been to unsettle the rulers in Baghdad and to force on them concessions to the shah in a running dispute over the Shatt al-Arab waterway. Once that aim was accomplished in 1975, the Kurds had been abandoned to the mercy of Baghdad yet again. And there had of course been the bitter experience in the Gulf War in 1991—the call to rebellion by the victorious American-led coalition, and the American abdication that followed. Out of that calamity, there had come the gift of autonomy and the protection of Anglo-American power, a measure of penance perhaps on the part of the Pax Americana for what it had done to the Kurds.

There were no sure guarantees that America was in Iraq to stay. Still, the Kurds wanted American protection and a promise that they would be spared the vengeance of the more resourceful nationalisms and more powerful political entities all around them. Loath to go it alone, they openly campaigned for a more extensive American military presence in their midst. The nationalism at play in Kurdistan appeared measured and restrained. The Anglo-American protection afforded Kurdistan had been vindicated. The Kurds threatening to turn away from Baghdad were still within the bounds of expediency and of political reason.

In the same vein, the interim President Sheikh Ghazi al-Yawar's claims of relative independence from American tutelage were of no harm to the American stewards. He himself had come from the ranks of a council that the American regency had chosen. He had an American graduate degree and a deep appreciation of America's role in Iraq. He would distance himself from American tutelage while still asking the Americans to stay on. The Iraqis were beginning to rediscover politics—after the simplifications and the terror of the despotism. In their collective memory, Iraqis still wrote and spoke of a time before the despotism when they had had the semblance of normal politics. Some of that history was consolation, but a good measure of it was true. The tribes had been independent and able to defy the state. The Shia jurists had been proud and autonomous. Indeed the supreme religious figure in Najaf, under the monarchy, never called on the monarch. An exquisite compromise had been arrived at: king and scholar would meet on the grounds of the Imam Ali shrine, on special religious holidays. The merchants too had their own role. The leading merchants were wealthier than the crown; it wasn't unusual for members of the royal household to be indebted to the merchants. Terror and oil had remade the country, of course, changed it beyond recognition. A new balance would have to be found, and the foreign soldiers and administrators could at best grant the Iraqis a chance to discover the truth of their country's political life.

No Iraqi poet was likely to sit down to write stirring poetry celebrating the transfer of sovereignty from the Coalition Provisional Authority to the interim government of Prime Minister Iyad Allawi, an event that took place, by surprise, on June 28, 2004, two days ahead of schedule. This was not quite "freedom at midnight," done to trumpets and drums. No jihadist was likely to see in the drama that played out in Baghdad reason to call to a halt the campaign of holy terror on the loose in Iraq's cities. That fabled Arab street, it was known, would dispose of this event with great ease, dismiss the new rulers as quislings doing the bidding of the Pax Americana. But the unadorned, brief ceremony that saw the American regent, L. Paul Bremer, to a C-130 at the Baghdad airport still had a dignity and a meaning all its own. He was escorted to that plane by one of this new order's best and brightest, the Kurdish leader Barham Salih, deputy prime minister in the interim government. True, there was staging and artifice and heavy-handedness in the affair—the timing of it made to coincide with the presence of the American president just across the border in Turkey, in the midst of a NATO summit. The handwritten note informing President Bush that the deed had taken place, on which he then scribbled,

"Let freedom reign," had less to do with Iraq and its burdens than with the political needs back home of an embattled president eager to show accomplishments and progress in an increasingly unpopular war. George W. Bush's needs—let alone those of his political adviser, Karl Rove—aside, this wasn't a charade that was pulled off in Baghdad. There had never been an American design to dominate and rule Iraqis. Over the horizon, Iraqis could now see the possibility of a time beyond that rule of the tyrant and the rule of the foreigners. Ahead of them lay the promise—and the hazards—of political freedom.

To be sure, it was not normal sovereignty that came to Iraq. A country with 160,000 foreign soldiers could not be described as wholly free. It was idle to pretend that the new American ambassador, John Negroponte, was an ordinary envoy. He had a huge reconstruction package to dispose of, and there was that formidable military force available to him. Negroponte himself was a man of poise and exquisite manners. As I observed him in August, only weeks into his tenure, there was mastery and skill to his performance: understated and calm, he seemed determined to stay in the background and to let the Iraqi leaders assume greater burdens—and higher visibility. He was no doubt aware that Bremer had had a heavy touch, and he wanted it known that the time of the American regency had come to an end. When I pressed Iraqis with the question of whether Negroponte was an ambassador or a viceroy, many were bemused and a bit uncertain as to how to characterize the American envoy. The consensus was that this was in truth a viceroy keen to carry himself as an ambassador and to observe with the strictest fidelity the transition to Iraqi sovereignty.

Iraqis knew a thing or two about the workings of foreign rule and foreign influence. At their fingertips they had that experience with the British presence in their midst. The British had ruled Iraq directly, from 1921 until 1932, and had then tried, over the course of a quarter-century, to shape and order its politics, working with native governments that alternately satisfied and thwarted British intentions. These present-day Iraqis knew that their prime minister had a close working relationship with the Americans. They could see his American security detail; they had access to the leaflets and the audiotapes of Abu Musab al-Zarqawi that dubbed Iyad Allawi the "Hamid Karzai of Iraq." The interim government operated in the Green Zone—under American protection. The leaders of this government moved about the country in American helicopters, and access to their homes was controlled by American soldiers. But freedom can't be a fetish. There were the needs of Iraq, and they were staggering. There was the nemesis of Iraq's freedom, an insurgency drawing its fire and pitilessness from the forces of the old regime, and from jihadists from neighboring lands who had come into Iraq. It was reasonable to assume that the Iraqis could live with this ambiguity in their political life and could grant this interim order the benefit of the doubt.

Proud and prickly, the Iraqis were a people who told the pollsters they wanted to see the departure of the American forces as they whispered in the ears of the American commanders in the field that they were nervous that the foreign soldiers might leave them to the chaos. There were some prerogatives available to this native government that no American proconsul could enjoy. It was one thing for Fallujah to pose as a citadel of Islam against the infidels, but an entirely different matter for that town to take up arms against a native government. Iyad Allawi could call the insurgents "enemies of Islam," as he did shortly after the transfer of sovereignty, while it was awkward, at best, for George W. Bush to insert himself into that fight over, and for, Islam. In the same vein, American officials had repeatedly warned Iraq's neighbors to keep their fires—and their misfits—away from Iraq, but there was something more true to the region when Mr. Allawi told his neighbors that Iraqis would not forget those who stood with them, and stood against them, in their time of vulnerability and disorder.

This is not a region given to charitable interpretations of America's motives. But there were Arabs who saw in the transfer of sovereignty evidence of America's good will and benevolence. In Kuwait, Ahmad Bishara, one of the principality's most distinguished and forthright and secular intellectuals (scion of a family of sea captains and traders, he studied at Columbia University in the tumultuous sixties, then went on for a PhD in engineering at the University of Michigan) spoke of this event next door to him in Iraq with deep feeling and appreciation. In a note drafted the morning after the ceremony in Iraq, he wrote, "History will record how a superpower went to free a people only to slip out in grace without fanfare. Only America can do that: put its might and spill the blood of its sons and daughters to save a nation from its own evil, without asking for anything in return. Not even a gun salute for a job well done. I hope one bright day in the future

Iraqis will revisit this moment and say: 'Thank you guys for a job well done.' That day will vindicate today's and yesterday's sacrifices."

Americans were not likely to stay long in Iraq. If there had been hopes that the place would be a forward base of the Pax Americana in the Persian Gulf, these hopes had been set aside. By the time Americans had turned over sovereignty, what triumphalism accompanied this campaign had long been abandoned.

That master of terror, Abu Musab al-Zarqawi, had foreseen the shape of things to come. In that letter intercepted in Iraq—a letter that Zarqawi had intended for Osama bin Laden and Ayman al-Zawahiri—the Jordanian had spoken of the impact of Iraqis' reclaiming their own country. "America is being bloodied in Iraq," he said, "but has no intention of leaving, no matter the bloodletting among its soldiers. It is looking to a near future, when it remains safe in its bases, while handing over control to a bastard government with an army and a police force." The fight against a native government, Zarqawi conceded, would be infinitely harder to wage.

Iraq had become a devil's playground: its porous borders were a magnet for jihadists looking for a field of battle. There were Jordanians and Syrians and Lebanese and Saudis and Palestinians, and Iranians, who made their way to Iraq. The lands nearby were seething with unrest and failure; the rulers winked at the boys of terror. Iraq was as good a dumping ground as any for the disgruntled and the restless of these neighboring lands. In Iraq, the self-styled *muhjahidin* would kill or be killed. The governments in Syria and Saudi Arabia could still insist on their innocence of what the purveyors of terror were doing in Iraq. But the neighboring governments had no interest in coming to the aid of the Americans—or the Iraqis. The Americans were getting their comeuppance in the streets of Fallujah and Baquba and Najaf. The big ideas of reform, those heady alien notions of remaking the ways of the Arabs, were being battered, and abandoned, by the day.

There was no need to run risks on behalf of the Americans. Nor were the Arab rulers beyond Iraq having an easy time of it themselves. There were manhunts and gun battles in a Saudi realm once known for its quiescence. There were armed militants determined to drive out the "expats" from the residential compounds in Arabia, convinced that the flight of those foreign workers and technicians would bring the economic life of the country to a standstill. If the purveyors of terror in Iraq had beheaded Nicholas Berg, a young man from Pennsylvania, in May of 2004, and presented the deed as a "gift" to the believers, the underground in Arabia would stage its own grim ritual in the month that followed. A man from New Jersey, Paul M. Johnson, an engineer who worked in Riyadh for Lockheed Martin, was kidnapped and murdered, and the event was staged by killers with an eye to the power of image and a feel for the darkness of the crowd and its appetite. The customary videotape was made; a frightened, blind-folded man could be heard haltingly repeating his full name, his American nationality, and the "confession" that he was in Arabia working on Apache helicopters. Secretive and averse to owning up to their furies and troubles, the custodians of the Saudi realm had insisted that these troubles came from grievances beyond their borders. There was rage over Palestine and the Palestinians, they said, and there was rage over the treatment of Iraqi prisoners at Abu Ghraib. The militants were quick to challenge this official version. In their video of the beheading of Paul Johnson, which made its way to the Islamist Web sites and to the satellite channels of the Arab world, they were to make specifically Saudi demands: the release of their "holy warriors" from three of the country's prisons. These militants were children of Arabia, their demands and grievances emanating from the conditions of the Saudi realm.

Conflict by proxy had played out pretty much the same way a quarter-century earlier, in the civil war of Lebanon. The Lebanese had slipped into civil war, and the neighboring lands had shifted onto Lebanon wider Arab quarrels. The money had come, and the volunteers, and Lebanon's war had become a proxy war for the wider struggles of the region. Iraq was a bigger theater still, and the jihadists spoiling for a fight had been given a place where their war against their own regimes, and against the Americans, could be fought. This was a war in broad daylight, under the gaze of the world, and in the glare of the new media. By the strict calculus of power, these jihadists could not win. But they were true believers, convinced of the righteousness of their campaign and of the "treason" and degradation of the regimes they were determined to overthrow. That standoff that had dominated Arab politics, between rulers in the saddle and ferocious, nihilistic oppositionists, was now playing out in Iraq. The Arab rulers could not be overthrown, but they had no genuine remedies for the ills of their societies. The oppositionists had their wrath and nothing else to offer.

An Iraqi society released from the grip of a terrible despotism was thus given the added burden of a wider Arab fight. The drifters who had made their way to Afghanistan in the 1980s were now in an Arab land.

The jihadists and the Arab governments were invested here; so were those spectators in Cairo and Damascus and Arabia reading their own world—and their needs—into Iraq. When Saddam was arraigned before an Iraqi judge, immediately after the transfer of sovereignty, ruler and ruled in Arab lands understood the meaning of the drama. The Saudi commentator Abdul Rahman al-Rashed wrote in the columns of *Asharq Al-Awsat,* that this was the trial of a "terrible era," a "whole bad time" in Arab life—of "Iraqis other than Saddam who took part in the making of that history, of Arabs who shall remain unnamed, of an entire Arab culture that defended him down to his last lies." This trial, he added, was a "nursery" and a school for teaching the meaning of responsibility.

Abdul Rahman al-Rashed was not alone in his recognition that the indictment of Saddam Hussein was loaded with symbolism for Arabs beyond Iraq. No one in the Arab world could miss the meaning of the foreign minister of Egypt's declaring the trial of Saddam Hussein a sideshow of no great importance. This representative of the Egyptian elite fully understood that there were Cairenes, reduced to political silence in their own city by despotism, who could see in Saddam's trial the spectacle of power being brought to account. There was no tradition in this region of the responsibility of rulers. Save for Lebanon, there was no experience of men in power serving a term or two and heading into the sunset. There is an expression—in Arabic it rhymes nicely—which describes the normal trajectory of the ruler as a passage from the palace to the grave; *min al-qasr ila al-qabr.* Now this most turbulent of Arab countries was offering an entirely different spectacle—a ruler brought up on charges of crimes against his people and against the people of Kuwait.

The willful and the true believers could dismiss this trial as the work of the American "puppeteers" of this government: they could charge, as they did, that the young director of the tribunal who brought the indictment, the American-educated lawyer Salem Chalabi, had an Israeli partner in a London firm and had ties to Douglas Feith, of the Department of Defense, forged when the latter was in private legal practice. But a new history—hesitant, and in the shadow of a mighty

insurgency and of an American military force that had "physical cus-
tody" of Saddam Hussein—was made the day a young, soft-spoken
Iraqi judge read to Saddam Hussein and to his principal lieutenants
the specific charges of their indictments. That painful Arab exceptionalism gave way that day. The sorts of trials that had come to fragile new
democracies in East Asia and Latin America had come to an Arab
land.

The dictator and his principal lieutenants could never give the
aggrieved a sense of satisfaction. You could not call back the victims of
Chemical Ali, now a frightened old man; there was no way you could
force on the silver-tongued Tariq Aziz, the dictator's apologist in foreign lands and forums, an acknowledgment of his own crimes. The
former had called the director of the tribunal "Brother Salem" in an
attempt to please, Salem Chalabi told me as he recounted the startling
banality and cowardice of this lot. For his part, Aziz had let it be
known that he would be eager to turn evidence against his old partners
in the regime. The dictator himself alternated between bluster and
panic. He dismissed the Kuwaitis as "dogs" who had wanted to turn
Iraqi men into "paupers" and Iraqi women into "ten-dinar prostitutes."
He "heard," he said, that there had been victims of chemical weapons
in Halabja, "under the presidency of Saddam Hussein." He wrote off
the trial, as he was bound to, as the "occupier's justice," berated the
young judge for doing the occupier's work. Peace in the streets of
Baghdad and Fallujah had not yet been secured. This fragile new history, though, was possibly the beginning of a break with a heavy
Iraqi (and Arab) legacy.

Wars of liberation, rather like revolutions, it would appear, devour
their own children. Salem Chalabi did not savor his moment in the
sun. Weeks after the charges were filed against Saddam Hussein, trouble reared its head for the director of the tribunal himself. A warrant
was served on him; charges were made that he was implicated in the
murder of a finance ministry inspector who had been looking into
property seizures that had taken place after the fall of the Saddam
regime. The knives had been out for Salem Chalabi's uncle, Ahmad,
and now the forty-one-year-old lawyer was himself in trouble. He had
clashed, it was reported, with a finance ministry inspector days before
assassins had turned up at the home of the inspector, Haitham Fadhil.
The inspector had been one in a long line of Iraqi officials who had
been gunned down by unknown assailants. The murdered man's wife,

it was said, had asserted that her husband had been warned by Salem Chalabi to refrain from pressing his inquiry into property seizures that the Iraqi National Congress, headed by Salem's uncle, had allegedly committed. For the lawyer who had been at work prosecuting Saddam Hussein and his lieutenants, who had had ideas of setting up in Iraq a "truth and reconciliation commission" based on the South African model, this was a stunning turn of events. The charges against him were brought by Zuhair al-Maliky, the same judge who had ordered the raid on his uncle Ahmad.

In early August of 2004 I was on my way to Iraq. At my hotel by the Gulf, in Kuwait City, I ran into Salem Chalabi. I had known him since his days as an undergraduate at Yale. My wife and I had taken to him: he would visit us in Manhattan now and then. We had stayed in touch while he attended law school in Evanston, Illinois, at Northwestern University. He was an unusually literate and engaging young man: we had many interests in common—Iraq, Lebanon, the state of Arab affairs. He knew Lebanon—my birthplace—and its politics with intimacy, and for years, when my connection to that country had snapped, he kept me abreast of the life and the ways of that country.

In Kuwait, he was inconsolable: we ate dinner together, then went out and sat by the beach, late into the night. He was on his way to London; his wife (herself a child of Iraq) was there. He had a thriving legal career in New York and London as a highly paid corporate lawyer. He had not really known Iraq. He had been born there, in 1963, and eighteen days later, when the first Baath coup d'état had come, his parents had left Iraq. Years later, he had visited Kurdistan, once or twice, when that part of the country had slipped out of the control of the Baath. To the ways of his ancestral country, he was a stranger. Lebanon and England and the United States were more familiar to him. But duty and history and old family expectations that one day what had been theirs would be restored had brought him back to Iraq. We did not talk of the charges swirling around him—at least not in a direct way, at the beginning. We talked of Saddam Hussein and his criminal lieutenants. He had read Arendt's *Eichmann in Jerusalem,* and he had been amazed by its insight into what he himself would feel and experience in his encounter with this group. He had been ready, he said, for an encounter with "absolute evil," and had been struck by the "ordinariness" and cowardice of this lot. He had never struck me as a religious man, but he let it slip that he had been nervous enough to recite for himself the opening chapter of the Quran, the "exordium," to calm himself down.

Salem Chalabi had been given a rare and unusual experience. But now it had all come to this, and there ran through our time and conversation together his bottomless sense of disappointment. He had wanted the trial of Saddam to be something of a model for the "legal reformation" in Iraq and in the Arab world beyond. He had not been prepared for the acrimony of the country or its deep schisms. He had put his legal career on hold. He had put in several years of preparation for this moment of Iraqi legal history, having been active in an effort that preceded the Iraq war to indict Saddam Hussein on charges of war crimes. He told me that he had lived off his savings, that his personal security had been a nightmare. There were no exact words of his that I could quote that gave away his disappointment, no sense of whether he would have done it over again had he been given the foresight of what was to come. But he spoke of Iraqi and American officials who had now distanced themselves from him in the aftermath of his troubles. In Kuwait, he had met with Prime Minister Allawi. The latter had told him "not to return to Baghdad until the matter is cleared." The clearing of his name would "take time," he was told. It seemed astounding to him that anyone would link him to a murder case. He didn't know what this new venture in Iraq would yield. But his concerns were now more personal—the redeeming of his own reputation. Taking leave of him, I could not shake off the sense that Iraq's ways had taken their toll on yet another life. I knew him well: his decency and courtesy, his love of books and reading, the courtliness of an older culture that clung to him even as a young college student. He did not have to tell me that Iraq had held endless surprises for him. I could see for myself the sorrow and bewilderment in him.

A week later, in Kurdistan, I caught an interview with Salem Chalabi on one of the satellite channels of the Arab world. He was in London, his interviewer in Dubai. He tried his best to convey his innocence; he was being interviewed in Arabic, and it was clear that college and law school in the United States put him at some disadvantage. His Arabic was labored and hesitant. The interviewer was keen to debunk the tribunal and its director. And he had something specific on his mind: he wanted to know of a purported business relationship between Salem Chalabi and one Marc Zell, an American-born lawyer and investor, who happened to be an Israeli citizen. Zell had come to

Baghdad, Chalabi said, looking for business opportunities, but he himself had not done business in Iraq, he said. It was enough for the interviewer that an Israeli businessman had turned up in Baghdad. And it was enough of an "indictment" of Salem Chalabi that he had once met Douglas J. Feith, Undersecretary for Policy at the Department of Defense. He had met Feith once, Chalabi said, for five minutes in the company of seven other people. The matter of the tribunal against Saddam Hussein had been pushed aside. In the best of worlds, it would have been hard to stay with the trial of Saddam Hussein, to establish in the Arab world, and on that Arab street, the precedent of holding a ruler responsible for the follies and crimes of his regime. Now those older Arab phobias had once again overwhelmed the new possibilities.

In a hectic fortnight in Iraq, it would be fair to say, I did not encounter any Iraqis who placed credence in the charges against Salem Chalabi. A Department of Justice lawyer, a Minnesotan, who served as an adviser to the Iraqi Criminal Court, gave the matter its most legalistic and severe tone. In a conversation with me, he said that these were "serious charges" that Chalabi would have to answer. But the Iraqis saw the matter through the prism of politics. The Chalabis had been too close to the Americans, ran the Iraqi verdict, and had then placed themselves at odds with American power. They were sure that Salem Chalabi would know redemption. On September 1, there was a break in Salem Chalabi's case. The warrant for his arrest was withdrawn; he would return to Iraq for questioning as an "informational witness," but he was relieved of his role in the tribunal. Beyond this lawyer's fate, the bigger quest for a political and legal culture of responsibility was yet to prevail.

This order struggling for its life always had the burden of its neighborhood's troubles. In late August 2004, as the most recent of Moqtada al-Sadr's rebellions in Najaf had been brought under control, Sheikh Yusuf al-Qaradawi, on a visit to his native Egypt from his home in Qatar, provided more tinder for Iraq's fires. In an astonishingly radical fatwa that obliterated what line still existed between religion and politics in an unsettled Islamic world, the "television sheikh" ruled that the killing of American civilians in Iraq was "obligatory on all Muslims." The Americans in Iraq, the preacher said, were all "combatants and invaders, and there is no difference between an American soldier and an American civilian in Iraq. . . . The civilians are there to aid the soldiers and the occupying forces." The man living in the safety of Qatar—among Americans of every profession present in that princi-pality—had no qualms about sanctioning indiscriminate killing of ordinary Americans in Iraq. The sheikh paid "moderation" a tribute: he drew a line at the desecration of the dead. It was impermissible, he said, to desecrate the corpses of the Americans.

It was a moment that illuminated the landscape of this Arab world. Qaradawi was not an Iraqi, but he had given himself the right to rule on Iraq's affairs. In this unguarded moment, he had given himself away. The crude politics of it all was further underlined by his plea, on the same occasion, for the release of two French journalists who had been kidnapped in Iraq. He let his audience know that he had told the French foreign minister that "all the Arabs and the Muslims support and appreciate France's opposition to American policies and its refusal to take part in the invasion of Iraq." This was vintage Qaradawi: a man of the street, and a man of the chancelleries. It was important to let the faithful know that he was in the circle of power, that foreign envoys called on him and sought his help. There was no religious pretense here: he urged the release of the French journalists so that "France's good way of dealing with Arab and Islamic matters would become a lesson, and an example, for other nations."

Qaradawi ignited a storm: this was on the eve of the third anniver-sary of September 11, and some Arabs had begun to speak publicly about the responsibility of the children of the Arab world for terrors the world over. It had become harder to deny and to dissimulate. The cult of terror—enticing in earlier years, playing out the yearnings and resentments of mainstream society—had begun to scare increas-ingly large numbers of Arabs. There were video stores doing brisk busi-ness selling tapes and CDs of beheadings; there were Web sites where the masked men of terror displayed the way they had brutalized those they had murdered. There was a group by the name of the Islamic Army in Iraq that had kidnapped twelve Nepalese laborers, murdered them in cold blood, beheaded one of them, recorded it all, and described the atrocity as carrying out the "rule of God" on those "infidels" who had come to Iraq to "fight the Muslims and aid the Christians and the Jews, those descendants of pigs and monkeys." Bar-barism had come to scare those who had winked at it.

The deference to Qaradawi—often bordering on an understandable fear of taking on a man of great sway and resources—was challenged by the Saudi Abdul Rahman al-Rashed, who had impeccable establishment credentials. The journalist had just stepped down from running the daily paper *Asharq Al-Awsat* and was now based in Dubai, at the helm of the Saudi-owned satellite channel *Al-Arabiya*. As a columnist, he had always been forthright and free of any trace of that debilitating mix of belligerence and self-pity so common in Arab writings. He minced no words about Qaradawi and his ruling. "Imagine a man of religion encouraging the murder of civilians, a man in the fullness of old age inciting young boys to murder when two of his daughters are studying in the United Kingdom under the protection of a presumably 'infidel' power. We can't redeem our youth unless we take on the men of religion who have turned into revolutionaries who send other people's kids to war while they send their own to European and American schools."

This rebuttal by Abdul Rahman al-Rashed, followed by words of protest by other writers appalled by the cynicism and cruelty of this call to murder, brought about a characteristic retreat by Qaradawi. A week or so later, the preacher found an appropriate setting, the Diplomatic Club in Doha. In the presence of a French and an American diplomat, he stepped back from the fire, or tried to: "I don't authorize the killing of civilians or their kidnapping . . . but the question is who is a civilian and who is not?" He had been misunderstood, he said, and detractors had "plucked and rearranged a word or two to build castles from grains of sand and to fish in muddied waters. If it is difficult for the believer to distinguish between a civilian and a soldier in an occupied country, it would be best to choose prudence and to know that it is not permissible to kill a human being unless it is established that he is a soldier."

Men like Qaradawi had long cast caution to the wind and given themselves unprecedented claims to political power. This time, Qaradawi had been caught. (Presumably the rulers in Qatar had a word with Qaradawi about his embarrassing and incendiary ruling.) But he and merchants of religion and freelance preachers of his bent were protagonists in this struggle between order and ruin at play in Iraq.

Religious zeal was apparently selective: Sheikh Yusuf al-Qaradawi instigated ruin in Iraq but preached on behalf of order in Qatar. Several months after his incitement against Americans in Iraq, terror came to Qatar. On March 19, a car loaded with explosives, driven by an Egyptian computer engineer who had lived in Qatar since 1999, struck a theater complex in Doha, as a British theater company was performing Shakespeare's *Twelfth Night*. One British citizen was killed and sixteen people were wounded, shattering the confidence of this tranquil realm. If Qatar had believed that its hosting of the Al-Jazeera satellite channel would spare it the wrath of the jihadists, this episode of terror was a wake-up call. A man of education and skill and good income, an immigrant with children and good possibilities, was chosen for the suicide mission. Qaradawi minced no words this time around. Gone was the dissimulation; the fire was now at his doorstep. "Such criminal deeds," he said, "threaten the society in its security and solidarity, and bring benefit only to the enemies of the Islamic community and the enemies of religion. Such deeds can never be committed by someone who accepts religious faith or can be said to be a man of reason." What had been aided and abetted in Iraq was clearly impermissible in Qatar. Qaradawi was under no obligation to explain this arbitrary way with the faith. It was safe to assume that Iraqis could see for themselves this selective morality that consigned them, and their country, to the deadly workings of religious and political extremism. (Iraqis saw for themselves the painful hypocrisy of Arab and Muslim jurists rushing to condemn the London transit bombings of July 7, 2005, as they passed over in silence the torments of Iraq. "They do not do their shopping in Iraq or send their pampered children to school in Baghdad," I was told by a young Iraqi businessman speaking in sorrow more than in anger.)

In Baghdad's predominantly Shia suburb of Kadhimiyyah, site of the tombs of the seventh and ninth of the Shia imams, Ayatollah Hussein Ismael al-Sadr (a cousin of young Moqtada's father), a scholar of reserve and moderation, noted the inappropriateness of religious scholars outside Iraq issuing rulings about its affairs. There are religious authorities in Iraq, he said, who "know the affairs of the country and who know its people. The fatwas that come from religious scholars outside Iraq do not rest on a precise knowledge of the country's condition and the country's crisis." It was important, the jurist added, that Iraq's borders be secured, and that "the infiltration of the foreigners be brought to an end."

I had read Hussein al-Sadr's lament about this cynical use of religion. I had my interest in the Sadr family, and I knew that this man was a son-in-law of the legendary Muhammad Baqir al-Sadr, the "first martyr." I was eager to meet him, if only to connect with this rich history. I was given the chance to visit with him in his home in Kadhimiyyah, and to have dinner with him. The place was modest, with a small garden by the side. I was led to a gracefully designed library with a high ceiling and thousands of religious and philosophical books, stacked in shelves that reached the ceiling, books bound in leather, in the traditional way here. There were two rows of cushioned seats against the walls. When he made his appearance, I could not guess the sayyid's age. He may have been in his early fifties, though he could have been a bit older. He had the black turban of a sayyid, and his beard was completely white; there was both dignity and diffidence in him. He had about him a sense of fragility, and I could not help thinking of his younger relative Moqtada al-Sadr. The two are said to be on terribly bad terms, and the difference between the men was clear. Where Moqtada moves about with force—he reminds me of a panther—and his eyes dart about conveying suspicion of things and people around him, this cleric conveys grace of manners, and perhaps a touch of shyness. His attire was neat and modest—the obligatory black *abaya,* a white *thoub*—and spoke of a man who did not seek or cultivate personal flair. I knew he was a scholar, and the books—and the conversation to follow—confirmed the reputation. He had had a meeting once with Secretary of State Colin Powell. There were many followers of his, and ordinary Shiites as well, who had not been happy with that decision. There clings to Shiism an unease with power and the powerful, and an attachment to the religious scholars' lack of interest in the pursuit of worldly power. "Who's Powell?" said a man who complained to me about that meeting. "Sayyid Hussein is a descendant of the Prophet, the inheritor of great honor and merit, and he should not have given the American the honor of that meeting."

When I said by way of pleasantries that I admired what he had been saying about the debasing of religion by radical preachers, the ayatollah did not miss a beat. He was emphatic, as he went over the same terrain. "Religion and politics are separate realms; if you mix them, you damage both. The religious scholar has to be a man of his time and place, he must be concerned with the ailments and problems of his society, he must guide, but he should keep his distance from the political realm." It was clear that he himself knew the details of Iraq's life: he spoke with sorrow of the corruption in official life, the high cost of living, the price of pharmaceuticals. But he had no patience for those issuing fatwas from afar: "The scholar must be able to ascertain the impact and the context of his rulings, and those who don't live with us can't rule on our daily life."

We stepped out into the garden; a buffet dinner was spread out for us. We ate standing up. The sayyid ate sparingly, making the rounds to talk with his guests. There could be heard pieces of several conversations, and an anxious man asked me if it was true that America was contemplating a precipitous withdrawal from Iraq. The man asking this question had sympathy for the Americans. "We have tried their patience. Heaven knows what will become of us if they really leave." Before my departure, the sayyid gave me one of his books on the revelation received by the Prophet Muhammad. It was a learned book, full of quotations, drawing on what Orientalists had written about the Prophet. One thing in the book drew my attention—a page devoted to the sayyid's pedigree. He writes that he had written this book, in the suburb of Kadhimiyyah, "home of the two Imams, Musa al-Kazim, and Muhammad al-Jawad, peace be upon them," and that he is the son of Sayyid Ismael al-Sadr, who is the son of Haidar al-Sadr, who is the son of Sadr al-Din, who is the son of . . ." Compulsively I counted thirty-nine ancestors—back to the "martyr Imam Hussein," and further back to "the commander of the faithful Imam Ali, son-in-law of the Prophet, husband of his daughter Fatima." The sayyid had written his book in 2001. The link to the past had led to Imam Ali, who had been struck down more than thirteen centuries earlier. I had not thought much of the complaint about the sayyid's meeting with Colin Powell. But for a fleeting moment, that believer's complaint about the meeting had reason, and legitimacy, of its own.

In the Arab world beyond Iraq, and among those for whom religion had become a weapon of combat or an instrument of power, Hussein al-Sadr was swimming against the current. It was as sure as anything that Qaradawi would be back when this particular storm subsided. There were other self-appointed jurists and religious sources eager to weigh in on Iraq's affairs. This was the Arab world's big story, and Iraqis would not be allowed to have their own country for themselves. From Beirut, even Ayatollah Muhammad Hussein Fadlallah—with his great knowledge of Iraq and infinitely greater care when pronouncing on its affairs—was now compelled to endorse the "resistance" to the American presence in Iraq. There was no fatwa from him authorizing the murder of civilians, but the hostility toward this transitional Iraqi project was unmistakable: "I am with the resistance to the American occupation, regardless of whether this occupation is directly exercised or concealed under an Iraqi cover, and regardless of whether this resistance is peaceful or takes the form of armed struggle." He could not "condemn or evaluate" the movement of Moqtada al-Sadr: he was not on the scene, he allowed, and would not give himself the authority to judge the deeds of those caught up in that struggle. What he knew and could be sure of was the futility of "non-violent resistance, unless it was massive and organized, and there was no such non-violent option in Iraq."

This cleric had always displayed a keen eye for the ways of power, for the balance of things that can and cannot be. And these remarks he offered at this time in Iraq's crisis were no exception. Iraq was not Vietnam, he said, and America was not destined to repeat its experience in Vietnam. He made a sharp distinction between "mud" and a "swamp"—or a quagmire. There was "mud" in Iraq, but Iraq was not a swamp: mud frustrates those stuck in it, but they are not likely to drown in it, he observed. Perhaps America could be driven out of Iraq by sheer "frustration" and impatience, as it had been a generation or so earlier when it ventured into Lebanon. But there had to be a realistic reading of Iraq, and of the American presence in that country.

Arab society and opinion had given despotism in Iraq more than three decades of indulgence. But now the judgments of this new Iraqi interlude were fast and severe. There had been a huge American presence and a powerful American role in the politics of the region—in Saudi Arabia and Egypt, in the Arab states of the Persian Gulf, and in Jordan. The Iraqis were now singled out for judgment, and the American role in that country had come in for a level of scrutiny the other Arab regimes had been spared. The willfulness of the intellectual class was on display here, seeing and judging what it wished to see and to judge. And so was the cunning of regimes in the saddle that sat in judgment of a tormented Iraqi population trying to find its way out of a terrible darkness.

The insurgents fought on in Iraq armed in no small measure with the sympathy given them by the Arab papers and the satellite channels and by elite and mass opinion in neighboring Arab lands. They fought for minority dominion within Iraq, but they could be forgiven the sense that they were battling for a wider Sunni Arab truth and that they were fending off Shia and Kurdish claims. Zarqawi himself was given to stating the sectarian darkness and bigotry at the heart of it all. In one of his typical audiotapes, made available less than a week before Iraqis were to cast their votes for a National Assembly, he dismissed these elections as a "big American lie" aimed at bringing the Shia to power, in violation of God's law and the tradition of the Prophet Muhammad. Once again in this Zarqawi statement, the Shia were identified as *rafida*, heretics and apostates, literally rejecters of Islam. Zarqawi and his band were admittedly brazen killers and outlaws. But there were many others, preachers and pamphleteers, in the Sunni Islamist movements in Europe and in the Arabian Peninsula, who described the Shia in exactly the same terms.

The broadcasters and the writers rolling together the causes of Iraq and Palestine—these would come to be tethered together—were under no obligation to own up to the sectarianism hidden within their pronouncements; they were not about to admit to deep-seated hostility to the Kurds and the Shia bidding for a legitimate share of their country's bounty and power. They had an easier time of it; they could in a time-honored fashion conceal older phobias and enmities in the garb of anti-Americanism. And they would—without appreciating the irony—fall back on a stringent kind of Orientalism, speaking of Iraq as a country with a terrible despotic tradition fated to tyranny. The weight of Iraq's own history was indeed heavy; the ways of the Arab world beyond and around Iraq made it virtually unbearable. Other Arabs might more decently have let Iraq and Iraqis be, granting them the time and the freedom to sort out their own destiny. But that the other Arabs could not do. Iraq provided a way that an unhappy generation of Arabs could give voice to a deeper unease about their place in the world. If the political life of Syria, Egypt, Saudi Arabia, Tunisia, and Jordan was off-limits to the peoples of these lands, Iraq and the American presence in it served as the safety valve for an Arab culture in the throes of a political crisis that goes on through bottomless anguish and expectations of reform and deliverance that never come.

The spectacle of Iraqis going to the polls—they were to do so three times in the course of 2005—was a challenge to the stagnant politics of the Arabs around Iraq. These millions of people flooding Iraq's streets could not be ignored. In all fairness, there were Arabs who extolled the "contagious" effect of this new Iraqi history. There was evident celebration in the way the pan-Arab daily *Asharq Al-Awsat* covered the first of these elections. Its banner headlines communicated unmistakable enthusiasm; its reporters were everywhere, gathering news of a people who defied those who had warned them that election day would be a day of terror. From the city of Basra the reporters wrote of an old man, ninety years of age, who had made the strenuous walk to the polling center and came out leaning on the shoulder of one of his grandsons, proclaiming that the day marked for him a day of his birth in a new Iraq. From Basra again, a laborer thirty years of age said that he had been unable to sleep the night before these elections, that he now feels a "new taste for this life in Iraq." There were other reports from towns and voting centers all over the country. And these were in a Saudi-owned paper, presided over by a young prince from the House of Saud. Liberty—with its vibrancy and joy—had broken through the old barriers.

But there remained surliness of course; my favorite example of the stubbornness of the old ways is the reporting in the leading Egyptian daily *Al-Ahram* on the morning after the election of January 30. There was studied nonchalance in the paper that day: nothing unusual had happened around and about Egypt. The front page had pharaoh himself, President Hosni Mubarak, attending an African summit in Abuja, Nigeria. In the picture, Mubarak is serenity itself, following the deliberations of the summit. Egyptians were told, in the paper's headlines that day, that their leader had brought to the summit suggestions about the development and the eradication of disease and about Sino-African cooperation in the year 2009. Iraq's news was buried by the military ruler's travels. And Iraq's news was covered in the way this autocratic regime typically filtered the reality for its people. There were reports of a violent day in Iraq—the killing and wounding of 122 Iraqis in more than thirty explosions, the attacks on polling stations. The pharaonic system was not to be shaken. Its message had not yielded: Egypt was bigger than the tumult of Iraq, and the dictatorship had sheltered Egypt from the violence that had befallen Iraqis. This new history playing out in Iraq had its work cut out for it.

A crime that took place in Beirut, as the first Iraqi election results were being released, was to make its own case, though, for the urgency of change in Arab lands. On Monday, February 14, 2005, Rafiq Hariri, a former prime minister of Lebanon, a businessman and a philanthropist of note, was struck down by a huge bomb that shattered his motorcade as it made its way on the city's seafront. Hariri was the unlikeliest of martyrs for the cause of Lebanon's independence. A

Sunni Muslim, he had risen from the obscurity and poverty of Sidon—on Lebanon's coast—to the upper reaches of Lebanese and Arab society, largely through the patronage of the House of Saud. He wasn't particularly articulate, or given to the call of political causes. He believed in the power of wealth and of pragmatism, and he saw Lebanon's mission in the time-honored way of Sidon's Phoenician heritage: commerce and trade, banking and tourism. He had made a vast fortune in construction in Arabia. But his country tugged at him, and he had found his way into its politics. He had given freely of his wealth. There were estimates that he had paid for the university education of thirty thousand Lebanese students. Over two long decades in politics, he had made his accommodation with Syrian power. He no doubt paid off Syrian intelligence operatives and officers, cut their sons and wives and daughters into business deals, did what he could for the restoration of his country, while staying on the safe side of Syria's hegemony in Lebanon.

For all his caution, Hariri had not been spared. In an Arab world that had grown perhaps indifferent to political violence, Hariri's murder was a jolt to Arabs in Lebanon and beyond. There was no blood on the man's hands; he had not led a militia or a political party. His murder in broad daylight in a city he had helped restore after a long, bitter civil war was an affront to decent sensibility. The man had been struck down as he had broken with Syria and with its satrap regime in Beirut. No one was fooled or taken in by the Syrian displays of horror at Hariri's murder. There was a saying in the hard hill country of Lebanon about killing a man and then walking in his funeral procession. The vast majority of Lebanon's people now wanted Syria and its informers and secret police and soldiers out of their land. The shock of this murder—twenty-two other people perished with Hariri—was the message that in the slaughterhouse of Arab politics, no one was safe from terror's reach. Here was a man of enormous wealth, with personal ties to French president Jacques Chirac and to the House of Saud, but violence had taken his life. Two months earlier, I had seen Hariri in Dubai at a conference on the Arab future. There were luminaries there—former President Bill Clinton, of course, on a speaking gig— but Hariri seemed adrift. A man of imposing physical appearance and boundless energy, he seemed more subdued than usual. He delivered a generic speech about reform and transparency. He never uttered a word about Syria. There was a tough operative of the Syrian regime in the audience, a Western-educated spokeswoman by the name of Buthaina Shaaban, close to the Assad dynasty, and Hariri knew he was being watched. He did not know what nemesis lay in wait for him.

Hariri had sought for his country a businessman's peace; his way was a break with the politics of charisma and ideology that had wrecked the Arab world. In the massive outpouring of grief for him—his burial ground, the site of the crime in Beirut's swanky hotel district, and his hometown of Sidon were all turned into instant shrines and overrun by mourners of every religious and sectarian creed—Lebanese and other Arabs expressed their desire to be rid of the car bombs and the horrific killings. The scandal of Syria's presence in Lebanon was now out in the open for all to see. Truth be known, this steady Syrian encroachment on Lebanon's sovereignty had been aided and abetted by the silence of the world. In one of those astonishing changes, the Syrian arsonists had come to be seen as the fire brigade of a volatile Lebanese polity. A generation earlier, the Pax Americana had averted its gaze from the Syrian destruction of the last vestige of Lebanon's independence. In 1991, American power had acquiesced when the Syrians put down the rebellion of a patriotic Lebanese officer, Michel Aoun, whose cause represented the devotion of the Christian Maronites to the ancestral independence of their country. That was the price paid by President George Herbert Walker Bush for enlisting Syria in the coalition that waged war against Saddam Hussein for his grab of Kuwait. Pity the Lebanese: they had cedars, Kuwait had oil. American power would restore Kuwait's sovereignty, as the Lebanese were consigned to their terrible fate in that Syrian prison.

A circle had been closed: it was fitting that the accommodation with Syrian power in Lebanon made during the first war against Saddam Hussein would come apart during the second American war in Iraq. (Fitting, too, was the fact that the protagonists now, Bashar al-Assad and George W. Bush, were sons of the men who had been there during the first campaign.) America now wanted Syria out of Lebanon. Damascus had not warranted membership in the "axis of evil" of President Bush back in 2002—the charter members, as we know, were Iran, Saddam Hussein's Iraq, and North Korea—but American power, it seemed, had had its fill with Syria. The rulers in Damascus had played cat and mouse with the Bush administration. They dreaded the massive American power deployed on their eastern border in Iraq but sought, by their own lights, to cut a deal with the imperial power.

They would, alternately, aid the infiltration of jihadists into Mosul and Fallujah and Ramadi and then offer promises of cooperation. They no doubt believed that the bazaar was open, that they could trade cooperation on Iraq for a free hand in Lebanon. The deal had not worked. And the Hariri murder, at once pathetic and brazen, had thrown Syria on the defensive.

News of America's demise in Arab opinion had been greatly exaggerated. In the streets of Beirut, in the discussions of other Arabs, there were appeals now to the great power—working this time with France—to push Syria out of Lebanon. To be sure, Iraq itself was still engulfed with violence. The Shia commemoration of Imam Hussein's martyrdom had seen predictable violence: jihadists had targeted Shia mosques and religious gatherings as they had the year before. A jihadist on a bicycle had hurled himself into a crowd of mourners; others had flung themselves on checkpoints in assaults on Iraqi police and army units. Still, for all this carnage, the message of Iraq's vote and that senseless death of Hariri in Beirut were remarkably different statements on the modern condition of the Arabs. The edifice of Arab tyranny, secure for a long generation or two, was suddenly under assault. Lebanese, terrified (and rightly so) by Syria's dictatorship, had suddenly found their voice. They wanted their country's dignity, and a reprieve from the culture of dictatorship and darkness.

"It's strange for me to say it, but this process of change has started because of the American invasion of Iraq," the hereditary leader of Mount Lebanon's Druze community, Walid Jumblatt, told an American journalist as he watched the people of his country heedlessly challenging Syrian power. "I was cynical about Iraq. But when I saw the Iraqi people voting three weeks ago, eight million of them, it was the start of a new Arab world. The Syrian people, the Egyptian people, all say that something is changing. The Berlin Wall is falling. We can see it." Educated at the American University of Beirut, Jumblatt had the usual leftist politics of West Beirut. He had never had any kind words to say about American power. He had come to his chieftaincy when his legendary father, Kamal, had been struck down by Syrian assassins in 1977. (The Druze are an esoteric Islamic sect who inhabit Syria, Lebanon, and Israel, and their chiefs wield enormous secular and religious authority.) He had done his best to live with Syrian power, even as he knew that the Syrians had murdered his father. On the other side of fear, Jumblatt now found a world of release. There were no "red lines" left, he announced, and the Syrian occupiers had to quit Lebanon. In an astonishing display of defiance, he challenged the Syrians to kill him, as they had his father, as they had Rafiq Hariri. His testimony about the contagious effect of Iraq's liberation was an illustration of all those Arab hopes grafted onto Iraq.

The Syrians had not assimilated how different the world had become after September 11 and after Iraq. In March 2001, the revered Maronite patriarch, Cardinal Mar Nasrallah Boutros Sfeir, had journeyed to the United States, where he sought an audience with President Bush—in vain. This was, after all, the time of realism: no one wanted to offend Damascus or stir up the passions of Lebanese nationalism. Four years later, however, a president who had "planted the flag of liberty" in Arab lands had no choice but to take up the cause of Lebanon's independence. The war on terror, and the vindication in Iraq, came to Lebanon's rescue. If the Middle East was to be repaired, then the establishment of a legitimate system of authority in Lebanon was of paramount concern.

The "Cedar Revolution" in Lebanon was heady, and even Syria itself was not spared the stirrings of change. On February 24, a group of prominent Syrian thinkers and oppositionists wrote an "open letter" to their Lebanese counterparts that was published in Beirut's most prestigious paper, *An-Nahar,* a national institution in its own right that had been fearless in its advocacy of Syria's withdrawal. The message was a moving tribute to Hariri, a message of condolence to the Lebanese people over the death of that leader. Hariri's murder was a "terrible ugly slaughter planned and perpetrated by those who do not wish to see Lebanon healthy, united and free," the letter read. "We fully support your demand for the withdrawal of the Syrian army from Lebanon, for the rectification of Syrian-Lebanese relations, for the building of a relationship based on equity, independence, and the free choice of both peoples. We have long expressed this view through all means available to us, for we as educated Syrians have always found in Lebanon a window for the expression of ideas not permitted us in our own homeland."

This was not quite a "Damascus Spring," but that tyrannical regime—in its fundamentals remarkably similar to the Tikriti edifice built by Saddam Hussein—was being questioned. Syrians long in the grip of autocracy were now in the crosscurrents of change. To their east, a new Iraqi democracy was struggling to take root and move away from dynastic rule and the cult of statues and supreme leaders. To their west, valiant (and stylish) young Lebanese were in the streets and plazas of Beirut proclaiming their attachment to liberty.

The Syrian rulers could not be sure that they would be spared a massive American strike. Their soldiers (but not their intelligence operatives) soon quit Lebanon, and the dominion acquired over the course of three decades was abandoned. The dark doings of the men who ruled Damascus would be put out for all to see; a United Nations inquiry, led by a soft-spoken German prosecutor, Detlev Mehlis, provided a portrait of the regime in Damascus worthy of Mario Puzo and the best tradition of Mafia chronicles. The trail of Hariri's murder went directly to the doorstep of Syria's ruler, and his closest collaborators— Assad's younger brother, Maher; his brother-in-law, Assef Shawkat, the head of Syrian intelligence; along with the key functionaries of the Lebanese intelligence services. In one memorable exchange, the young Syrian ruler personally threatened Hariri that he would "break Lebanon" over his head and that of Hariri's Druze ally, Walid Jumblatt. "So you either do as you are told, or we will get you and your family wherever you are."

The regime in Damascus would do its best to stonewall all international inquiries into its reign of terror in Lebanon, but the suspicions of how this regime worked now had the authority of a detailed legal text. Lebanon still had a way to go before it completely broke free of Syria's reach and terror, and several Lebanese leaders of note would be struck down by assassins in the months to come. Indeed as Iraqis were about to vote for a four-year National Assembly, in December 2005, terror hit Beirut once again, and a "prince" of the Cedar Revolution, the young journalist and parliamentarian Gebran Tueni, was murdered by a massive car bomb. The regime in Damascus had not been completely chastened, but the Lebanese displaying greater courage in their dealings with Syria were beneficiaries of the assertion of American power so close to them in Iraq.

"George Bush has unleashed a tsunami on the region," a shrewd merchant from Kuwait wrote to me, as he watched the entrenched systems of control in the Arab world beginning to give way. It was a terrible storm, but the perfect antidote to a foul sky. There was no way of knowing how these events would shake out. New and old were battling it out. In Cairo, the pharaonic regime of Hosni Mubarak was challenged by men and women who had had enough of that mediocre autocracy. In Kuwait, a long fight over granting women the right to vote—the fight of two decades—was decided in favor of the liberal-secular alliance. The tremors of Iraq were no doubt felt in Kuwait: eighty-seven women had been elected to Iraq's National Assembly, 32 percent of the seats. Suddenly, it seemed like the autumn of the dictators. But the old Arab edifice of power, it is true, has had a way of surviving many storms. It has outwitted and outlived predictions of its imminent demise. Something different, though, had been injected into this fight. A great foreign power that had upheld the autocrats and feared what mass politics would bring in its wake in Arab lands now braved the storm. It signaled its willingness to gamble on the young and the new and the unknown. Autocracy was once deemed tolerable, but death pilots nurtured in autocracy's shadow, in its prisons and its schools, came America's way on 9/11. Now the Arabs grasping for a new world, and the Americans who had helped call up this unprecedented moment in Arab life, were together riding this storm wave of freedom.

Little more than two years into this American undertaking in Iraq, there was to this moment of Arab history the feel of a reenactment of Europe's Revolution of 1848—the springtime of peoples. That revolution, it will be recalled, broke out in France, then spread to the Italian states, to the German principalities, to the remotest corners of the Austrian empire. There must have been fifty of these revolts—rebellions of despair and contempt. These rebellions spread with velocity and were turned back with equal speed. The fear of chaos dampened these rebellions.

As I grappled with the meaning of this Arab moment, I picked up a meditation that Massimo d'Azeglio, a Piedmontese aristocrat who embraced that "springtime" in Europe, offered about his time, which speaks so directly to this Arab time: "The gift of a liberty is like that of a horse, handsome, strong, and high-spirited. In some it arouses a wish to ride; in many others, on the contrary, it increases the desire to walk." It would be fair to say that there were many Arabs today keen to walk—frightened as they are by the Islamists coming to power and curtailing personal liberties, snuffing out freedoms gained at such great effort and pain. But more Arabs, I hazard to guess, now had the wish to ride.

The skeptics about this Arab springtime had the examples of Iraq's pain and violence, and the victory of the radical Hamas movement in the Palestinian elections of early 2006, as proof that this moment of promise would not last. Nor were these skeptics willing to accept that the American campaign for liberty was a serious effort to change the ways of Araby. But a break had been made with the complacent ways of the past. Hitherto, American diplomacy had granted the Arab world absolution from the laws of historical improvement. American power explained away its complicity in the historical decay of that region as the price paid for access to its oil and as the indulgence owed some immutable Arab-Islamic tradition. To be fair, America had not been able to find its way to the politically literate classes of the Arab world, for they were given to a defective political radicalism. Now the pact with Arab tyranny was being challenged. The ballot was not infallible, as the Palestinian elections were to show. But the Palestinian world had its own political maladies, and in truth there was precious little difference between the masked men of Hamas and the masked men of Yasser Arafat's Fatah movement. This broader Arab demand for a new political way was playing out in Arab lands. Those "immutable" Arab ways were now contending with a new history.

It was Iraq of course that had given impetus to these Arab stirrings. It had been the success of the first Iraqi election that had emboldened the custodians of American foreign policy to bet on these possibilities. In Iraq itself, it would take three months before these elections would yield a new government. The interim government of Iyad Allawi had had its run. Allawi's was a mixed record. He had been a transitional figure. He had conveyed a sense of toughness, and some of that was needed at the time. But it had proven difficult for his government to strike the right balance between reliance on American protection and the need for some distance from the Americans. Allawi himself may have hoped that the Americans would anoint him as their man in Baghdad. He had made his way in the Arab councils of power. He had in mind a "soft authoritarian" state and an "efficient crony capitalist state," as one highly informed Iraqi official put it to me. He was close to the Jordanians (he spent a fair amount of his time in Amman), and he had reached out to the Saudis. He had spent lavishly on his campaign. There was a widespread belief that the American regency, and Central Intelligence, had bankrolled his campaign.

Allawi's slate had done reasonably well—15 percent of the vote for forty seats in the National Assembly. But the new order would not be his. He did not help his own cause when he bristled at the results of the elections and began spending a good deal of his time in Jordan. There had been corruption aplenty in his government, and that too was costly to his reputation. It was widely known that there had been chaos and mismanagement in the Ministry of Defense during his interim cabinet. The Iraqi Board of Supreme Audit would confirm the rumors of official corruption and sloppiness. Thus it came to light that perhaps $1 billion had been drained from the country's defense allocations between the end of June 2004 and the end of February 2005. Contracts had been awarded without competition; shoddy equipment of little use had been procured; forty-three out of eighty-nine contracts had been given a sole contractor, a dual Polish-Iraqi national by the name of Ziad Cattan. The Ministry of Defense had been headed at the time by Hazem Shaalan, a Shia from the southern part of the country, who had made a name for himself as a bitter rival of the Shia clerical estate and a critic of Iran's role in Iraq. Now the stench of corruption dispensed with all that. Allawi himself even provided a graphic image of what had transpired on his watch and that of the American regent, Paul Bremer: "There was no auditing. Airplanes were flying in and the money out in suitcases," he explained to the Iraqi Board of Supreme Audit.

Precious funds needed to equip and pay the troops had disappeared, Saadoun Dulaimi, the successor defense minister would say of what had transpired under the interim government. I spent the good part of a day in the company of Dulaimi. We had gone out to the military and police academies and the training centers of Iraq's troops. A British-educated sociologist, a Sunni Arab fifty-one years of age, quiet and well mannered, and given to a touch of melancholy perhaps, he had never expected to come into this assignment. He was determined to do his best, and to pick up where the preceding government of Allawi had failed.

No emotional bond had been forged between Allawi and the Shia underclass. The roots of his political movement, the Iraqi National Accord, were in the Baath party and among former operatives of the Saddam regime. A quintessential "man of the shadows"—a great description of him once offered by his relative Ali Allawi—he was not to find his way to the sentiments of his own community. He did not share its sense of exclusion; he could not call up its sacred history, and he did not try. This connection came naturally to his rival Ahmad

Chalabi; it came as well to Ibrahim al-Jaafari, of the Daawa Party, who would emerge as the prime minister of the new government that was finally cobbled together by the end of April 2005. If Allawi had been inducted into politics through the Baath, Jaafari had come through Shia politics; he had spent years in exile in Iran before moving to London. The Daawa Party had drawn on the inspiration and leadership of the great "martyred" cleric Muhammad Baqir al-Sadr, who had been executed, it shall be recalled, in April 1980. That a follower of Sadr would assume political power on the twenty-fifth anniversary of Sadr's execution was not lost on the Shia of Iraq. As in the best of the annals of Shia martyrology, the followers and devotees of Sadr had lived to see the vindication of heroic virtue and the punishment of the wicked. (Fate obliged the believers, for April 2005 was the second anniversary of the fall of Saddam Hussein.) On April 10, the party's newspaper *Al-Daawa* commemorated its martyr's death, and the fate of his executioner "caught like a rat and now rotting in a jail cell." The writers and memorialists grieved for Sadr but remembered his courtesy and manners and high culture, the way he took on the tyranny, the manner in which he fought for the faith when others had given in to despair or had turned to secular ideas. The front page of the paper had a serene photo of the martyr—a handsome man in clerical attire and the black turban of a descendant of the Prophet Muhammad, his hands neatly and delicately placed on his knees. On the same page, in a low corner, there was the seminal photo of the fall of the dictator's statue in Firdos Square in Baghdad two years earlier.

At Baghdad University, the paper reported, Prime Minister Jaafari had given a eulogy in honor of the martyr, and he had read into Sadr's life devotion to the public interest and to the unity of all Iraqis—Sunnis and Shia, Arabs and Kurds. History had come like this: the cruel murder of a noble man at the behest of a tyrant, and then the seeing of this story to its rightful and proper end. "Baqir Sadr, from us, *salam,* greetings of peace," read the paper's banner headline. As one drove through the streets of Baghdad on this occasion, the city appeared to belong to the martyred man: his words and portraits, colorful sketches of him, were everywhere. They adorned balconies; they were scrawled on the walls. The kind of justice that would be claimed in Sadr's name would now depend on men and women suddenly released from historical shackles. Sadr's followers had his memory, but they were of course on their own. Sadr's second life, as it were, would depend on what his devotees would do with the memory and the power.

In the hagiography of Muhammad Baqir al-Sadr, the life of the faith is free of sectarianism. The treatises of Sadr had never been exclusively Shiite. This was the way *Al-Daawa* commemorated him; this was the way that Jaafari, the newly designated prime minister, spoke of him. But there was a different truth gripping the country. As far as I know, no Sunni Arabs stepped forth to eulogize Sadr. A raging insurgency drew on their resentments and on a powerful sense that the order of the world had been violated. The predicament of the Sunni Arabs alternating between truculence and a bewildered response to the loss of power was conveyed to me by a leader of the Association of Muslim Scholars, Dr. Isam al-Rawi. A geologist by training, with a history of activism in the Muslim Brotherhood behind him, a faculty member of the University of Baghdad's department of earth sciences, Rawi, a man in his midfifties, had emerged as the principal spokesman of that powerful Sunni Arab organization. Rawi is clearly given to political exposition: sitting down to a meal with Leslie Gelb and myself, he was eager to talk. He knew English, but he spoke in Arabic; the translation for Les Gelb's benefit was done by one of the American embassy's most gifted young people, Jeffrey Beals. (Beals, a political officer twenty-eight years of age, never faltered; the precision of his Arabic, his ear for its cadence and for its allusions, was pitch-perfect.)

Rawi's presentation and manners were familiar to me from prior dealings with Arab scientists and engineers drawn into Islamist politics: a curious mix of diffidence and steely belief, the reasonable, quiet presentation of audacious views. He had spent four years in prison, he told us, under the "secular tyranny" of Saddam Hussein. It was galling to him, he said, that the Sunni Arabs are now depicted as the henchmen of the dictator. "He was severe with everyone, Saddam Hussein, particularly with the Muslim Brotherhood. Who ruled whom? So many of Saddam's men were Shia and Kurds. It is a travesty that the past is so distorted, that the honor of the Sunni Arabs is sullied as it is today. When they came in, the Americans had a real chance to reach an accommodation with the Sunnis. Everything was quiet at the beginning. The American soldiers played football with the children, shared soft drinks and ice cream with them. For our part, we were determined to get along with the Americans. We knew that we could not fight them; we knew the magnitude of American power. But the Americans had no understanding of Iraqi traditions. We tried to tell them—I myself tried—about our traditions. We warned against violating the sanctity of our mosques and cemeteries. But it was to no avail. In the first four months of the occupation, forty of our mosques were stormed. The Americans were determined to marginalize the Sunnis. Gradually, it became obvious that there was a heavy religious dimension to this war. I myself did a lot of reading about Bush, and about the preacher Billy Graham. The more I watched this American project, the more convinced I became that our Islamic religion is under attack." He himself was a believer, he added, and could see the "believing warrior" in George Bush as well.

Isam al-Rawi had no use for this new order hatched by the elections of January 30: "We tried to secure a delay of six months, so we could be ready to participate in the elections. But no one wanted us at the table, and no one wanted our participation. No, I don't consider Jalal Talabani a legitimate Iraqi president. In all of Talabani's offices, there is no Iraqi flag, no Iraqi map. There are the flags and the maps of Kurdistan, and that is all. Nor can I take comfort from the role played by Ayatollah Ali Sistani. How can we trust Sistani, how can we accept his authority in the affairs of Iraq? He is never seen or heard. It is strange, this mystery. The Prophet Muhammad himself, peace be upon him, was seen and heard by the believers on a daily basis, shared their life, and was accessible to them. Sistani kept to himself and for thirteen years was never seen in public. This state that the Americans have assembled has no legitimacy. In the south, the anniversary of the Iranian revolution is now celebrated by the Iraqi Shia as their own. For our part, we have to fill the void left by the fall of Saddam Hussein; we have to build a viable alternative. We can't fight the Americans, but we can't give them our consent either. They're occupying our presidential palaces, they dominate our life. They talk about drawing down their forces, withdrawing to military bases outside the major cities. But they are everywhere, and their checkpoints are everywhere. I see them every day on my way back and forth between my home and the university. They talk about granting us liberty, while they are slowly laying down the foundations of a permanent presence in our country."

Of his community of Sunni Arabs, al-Rawi spoke as one speaks of a people cast adrift and at the mercy of the elements. "We have no leaders; Sheikh Ghazi al-Yawar is a little too friendly and eager to please; National Assembly leader Hajem Hassani has no history in this country and no power base. We can't rely on the police and army units, for they are truly extensions of the Kurdish and Shia militias." For all this bitterness and this political alienation, there was still moderation, he added, among the Sunnis. He singled out an important fatwa that his association had just issued, with the support of sixty to seventy leading scholars and luminaries, authorizing joining the ranks of the army and police forces. The fatwa was subtle, and he was proud of its political dexterity. It had authorized military and police service by Sunnis so long as the "intentions of the recruits are pure," and on condition that the soldiers refrain from being "pillars of support for the occupiers against the interests of the people." Necessity had to be acknowledged; it was important to "safeguard the faith and the country." He had given the fatwa its due and its religious warrant. But he had let it slip that it was a bow to the logic of necessity. His community could not declare total war against the new order of things. The Sunni Arabs had all but stayed away from the national elections. A community that had dominated this land now claimed a mere sixteen seats (6 percent) in the National Assembly. There had settled upon that community doubts as to the wisdom of its truculence. Al-Rawi was honest enough to admit that that strategy had backfired. The Sunnis were now dependent on the good will of the Shia and the Kurds, and on the recognition by one and all that the peace of the country depended on capping the volcano in the Sunni Triangle.

"We are orphans; we have no one save Allah," another Sunni Arab leader, Sheikh Mohamed Khalil Nasif of Kirkuk, would say in an open meeting in April 2005 that brought together the leaders of that contested, volatile city. The speaker was a dashing man dressed in traditional Arab attire, in his early forties perhaps. He had been jailed by the Saddam dictatorship because his tribe, al-Jubur, had been at odds with the dictator. After the fall of the regime, he had made his way to Kirkuk's provincial council. "In Kirkuk, we have no television satellite channels of our own, no radio stations, no way we can reach or educate our people. Our Kurdish brothers are supported by the government and by the resources of Kurdistan, our Turkoman brothers are supported by Turkey, and the Shia have Najaf and Sistani. Look at us, look at our city: Kirkuk sits atop an ocean of oil, but its streets are wrecked and misery is everywhere. Everyone is convinced that we were the masters of the old regime, but we were its victims, and its spoils were denied us. There is no democracy here, and certainly not in

Kirkuk. These American-sponsored elections came, and everyone voted for their sect. Only the Communists voted for Iraq and as Iraqis, and the Communists got only two seats in the National Assembly. We are not afraid of the terrorists; we defied them; we went to the polls in record numbers. The voter turnout was higher here than in any other city in Iraq, but elections are not enough. There has to be order, and this city will have to be shared." The Kurds dominated the provincial council of Kirkuk, where the political and demographic pressure of Kurdistan was intensely felt. Nasif spoke with a tone of resignation. Kirkuk was at some remove from the central part of the country and from the Sunni Triangle. Here the Sunni Arabs were on their own, and in the shadow of Kurdistan.

Disinheritance was not the sole and exclusive property of the Shia. From this man in Kirkuk, even from the leader of the Association of Muslim Scholars in Baghdad, there could be heard the anxiety of a community awakening to a changed world.

A measure of caution was settling upon the Sunni Arabs. In early July 2005, a new association, the Sunni Endowment, made its appearance. Its leader, Adnan Dulaimi, called upon his community to renounce violence and to opt for a new political way. "I ask all Sunnis to register their names for the next election, because we are in a political battle that depends on the vote." The political process, Dulaimi said, was not perfect, but it was the best that could be had. Dulaimi would find the doors thrown open before him. The constitutional drafting committee would take into its ranks fifteen Sunni Arabs without any regard for their political past including any association they might have had with the Baath. A month later, a colleague of Dulaimi in the leadership of the Sunni Endowment, Ahmad Samarrai, would go a step further: he condemned the Arab jihadists who had come to Iraq and said that the country had no need of them: "We reject their presence in our country and we ask that they be severely punished, particularly those of them who killed Iraqis."

Moderation among the Sunni Arabs, it has to be conceded, had become particularly dangerous. Dulaimi and Samarrai were running enormous risks. Mijbel Sheikh Issa, a Sunni Arab from Kirkuk, by all accounts a hard-liner who had had a difficult time accepting the legitimacy of Shia demands, had nonetheless been struck down by assassins for his participation in the committee drafting a constitutional document. There were leaders who knew that violence offered no way out, but they could not openly challenge the insurgents. In the shadow of the terror, the best they could do was to advocate a "return" to the political process lest their community be left out of the political struggle for the country's identity and resources. This was the opening that had permitted the emergence of the Sunni Endowment and the National Dialogue Council, a new political bloc representing the Sunni Arabs. The vast American presence had to be accommodated, and these groups could rightly claim that it was unwise to leave the political field—and the patronage of the Americans—to the Shia and the Kurds. A narrow path would be tread between the insurgency and the requirements of the open political game.

"I can't condemn kidnapping and terror. I have no protection," I was told by a fairly influential member of the National Dialogue Council. My informant came from the town of Abu Hishma, a Saddamist stronghold, but now resided in Baghdad. A man in his late forties, with a dark complexion and a close-cropped beard, he wore traditional attire—a white *dishdasha* and a brown *abaya,* a white kaffiyeh with a brown *agal* (the cord for the head cover). He was accompanied by an older colleague from the same movement. There was a winning way about the younger man; he was free of bluster and spoke with care and a measure of resignation about the state of things. He had been warned by the insurgents to keep his head down; he had received death threats replete with the make of his car, his physical description, the places he frequents. It had not been easy for him in recent months, and the strain showed. He was no friend of the old order, he said, his hometown notwithstanding. But he had been picked up by the Americans and kept in detention for twenty-one days. He was charged with providing a safe house for the insurgents. The Americans, he said, were owed a "word of truth": they don't abuse, and they don't torture. That is the specialty of the Iraqi forces, he ruefully observed. "Nothing has changed. The Iraqis doing the interrogation are the same ones who did so under Saddam. They have worked their way into the good graces and the protection of the Americans. The latter believe that they have trained forces of order. But these forces are in it for what they can get. When they raid houses, they will strip people of their jewelry, their cell phones, their money, and keep it for themselves. The Sunni Arabs are now on their own. The government belongs to the Shia and the Kurds. The extremists who come from Arab lands show the Sunnis no mercy either. In

Fallujah, the *mujahidin* moved into people's homes, married their daughters against their wishes, imposed their tyranny on them." He had no problems with the Shia, he said, but admitted to a worldview he could not shed: the Sunnis are more worthy, more entitled to power. He gave me a statistic making the rounds: the Sunni Arabs, he said, accounted for 42 percent of Iraq's population and were thus the country's single largest minority. They had governed, and they are the ones who could keep Iran and its influence at bay.

The older man—an engineer from Baghdad, trained in Moscow— then offered his own biography: his father was a Sunni, his mother was a Shia, and he had had for her more reverence and affection than he did for his father. But he had a dread of Iran's influence. "The Iraqi Shia are ourselves, Arabs like us. But the Safavids are another matter, they are strangers." I had not heard this term in this country; the Safavids had imposed Shiism as a state religion in Iran in the sixteenth century. Their domination is long gone, but this man saw their ghost stalking his land. The term he chose, I sensed, took in Shia political parties in Iraq and seminarians in Najaf. And he too, raised by a Shia mother, saw political rule as the natural right of his father's people.

I had been given these two men's reading of things. And once again I could not shake off the feeling—and told them so, to some bemusement on their part—that there was a distinctly Shia tone to the way they spoke of their condition. Power—Sunni power and the way it was exercised here for centuries—had been undone. But normalcy was yet to come. Old, sly Baathists were still around: they had the "social capital" of their old hegemony, the habits of command, and some skills in dealing with the world. They would come back now as the representatives of the Sunni Arabs. They found their way into the drafting of a new constitution. When the American regency added fifteen Sunni Arabs to the constitutional drafting committee, the majority of them were old Baathists. There was no serious vetting of them. They came back unapologetic. In the way they returned, they were heirs of an old tradition. This time too, they were there as the self-professed bearers of nationalism against the "secessionists" in the north (the Kurds) and against the seminarians in Najaf, and the Shia of the south. Once again, there were claims that they represented progress, modernity. The unitary state, the command economy: these were the goals they had come to defend.

It was known that had the Sunni Arabs had the oil wealth in their region, they would have struck out on their own and left the high-landers of the north and the Shia of the Middle Euphrates to fend for themselves. These Baathists may not have been children of enlighten-ment. But a worse alternative lurked in the wings. As the country entered the final phase of its quest for a constitution, the followers of Abu Musab al-Zarqawi posted a message on an Islamist Web site on August 21, 2005. The group was Ansar al-Sunna, and the message was one of fire and brimstone, a warning to those among the Sunni Arabs who would partake in the country's political and constitutional life. Such a choice, the men of darkness warned, amounted to a "rebellion against God's law, and against his sovereignty on earth." It would con-stitute apostasy, grounds for banishment from the "community of Abraham," it was proclaimed, a surrender to "the Crusaders" and their allies—the "Shia heretics" and the "Kurdish apostates." Baathism was being outflanked. It remained to be seen whether those who winked at terror and saw its usefulness could manage to break free from its hold.

No surprise, the surviving remnants of the old regime, now posing as defenders of the Sunni-Arab community, simultaneously claimed and disowned the terror raging in the country. The insurgency was theirs and not quite theirs, the old Baathists would maintain. They kept an arm's-length relationship with the terror. The insurgency was what gave the remnants of the old regime their power, and their leverage with an America eager to limit its burden and its "exposure" in Iraq. Having empowered a group of Baathists in the work of draft-ing a constitution, the American stewards had to live with the conse-quences of their handiwork. No massive wave of revenge killings had been unleashed on the Sunni Arabs by the Shia and Kurdish victims of the Baath tyranny. No effort had been spared to bring the Sunnis into the new political world. There remained that stubborn belief by the Sunni Arabs that Iraq was now a "stolen country." Their deeply rooted conviction was not unique to them, it has to be said. All around them, in the neighboring states whose ethos they shared, whose polit-ical culture and media they drew upon, political power was a monop-oly, the inheritance of a political caste. It would be hard for these men to see their way to a new conception of things.

It was the Sunni Arabs of Iraq—out of their need for disposable jihadists who would hurl themselves at the Iraqi Shia and at the Americans—who had given the Arab drifters and holy warriors shelter and sanctuary. And the hope could be entertained that the hosts would cut these pitiless warriors adrift. As the political process put down roots, the zeal and bigotry of the outsiders had become a burden to the hosts themselves. In the Turkoman town of Tal Afar, by the Syrian border, there was talk of Wahhabi zealots who had come into this mixed Sunni-Shia community with phobias alien to this place. The people of Tal Afar, its Sunni and Shia, were related by blood and intermarriage, and for the jihadists this world of ambiguity had to be struck down. An Iraqi friend in Baghdad, Hassanein Muallah, a high official in the Ministry of Education with a deep knowledge of his country's provinces and politics, told me of a tribal sheikh in Tal Afar who was ordered by his sons not to shake hands with the Shia *rafida* (heretics). The old man had Shia relatives, but the jihadists had gotten to his sons and had inducted them into a wholly different idea of the faith. This new bigotry would have to war with the older ways of this land.

Nearly three years into this war, a growing split could be discerned between the Sunni Arabs and the jihadists. In Baghdad, I met a man of the Dulaim tribe, from the Anbar province, Faris Muhammad al-Faris, from the Bou-Fahd clan of his tribe. (The tribes are particular and precise about these matters). Earlier in the day, his cousin, Nasr Abdul Kareem, an influential man in Ramadi, a tribal sheikh and a professor of languages and history at the local university, had been assassinated by Zarqawi's thugs. The assailants had been a band of four Iraqis, two Syrians, and a Saudi. The Arab jihadists had been ambushed and killed, the Iraqis had been captured. The victim, I learned, had once believed in the idea of "noble resistance" to the occupier and had been sympathetic to the insurgency. But he had entertained growing doubts about the efficacy of violence. He had begun to separate himself from the insurgency; he was struck down in the midst of this transformation. And the cousin telling the story had received a death threat of his own. He was on his way to Syria, he said, where he would wait out this moment of peril. The jihadists and the Sunni Arabs of Iraq had taken a ride together, but their ultimate aims were not the same. There remained that hope offered by the noted Iraqi author Hassan al-Alawi that the jihadists had their gaze fixed on the green fields of paradise, while the Sunni Arabs of Iraq were fixated on the Green Zone in Baghdad—the division of spoils, their claim on the bounty and the patronage of American power.

• • •

By the summer of 2005, the effort to "stand up" Iraqi military forces, it was announced, would now be led by a new American commander. David Petraeus would hand over to Lieutenant General Martin Dempsey, and Petraeus would be given a new assignment, commanding general of U.S. Army Combined Arms Center and Fort Leavenworth in Fort Leavenworth, Kansas. The change of command was to take place on September 8. After that Petraeus was scheduled to go to Afghanistan on a brief visit to look at the Train/Equip Program in that country. There would be some "out-briefs" at the Pentagon, family obligations—a visit to his aged father in California, a parents' weekend at MIT for his son—and then drive to Fort Leavenworth. He had known Dempsey for a long time, he told me. They had grown up in neighboring towns in New York; they had been classmates at West Point and fellow division commanders in Iraq—Petraeus in Mosul, and Dempsey at the head of the First Armored Division in Baghdad.

This was a bittersweet time for Petraeus. He had been deployed—first in Bosnia, then in Iraq—for forty out of the preceding fifty-two months. Fort Leavenworth was a big new assignment. There would be a large house, and a front porch overlooking the Missouri where he would put up his feet and sip a beer. He would have a chance at family life. It was time to go home and make his peace with normal life. But he had known combat and fellowship. There had been the thrill of his command in Mosul. *"Ana Mosulawi"* (I am from Mosul), he would proclaim in that city. He had been undisputed master of Mosul; he had governed wisely. Then he had received this assignment, training Iraqi forces. *"Ana Iraqi"* (I am Iraqi) became his new mantra. He had his boundless energy, and a way with recruits. *"As-salam 'alaikum Sadiqi,* greetings friends, *mabrook,* congratulations on your graduation,"* he would tell the recruits and SWAT teams he visited, startling the Iraqi soldiers used to command by remote control. He had an infectious enthusiasm for the soldiers' mission. He had his protégés among the younger Iraqi commanders, ones who seemed to imbibe his code of physical fitness and responsibility for their troops. He loved being on the scene, the three-star general turning up in places of danger when least expected.

Petraeus had garnered a lot of press attention in a military on the lookout for any "hotdogging" among its commanders. He had had a hard time living down a *Newsweek* cover with a photograph of him and the provocative title "Can This Man Save Iraq?" Members of Congress had come to him seeking a quick fix on the war. At his commands in Mosul and in Baghdad, people dropped in eager to rub shoulders with a celebrated soldier with a record of accomplishment. (I must in part be describing myself, for he opened his door to me, but I like to think that more than that passed between us.) He knew the double-edged nature of fame, knew that the crowd could be fickle, that American opinion on the entire Iraq undertaking had undergone a sea change. For every administration official who invoked Petraeus's authority as to the progress on the ground, there was a "dovish" critic of the war calling into question the quality and depth of the training effort. Petraeus had done his best by Iraq: he knew the political class of the country, and their ways and foibles. He had for the young Kurdish politician Barham Salih a special regard. He admired the smarts and the work ethic of the Shia leader Ahmad Chalabi, came to see him as the brightest member of Iraq's cabinet. There was knowingness in Petraeus; his hopes for Iraq were tempered by a street-smart knowledge of the country's ways. He had had money and power and military equipment at his disposal; he was unillusioned about the people he had lived and worked among. "This is the imam society," he said of Iraq. "Iraqis respond to good leadership, but they can also be led astray by bad leadership."

The Petraeus restlessness: it still drove him as he was taking stock of his time here, conscious that this mission was coming to a close. One afternoon, he invited me to tag along on a visit to an Iraqi unit, the Muthanna Brigade, led by one of his star protégés, a brigadier by the name of Aziz al-Dhalmi. What I thought would be a routine visit to the brigade's headquarters was to be more than that. Petraeus wanted to "walk the beat," to do a foot patrol with his Iraqi protégé. The things about the Iraqi brigadier that endeared him to Petraeus were on full display. General Dhalmi was a short, gregarious man, with an easy and confident air. On a piece of paper, he scribbled for me the basic facts of his life: his birth in 1960, in Diwaniyya, in the south; married with five children; entered military service in 1982. He had taught himself English, I concluded on my own, and his confidence with the language was of a piece with his overall air of endearing authority. From Petraeus I had learned that the brigadier was a superb officer who would train units only to lose them to more senior commanders who would "borrow" these units for other assignments.

On this outing, we were to visit the difficult neighborhood of Abu Ghraib, on the outskirts of the city. Ours would be a mixed Iraqi-American contingent: Petraeus's people and the officers of the Muthanna Brigade. By the time we got there, the afternoon heat had grown ferocious. The asphalt of the paved road felt like chewing gum. We came in a convoy of Humvees; there were helicopters overhead, and Iraqi sharpshooters lined up by the side of the road. They were there in full gear, the Iraqis, with masks. Their patience in the heat of the day made an impression on an American officer walking with me. "Don't tell me that the Iraqi soldiers lack dedication; look at them standing politely in this killer heat." (The masks serve a double function, providing both anonymity and protection against the swirling dust.)

There was a small neighborhood market, our principal stop, with stalls for fruits and vegetables and spice sellers. It had begun to empty out by the time our convoy arrived. General Dhalmi was keen to show his knowledge of the place, his familiarity with the vendors. Two young spice sellers in their stall, taking in the large contingent of visitors, said that the brigadier had done well by this neighborhood. A young man wheeling his cart seemed eager to make his way home past all this commotion. Petraeus dropped in on a small shop that made its own ice cream; the vendor was thrilled by the crowd that had descended on his place; the shop, cool with ice blocks, was a respite from the heat outside. The American commander had a huge chunk of time behind him in Iraq. He took the ice cream offered him, consumed it on the premises, insisted on paying for it, and complimented the vendor on his product. An hour or so later, after a walk to a dilapidated bridge at the end of the road, we took the Humvees back to a landing zone where the helicopters waited to take us back to Petraeus's headquarters. This was Brigadier Dhalmi's world, after all. The quality of mercy he would show the people at the receiving end of his brigade's power, the ability to forge a military bond across the sectarian divide: those would remain after Petraeus had packed up and left. The insurgents were not going away, and the forces of order—army and police units alike—were daily targets of the insurgency.

In that very American desire to document and count things, the training effort could boast of what it had done: In the course of fifteen months, from mid-June 2004 to early September 2005, Iraqi security forces had been given 172,000 AK-47 automatic rifles, 163,000 pistols, 8,000 heavy machine guns, and 195,000 sets of body armor. Some 100,000 Iraqi security forces had been trained. This had been, by the American military's reckoning, the "largest military procurement and distribution effort since World War II," at a cost of $11.1 billion. No money or effort had been spared. But it was Brigadier Dhalmi and his troops—and the larger society from which his brigade was drawn—who would determine how this battle for Iraq would unfold.

Slowly, and in fits and starts, the American stewards were shifting the military burden onto the Iraqis. After the rebellions of Moqtada al-Sadr, and the running battles between his ragtag Mahdi Army and the Americans, an uneasy peace had come between the American forces and the militias in Sadr City. I saw this in a meeting in that impoverished quarter of Baghdad in late July 2005. The setting was the municipality of Sadr City, where a group of American officers, led by Colonel Joe DeSalvo of the Third Infantry Division, had come with their translators to discuss the security of Sadr City with local leaders and with representatives of the Mahdi Army. This was not quite peace, but the deliberations had to them a tone of reconciliation. The foreign power had accepted the legitimacy of the Sadrists, and the latter, now made more respectable by their representation in the National Assembly, were determined to show that they were men of order and responsibility.

There was something unexpected for me about the local leaders gathered around a huge rectangular table: they were men of the countryside, people from the south and from the Marshes who had made this part of Baghdad their home. This was not the world of the bourgeoisie and the professionals in the affluent districts of Baghdad. Almost to a man, they were dressed in traditional attire, a colorful display of brown and black *abayas,* matching *kaffiyeh* and *agals.* Some were self-consciously stylish in the way of men aware of their status in the world. The most dashing was the "hero of the Marshes," the legendary leader and anti-Saddam fighter Sheikh Abdul Karim al-Mohammedawi. He carried himself with quiet dignity; dark and striking, he needed and sought no attention. He was a "doer" not given to excess, and his presence underscored the seriousness of what was transpiring that day.

New "rules of engagement" were being negotiated. Colonel DeSalvo earnestly set out what he took to be a time of accord with the people of Sadr City. "We want to help Sadr City improve the quality of life for all its inhabitants. The better the security on the ground, the less the need for an excessive military presence on our part. A lot of the security forces in Sadr City are sons of Sadr City." The colonel's choice of words, "sons of Sadr City," was true to the sensibility of the place; it is the way people of this neighborhood would speak of themselves. "American forces consider the Sadr movement a legitimate political entity," he added, using again the term the Sadrists use about themselves. "All you have to do is follow the rule of law."

The men assembled here were the leaders of a huge urban mass, four million people. A phenomenon familiar throughout the lands of the Arab-Islamic world was on display here—the ruralization of the cities. The south had simply spilled into this part of Baghdad. And these people still had their bitter sense of exclusion. They had been brutalized by the dictatorship, and they had come into conflict with the American forces. They sought "sovereignty" over Sadr City, but did not quite know what it meant. And they still nursed their resentments. "The Iraqi Army left the hot areas alone to concentrate on this place. The Iraqi Army is nothing but an instrument for dominating Sadr City and the Sadrists," one participant asserted. The head of the municipality then spoke of the official neglect that afflicts this place. He said that he lost nine of his staff to violence, that the government had promised $382 million in aid to Sadr City but that none of that had materialized, that Sadr City still awaits the help promised it.

Colonel DeSalvo could not grant Sadr City what it wanted by way either of money or of "sovereignty." He was still an outsider, and to the diehards still an "occupier." But a corner had been turned in that there was no animus in the room. No one objected when Deputy Prime Minister Ahmad Chalabi, who sat in on the meeting, told the crowd that they would not be assembled in this fashion, and in this place, had it not been for the Americans and the war they had waged. "Sheikh Abdul Karim would not be here, and would have been driven out of Iraq had it not been for the protection of military planes," he said of the hero of the Marshes, who nodded in agreement. The issue of sovereignty, Chalabi said, was not DeSalvo's to grant or deny; it was up to the National Assembly to work out the terms of America's military presence in Iraq.

The people of Sadr City had fought the Americans and had now made peace with them. This fragile peace rested on the palms of a devil, as the Arabs would say. There was no guarantee that Moqtada al-Sadr would find this peace to his liking. But a military contingent made up of "sons of Sadr City" held out the decent hope that the foreign power could extricate itself and leave a modicum of order on the ground.

I was given this sense of cautious confidence in the company of the defense minister, Saadoun Dulaimi, when I accompanied him one day inspecting military police academies. There was no bluster in him, but he clearly relished visiting with his soldiers. "We don't need huge armies, all we need are good faithful units," he said. He never spoke of his burden as a Sunni Arab from one of the country's great tribes, the Dulaim, but his colleagues told me that he deeply felt this sense of obligation, and that it fed in him a desire to bring the insurgency under control. Some weeks after I saw him, there was a battle for an insurgent stronghold, the town of Tal Afar by the Syrian border. A joint American-Iraqi raid entered a city that the insurgents had all but claimed as a new base, where they had killed and terrorized at will. The insurgents had fled; the dispatches of September 11, 2005, quoted the soft-spoken scholarly man, the sociologist with a British education, threatening the insurgents and those who harbor them with a dire fate: the forces of order would "cut their heads and cut off their tongues." The security forces, he announced, would hold the city; there would be no repeat of the cat-and-mouse game of claiming cities from the insurgency only to vacate them and witness the return of the perpetrators of terror.

Dulaimi's language was unusual for him; the man had not changed, but Iraqis in power had begun to recognize that this fight was theirs, and that the American regency, for all its might, could not pacify Iraq. Petraeus had left by the time Tal Afar was launched. But the teacher in him, I knew, no doubt delighted in the dispatches that came out of that embattled city. "Iraqification" was gaining ground if only because the American stewards had begun the search for their own deliverance.

Iraq had not been delivered into Shia hands, but the Shia would now begin their own reckoning with the wages of political power. Thus it came to light, in mid-November 2005, that Iraq's ministry of interior, now in the hands of elements drawn from the Supreme Council for the Islamic Revolution in Iraq, and headed by a Shia minister, had run a secret detention center where 173 Sunni Arab detainees had been held and subjected to abuse and torture. American forces had happened on this center in the course of a search for a missing young man. The Badr Brigade, an organization that had been launched in Iran during the time of Saddam Hussein, was doing the dirty work. The restraint of the Shia had been remarkable given all that had been thrown at them. Now the Shia narrative of victimhood and virtue had to yield to what power brings with it—the possibility of victimizing others.

"People are doing the same as in Saddam's time and worse," Iyad Allawi, the former prime minister, would say in the aftermath of these disclosures. "We are hearing about secret police, secret bunkers where people are being interrogated. A lot of Iraqis are being tortured or killed in the course of interrogations. We are even witnessing sharia courts based on Islamic law that are trying people and executing them." These remarks were made a fortnight before the country's national elections set for December 15; Allawi was running his own slate of candidates, and his platform was that of a secular man of the Iraqi state, a nationalist at odds with religious identity. The Badr Brigade and the Ministry of Interior were fair targets of Allawi, for the old Baathist had scant support among his own Shia kinsmen. He had proposed a political program that set him apart from the other Shia contenders. He was critical of the entire de-Baathification effort, seeing it as a factor in the rise of the insurgency. He had no kind words for dissolving the Iraqi Army a year or so earlier. He was running a slick, well-financed campaign, with steady advertisements on the Saudi-owned satellite television channel Al-Arabiya and a series of long interviews with him in the London-based Saudi-owned paper *Asharq Al-Awsat*. On the eve of the elections, he was granted a hugely publicized visit with the Saudi ruler, King Abdullah. His message was his ease with the rulers of the region, the promise of normalcy for Iraq in its Arab habitat.

The Saudis had made no secret of their fear that Iran was gaining primacy in Iraq, and Allawi presented the perfect antidote: a Shia "man of the shadows," a shrewd man who could strike bargains and enforce them, a kind of Iraqi Hosni Mubarak, if you will. There were hints that Washington still favored him, despite promises of American neutrality. There were the old arguments for him, the strongman who had all the "phone numbers of the insurgent leaders in his Rolodex." In Najaf and in the Shia towns of the south and the Middle

Euphrates, there was of course little appreciation of Allawi, or of his laments for the old Iraqi Army or of his worries that de-Baathification was alienating people who ought to be brought into the fold. Shortly after this hugely publicized comparison with Saddam's time, Allawi turned up on the grounds of the Shrine of Imam Ali in Najaf. In retrospect, this was not the wisest of choices. A melee broke out, and the crowd ran him out of the shrine. He was pelted with shoes and sandals. His security detail hustled him out of the place. There was no Shia monolith in this land; here was a man of the sect casting his lot with the Baathist apparatus from which he hailed. He had come to Najaf for a politician's obligatory visit. But he did not share his community's sorrow; he did not partake of its history of lament and exclusion.

On Allawi's watch as interim prime minister, there had been assaults on (Shia) Najaf and (Sunni) Fallujah. This was a claim of sorts to secularism, proof that he was above sectarian loyalties. He had ridden America's coattails, but he now presented himself as a man who had stood up to American power. He hinted, furtively, that the old, "honored" Iraqi role in the Israeli-Arab struggle had been cast aside in favor of a more forgiving attitude toward Israel, and that he himself would return to the old verities. The Iranians were out to get him, he said, because he was an Iraqi patriot, a decisive leader who would check Iran's meddling in his country's affairs. The Shia world in Iraq (and in other Arab lands) had always been checkered, and it had never had to itself, unchallenged, the loyalties of men and women born into the faith. Born and raised during the twilight of the monarchy, this politician had come into his own at a time when the Shia elites were at home in the social and political world of Iraq. He had then taken to the Baath, as so many of his Shia peers had done. His ease with power was its own statement that these "compact communities" were always riddled with holes, that countless men and women walked out of the sects to knock at gates beyond.

For the third time in eleven months, Iraqis were to go to the polls, on December 15, 2005. On the eve of these elections, a huge number of Sunni religious men issued a fatwa calling on their community to turn out to vote. It was reported that no fewer than a thousand preachers had signed this fatwa. There would be no boycotting the elections this time around. There was no need to sing hymns in praise of this new order; it was enough to say that the Sunni Arabs did not want to leave the spoils of power to the Shia and the Kurds, and that the vote would make it easier to get "the occupier" to quit Iraq. In their fashion, the insurgents complied; they too let this national election go forward. There was enough firepower—Iraqi and American—to secure the voting. It was too early to claim that this new Iraqi history had prevailed and that the Sunnis were done with truculence, but the power of this new way had made itself felt, and the people of the Sunni provinces had made their own claim to this new political way. Two months earlier, the Sunni Arabs had come close to upending the new constitution; a change of no more than eighty thousand votes in Mosul and the larger Nineveh province would have doomed the constitution. Oddly, this had paved the way for the new turn toward political compromise on the part of that community. The Shia had had their "coming out" a year earlier; now the Sunni Arabs had stepped forth to assert their political claims.

The election confirmed the sectarian and ethnic breakdown of the country. A shrewd Iraqi observer, Nibras Kazimi, had it mostly right when he observed, a week after the elections, that Iraq had held a census rather than an election. Those who had bet against "identity politics" were not vindicated. The big Shia slate, the United Iraqi Alliance, swept, with a huge margin, the nine Shia provinces in the south and the Middle Euphrates; the Kurdistan Alliance claimed three provinces in the north and, by a considerably smaller margin, Kirkuk as well; while the Sunni Arabs delivered their votes to rehabilitated elements of the Baath and to the Sunni Islamist groups that had emerged as their standard-bearers after the fall of Saddam. Baghdad voted its complex and checkered identity: the Shia slate had polled 59 percent of the vote, the Sunni parties had taken 19 percent, and the "secular" slate of former prime minister Iyad Allawi had taken 14 percent.

Grand Ayatollah Ali al-Sistani had declared his "neutrality" in this round of elections; he had not endorsed the United Iraqi Alliance. But there was enough vagueness in his position that the United Iraqi Alliance could still claim that it had on its side the authority of the Shia hierarchy in Najaf. The operatives of the big Shia list were not above dissimulation, and they were good at the political game. Vast numbers of Shia men and women, filled with piety, did not have it in them to go against the clerical institution of their sect. In the countryside, there were reports of clerics and seminarians warning women voters that their marriages would be null and void were they to go against the authority of the grand *marja' al-taqlid,* Ayatollah Sistani. And there were reports of clerics at the entrance of polling stations asking voters to swear on the Quran that they would vote for the United Iraqi Alliance—the slate of Imam Ali, its promoters were to call it. There was little room for candidates running on competence and managerial skills or betting on nonsectarian nationalism. The Shia were being hunted down by jihadists, targeted solely for their identity and faith, and they would vote that identity. It did not matter that the Shia-led cabinet of Prime Minister Ibrahim Jaafari had not been skilled at governance. The Supreme Council for the Islamic Revolution, perhaps the United Iraqi Alliance's most powerful bloc, had money and man-power, the weight of its own television station, the patronage of the resourceful Iranian state next door. It had going for it the powerful Shia sense of old persecution and the sense of deliverance from old weakness to power and redemption. It would be difficult for political men like Iyad Allawi and Ahmad Chalabi to withstand this sort of power. Neither "toughness" nor bureaucratic ability would match the force of sectarian loyalty. Chalabi had been offered a place within the United Iraqi Alliance, six sure seats for his Iraqi National Congress, but had opted to run on his own, and the gamble had not paid off. It was not yet time for "modern" politics beyond the sect. Anticlerical Shia voters and some old Sunni Baathists went with Allawi, but there were not enough of them. He would lose to the Shia slate in the south and to the Sunni parties in western Iraq. He managed to pick up 8 to 10 percent of the vote in the Shia provinces and roughly the same in Sunni Mosul. There were Communist voters, but there were not enough of them either.

In their pride, Iraqi secularists would claim that this sectarianism had been bred by the American regency, that the foreign stewards had empowered the Hakim family of the Supreme Council and the Sunni Baathists and the Barzanis in Kurdistan, that they had not shown suf-ficient respect for Iraqis "in the middle," men and women long severed from the claims of sectarianism and ethnicity. The political writer Tamara Chalabi observed, in this vein, that the American approach to the country ignored eighty years "of an active Iraqi national identity, where politics took many different covers that were not always defined by identity." Admittedly, there was a measure of truth in that lament because a foreign power eager to reduce its exposure in a hostile, unfamiliar place is by the nature of things driven to accommodate those who pose as the empowered defenders of their respective communities. Men and women "in the middle" always risk seeming inauthentic in places and times of great contest and polarization. But it would be fair to say that this was the Iraq America found, and that Iraqi identities had been sharpened by a great, inevitable struggle over the country's spoils and over its very definition. The unease of the Kurds with Iraq was not an American invention. A visitor to Barzani's solitary, windswept mountain abode who is treated to a quiet and bitter rendition of the crimes of the Iraqi Army against the Kurds is not listening to some American-inspired tale. The narrative proceeds from the very founding of the Iraqi state in 1921, and to the cruelties of an army that Kurdistan had never seen as its own. Nor could one expect the Sunni Arabs to vote anything beyond their rage at their loss of dominion, and their determination to keep the Shia seminarians and their militias, and their newfound power, in check.

Elections offered no panacea, just the promise that the struggle over the country would be pursued through nonviolent means. The transitional Assembly had had scant Sunni Arab representation—6 percent in all. There would be larger representation by that community this time around. It was as sure as anything that it would not satisfy a community that still believed in its right to rule. To be sure, there remained the possibility that these elections would be the starting gun for a more deadly conflict among the communities. But the elections were still Iraq's—and America's—most reasonable way out of the prevailing stalemate.

Washington was in no mood to look too closely at the results of the election. President Bush had gone out to sell the Iraq war yet again, and the drama of that Iraqi election was the centerpiece of a hectic effort to explain and justify the war. There may have been "irregularities" in these elections, but they were not excessive, administration officials would assert. The results had been exceedingly favorable to the United Iraqi Alliance, and the Sunni Arabs had taken to the streets to proclaim that they had been robbed of their proper share of the vote. They had been joined by a coalition of secular parties. Washington, and its envoys on the scene, fell back on a discreet silence in the face of these protests. They could in no way disown these elections; what they did was to press for a broad ruling coalition that would rein in the diehards of the United Iraqi Alliance. The weight of numbers was not enough in a society with such deep schisms. There was no exact science that could come up with a National Assembly that truly reflected the communities in the land. The logic of numbers still had to be "corrected" by a political process that gave the Sunni Arabs reason to turn away from the insurgency and to trust that a newly constituted government would not be an instrument of the Shia religious parties.

Beyond the Sunni-Shia fault line, and the struggle between the United Iraqi Alliance and the Sunni blocs, lay the disheartening performance of independent men and women of reasonably open and secular orientation. A political activist in his midforties allowed himself a dark reading of what had transpired in that election. "You could read this as the defeat of a liberal generation. Anyone who broke with the United Iraqi Alliance was severely punished. How do younger men and women who don't want to be part of these religious blocs find their way into politics?" He then ticked off a list of names for me, people of impeccable credentials and pedigree who were overwhelmed by the victory of the big Shia bloc. There was the "prince of the Marshes," Sheikh Abdul Karim al-Mohammedawi, a hero to people in the south, who had managed to secure only a handful of votes. In Karbala, there was a political man of genuine standing and education, Ali Dabbagh, who had been a member in the American-appointed Governing Council and in the transitional National Assembly and had made it to the Assembly in that earlier round of elections as a member of the United Iraqi Alliance. He had gone to his hometown, sought a seat there, and been resoundingly defeated, even though he had always been a protégé of Ayatollah Ali al-Sistani. There was the case, as well, of a woman of genuine standing, Dr. Salameh Khufaji, a former member of the Governing Council who had lost her eighteen-year-old son to an insurgent attack: she too failed to secure a parliamentary seat. Organizational muscle had carried the day, and there was no place for loners striking out on their own. Men and women who were political icons in their own right had been swept aside.

The man treating me to this narrative was no fan of Iyad Allawi, but he saw his poor showing as part of the same story line: Allawi had gotten 15 percent of the vote a year earlier, and he now had gotten a mere 8 percent, even though he had folded into his slate old Baathists, the Communist Party, former interim president Sheikh Ghazi al-Yawar, and Hajem Hassani, Speaker of the transitional National Assembly, among others. It was too early to draw big conclusions about some dark theocratic future for Iraq, this man said. But the prospects looked bleak to him. Iraqi liberalism was a fragile reed, he conceded, and the landscape all around Iraq—the pressure of the Arabs, the pressure of Iran—made the prospects bleaker still. There ran through his analysis a muted disappointment that the Americans were averting their gaze from what had really transpired in that election. It was not the standard Arab propensity to find fault in American policy, for this man favored the American war and was unabashedly pro-American. It was the recognition of the difficulty of changing his homeland that seemed to overwhelm him as he took stock of a dramatic and seminal event in his country's history.

But the sky had not fallen. The United Iraqi Alliance had secured a victory but had fallen short of political domination. And when the dust settled, two months after this election, the United Iraqi Alliance had put forth as its choice for prime minister the incumbent Ibrahim al-Jaafari, a physician not known for great ideological zeal. True, he had left his country for Iran in 1980, but he had given away a great deal about himself when he had quit Iran for London in 1989. He had chosen exile in Europe, and even his detractors who faulted him for poor management and leadership skills conceded that he had no blood on his hands and was untainted by corruption. He belonged to the devout middle classes, was religiously and socially conservative; he partook of the piety of mainstream Shiism. But nothing in his past, and nothing in his muddled stewardship of the transitional government, suggested that religious utopia was in the air, that a Shia reign of virtue was about to descend on Iraq.

This being Iraq, and this moment being a time of sharply drawn identities, the biography of Jaafari put out by his promoters had a none-too-subtle message to the Sunni Arabs. It was noted that he had been born in Karbala, in 1948, that he had been educated in Mosul, and that his ancestors had emigrated to Iraq from the Arabian Peninsula, from the town of Shaqra in today's Saudi Arabia. Iraqis could discern the message of this announcement. Jaafari was an Iraqi and an Arab. He may have sought refuge in Iran, but his roots lay in the most Arab of places, in the Peninsula itself. He would not front for Iran or serve its interests in Iraq. Whether his detractors in Fallujah and Ramadi would cede him this precious Arabism was an altogether different proposition. After quiescence the Shia had begun to fight back, and the instruments of the state were now available to them. The historic sense of Sunni power and Shia submission—"To us political power, *al-hukm,* to you *al-latm,* weeping and grief" went an unsentimental proverb in this land—had been overturned. The policeman at the door was now more likely to be a Shia than a Sunni, and the mild-mannered and inoffensive politician chosen to head the permanent government was caught up in this overturning of the order of power. He could boast of his Arab roots in the Peninsula, but a new compact between the Sunni and Shia children of this land had not yet been struck.

The Shia could be forgiven the sense that they needed the protection of political power, that they had to claim for themselves instruments of state power. They were in no mood to hear that they had overreached or that their appetite had to be curbed lest they frighten the Sunni Arabs. On February 22, in the midst of the deliberations over the makeup of a potential new Jaafari government, soon after the American stewards had issued a warning to the Shia that "sectarian" militias could not be allowed the run of the key ministries of interior and security, a bomb in the city of Samarra shattered the golden dome of one of the most sacred shrines of the Shia. The shrine of al-Askariya, the burial place of the tenth and eleventh Imams, was in a predominantly Sunni city; established in the ninth century, it had developed into a major center of Shia pilgrimage. It was there, in its vault, the faithful believed, that the twelfth imam, Muhammad al-Mahdi, then an infant, had hidden and gone into occultation—that is, disappeared to the eyes of ordinary men. The bombers had struck the shrine in the hope that the Shia would be goaded into full-scale sectarian warfare.

Grand Ayatollah Ali al-Sistani was to appeal for calm as the Shia hacked away at Sunni mosques. For once the great jurist showed his impatience: "If the government security forces cannot provide the necessary protection, the believers will do it." There were more politicians who were quick to assert that the Americans had given the green light for this deed because their envoy had been pressing the Shia to make concessions to the Sunni Arabs. But even those making the charges no doubt knew better. It would be harder in the shadow of this terrible deed to ask for Shia restraint and to remind the Shia leaders of the need for magnanimity. Yesterday's subjugation may have ended, but "normal" political life had not set in.

The occupying power was a stranger to this Sunni-Shia fight—but not quite. Its envoy, after the imperious Paul Bremer and the hands-off John Negroponte, who didn't stick around long enough to make a difference at any rate, was the Afghan-born Zalmay Khalilzad. He had been dispatched to Iraq in the hope that he would have a better feel for the place and its complexities than his predecessors. He was giving it his all, threatening and cajoling the Iraqi political class, pushing them toward a national unity government that would rein in the militias. It was now noted by the Shia preachers in Najaf and Karbala and Baghdad that the American envoy was a Sunni Muslim, after all. It was thus that a distant power—"globalized," made up of immigrants who buried their past—was turned into a player in the civil war of Islam between its Sunni and Shia children. This was the classic no-win situation: Dispatch Bremer and you will have dispatched a total stranger with no knowledge of the place. Dispatch Khalilzad and you will have inserted the foreign power into a very old, local feud.

In no time, Shia political operatives had given Khalilzad a most Sunni of names, Abu Omar. The Bush administration had come face to face with the classic dilemma of an occupying power: it had thrown its weight against the extension of Prime Minister Jaafari's tenure while still insisting that it respected the democratic choice of the Iraqi people. Jaafari had prevailed by a single vote within the United Iraqi Alliance; he had been put forth as the Shia candidate for prime minister with the crucial support of Moqtada al-Sadr's bloc of deputies. It was an open secret that Washington and its envoy on the scene favored a rival of Jaafari's, Adel Abdul Mahdi, a more worldly man of the Westernized class, fluent in English and French, more familiar and accessible to the Americans. Jaafari had not governed well—nor, it should be added, had his predecessor, the CIA favorite, Iyad Allawi. But for the vast majority of the Shia, Jaafari was one of them, his rejection by Washington another indication of the capitulation of American power to the will of the Sunni Arabs within and beyond Iraq. The American regency had a dread of Moqtada al-Sadr. But Jaafari could plead that the young inheritor of the Sadr legacy was a fact of life, that he "owned" the streets of Sadr City, and that he, Jaafari, had the best chance of bringing Sadr into the fold.

It was an uneven fight, the drawn-out standoff between Jaafari and American power. Four months after the elections of December 15, Jaafari was still unable to form a national unity government. American opposition to him had emboldened his rivals in the political class, and he faced a veto by Jalal Talabani. Nor was all secure within the big Shia bloc, the United Iraqi Alliance, where other contenders for the prime ministership hedged their bets and waited to make their own bids for that position. Washington had sung the praises of democracy, but was now determined to have its way. There were no good, viable alternatives to Jaafari. And the Americans were to win a pyrrhic victory. When Jaafari concluded that he was a beaten man, the Shia politician chosen to replace him was Nuri al-Maliki, an operative of Jaafari's own party. There were many people who said that he was no more worldly than Jaafari, that he would not be more forthcoming toward the Sunnis and the Kurds—and the Americans—than Jaafari had been. It had not been a pretty spectacle: a democratic caucus that had chosen Jaafari had been overruled, and an occupying power had been forced—by the truculence of the political class in Iraq and their machinations, by its own desire to dominate the political process even as it vowed again and again to hand over real power to the Iraqis—to walk away from its own commitment to democratic ways. Jaafari's setback was both his own and a demonstration that the Shia journey to political primacy in Iraq would not be an easy affair. Whether they knew it or not, the American officials who pushed Jaafari aside had taken on added burdens of their own.

CHAPTER 8

Waiting for Rain

The face of my country frightens me," Ali Ghaleb, a physician who directed Iraq's system of public health, was to observe to a French author, Pierre Rossi, in the early 1960s. I came upon this quotation in the course of reading at random about Iraq; its truth was indisputable. The physician was no doubt thinking of the regicide of 1958, and of the bloodletting that came in its aftermath. In the scheme of Iraqi history, he was hardly unique. Iraqis understand the terrors of their own history. They know the temper of their country. The great poet Muhammad Mahdi al-Jawahiri, looking back on decades of his own life, and on his country's tumultuous modern history, spoke of Iraq as a country hard on its rulers and on its own people. The poet had known the first Hashemite king of Iraq, Faisal I, and had briefly worked in his court. He wrote of that monarch with sympathy: the Hashemite ruler would have been a happier man, Jawahiri wrote, had he had a throne in Syria, for Iraq was a hard, unforgiving land and cruel to its own.

For Iraq's sorrow and the pain of its history, for its expectations of better days that never came, Jawahiri had chosen a fitting literary metaphor: he was born, he said, in Najaf, on a parched piece of ground, and the Euphrates River was just achingly nearby. There was water in Iraq, the confluence of two rivers, but the land was fierce and parched; there was oil wealth, but the prosperity was always a day away. There were the claims—and realities—of an elite secular culture that once took in Jews and Christians and Sunnis and Shiites and Kurds, but the elite culture always cracked under pressure, and the sectarianism of the country trailed it like a steady curse.

"My father is Shiite, my mother is Sunni, and on my father's side the family is half Arab, half Kurd," a young man in the lecture hall of Iraq's Foreign Ministry said in a tone that mixed pride and bewilderment. It was a contribution to a discussion I was party to. "Where do

I go, in a country that would split along ethnic and sectarian lines?"
He had his rich and complicated background; he had a noble and high
idea of his country, but outside the protection of this official building,
his country was ablaze with sectarian feuds, riven with suspicions. A
history more difficult than this young man may have bargained for
cast its shadows on his—and his country's—possibilities.

In an indispensable work of historical interpretation, *Ancient Iraq,*
by a French scholar who studied the country's archaeology and culture,
the author, Georges Roux, writes that Mesopotamia did not "offer
ideal conditions for the development of an original civilization." The
civilization had developed, Roux observes, in the "extreme south of the
country, on the fringe of the swamps. . . . Whatever man achieved in
ancient Iraq, he did it at the price of a constant struggle against nature
and against other men, and this struggle forms the very thread of history in that part of the world." There was no uniformity in this land
of contrasts that pitted the northern steppe against the southern
marshlands. This kind of geographic determinism can be pushed too
far. But Roux's view of the opposition between the north and the south
has a power readily apparent to anyone given the most superficial contact with Iraq. The political cartography that threw together in one
realm the Kurdish highlanders and the Arabs of the Middle Euphrates
had dispensed with deep historical differences, had glided past them.
The violence that has hovered over this country issued from these deep
contradictions.

In the scheme of such categories, Iraq has been the borderland
between the desert Arabs of the Peninsula and the Persian Gulf and the
Levant Arabs of the eastern Mediterranean. It has lacked the intimacy
and familiarity of desert society, and the mimicry and inauthenticity
and polish of the Levant. It has been a place apart, and Iraqis have
been aware of their separateness. The medium of expression of this
land has been poetry, and the Arab revival of letters in the twentieth
century is heavily indebted to the Iraqis. The list is long, but there can
be no doubting the literary genius and talent of Iraq's great modern
poets. There was Muhammad Mahdi al-Jawahiri, his poetry a veritable chronicle of his country's odyssey in the twentieth century. There
was Badr Shakir al-Sayyab, of the city of Basra, who died in 1964, in
his late thirties, and whose poetry owed much to the influence of
T. S. Eliot and Edith Sitwell. (The reverence for Sayyab was extraordinary; a statue of him erected in Basra became a shrine for young

poets, evidence of devotion to the place of poetry in the country's culture and public life.) And there was Buland Haidari, a Kurdish poet of luminous gifts, born in Arbil in 1926 to an aristocratic family, who played a signal role in the development of free verse. Haidari died in exile in London in 1996, after nearly five decades of steady, brilliant output.

There was, of course, no single poetic tradition in Iraq, but the poetry was unmistakably dark and brooding, an expression of the country's pain and its recurring sense of grief and disappointment. Shaker Laibi, an Iraqi poet and literary critic born in 1955—he would have come into his own in the age of the Baathist tyranny, and like so many of his contemporaries was destined for a life of exile—has written of this flight to poetry in Iraq. In that medium of expression, Laibi saw Iraq's distinct ways and the weight of its cruel history. He contrasted Iraq with Egypt and Lebanon: the Egyptians, he said, were people of song and dance, and the Egyptian, in a long settled history of tranquillity, was able to express the joy and contentment of life, to alternate in an easy way between the sacred and the profane. For their part, the Lebanese had been lightly governed and free to speak, in prose, in their parliament, and to seek their destiny through their travels to distant places. In contrast, the Iraqis had their poetry: it was the medium that their troubled life and their repressive regimes made possible.

In the early 1980s—at a time of war and violence in Lebanon—Laibi estimates there were nearly five hundred men and women of poetry and letters—as well as people of the visual arts, including sculpture and painting, at which the Iraqis also excel—in Beirut. The cruelty of the regime, the privations inflicted on Iraq by its war against Iran, had forced countless younger people to flee the country. Beirut was one destination, but homes were also made in the cities of Western Europe and North America. Iraqis were not given to emigration and wanderings; they were not like the Lebanese, who were quick to quit their small country for other shores. This tyrannical regime had changed all that. As with the Russians in the second half of the nineteenth century, an exile tradition of letters preserved those inert—and beloved—memories of a fabled country. There were the usual quarrels of the exiles, and the Arabic dailies and literary periodicals in London and Beirut chronicled the yearnings of two or three generations of Iraqis. Their subject was always their country; its hold on them never weakened. They lived on the expectation that the country they knew would be there awaiting them when the despotism gave way.

From Sweden and Denmark, the exiles wrote of the palm groves of their homeland, of evenings on the banks of the Tigris, of the nights of their beloved Basra. Tyranny paid them no heed; it had money and the whip, and the false grandeur of the state. Moreover, the tyranny had its own manufactured literary culture—the "fighting poets" and the "Baathist poets" of the regime, and the sycophants posing as historians in the service of the ruler, telling of his exploits and prettifying his deeds. Some of the exiles knew that theirs was a journey of no return. The American demolition of the Baath regime had given them the chance to return to their homeland. Time is cruel, and those who chose to return came back to a world that had not been waiting on them. Here is the writer Khalid al-Maali recalling both his forced departure from his country and the shock of his return: "We had left, each of us carrying a bundle of dreams and illusions, finding a place somewhere to rest, or to keep moving even faster so as to keep the past at a further remove. Year after year, we would chew on our words, fight our own words, and among ourselves, until we took leave of ordinary life. We held on to our illusions in the hope that these would rescue us from calamity. Because fate is merciless, we were returned to our land and our people, to find that some of them had departed to that place from which mortals do not return. We wanted to behold our country, and to talk to those who had survived, to mourn those who departed. . . . We looked in vain for familiar faces, for high walls that were now demolished, for familiar street corners, for a once overflowing river now running low and shriveled and its fish dead and gone. We found palm trees that no longer bore their fruit, and nights no longer illuminated by the stars."

A prolific peer of this poet, Najm Wali, who had made a home in Germany, wrote in a similar vein of the home and the life that could not be retrieved. Wali had left Iraq in 1980, in that time of darkness when Saddam Hussein had begun to close up the political universe at home and to begin his wars beyond Iraq's borders. He remembered the date of his departure, October 28: "I turned my back on the country that had been my home for 24 years. . . . I knew that my journey was irreversible, that I couldn't look back, and just as you can't step twice in the same river, you can't live twice in the same homeland. I am not the first person to know this fact. From the very dawn of human history, ever since frontiers and borders were known, exiles knew and understood this bitter truth." Wali went back to that "great son" of Iraq, the poet Muhammad Mahdi al-Jawahiri: he recalled his fate, dying in exile, in Damascus, "a thousand kilometers from his birthplace." This had been Iraq's fate in the "age of terror and the policemen." The dictator who had announced, in 1979, that "he who does not like us can leave" had claimed the country for himself and his own, Wali wrote. "Now when the exiles go back, there is the recognition that this is another form of exile."

It wasn't just the ravages of time, of course, handing out surprises—and disappointments—to the men and women returning after three or more decades away from their country. They were coming back to a place in the grip of a new kind of terror—the anarchy, an insurgency that refused to go away, the assassinations that targeted men and women of letters and the law and the other professions. In this dangerous time, there was a stubborn determination to go on with the life of culture and letters. An Iraqi writer, Salah Hassan, who had been living in Holland, caught this juxtaposition between literary life and the breakdown of public order in Basra and Baghdad in May 2004. A poetry festival had taken him to Basra. The meeting had taken place in one of the city's hotels. Outside, in the streets of Basra, there was now a small war between the British forces and the militia of the young cleric, Moqtada al-Sadr. Salah Hassan had stepped out of the confines of the hotel, with a Kurdish woman poet, for a walk in the neighborhood nearby. Hotel security had advised him against the venture: the poet was unveiled, and the two of them, they were warned, were at risk of being kidnapped. On a street that ran parallel to the hotel, the two of them saw the dereliction of the life of Basra: heaps of garbage, stray animals, impoverished children picking their way through the mounds of filth.

Hassan witnessed more of the same degradation in Baghdad, at the National Theater. At first glance, from the outside, the place looked reasonably orderly and clean. But in truth, it was run-down, some of its walls long decayed, and there was something sad and unsettling about the advertisements posted on the walls for an exhibition of the work of the country's sculptors against the background of gunfire and explosives. It wasn't just these scenes that pained this man of letters. There was the psychic landscape he encountered: there was cynicism everywhere. He had taken the initiative to acquire some fifteen thousand scientific books for the University of Basra. No one he encountered in Iraq had believed that the effort had been motivated by regard for the country's intellectual life. They were quick to assume that the thing was a scam, that Hassan was in it for personal advantage and for money. "When I told them that this was a gift from Dutch universities for the universities of Iraq, they mocked me and thought that I had taken leave of my senses. There was a proverb in Iraq that maintained that behind every palm tree there was a poet. In the age of Saddam, they should have added the word 'mercenary' to that proverb." The dictator's terror had wrecked Iraq's intellectual life. Salah Hassan had found literary and cultural desolation in his home-land.

Liberty had come after a long season of terror, followed by a devastating time of siege and sanctions that had all but pulverized Iraq's intellectual and cultural life. (War, to be sure, when it came, was costly, but the slow death of the country, in the 1990s, under a sanctions regime that visited hell on Iraq's people but spared the ruling apparatus needs to be recalled when drawing up an audit of the American war in Iraq.) Decades of culture, the social capital of a modernism slowly and painfully nurtured in Iraq, had been all but wiped out. The proud country and its middle classes and literati and professionals had been brought to their knees. We know the broad outlines of this descent into hell and pauperization, but we are yet to have the telling details of it all. It is still perhaps too early for Iraqis to tell what happened to them over the quarter-century that preceded the American war. Pride in a culture where people are loath to dwell on the violations inflicted on them no doubt impedes a full reckoning of what occurred. Time too is needed before a people bare their terrible secrets. But a little-known work of autobiographical fiction by a brilliant Iraqi woman of letters, a professor of Russian literature, offers a heart-breaking portrait of what became of this proud and vital tradition of Iraqi modernism. The author was Hayat Shararah, born in Najaf in 1935 to a family of great learning, and her book, *Idha al-Ayyam Agh-saqat (If the Days Darken)*, was published in 2002 with an arresting introduction by a sister of hers, now living in London. Hayat Shararah and one of her two daughters committed suicide in Baghdad in the summer of 1997. The novel was the work of a sensitive and rebellious soul watching the unraveling of an entire world around her. The sister supplying the introduction and the narrative of Hayat's life was discreet; she did not give the details of the suicide. It was gently and elegantly touched upon: Hayat was depicted as "leaving" Baghdad, a city she once loved but now a place strange in its filth and squalor, its people degraded by fear and humbled by hunger.

Hayat's father, Mohamed Shararah, had been a celebrated poet and teacher who had known both fame and the prisons of Iraq under the monarchy. He had been a devoted father, and his home had been a literary salon frequented by the greats of Iraqi letters and poetry. A precocious child, Hayat had taken in these comings and goings, the poetry evenings, the love of language, the mix of literature and politics, and the dreams of the country's emancipation. We see her as a young child with a notebook taking down the lines recited by the legends of Iraqi poetry—Muhammad Mahdi al-Jawahiri, Badr Shakir al-Sayyab, and the woman poet Nazik al-Malaika. A child bred to independence, Hayat was to make her way into the Communist Party, schooling in Egypt, and five years in Russia, where she obtained a doctorate in literature. Along the way, she married a like-minded soul, a dedicated physician. They had two daughters. Hayat turned away from politics to the consolations and demands of literature and teaching, but this was Iraq and their lives would unfold in the shadow of its political terrors.

Iraq had known violence and political turbulence, but the 1980s and 1990s—Saddam's time, and the time of his wars, and the economic siege imposed on Iraq by a broad coalition that had defeated him but left him in place to torment his own people—were to devour every little saving grace this country had known. Hayat's husband was imprisoned and tortured, and died an early death. Her father died a disillusioned, broken man. She was left with her daughters, and her fiction catches the time of terror and hunger that befell Iraq. She was a university professor, and her unsparing portrait documents the struggle of her peers, her professional class, for shreds of dignity, for increasingly scarce supplies of food and tea and coffee. The great centers of learning were now in the grip of terror, the boys of the *mukhabarat* (the secret police) granted special admissions and exempt from attending classes, had the run of the university. The administrators were petty tyrants—Little Hitler, one such administrator was called—and informers who gave and withheld favors as they wished.

Hunger was a companion of this fear. A large country with good soil and abundant water now dreamt of food, and accomplished people would stand in line waiting for handouts from the regime's oper-

atives. There may have been old pride, but men and women now did
what they had to in order to survive. They took down old personal
libraries, books they treasured and loved, and brought them to street
vendors, bullies who knew the despair of the sellers, knew that a
world had spun out of control and that there was little room in it for
books and learning. There may have been old notions of honor and
propriety, but women now knew that the old notions warred with the
new realties of the country. This was a big prison, and the jailers
decreed that women under forty-five years of age could not leave the
country without a "male protector." Hayat thus could not go abroad
with her daughters, nor would it be easy for her to publish what she
wrote—studies of Turgenev, Tolstoy, and Dostoyevsky—or collections of her father's work. The country was at war and regimented by
a master who even decreed the proper weight of his people—and
how these people in the university dreaded *yawm al-wazn,* the day of
weighing. This was not the place or the time for people given to sen-
sitivity or honesty; it was best not to look into things or to name them
as they were. Hitherto emancipated women in Hayat's fiction suddenly
take to religion; scholars of great accomplishment are pushed out of
the university and seek the safety of living behind closed doors.
Bananas, chocolates, coffee, even tea become the stuff of obsessions.
We are reading a work whose conclusion we know: this bleak world
offers no way out, and this sensitive woman, Hayat Shararah, too
proud to bend and to grovel, chooses death on August 1, 1997. So
does her daughter Maha. (Another daughter, Zainab, survives and now
lives, I am told, in New York City.) For the two of them who perished,
this new gift of dangerous liberty would come too late. There would
come a time when the era of Saddam Hussein would be recalled as a
time of secular primacy, when religion was kept in check, and social
and cultural liberties kept intact. But those who know the country well
tell a different story. In the final years of the regime, around the year
2000, the Baathist tyranny reinvented itself as a conservative Islamic
state. The regime was digging in; it had closed on itself. The half-
finished mosques all around Baghdad bear witness to this new, false
piety. Saddam Hussein had gone on a mosque-building binge, but the
shortages and the sanctions, then the American invasion, had cut
short this spree. It was during this period as well that countless prostitutes had been rounded up and some of them beheaded, and a show
was made against the public consumption of liquor. The society was

being recast, and a secular Baathist regime was falling back on a contrived piety.

The claim that the tyranny had at least respected the canons of secularism was, in truth, hollow. It was not a surprise that the Baathists would reincarnate as Islamists—the Islamic Baath Party was the ironic name given the Baath by Defense Minister Saadoun Dulaimi—in the aftermath of the American war. One of the principal leaders of the Sunni Arabs to emerge in the time of the Americans was Tariq al-Hashimi, of the Iraq Consensus Front, which gained a respectable forty-four seats in the elections of December 2005. Hashimi was a "false Islamist," an Iraqi leader in the know told me. For Hashimi was an old Baathist, a former colonel in the Iraqi armed forces. His Baathism had yielded to "Islam," but at the heart of the change was expediency and the drive to power. This was perhaps fitting, for even the founding theorist of the Baath, Michael Aflaq, had conceded the primacy of Islam and was said to have left the Greek Orthodox Church for Islam out of recognition that secularism could never give Islam meaningful competition in Arab political life.

"Under Saddam, we lived in a big prison; today we live in a kind of wilderness. . . . I prefer the wilderness." The words are those of an educated Iraqi woman, Dr. Lina Ziyad. Perhaps it was inevitable that this new liberty would come at such a terrible price. There were enforcers of virtue in Lina Ziyad's country keen to impose on this historically secular country new codes of "Islamic" practice and ritual and dress. There were car bombs and rampant insecurity. There were vigilante squads attacking liquor store owners and demanding that Iraqi women don the veil. Still, there were men and women willing to bet on an uncertain future.

There was unmistakable nostalgia at play. A society violated by a merciless despot who had shown its order and its ways scant, if any, regard seemed to fall back on the old ingredients of *nasab* (pedigree) and inherited merit. The old social order seemed to reemerge. Among the clerics, there were the Hakims and the Sadrs, harking back to an earlier time. Among the politicians there were the Chalabis, the Pachachis, the Chederchis, the Allawis, the Hamoudis, heirs of men who had been figures of consequence under the monarchy. And there was perhaps the most quaint piece of nostalgia: the return of a standard-bearer of the Hashemites, Sharif Ali ibn Hussein, proclaiming the cause of constitutional monarchy. As in the tales of *One Thou-*

sand and One Arabian Nights, Sharif Ali, then two years of age, had survived the regicide and the revolution of 1958. He and his parents had been given shelter by a family of ordinary Iraqis, and had then been given asylum and a way out of the country by the Saudi embassy. He had grown up in Lebanon and London; he had made a living in investment banking and had been active in exile politics. If the country needed or hankered for a king, he was at the ready. The sacking of the Saddam regime had made it possible for Sharif Ali, a man who exuded the gentility of the Hashemites, to return to his birthplace. When he contested the elections to the National Assembly, nostalgia and restoration were what he had to offer the turbulent country. His basic message was simple: he was the heir of Faisal I, founder of modern Iraq, and he would be above "partisanship and sectarianism." The constitution would be respected, and the "dictatorial practices" of the intervening decades would be brought to an end.

The cause of monarchic restoration was doomed. Sharif Ali sought a seat in the National Assembly, but his bid was turned back, both in the first national elections of January 30, 2005, and in the second cycle eleven months later. A big history swirled around him, and I was curious about the promptings of his return to a country he had never known. Politics is the "family business," he said to me, when I called on him a fortnight after the distressing results of the second election. "Some families go into commerce or the military, and we have been in the business of politics and leadership for centuries." Tall and thin, with the high forehead and fine features of his family, elegantly dressed in a dark suit, the sharif had received me in a lightly guarded villa just beyond the security of the Green Zone. His manners were exquisite, his English courtly and polished. No, he said in response to my query, he had not been nervous about coming back to Iraq. He thought of it as a calling, and he presented to the Iraqis a program of constitutional monarchy. He was bitter about the results of the second election; he had run on the Ahmad Chalabi list and deeply believed that his slate had been the victim of fraud and foul play. "People came to see us, local leaders from Sadr City had called on me repeatedly. We may not have swept Sadr City, but we knew the scale of our support." He would not quit the field, he told me, but would still search for a role in this new Iraq. He thought that the presidency might in time come his way, or the chairmanship of the National Assembly. He had high hopes that Iraqis would turn to him: he had the special claim of the

Hashemites—Sunni rulers, *ashraf*, descendants of the Prophet, quite acceptable to the Shia, known to have been merciful during the four decades they had governed Iraq.

Sharif Ali conceded the odds against him: he understood that the Shia clerical institution in Najaf had trouble getting its mind around a descendant of the Prophet who adhered to Sunnism. He had the added burden of a campaign waged by the Jordanian monarchy against his claim to the Hashemite mantle. But he would not give up hope, he said. He saw monarchic restoration as the gift he would put before a country stalked by sectarian antagonisms. He had a more flattering image of Iraq than the one he had seen emerge out of the elections—and the anarchy in the streets. The nostalgist in me could only wish him well, for monarchies in the Arab world had proven better and more merciful than the despotic regimes and the national security states that had run down this unfortunate Arab political order. A petty thug from Tikrit had made himself master of all that was within sight; the country could do worse than give the nod to a prince bred to good manners and decorum and restraint. The past—imagined, prettified—wasn't going to rehabilitate this country. But forgive the Iraqis their understandable search for a usable past.

There had been that eccentric ruler Abdul Kareem Qassem, who had overthrown the monarchy. He too has been rehabilitated in this new wave of nostalgia. He was brutally executed, it shall be recalled, in 1963. No grave commemorated him; his body had been dumped into the Tigris. Now a bronze statue of him rose in a Baghdad square. The country now thought better of Qassem. It was recalled by those reviving his cult that he had no private residence of his own, that he had died with a meager sixteen dinars to his name; he was now eulogized as the "leader of the poor," a dreamer, at worst a tragic figure who had wanted the best for his country but had been unable to bring it about.

The past and its pull were captured for me during a visit I made to the home of the finance minister, Ali Allawi, in the summer of 2005. He lived in the Mansour district, one of Baghdad's wealthiest neighborhoods, in what had been his family home during the days of the monarchy. There were armed guards at the entrance, and I had to wait in a small trailer packed with armed men. The house was at once elegant and subdued, a split-level home with a garden, a living room on one side, a library on the other. The furniture and the wood paneling had the mark of an older era, the time of the urban high bourgeoisie. Allawi, himself a polished and slightly reserved man in his midfifties, bespoke that era. He received me in the library; he had been recovering from a knee operation, and the cane he carried added to the aura. On the wall of his library, there was a picture of his father, in formal attire. It had been taken in 1953, I believe, when his father, Abdulameer, had been sworn in as minister of health. The son would have been a boy of five then, an heir to a distinguished pedigree. In one of these twists of family background, Ali Allawi was a second cousin of Iyad Allawi and a nephew of Ahmad Chalabi, two rivals for power in the world of Iraqi politics. He apologized to me for the heavy security. A month earlier, six of his bodyguards had been killed when a Sudanese jihadist had detonated himself at a restaurant where Allawi was having a meal; four of his guards had lost their limbs as well. He told the story of the Sudanese with baffled astonishment, as if never quite grasping the idea that a man from the Sudan would come into Iraq on such a cruel mission.

I began with his father's picture, for I sensed that this was where the story began. I had been told that his father had been one of Iraq's most distinguished physicians, that he had served as dean of the Royal College of Medicine. The family had quit the country after the revolution of 1958, and his father had made a new life in London. The son had been given the best of American education; he had followed his uncle Ahmad Chalabi (his senior by only four years) to MIT, then earned a doctorate at Harvard. To the Baghdad he had left as a boy of ten, he had come back once, in 1967, on a short visit. After that, his country became a place of memory, and of the imagination. He prospered in international business, working out of London, and his three grown children had worlds of their own beyond Iraq. Still, his country's pull was irresistible: he came back in the aftermath of the liberation. He served as minister of commerce in the first interim government that the Coalition Provisional Authority had put together; for a brief stint of two months he had been minister of defense. He had had a difficult relation with Paul Bremer. He joined the cabinet of Ibrahim al-Jaafari formed after the national elections and was given the task of organizing the country's chaotic finances. There had been massive corruption in the interim government; Ali Allawi had been brought in to bring the chaos—the costly subsidies of fuel and food, and the waste of public treasure—under control. By all accounts, he was a man of

unblemished reputation, worthy of the trust granted him by his colleagues.

I was curious about the impulse that brought him back to Iraq. "It
would have been rather odd if I had not come back," he said. "Away
from Iraq, we spent so much time replaying the things that could have
averted the destruction of the monarchy. It was endless. If only the
regent had done this or that, if only Nuri al-Said had been more
careful or, conversely, more decisive, our world would have held. I had
to come back." Turgenev would have loved this man, I thought: the
liberal caught up in a world of intense violence and controversy. He
was a reader of history, an observer; a knack for finance was only one
dimension of this immensely decent and literate man. He took the
long view of things; his interests were eclectic—the sacking of Baghdad by the Mongols in 1258, the mind-set of the Arabs toward the
Shia, the high Persian culture that predated Shiism and formed the
culture of the world around him.

His country interested him in the way it would hook a stranger; he
saw it through the prism of his Western education and the adult life he
had lived abroad. "Nothing here is what it seems. If you see an ele-
phant—it is probably an ostrich." He delivered the verdict without
self-righteousness. A "compressed Darwinism" had taken place under
the Baath tyranny, he said. There had occurred in the country a
"rewiring of the Iraqi mind as people coped with that frightening
order. That kind of change would ordinarily take countless years,
perhaps many decades. But the terror was intense and perverted,
hence that compressed Darwinism." There was weariness in him and
a dose of jilted idealism. It had taken him six months to repair his family home; it had been an interrogation center under the Baath. He had
found it full of filth and excrement; a kind of evil clung to it. He had
also found a cache of documents: the Baathists were neurotic about
recording their deeds of brutality, keeping records of the people they
had victimized. The repair of the "Iraqi mind," he said, would "take
two or three generations. But this is a young man's work, and we are
old and weary." He did not know how the repair of the Iraqi mind
would take place, but the very process of brutalizing the country
offered the consolation that people adjust to all sorts of things, that
they are immensely adaptable.

Ali Allawi knew America well, and he was devoted to its culture and
practicality; he would not second-guess the justice of the war that had

made possible his homecoming. But he had not been prepared for the incompetence and amateurism of the Coalition Provisional Authority. He had read widely about the American rehabilitation of Germany and Japan in the aftermath of the Second World War. America had "sent the best of itself" to these places, he said. In Germany, he added, there had been Americans of German ancestry who knew the language and the ways. "Here the ignorance was pervasive." The Americans who came here were of three types: there were "wet-behind-the-ears" young people who were given vast responsibilities and power; there were "worn-out bureaucrats" having a second run at things. Finally there were the "half-baked ideologues" who had their own wild notions of Iraq and who quit in a hurry when the country disappointed them.

At the heart of this great American undertaking Allawi saw the fundamental ambivalence: America had liberated the Shia but was determined to check them. "In the short time I was minister of defense, I tried to tell Paul Bremer that Moqtada al-Sadr did not pose the kind of threat posed by the former regime loyalists. I did not succeed. The Americans came with their own model of a menacing Shiism and imposed it on the reality here. It was naïve to bring to Iraq the lessons of Iran." Iran's influence was huge in this region, he believed; there was a natural cultural preeminence to Iran that went beyond the Shia community. He recalls visiting Iran with a delegation that included the Kurdish leader Jalal Talabani. There were translators present, but Talabani surprised him by speaking fluent Farsi and by saying that he thoroughly admired the language and culture of Iran. "No one accuses Talabani of subservience to Iran; this remains the burden of the Shia alone." He did not much like the facile analogy that compared the coming of the Americans to Iraq with the fall of Baghdad to the Mongols in 1258; he was not given to that kind of simplification. But there were historical parallels that appealed to him. "Go back to that episode: the Abbasid rulers goaded the Mongols, who had other priorities. The Abbasids had not believed that the Mongols would strike. They did, and the great devastation liberated the Shia. This was not the tale of betrayal that the nationalist Arab historiography tells; the Shia had not opened the gates of Baghdad before the Mongols. But the liberation of the Shia was an outcome of that historic event. A strange thing happened then: the Mongols converted to Islam and became fanatically orthodox, persecutors of the Shia. The Americans of today could not take to the Shia. Perhaps this unease was transmitted to them by the Sunni Arab regimes they had worked with for so long. That Arab mind-set is most certainly unique in its inability to deal with Shiism and to take it into the fold."

He spoke of the Shia with the tender regard of a man moved by the condition of less fortunate kinsmen. He had seen Shia towns of unimaginable destitution. His government work had taken him south to Amarah, in the Middle Euphrates. In the early days of the monarchy, the agricultural province of Amarah had been prosperous and blessed. But that was long ago. Misery had come to Amarah: land had gone out of cultivation; canals had silted up. He had been surprised by the poverty of the land and the defeat of the people, their gratitude for a little project he had brought with him. "It was barren earth of white salt, nothing save poverty, in a country of huge oil reserves and abundant wealth. Closer by, in Baghdad, in Sadr City, there is a great mass of people, and even the upper orders in the Shia community don't know what to do with them." He was anxious about the future. He did not believe that the Sunni Arabs had accepted the passing of their hegemony. "They are a minority in Iraq, but they have a majoritarian mind-set because of the large Sunni Arab world around them. They are convinced of their own title to the country." Iraq had to be "regionalized," he thought, with power pulled away from Baghdad, and the Sunni Arabs given more than their share of power and bounty to conciliate them. He gave the loyalists of the old regime their due; he never thought that they would wage as fierce and tenacious an insurgency as they had. Other Shia leaders, he conceded, are convinced that their people could hold their own, that the young men of Sadr City, the underclass, would fight, and the Shia would never return to their prior subjugation. But this was not his view, for the brooding pessimist in him saw the Shia weighed down by a tormented history. "The Shia defer fights, run away from them at times, and then come back and pay a heavier price than the one they would have paid had they stood firm in the first place. It had happened this way with Imam Hussein. That battle could have been easily won had people in Kufa gone out to defend the man they had invited into Iraq. They didn't and they were to pay dearly for that abdication. They continue to pay to the present day."

Events were open-ended in Iraq, Allawi said. There was so much to do; he had been appalled by the country's condition. It was hard to cash a check here, he lamented, let alone institute a business culture of transparency and adherence to the law. But he was giving it a try. It was midmorning as we spoke; he had been generous with his time. In the late afternoon we met again at the poolside estate of his uncle, Ahmad Chalabi, where Allawi was doing some water therapy for his knee. He had nearly drowned in this pool as a young boy, he told me. A beloved uncle—"may God rest his soul"—had saved him. The pool was in a garden of tall palm trees, behind high walls and a heavily guarded gate. Memories of old Baghdad and tales of new cruelties alternated as we talked in the pool's shallow end. Dusk had come; within this garden—where a beautiful *mudif* (guesthouse made of the reeds of the Marshes of the south) had been added to this rambling estate—there was a beguiling kind of peace. From behind the high walls there was the echo of mortar rounds, the sound of police sirens, and nearby, in the Baghdad way of traffic control, policemen could be heard firing into the air. Before me was a man of refinement and means and education. Next morning when I tried to write down and make sense of what I had seen, I was convinced that it was the picture of Ali Allawi's father in the library and the memory of a beloved uncle pulling him out of the water that had brought this man back to a country on the boil, a place where a Sudanese bigot kills and maims without a moment's sorrow or a moment's pause.

The political whirlwind had devoured nearly five decades of the country's life. Two generations had been lost to wasteful tyranny. This man may have been admittedly weary, but the place needed him, needed both the old memories and the skills acquired in foreign lands.

The country's needs, and the two generations lost to war and tyranny: I saw these in a young man I had taken to, named Ammar, a graceful, handsome man, twenty-five years of age, of winning manners. He worked for a friend of mine, and there had been enough time for us to feel comfortable with each other. He had been an excellent chemistry student, he had received a graduate degree, and he ached to get out of Iraq to the United States. A former professor of his had received his doctorate from the University of Miami, so there was magic attached to the name of that university. Young Arabs, Ammar knew, were not in demand on foreign shores. He was trapped here, and I could offer him no consolation. He was a young man of enormous dignity; he would not hustle strangers for favors. He felt intensely his country's wounds: "We have been ruled by cruel men because our people are backward and full of superstitions. How else can we explain that men with no culture or education disposed of our fate?" He was stoical about his, and his country's, prospects. He would learn and master the business skills he could, knowing that the science that he had learned at the university lagged behind the science of the world outside. He saw no end in sight to the insurgency. We talked once late into the night; we had left the television on, and the escapism of the Arab world played out on the screen. We were half watching a particularly glitzy channel, Rotana, and there were young Lebanese women, pop singers, scantily clad, and music videos that would make Britney Spears envious; there were scenes of trendy Egyptians, bleached blondes on large yachts, in some fantasy of Egypt that bore no relation to that crowded land. I thought that these images must make for an odd contrast to his world. There was no bitterness in him as he spoke of what life heaped upon the people he knew. The night before, a guard he knew had been killed on the road south of Baghdad, on that "triangle of death." He remembered him well, drew a measure of consolation from the fact that the man who was killed had been young and had no children. He knew that there would be more grief to come. He bade me farewell for the day and headed home as darkness descended on Baghdad.

New, fragile buds were struggling to be born—new forms of political expression. Iraqis with a memory of a time before the tyranny could claim these political forms as a return to the old ways of the country. They could be forgiven this consolation, the claim that there had been the semblance of political life in their recent history. Few Iraqis had a living memory of the last time their country had known parliamentary elections. A good half-century had passed since the last election in 1954. But some Iraqis could be heard claiming parliamentary politics as a restored inheritance. Others did not quibble: they were eager to partake of the liberties afforded them by a native government still under foreign tutelage. The deadline the American stewards gave for the drafting of a constitution may have been exceedingly tight and unrealistic—a mere ten weeks between the forming of a government in April 2005 and the first deadline of August 15 of that summer. But the Iraqis—battered and exhausted by a stubborn insurgency—still preferred the promise of constitutional politics to the unchecked tyranny of the former regime. After a brief hiatus, the work of the constitutional drafting committee was completed. And two months later, the constitution was ratified in a popular referendum. To be sure, the Sunni Arabs had opposed it by large majorities and the Kurds and the Shia had given it a huge margin of approval. But this conflict was better than outright combat and better than the past.

Coming into Iraq as the election results of December 15, 2005, had been tallied and assimilated, I could hear both disappointment and resignation. The sky had not fallen, the United Iraqi Alliance had prevailed, but its share of the parliament—128 out of 275 seats—put it well short of political domination. Its leaders would still have to scramble to put together a ruling coalition, it would still have to contend with the Kurds and with the Sunni Arabs, and it would still have to maintain discipline within its ranks. The talk of "theocracy" and of a "second Islamic republic" was overblown; the jurists in Najaf gave every indication that this was not their program or their utopia. Iran was present in Iraq, as was inevitable; geography could not be annulled. But the Iranian theocratic model was an altogether different matter. What was worrisome to secular Iraqis was the rise to considerable power of the Badr Brigade, the militia of the Supreme Council for the Islamic Revolution in Iraq. These were the forces of the political cleric Sayyid Abdul Aziz al-Hakim, who had inherited the mantle of his older brother, Ayatollah Muhammad Baqir al-Hakim, who had been assassinated in the summer of 2003. The Badr Brigade had infiltrated the Ministry of Interior and made its way into the governorates and police departments in the Shia provinces of the Middle Euphrates and the south. A turbaned man, Hakim would not rule; he would be the éminence grise of the Shia political establishment, the kingmaker of cabinets.

I never met Hakim. I caught a glimpse of him in the delegates' lounge of the National Assembly—a small, bespectacled man, dressed in clerical attire, with the black turban of a sayyid. He moved fast as he took in the greetings of other parliamentarians. He seemed coiled and entitled, a dour man. Above all, I formed my impressions of Hakim watching him on television, as he claimed a fair amount of airtime on his own television station, Al Fourat. I watched him once on the occasion of a Shia religious ceremony. He was seated, and his tone was both banal and hectoring. I had seen a reference to him in the literature of his movement as *hujjat al-Islam,* a rather middling religious rank, well below that of ayatollah. The content of his oration was superficial, but his self-confidence was unnerving. He was not trying to please his audience or to engage them. (The religious tradition has great orators; I have listened to one or two religious scholars who could really hold an audience.) What he had was his distinguished pedigree—his father who was the preeminent Shia jurist of his time, his murdered older brother, and the sixty-odd members of the Hakim family killed by the Tikriti regime. He had no doubt as to his claim to this new order of power. The elections had vindicated him, and his power was presented as the redemption of all that had been heaped on the Shia in the time of the great oppression. This was not a man to apologize for power, or to be reticent in the face of its temptation.

Hakim's Arabic had a Persian cadence to it; this was an aspect of him that several of his Iraqi detractors had pointed out to me. I could safely assume that the man's orations would not play in the Anbar province. It was said that he had flirted with the notion of putting himself forward as a "political *marja'* " (political guide)—a novel reading of the status of *marja'* that Sistani claimed in its proper religious sense. The idea smacked of the Iranian theocratic republic and its ways. The claim had not caught on, but Hakim's power was still considerable. The secularists bemoaned the American indulgence granted Hakim, his courting by President Bush and by the American embassy. He had not spoken kindly of the American war, it was said, but there he was reaping its dividends.

The saving grace of Iraq was that Hakim's will would always run into and clash with the worldview of other centers of power. It was not known with any precision what kind of moral order Hakim would impose were he to have his chance to mold Iraq. He was not a philosophical man. By the accounts available, his was a simpler drive for power. There were reports that social freedoms in the Shia heartland were increasingly restricted, that it had become harder to get a drink in Basra, harder for men and women to mingle together in the open; public piety had become the rule of the day. But this was not Iran, and this was not Khomeini's theocratic state come to Iraq. The Badr Brigade, and the Sadrists, were "living off the land," an unsentimental security man of a rival political group said to me. They had stepped into the "political vacuum": they had seized the properties of the former regime, cars and public buildings. They had found their way into the governorates and the police stations and put together profitable enterprises—the smuggling of crude oil and subsidized gasoline.

There was money as well that came from the traffic of pilgrims. "The security structures reinforce the business rackets," he said. "This has nothing to do with religion, though people can drape it in Islamic colors."

The very diversity of Iraq will help redeem it: this is the consoling thought of many Iraqis. One can be forgiven this thought, for this is a country of many truths. Hakim's writ—or Moqtada al-Sadr's—may run in the town of Nasiriyah, but the mountains of Kurdistan yield the truth of their people. Flying from Baghdad into Kurdistan in the winter of 2006—barely a month after this seminal second election—one has the impression of crossing countries, and states of mind. The hills dusted with snow, their very enormity and solitude after the clutter of Baghdad, and the quiet of the villages speak of a different land. I flew on an American military aircraft to Arbil, courtesy of President Jalal Talabani. He had come to celebrate the merging of the two regional governments of Kurdistan—his own, based in the more urbane city of Suleimaniyah, and that of his old nemesis Massoud Barzani, based in Arbil. This was an event of note for the people of this hill country. These two turfs had known rivalry and outbreaks of intermittent war. There was no love lost between these two leaders, and stylistically they could not be more different—Talabani the gregarious raconteur, a man who abhorred being alone and savored the talk and the company of strangers, and Barzani the tribal chieftain secluded in his mountain retreat. But Iraq had been remade, and these two leaders now wanted amity in Kurdistan.

Barzani was waiting just beyond the tarmac for Jalal Talabani and the diplomats who were coming with him from Baghdad—the ambassador of the United States, the ambassadors of Britain, Iran, France, and China. Talabani arrived dressed in a dark blue suit, his signature attire. Barzani was the Kurdish leader at home: he was dressed in the traditional Kurdish way, the *jamadani* (headdress), the *shirwal kamiss* with the cummerbund. Barzani was gracious in his welcome, with intelligent, probing eyes, a subdued contrast to the voluble Talabani. The airport was small but orderly; its mere presence amid these barren hills was a testament to will and accomplishment. These people could not have taken this small airport for granted. What progress had been carved into these hills had been earned the hard way, redeemed by immense Kurdish suffering.

The ceremony itself, held in the parliament of the regional government, was festive, almost rambunctious. The two leaders sat down before a bank of microphones. The hall was packed with the leaders of both regions, the gallery packed with young people who had come to celebrate this occasion. There were seated together men and women with modern flair and clothing, and "traditional" people in the attire of these hills. A woman dressed in colorful, traditional garb, seated next to me, was eager for me to know that this was a special day, that this unification would make it easier for people like herself, people who do "civil society work," she said, to get their work done. She had about her a winning air of confidence, and the talk of "civil society" struck me as neither false nor contrived. When Talabani spoke, he spoke in Arabic, fitting for an Iraqi head of state. (He is fluent in Arabic, Kurdish, Farsi, and English; he even tried what French he had learned as a young boy in Baghdad on the French ambassador.) The speech was vintage Talabani, laced with hope, and optimistic. The Kurds had a time-honored expression that they had no friends but the mountains, and Talabani recalled it as he told his audience that they had friends the world over. He pointed to the foreign ambassadors who had come for this occasion, a reminder that the solitude of the past had come to an end. He recalled Kurdish suffering but did so without self-pity. He talked of the "Anfal campaign," the notorious campaign of terror and extermination that the Baathist tyranny had unleashed on the Kurds in 1987–88 and that had taken a toll of 180,000 lives and scorched thousands of hamlets and villages. This was behind them, he said, and the Kurds could look forward to a federal, democratic Iraq.

Barzani was less articulate. He spoke in Kurdish, in a conversational style, and the woman seated next to me was eager to render into Arabic what he said. "We have tried other means," he said in a coded reference to the fratricide among the Kurds. "Now we choose this merger of our two governments." It was understood that with this union the Kurds were being readied for the political fight over the country. There was talk of Kirkuk by the two leaders, and there was more candid talk of it in the three days I would spend in Kurdistan. Over breakfast the next day in Talabani's guesthouse, Talabani, in a nostalgic mood, recalled that the Baathist regime's apologist, Tariq Aziz, once told him that the Kurds had one right in Kirkuk: as they passed through it, they could weep for it, and nothing more. "This is generous of you," Talabani had told Tariq Aziz, "for weeping is a right you deny the Shia." History had turned: Tariq Aziz was now in prison pleading illness and old age, and Talabani was at the helm of the state. It was hard to imagine the spirit of this man being crushed by adversity. He had lived to see fulfillment; he had brought the Kurds to Baghdad, as it were. He was the master of the political game; no government could be formed without his participation. He had stretched the ceremonial powers of the presidency, for he knew all of the protagonists. He was free of sectarian animus, and this was his strength, for he was the right man for a country that yearned for consensus. (Memories of the terror are never far in this hill country: one day after the ceremony in Arbil, a road repairing crew came upon a mass grave in the outskirts of Suleimaniyah, and Kurdish television showed the familiar footage of families grieving amid the human remains, sorting through the identity cards of the dead.)

A young aide of President Talabani, Aram Yarwaessi, thirty-three years of age, elegant and Westernized, with a British accent and gentle demeanor, had put a successful business life in England behind him to join Talabani's staff. He told me of his life, and of the sorrows that had befallen his family. His father, Shawkat Haji Mushir, had been a colleague of Talabani and one of the founders of the Patriotic Union of Kurdistan. In 2003, on the eve of the American war, Aram's father, then fifty-six, had been assassinated by a terrorist group associated with Al Qaeda, Ansar al-Islam, that had put down an extensive infrastructure in Kurdistan. He had been shot, at close range, as he was signing a cease-fire agreement with Ansar al-Islam. It had been a trap, and Aram's father had paid with his life. Then the American invasion had come, and on the fortieth day of mourning for Shawkat Haji Mushir, the Kurdish forces had overrun the positions of Ansar al-Islam. It had been a devastating time for Aram's younger brothers. This young, gentle man, who recalled these events for me late at night in Suleimaniyah, at Talabani's guesthouse, was clearly devoted to Talabani, grateful for the work and for the chance to be part of this story of Kurdish redemption. It was easy to see that Aram's love for his father had flowed into devotion for Talabani. The hills of Kurdistan were worlds away from London, and his girlfriend was in England. But this young man had no doubts as to his purpose: he would work to see the coming of a secular republic that would give the Kurds their due. He had no patience with theocratic government; it wasn't the cause for which his father had died.

We flew back to Baghdad from the airport at Suleimaniyah, on the outskirts of the town. The officials and the notables were there to see Talabani back to the capital. A year earlier, this airport had been just a gleam in the eye of my friend Barham Salih. He had taken me to see it, and the furniture, brought from Turkey, was still in plastic covers. Now it stood, another monument to dreams fulfilled. Barham was there to savor this moment, and he loved the irony of a Kurdish airport built in this country by a Turkish company. Always restless, he carried onto the plane a prospectus of his next project: an American university in Suleimaniyah. He took pride in the name, American University of Iraq in Suleimaniyah. It would be for all Iraqis, and the design of the campus was the familiar design of an American college with labs and dorm rooms and open, green spaces. The country needed it. There was wealth in Iraq, and there was a desperate need for an educated class. This university was a bet on that secular, democratic future. Some eleven hundred professionals—physicians and engineers and teachers—were quitting Iraq everyday, it was reported, terrified by the brigandage and kidnappers, and discouraged by the dereliction. This new order was always on its heels, its hope a stubborn belief that the country would still turn a corner and prevail.

There were other forms of rehabilitation under way: an engineer by the name of Azzam Alwash, who had left Iraq in 1978 for a career and a new life in Los Angeles, had returned to pick up an old "romance," as it were, and to do what he could for this new order. His father had been one of Iraq's leading irrigation engineers. As a boy in Baghdad, Azzam Alwash had accompanied his father as he made periodic visits to the Marshes, at the junction of the Tigris and the Euphrates, the vast delta covering some six thousand square miles. The boy had picked up his father's passion for this "water garden" of Eden—its people, and its magical ecosystem. In 1991 Saddam Hussein had struck at the very ecosystem of the Marshes. The dense reed beds and the waterways had given shelter to the regime's opponents. This was southern Iraq, Shia country, and Saddam Hussein ordered a massive assault that burned and poisoned the reed beds. As the journalist Pat Twair, in a report on Alwash's return home, has written, "The wetlands were turned into a dust bowl." When the reed beds were burned, an estimated 250,000 people were killed or dispersed. These reed beds had sheltered rebels and dissidents, and a wholly different way of life. No preceding regime—Abbasid or Ottoman or Persian—had had the dark vision of so brutal an assault. Away from his homeland, Alwash had founded Eden Again, an organization devoted to the revival of the marshlands. He would get his chance after the fall of the Baath. He returned with the new order. He would do what he could to reinundate the Marshes. It was not easy work: some of the damage could not be undone. A year into his project, Twair tells us, roughly 40 percent of the marshlands have been reinundated, and about 20 percent of the original population have returned. The engineer's prognosis: partial recovery of the Marshes. "We can never expect to restore all the original wetlands."

This state was an affliction, and a curse, for the people of this land. There was the personal pathology of the Tikriti ruler, to be sure. But the alienness of the state, and the independence from the society afforded it by the oil revenues, turned it into a criminal enterprise, bereft of mercy or restraints. Some three decades before the assault on the Marshes, the great explorer and travel writer Wilfred Thesiger recorded the life on those reed beds. Thesiger was fearless, and heedless of comfort. He lived among the Marsh Arabs from 1951 until 1958. He partook of their hard lives. He was in London when he heard that the monarchy had been overthrown. Thesiger was a man with a brooding and dark view of what "modernity" brings in its wake. In *Arabian Sands,* a classic of travel writing, he had caught the twilight of the desert Arabs, on his last exploration of the Empty Quarter, in 1946, and had written that their world was marked for extinction. Now a similar premonition came to him about these "desert waters." In his second classic work, *The Marsh Arabs,* he was prescient: "Soon the Marshes will probably be drained; when this happens, a way of life that has lasted thousands of years will disappear." He gave his hosts the honor of a memorable portrait—made all the more poignant by what befell their world at the hands of the Baath regime:

> Memories of that first visit to the Marshes never left me: firelight on a half-turned face, the crying of the geese, duck flighting in to feed, a boy's voice singing somewhere in the dark, canoes moving in procession down a waterway, the setting sun seen crimson through the smoke of burning reedbeds, narrow waterways that wound still deeper into the Marshes. A naked man in his canoe with a trident in his hand,

reed houses built upon water, black, dripping buffaloes that looked as if they had calved from the swamp with the first dry land. Stars reflected in dark water, the croaking of frogs, canoes coming home at evening, peace and continuity, the stillness of a world that never knew an engine.

Thesiger's Eden can't be recreated. But the "partial recovery" that Azzam Alwash sought was good and noble still. The Tikritis had hacked away at everything: even the palm trees had not been spared. By one estimate, there had been 38 million palm trees when Saddam Hussein had risen to power; there were 11 million trees by the time his regime had been decapitated. This had been part of the tyranny's war against the people in the south, part of the pauperization the man sought for a part of the country he had never taken to. In the lore of this land and its people, the palm tree is graced: the Arabs describe it as having its feet in water and its head in the scorching sun. The Baathist tyranny had paid that romance, and that grace, no heed.

No one can be sure of the nature of the culture that the tyranny has left behind. I have listened to Iraqis switch back and forth between fierce pride in their country's modernism and utter despair over its condition. I have seen secular and worldly Baghdadis return from the south with reports of a country that seemed foreign to them. They return taken aback by the piety and the religious superstitions, and by the disheartening poverty. There are reports, exaggerated by the telling, that Iranian charities and political-religious operatives from the larger Persian state next door are running away with Iraq, that they will recast it in their image, that they are training Shia activists in media and political work designed to impose an edifice of power akin to Iran's. There is an Iranian television channel, Al-Alaam, that airs in Arabic, and those worried about theocratic politics point to it as evidence of Iran's reach into its neighbor. Those keen to see that "Shia crescent" conjured up by King Abdullah of Jordan rise over Iraq speak of Iranian money flooding Iraq, of book fairs that bring to Iraq the literature and religious books of Iran. On the eve of Iraq's first national elections of January 30, 2005, there were charges—unsubstantiated but nevertheless uttered with great confidence—of huge numbers of Iranians crossing into Iraq to participate in the elections and to tilt the balance in favor of the Shia parties. These fears had going for them the widespread view of Iranians as people of guile and mystery and concealment—the double burden, in Arab eyes, of their Shiism and their Persianness. *Etelaat* agents (Iranian intelligence) were everywhere in Iraq, it was asserted by the Sunni Arabs within and outside Iraq. And the Sunni Arabs were not the only purveyors of this view. For the American and European critics of the war, this was an irresistible rebuke to the war—an American project that had "delivered" Iraq into Iranian hands. It was in this vein that the foreign policy writer and activist Peter Galbraith wrote of Iraq when he described it as George W. Bush's Islamic republic. And it was in a similar vein that a reporter for the *Wall Street Journal,* taking leave of Iraq in early 2006—she herself of Iranian ancestry—spoke of a country where Iran was now everywhere.

But Iran is not about to run away with Iraq. This is not Lebanon, where a small investment of Iranian money would secure for the Islamic republic a presence by the Mediterranean. Iraq is a big country with wealth and resources of its own. Najaf is a proud Shia city, *the* sacred city of Shiism, the sun around which all Shia planets turn, the influential and shrewd jurist of Najaf, Sayyid Muhammad al-Ghurayfi, was keen to remind me in a visit described earlier in this book. Granted, geography could not be annulled, and that nine-hundred-mile border between Iran and Iraq would make its impact felt on both sides of the frontier. But the barriers of language, and the pride of an Iraqi political class that made its home in Baghdad—not down in the south—were a better bet as to the shape of things to come in Iraq. Few Iraqis watch Al-Alaam. It is too clumsy and repetitive; there is more glitzy fare from Dubai and Doha and Beirut and Cairo, Arabic material more congenial to the taste of Iraqis. The country was never the secular, modern haven of the exiles' imagination. And it was not about to take to sudden, excessive piety.

Theocracy was a scarecrow, breakdown the more serious nemesis. "I am worried about Iran and I am not worried," the shrewd president of Iraq, Jalal Talabani, observed to me on the shores of Lake Duqan, not so far from Iraq's northeastern border with Iran. "It depends on us Iraqis. We can have decent relations with the Iranians as sovereign states if we order our own house. If we don't, then the bets are off." Talabani knew Iran and its politics and its language. He treasured an exchange he had had with the "Supreme Leader" of Iran, Ayatollah Ali Khamenei, where the Iranian cleric said that both of his parents had been born in Najaf. "Then you are an Iraqi," Talabani had said with his customary good humor and relish. Talabani then supplied the ironic twist on this story: he told Khamenei that his own tribe traced its descent to Iran. "So here you have it, an Iranian leader with Iraqi connections, an Iraqi leader with roots in Iran." There was no complacency in Talabani's view of this matter. He had an Iraqi patriot's calling; he had come into his role now, in his early seventies, as the standard-bearer of Iraq's nationalism. He was sure that once peace came, Iraq would hold its own in the contest of nations around it.

An astute reporter, Shakir al-Anbari, dispensed with the Iranian scarecrow and caught the cultural dilemma of his divided homeland. "Iraq has passed from the culture of tyranny to the culture of victimization," he observed. "Everyone now feels victimized and persecuted, the oppressor and the victim alike. What's strange now is that an Iraqi in Mosul does not know much about the culture of Basra. This is true, as well, for someone in the town of Hit in western Iraq when it comes to the culture of the city of Samawa, in the Middle Euphrates. All these cities are isolated islands, each a world in its own right. It is thus difficult to speak of a national culture in this time of sectarian cities. There are some isolated sparks of enlightenment but they all die out in this dark night."

Identity was historically checkered here, but the new culture and its lines were being drawn by violence. Iraqis may have glided past the sectarianism of their land—and I have made this argument in this text—but there was a great deal of truth as well in their claim that their world was always a place of conflicting loyalties. Mixed neighborhoods were targeted now; it wasn't quite "ethnic cleansing" of the Balkan variety, but "borders" were rounded out, Iraqis were fleeing to live amid their kinsmen. A reporter for the pan-Arab daily *Asharq Al-Awsat,* on March 25, 2006, filed a poignant story about twin boys in Baghdad, Omar and Ali, fourteen years of age, hitherto attending the same school in the Shia neighborhood of Karkh, now being forced to take different paths. (Ali is, of course, the quintessential Shia name, the name of the Prophet Muhammad's cousin, the first of the twelve Imams, while Omar, the name of the second caliph, a rival of Ali in the great "civil war" over the Prophet's inheritance, is particularly objectionable to the Shia.) As it were, the twins hailed from a mixed home—their father, Tahseen al-Juburi, was a Shia, and their mother, Hana Tawfiq, a bank employee, was a Sunni. In the neighborhood school, it was Omar who was subjected to harassment; he had pleaded with his parents to change his name to Hassan or Hussein. An Arabic language instructor had queried the twins, and their classmates, about their sectarian background. He had made Omar squirm about his name. When Tahseen al-Juburi looked into the matter, he learned that the teacher belonged to one of the "sectarian Shia parties." He had pressed the educational authorities about the behavior of the teacher but was waved off. "Brother, why don't you change your son's name and end all this trouble. Is there a reasonable person who would name his son Omar at this time?" a clerk in the education department told him. Juburi was appalled: "I am a Shia, a government employee, this is my home and I can't sell it and move elsewhere, my tribe is half-Shia, half-Sunni, and we never bothered with such matters. My proof is that when I asked for my wife's hand in marriage, I didn't know that she was a Sunni. Iraqis were strangers to this kind of discrimination, which now blows away from beyond our borders and aims to shatter the fabric of our social life."

The twins' mother, Hana Tawfiq, offered her own sorrowful lament of what had befallen her country: "Until today we would have been too embarrassed to ask if someone was a Shia or a Sunni, or even a Muslim or a non-Muslim. We used to visit the church of the Virgin Mary in Midan square and light candles for her. We had a fellow worker whose name was Joseph who visited the shrine of Imam Ali and the Sunni mosque of Abu Hanifa, with his wife, to ask God to grant them a child. Thus we were, and such were our habits." Perhaps the past was being prettified, and all the more so against the background of the new sectarian struggle. Perhaps Tahseen al-Juburi "knew" that his wife was a Sunni; what mattered was that the marriage had taken place, that deference had been paid to an inclusive idea of belonging, that a son had been given the name of Ali and another the name of Omar. Now that sort of malleability had become harder to sustain. Iraqis could console themselves that all this sectarian antagonism had been let loose in their midst by (Shia) Iran and by the Sunni Arab regimes nearby. There was truth in that lament. But Iraqis would delude themselves were they to think that strangers had inflicted all this on them. The past had not been so pretty or so harmonious to begin with.

I want to return to the life and work of the Kurdish poet Buland Haidari, for the man's ordeal catches the struggle of Iraq's best minds for a way out of the cruelties of the country's history. There was a nobility to his work and his life, an unmistakable decency and humanity to his voice. Haidari, born to hope in the mid-1920s, was to know his country's promise—and terrible disappointments. A few years back, I opened my work, *The Dream Palace of the Arabs* (1998) with his death in London. I read into that death the larger theme of his generation's odyssey—its early hopes of modernism, its fight with the dictators and the autocracies, and the death of so many of these pioneers of letters and culture, often away from the burning grounds of the Arab world. My account of Haidari was brief, but I was struck by this man's genius, and by his journey out of Iraq, his years in exile in Beirut, then his death in London.

In my book, I laid out the bare outlines of Haidari's life. It was only three years later that I was given a more intimate view of this great poet's trail. It came to me as the unexpected offering of a renowned Israeli literary scholar, Nissim Rejwan, himself a child of Baghdad, two years older than Haidari. They had been close friends and literary companions in the time before the terrors of Iraq blew away a whole world of Iraqi life. Nissim Rejwan opened up that world to me: a band of young poets and literati, Muslims and Jews, in the mid-1940s, savoring the life of letters, clutching the latest of world literature as precious possessions. Rejwan was "deeply touched," he wrote to me from Jerusalem, in April 2001, by the pages I had devoted to his "friend and soul mate Buland." It was "high time" that Buland got the credit he deserved as a "pioneer of the New Poetry—and as a rebel." To his letter, he attached an essay he had written, in Arabic, back in April 2000, for *Al-Sharq,* an Arabic periodical published in Israel. It was a farewell to his friend and included copies of several letters that Haidari had sent him in the months that preceded his death.

From Rejwan's account, and from the letters written by a man fully knowing that the end was near (he would die of heart trouble), I could make out Haidari's life and behold a piece of Baghdad's history now irretrievably gone. Rejwan had been at the center of a literary band. In the mid-1940s, he had been in charge of Al-Rabita Bookshop, an offshoot of a cultural association of leftist intellectuals. In a city where the people were provincial and had a limited knowledge of foreign languages, this bookshop became a gathering place of the avant-garde. Rejwan stocked it with the latest in literature—the poetry of T. S. Eliot, Ezra Pound, W. H. Auden, Stephen Spender; the fiction of Joyce, Kafka, Orwell, Greene, Bellow. Young Buland made his way into this literary oasis of Baghdad. He broke with his aristocratic family and lived what Rejwan describes as "the life of a real tramp, roaming the streets during the day and sleeping in public parks and under the bridges of the Tigris." His passion was poetry and free verse. (Free verse, as Rejwan reminds us, was pure literary and cultural heresy, a break with fifteen centuries of classical, rhymed Arabic poetry.) In 1946 Buland published his first collection of poetry, *Heart-throb of the Mud (Khafqat el-Teen)*.

But this literary band's entire world was in the wind. Nationalism was blowing in; a deadly fight for Palestine would bring its troubles right to the heart of Baghdad. It overwhelmed this comradeship, and the old ways. There was anti-Jewish rioting in Baghdad. Nissim Rejwan and his family were soon on their way to a new life in a newly established Jewish state in Palestine. The man who had launched the bookshop, an old, decent leftist by the name of Abdel Fattah Ibrahim, was anxious about Nissim's departure and pleaded with him to hold on in Baghdad. "You Jews are the salt of the earth. How do you think you are going to manage to live in a state of your own—all cooped up together in one place? All right. Have it your way! Have a bloody state of your own! Come to think of it, why should we be the only sufferers? You will soon discover what a burden it entails." In February 1951, Nissim Rejwan quit Iraq with his family. The cocoon of these literary aspirants—and the life of Baghdad's Jewry—had come to an end.

Some forty-odd years would pass before members of this Baghdadi band found each other again. Rejwan had kept up with Buland's literary output. He had reached out to him. In early 1995, a letter came from Buland Haidari, from his home in London. It was brief, something of a declaration of a bond that time and "passing events" could not overcome. He wanted to know of Nissim's doings: "I stretch out my hand to you my dear friend."

In the correspondence that followed, Buland told of his life's—and Iraq's—disappointments and grief. It was a life of "tragedies," he wrote, and "many places of exile." He had married a Baghdad-born artist, Dalal al-Mufti, in 1952. He had worked for the Soviet cultural center. In 1963 he had had a close brush with death: he had been sentenced to die by the dictatorship of Abdul Salam Aref. He had been lucky to escape execution: the intervention on his behalf of a Kurdish vice president had spared him. He then made his way to Beirut and put together a new life. But trouble trailed him there, Lebanon was set ablaze, and he quit that country in 1977. He drifted to Athens but found no work there. He made a brief return to Baghdad, but the Baathist tyranny of Saddam Hussein was closing up Iraq's world, and Haidari ended up in London, his final place of exile. He had a hankering to visit Haifa, he told Nissim in a letter in April 1995. But he was in poor health; he had a blocked artery, and knew he did not have much time left.

To the very end, Haidari wrote of his doomed and beloved country: "Release me of my dream of return one day to my Iraq/For what remains of my country is like me, and not much remains." He wrote of the politics of the exiles dutifully, but with a tone of despair. He was through with political hope: he gave voice to a deeper truth. "Forgive me Baghdad," he wrote in another verse. "The dawn will come/And the sun will rise again/Even if the grave awaits." In the same poem, he saw his native city, "dressed in the garb of mourning, black ruins traversed by death, with no sound save that of the ashes." For this poet— let alone for his old friend now in Jerusalem—there remained a fidelity to a world that had been provincial but whole. Nothing prettier, nothing better had risen in its place.

On June 4, 2004, the Arabic papers in London carried the obituary of the sculptress Dalal al-Mufti, Buland's widow. She had survived him by eight years. In one of the papers, there was a picture of her, a woman of striking beauty and grace. The life, as recounted in those obituaries, was the life of a whole Arab generation unable to transmit its ways and to bequeath them to their sons and daughters. This woman was a child of the upper bourgeoisie. Born in 1931, she had studied at an elite school in Alexandria. She had graduated from the American University of Beirut; she had met Buland through his sister, a friend of hers. They had married, they had had a son, and had retained a commitment to the making of a new, more emancipated culture in their homeland.

Dalal al-Mufti had been active in women's causes and in the teachers' syndicate. She had not been spared political troubles of her own: she had been imprisoned in 1963, the year her husband had been sentenced to die. She had followed him into exile. She had done a great amount of work as a sculptress but was averse to holding exhibitions of her work. By all accounts, she was a modest, refined woman, "her home open"—as the Arabs would say—to all Iraqis who sought her help. She died as a new battle for her country was being fought. She had witnessed, from afar, the fall of the despotism, and could not know for sure if the country would bear out Buland Haidari's darkest fears, or the fragile hopes both of them and their contemporaries had for their tormented land.

The ghost of Haidari stalked the first visit I made to Kurdistan in the summer of 2004. I had been thinking—and writing—of him; I had learned of his wife's death weeks before the trip. He was my literary connection to my Kurdish hosts. Their love for him and their pride in him were moving. My friend the Kurdish leader Barham Salih told me that in his final years, Haidari had given up on the dream of Kurdish assimilation into Iraq. He had "retreated" and had fallen back on Kurdish nationalism. It was the classic tale of the rejected *assimilé.* He had enriched Arabic letters but had then despaired of the Arabs. Younger Kurds had come to express themselves, more than ever, in their own language—and to aspire to mastering English. Buland's generation, and its larger universe, was of a different culture and a different age.

It was in 1960—before the mass graves, when a count could still be kept of the victims of official terror—that the gifted poet of Basra, Badr Shakir al-Sayyab, penned what remains, for countless Iraqis, their country's noblest and truest poem, "The Song of Rain." Here are some of its lines, superbly rendered into English by the literary scholar Issa Boullata:

> Your eyes come to my fancy with rain,
> And across the Gulf's waves lightning burnishes
> With stars and shells the coasts of Iraq
> As if they are about to shine
> But night covers them with a robe of gore.
> I cry to the Gulf, "O Gulf,
> O giver of shells and death."
> I can almost hear Iraq gathering thunder
> And storing up lightning in mountains and plains . . .
>
> Ever since we were young, the sky was
> Clouded in the winter,
> And rain poured,

Yet every year when the earth bloomed we hungered.
Not a single year passed but Iraq had hunger.
Rain . . .
Rain . . .
Rain . . .
In every drop of rain
There is a red or a yellow bud of a flower.
In the young world of tomorrow, giver of life.
Rain . . .
Rain . . .
Rain . . .
Iraq will bloom with rain.

The chroniclers say that the Abbasid caliph al-Mansour (the victorious), who laid down Baghdad's first brick by a wide bend in the Tigris in 762, had high hopes for his new capital: he dubbed it *madinat al-salam,* the city of peace. His city was to know grandeur and heartbreak. Peace, it must be conceded, hasn't been its lot. It awaits the peace its founder wanted for it, and it awaits the rain of mercy that al-Sayyab longed for. The foreign power that blew into Baghdad happened onto a tangled and pained history.

A British officer who served with the U.S. Army in Iraq, Brigadier Nigel Aylwin-Foster, offered the (gentle) critique of a friend who saw America and its forces up close in Iraq. The Iraq undertaking was "forbiddingly difficult," he said, and "might not have seemed as appealing had the U.S. forces not recently achieved a sudden and decisive victory in Afghanistan." There was truth in this observation, and there was insight, as well, in his remark that the "can-do" approach of American military leaders nurtured an attitude of "damaging optimism" in the chain of command. Junior commanders were "unfailingly positive," he wrote, and their reports were laced with a "misleading degree of certainty." Beyond the military dispatches lay the broader, deadly contest between American optimism and the overwhelming difficulties and complications of Iraq.

This battle, fought under Arab eyes, and under the gaze of Iran, often seemed like a struggle between American will and the laws of gravity in the region. The local spectators did not know how the play would unfold, but they were secure in the knowledge that they "knew" Iraq and its defects, and that the foreign power didn't. These spectators had their age-old pessimism about their world. The American assertion (and hope) that Iraq, and the region around it, could change was the first challenge in a very long time to the settled pessimism of a people who had seen the coming and breaking of many storms, who had witnessed many false dawns. The Arab world's troubles were no longer its own. America had hitherto beheld that region at some distance, but American power was now on the ground in Iraq. Autocrats and embattled liberals alike would read their hopes, and their fears, into that searing battle.

This war in Iraq, and its forerunner in Afghanistan, was destined to test America in ways it hadn't been tested before. There would step forth regimes in the Islamic world (and beyond) asking for indulgence for their own terrible wars against Islamists. There would be rulers offering the bait of secrets that their security services had accumulated through means at odds with American norms. There would be chameleons good at posing as America's friends but never turning up when needed. There would be one way of speaking to Americans, and another of letting one's population know that words are merely a pretense intended to delude the foreign power. There would step forth informers, hustlers of every shade, offering to guide America through the minefields and the alleyways. America now had to stick around Eastern lands. It may not have wanted an imperial edifice in the Arab-Muslim world. But one had risen, or been acquired, and we now watch as the terms of engagement unfold before our eyes.

APPENDIX A

Turning Points
in the American War in Iraq

2003

MARCH 20 The military campaign against the regime of Saddam Hussein begins.

APRIL 9 Baghdad falls, with the celebrated destruction of Saddam Hussein's statue in Firdos Square.

MAY 12 The American "regent," L. Paul Bremer, arrives.

JULY 13 The Governing Council, composed of twenty-five Iraqi leaders, convenes.

JULY 22 Saddam Hussein's notorious sons are killed in Mosul in a confrontation with American forces.

AUGUST 19 A huge blast shatters the UN Headquarters in Baghdad, killing the UN envoy, the Brazilian-born Sergio Vieira de Mello.

AUGUST 29 A blast in the Shia holy city of Najaf kills the noted Iraqi Shia leader Ayatollah Muhammad Baqir al-Hakim.

DECEMBER 13 Saddam Hussein is captured on the grounds of a run-down farmhouse on the outskirts of his hometown of Tikrit.

2004

JANUARY 15 A new Iraqi currency is introduced.

MARCH 2 Massive terror attacks on Shia mosques in Baghdad and Karbala take a toll of 171 victims.

MARCH 31 Four American contractors are ambushed, killed, and mutilated in Fallujah.

APRIL 4 and 5 The first of the rebellions by the young Shia radical cleric Moqtada al-Sadr occurs.

MAY 17 Ezzedine Salim, a Shia man of letters who was then head of the Governing Council, is murdered.

MAY 20 An American-Iraqi force raids the home of Governing Council member Ahmad Chalabi.

JUNE 1 The Governing Council is dissolved; an interim Iraqi government under Iyad Allawi takes office.

JUNE 28 Paul Bremer, head of the Coalition Provisional Authority, leaves Baghdad.

AUGUST 26 Grand Ayatollah Ali al-Sistani secures a truce in Najaf and a halt to a rebellion by the forces of Moqtada al-Sadr.

NOVEMBER 8 The Americans mount a major assault on the city of Fallujah, a hotbed of the Sunni Arab insurgency.

2005

JANUARY 30 In the "Purple Revolution," Iraq holds national elections, drawing a huge turnout of Kurds and Shia but scant Sunni Arab participation.

FEBRUARY 28 A Jordanian-born terrorist strikes in the Shia town of Hilla, killing 130 of its people.

APRIL 6 Jalal Talabani, one of the two principal Kurdish leaders, is elected president of Iraq by the National Assembly.

APRIL 28 A cabinet is formed under the Shia leader Ibrahim al-Jaafari.

JULY 5 A committee of the National Assembly begins deliberations over the drafting of a constitution.

AUGUST 22–28 A constitutional draft is submitted to the Assembly.

OCTOBER 4 The Jordanian-born terrorist Abu Musab al-Zarqawi calls on Sunni Arabs to boycott the referendum on the constitution.

OCTOBER 15 The constitutional referendum is marked by a substantial turnout and a marked absence of violence. The Sunni Arabs "return" to the political process. The constitution is ratified with 78 percent approval, thanks to the support of the Shia and Kurdish communities.

DECEMBER 15 In a nationwide election for a permanent National Assembly, 11 million Iraqis cast their votes. The ballots reveal the triumph of "identity politics," with the voters splitting along sectarian and ethnic lines.

2006

FEBRUARY 22 Terrorists attack the sacred Shia al-Askariya shrine in Samarra, triggering a period of greater sectarian violence.

MARCH 16 On the outskirts of the Kurdish town of Halabja, protestors destroy a renowned monument that had been erected to honor the Kurdish victims of poison gas attacks under the Saddam Hussein regime.

MARCH 19 The day marks the third anniversary of the American invasion of Iraq.

Notes

I made six trips to Iraq. I kept fairly extensive notes, and I relied on these notes in the writing of this book. The writing was prompted by my first trip in October 2003. The trips to come offered me a view on the shifting nature of this expedition to Iraq. I carried on extensive correspondence with U.S. military officers I met there, and with Iraqis. I drew on these as well, as my text makes abundantly clear.

As this book is, in part, an inquiry into the wider Arab response to (and the origins of) this war, I monitored the Arabic press tightly. Two papers, in particular, were helpful, both Saudi-owned but published out of London, *Al-Hayat* and *Asharq Al-Awsat*. The latter was better: it had more sympathy for the Iraqis and a lighter dose of anti-Americanism. I monitored, intermittently, the Iraqi press and the Egyptian daily *Al-Ahram*. As my notes make clear, a number of other Arabic periodicals were relied upon.

Introduction to Paperback Edition

The controversial memo, obviously an intended leak, by National Security Advisor Stephen Hadley was published in *The New York Times,* November 29, 2006.

The Report of the Select Committee on Intelligence, *Postwar Findings About Iraq's WMD Programs and Links to Terrorism and How They Compare with Prewar Estimates,* was published on September 8, 2006.

Leon Wieseltier's reflections are from his essay, "Try Anything," *The New Republic,* November 27 and December 4, 2006.

The data about the flight from Iraq and the scale of violence are drawn from the quarterly Pentagon report, "Measuring Stability and Security in Iraq," November 2006.

The Iraq Study Group published its recommendations in book form, *The Iraq Study Group Report, The Way Forward—A New Approach,* New York, Vintage Press, 2006.

James Baker's revealing quotes are from his memoir, *Politics and Diplomacy,* New York, G.P. Putman's Sons, 1995.

PREFACE AND CHAPTER 1

Leon Wieseltier's statement about the justice of the war is from *The New Republic,*
    May 10, 2004, "The U.N.'s Revenge."
On the Abu Ghraib prison story, I consulted the "Schlesinger Report," *Final Report
    of the Independent Panel to Review DOD Detention Operations,* James R.
    Schlesinger, Chairman, August 2004.
Hassan al-Alawi's book *al-Iraq al-Amriki (American Iraq)* was published in London,
    2005.
The Saudi-owned daily *Asharq Al-Awsat* (January 3, 2005) broke the story of the
    Saudi jihadist who struck a Mosul mess tent on December 11, 2004.
The Churchill quote about Iraq as an "ungrateful volcano" is from David Finnie,
    Shifting Lines in the Sand (Cambridge, MA: Harvard University Press, 1992).
President George W. Bush's statement on the election of 2004 as an "accountability
    moment" is from the *Washington Post,* January 16, 2005.
The Egyptian prime minister's (standard) promise that reform in his country is
    on the way is from Alan Friedman and Frederick Kempe, "Egyptian
    Order Pledges to Assist in Mideast Peace," *Wall Street Journal,* January 27,
    2005.

CHAPTER 2

The estimates as to the subsidies the Arab jihadists provided the Taliban can be
    found in *Joint Inquiry into Intelligence Community Activities before and after the
    Terrorists Attacks of September 11, 2001,* Report of the U.S. Senate Select Com-
    mittee on Intelligence and U.S. House Permanent Select Committee on
    Intelligence, December 2002.
Professor Saad Eddin Ibrahim's remarks on the atrocities of the Arab world are from
    his essay "Reviving Middle Eastern Liberalism," *Journal of Democracy,* Octo-
    ber 2003, 6–10.
The weary shopkeeper who opined that a just foreign ruler is better than a home-
    grown tyrant was quoted in *Asharq Al-Awsat,* April 18, 2003.
The Egyptian Mohamed Heikal, arguably the Arab world's most popular author and
    pundit, wrote a typically fierce condemnation (in Arabic) of the American
    presence in Iraq, *The American Empire and the Attack against Iraq,* Cairo,
    2003.
The Lebanese volunteer quoted about the reality of the Iraq war was reported in
    Al-Hayat, April 17, 2003.
Sheikh Yusuf al-Qaradawi's rulings and sermons are widely circulated and reported
    on in the press. For an early sermon on the Iraq war on March 7, see *Al-Hayat,*
    March 8, 2003. See also IslamOnline.net, March 8, 2003. On the edicts of

other religious scholars, see the excellent reports gathered and translated to English by MEMRI, the Middle East Media Research Institute. Of particular interest is their special report of April 11, 2003, titled "Arab and Media Reactions to the Fall of Baghdad."

The view of the Palestinian official Adley Sadeq of the Iraq war and of Saddam Hussein is from *Al-Hayat Al-Jadeeda,* April 10, 2003.

For a critical account of the Arab media's reading of Iraq, see Abdul Rahman al-Rashed, "Worse than the Media of 1967," *Asharq Al-Awsat,* April 1, 2003.

The two passages by the celebrated poet and author Adonis are from *Al-Hayat,* April 17, 2003, and August 28, 2003.

CHAPTER 3

Gertrude Bell's remarks on the Sadr family of Iraq are from *Lady Bell: The Letters of Gertrude Bell* (London: Ernest Benn, 1927).

Chibli Mallat provides an excellent account of the life of the celebrated cleric Muhammad Baqir al-Sadr in his book *The Renewal of Islamic Law: Muhammad Baqir al-Sadr, Najaf, and the Shia International* (Arabic edition, Beirut, 1998). The more controversial life of Muhammad Sadiq al-Sadr is told by Mukhtar al-Assadi, *Al-Sadr al-Thani: The Second Sadr, the Witness and the Martyr, the Phenomenon and the Response* (in Arabic, Iran, 1999).

On Ayatollah Sistani's carefully hedged rulings on the American presence and on permitted dealings with Americans, see *Al-Hayat,* October 12, 2003.

Reuel Marc Gerecht's *The Islamic Paradox* (Washington DC: American Enterprise Institute Press, 2004) has a careful (and sympathetic) portrait of the Shia clerical institution.

Hussein Khomeini's unusual message to the Iraqis, and his criticism of the Iranian theocracy, can be found in a long interview with him in *Al-Hayat,* August 10, 2003.

CHAPTER 4

Captain Luke Calhoun's statement on America's lack of knowledge of Iraq is from the *Wall Street Journal,* October 6, 2003.

An incomparable and old-fashioned (and quite generous) reporter, Edward Pound of *U.S. News & World Report,* acquired thousands of pages of intelligence reports, covering the period July 2003 through early 2004. Those reports, which he gave me access to, were prepared by the CIA, the Defense Intelligence Agency, the Iraq Survey Group, and various military command units in the field. Pound drew on these documents in his own reporting; see "The Iran Connection," *U.S. News & World Report,* November 22, 2004. The raw documents themselves were a unique source of insight into the early dilemmas of the American mission in Iraq.

Text of Saddam Hussein's audiotapes is from *Asharq Al-Awsat,* November 17, 2003.

Dexter Filkins's "Attacks on GI's in Mosul Rise," *New York Times,* November 27, 2003, was a particularly powerful dispatch.

Secretary Donald Rumsfeld's statements about the "contradictions" of the war can be found in the *New York Times,* December 2, 2003.

Marine Sergeant Major Gregory Leal's quote about the lack of a book on liberating a foreign country is from Christopher Cooper, "How a Marine Lost His Command in the Race to Baghdad," *Wall Street Journal,* April 5, 2004.

See John Dower's seminal book *Embracing Defeat: Japan in the Wake of World War II* (New York: W. W. Norton, 1999).

Leon Wieseltier's essay "Still," *New Republic,* September 22, 2003, vividly captures the American public's short memory.

See Richard A. Clarke's book, *Against All Enemies* (New York: Free Press, 2004).

The text circulated by those who pulled off the gruesome deed on March 31, 2004, of killing four American security contractors and desecrating their bodies was printed in the London-based radical paper *Al-Quds Al-Arabi,* April 2, 2004.

Moqtada al-Sadr's proclamation to his followers can be found in *Al-Quds Al-Arabi,* April 5, 2004.

CHAPTER 5

The Mahdi Army's warning to the army and Civil Defense Corps is from *Al-Hayat,* April 12, 2004.

The ordinary Baghdadi's rumination on the violence of his city is from *Al-Hayat,* April 19, 2004.

On the fragile Sunni-Shia unity, see Jeffrey Gettleman, "Ex-Rivals Uniting," *New York Times,* April 9, 2004, and *Asharq Al-Awsat,* May 17, 2004.

On Fallujah, and the murder of six Shia truckers in that city, in June 2004, see the Egyptian (Islamist) columnist Fahmi Howeidi, in *Asharq Al-Awsat,* June 23, 2004.

The statement by the governor of Karbala on Fallujah's suffering as an act of God is from Yochi Dreazer and Jabbar Yasseen, "Iraq Vote May Deepen Ethnic Strife," *Wall Street Journal,* November 9, 2004.

The facile analogy between Iraq and Palestine was made by Jihad El-Khazen, in *Al-Hayat,* April 29, 2004.

The controversy about the Iraqi flag was covered by Ernest Beck and Julie Lasky, "Flag Design, Too, Comes Under Fire," *New York Times,* April 29, 2004. Chederchi's interview appeared in *Asharq Al-Awsat,* June 14, 2004.

Gertrude Bell's high hopes for the Iraqi kingdom can be read in Janet Wallach's biography of Bell, *Desert Queen* (New York: Anchor Books, 1999). The British ideas of the 1950s about Iraq's potential are from William Roger Louis's masterful account *The British Empire in the Middle East* (New York: Oxford University Press, 1985), 592–93, as is the passage about the British affectations of the Hashemites.

The story of King Farouk and of Egypt's peaceful coup d'état of 1952 is told by William Stadiem, *Too Rich: The High Life and Tragic Death of King Farouk* (New York: Carroll & Graf, 1991).

On the Arabness of Iraq's Shia, see Yitzhak Nakash, *The Shi'is of Iraq* (Princeton, NJ: Princeton University Press, 1994).

On Iraq's Jewish community, see the work of the late Elie Kedourie, and in particular his essay "The Jews of Babylon and Baghdad," in Sylvia Kedourie, ed., *Elie Kedourie 1926–1992* (London: Frank Cass, 1998), 11–23.

On the life and terrible legacy of the educator and propagandist Sati al-Husri, see Elie Kedourie's masterful essay "The Kingdom of Iraq: A Retrospect," in his collection *The Chatham House Version and Other Middle Eastern Studies* (Hanover, NH, and London: University Press of New England, 1984), 236–82.

The great Iraqi poet Muhammad Mahdi al-Jawahiri wrote a book of personal and Iraqi history, *Dhikrayati (My Memories)* in Arabic, published in Damascus in 1988.

On Abu Musab al-Zarqawi, see a very good report by David Cloud, "Elusive Enemy," *Wall Street Journal,* February 10, 2004. A full Arabic text of Zarqawi's important letter cited in the text was published in *Al-Hayat,* February 12, 2004.

The history of the Baath Party—the early hopes, then the great distortions—is told by one of its leaders, Sami al-Jundi, in *The Baath* (Beirut, 1969).

Hanna Batatu's *The Old Social Classes and the Revolutionary Movements in Iraq* (Princeton, NJ: Princeton University Press, 1978) is by common consent the single most authoritative source on contemporary Iraq.

The life history of Taleb Shabib is told in an obscure (Arabic) book by Ali Karim Said, *Iraq: February 8, 1963* (Beirut, 1999).

Colonel Nathan Sassaman is quoted in Dexter Filkins, "Tough New Tactics by U.S. Tighten Grip in Iraqi Towns," *New York Times,* December 7, 2003.

CHAPTER 6

Hannah Arendt's book is *Eichmann in Jerusalem* (New York: Penguin Books, 1977). On Syria's Kurds, see Neil Macfarquhar, "Kurds Vent Anger in Syria," *New York Times,* March 24, 2004. See also Katherine Zoepp, "New Hope for Syrian Minorities: Ripple Effect of Iraqi Politics," *New York Times,* December 29, 2004.

Ghassan Charbel's column is from *Al-Hayat,* March 27, 2004.

Ghassan Tueni's *Dialogue with Tyranny* (in Arabic) was published in Beirut, 2004. Tikrit's second thoughts about Saddam Hussein are described in "Tikrit Looking for a New Role," *Al-Hayat,* January 15, 2004.

Tariq al-Homayed's thoughts about radical preachers and their style are from "The Crisis of Every Crisis," *Asharq Al-Awsat,* April 12, 2004.

Professor Wamid Nadhmi's reflections on the growing role of religion are in Farnaz Fassihi's "Some Early U.S. Decisions Are Haunting America's Efforts," *Wall Street Journal,* April 19, 2004.

The Fallujah Sunni cleric's thoughts about America and Israel are from *Al-Hayat,* April 19, 2004. On the "reign of virtue" that the jihadists brought to Fallujah, see *Al-Hayat,* May 24, 2004. The quote from Fallujah cleric Muhammad al-Hamdani is from *Al-Quds Al-Arabi,* April 22, 2004.

The passages are quoted from Amin Maalouf's allegorical novel *Leo Africanus* (New York: New Amsterdam Books, 1992), 123–24.

The Wahhabi preacher Saud al-Shraim is quoted in *Al-Hayat,* April 10, 2004.

Ayatollah Muhammad Hussein Fadlallah, "The Tyrants Past and the Current Occupation," *Al-Hayat,* April 5, 2004.

For Laurent Murawiec's view of Saudi Arabia, see his book *La Guerre d'Après* (Paris: Albin Michel, 2003).

See Bob Woodward, *Plan of Attack* (New York: Simon & Schuster, 2004), 228–32, for the Saudi view of the war against the Iraqi regime.

On Israel's Lebanon experience, see Fouad Ajami, *The Vanished Imam* (Ithaca, NY: Cornell University Press, 1986), and Clinton Bailey, "Lebanon's Shi'is after the 1982 War," in Martin Kramer, *Shi'ism, Resistance, and Revolution* (Boulder, CO: Westview Press, 1987).

On the sociology of the Iraqi Shia, see Ibrahim Haidari's outstanding book *The Tragedy of Karbala: The Sociology of Shia Discourse* (in Arabic) (London: Dar Al Saqi, 1999).

Hassan al-Alawi's discussion of "the sect of the rulers" and "the sect of the ruled" can be found in a probing interview with him in the Lebanese weekly *Ash-Shiraa,* April 25, 2005.

On Bell's meeting with Abdul Rahman al-Gailani, see Wallach, *Desert Queen.*

The wider Sunni Arab animus toward the Shia is conveyed in Paul Bremer's book *My Year in Iraq* (New York: Simon & Schuster, 2006), 71.

The Shia and Kurdish rejection of U.N. envoy Lakhdar Brahimi's proposals was reported in *Al-Hayat,* May 9, 2004.

Osama bin Laden's offer to kill Paul Bremer or the Algerian envoy Lakhdar Brahimi was reported in *Al-Hayat,* May 8, 2004, and *Asharq Al-Awsat* on the same day.

See Sami Shoursh, "The Harvest of This Arab Week," *Al-Hayat,* May 23, 2004, for a moving account of the life and murder of Governing Council member Ezzedine Salim.

Robert Pollack's superb retrospect, "The Chalabi Comeback," *Wall Street Journal,* August 29, 2005, documents the tenaciousness of Ahmad Chalabi. On the

Chalabi controversy, Jim Hoagland's "Cutting Off Chalabi," *Washington Post,* May 21, 2004, was particularly illuminating.

The Robb-Silberman Report, submitted to the president of the United States, *The Commission on the Intelligence Capabilities of the United States Regarding Weapons of Mass Destruction* (March 31, 2005), 108–9.

Chalabi's own statement on his dealings with the Iranians was reported in *Al-Hayat,* January 3, 2005.

The Shia cleric Qabanji's statement that his community now wanted its share of political life is in *Al-Hayat,* January 27, 2005.

The statement by Najaf's clerics against recruiting women into the armed forces is from *Asharq Al-Awsat,* February 7, 2005.

CHAPTER 7

King Abdullah's remarks on the "Shia crescent" and on Iraq's need for a strongman can be found in the *New York Times,* May 18, 2004, and the *Washington Post,* December 8, 2004.

On the popular mood in Jordan, see James Glanz, "In Jordanian Case, Hints of Iraq Jihad Networks," *New York Times,* July 29, 2005. See also a first-rate report by Rana al-Sabbagh in *Al-Hayat,* August 1, 2005, which illuminates the split between the regime and the "Jordanian street."

The statement by a group of Iraqi intellectuals on Abu Ghraib and on the prisons of the old despotism was reported in *Asharq Al-Awsat,* June 1, 2004. Abdul Hadi al-Hakim's plea to keep Abu Ghraib intact was expressed in his essay "Don't Demolish Abu Ghraib," *Asharq Al-Awsat,* June 12, 2004.

UN envoy Lakhdar Brahimi's bitter departure from Baghdad was described in *Al-Hayat,* June 4, 2004.

Interim Prime Minister Allawi's statement about his dealings with foreign intelligence agencies was quoted in *Asharq Al-Awsat,* June 10, 2005. The allegations about Allawi were reported by Seymour Hersh, "Plan B," *The New Yorker,* June 28, 2004. The text of a sermon against Allawi by a Sunni prayer leader in Baghdad was reported by *Al-Hayat,* June 12, 2004.

Ghassan al-Imam's dark view of Shia intentions was expressed in his column in *Asharq Al-Awsat,* January 25, 2005.

Zarqawi's warning to Allawi was reported in *Al-Hayat,* June 24, 2004.

The text of the Barzani-Talabani statement was in *Asharq Al-Awsat,* June 8, 2004. Dexter Filkins provided a treatment of it in "Kurds Threaten to Walk Away from Iraqi State," *New York Times,* June 9, 2004.

Abdul Rahman al-Rashed's view of the importance of putting Saddam Hussein on trial was in his column in *Asharq Al-Awsat,* July 1, 2004.

I followed the Salem Chalabi affair in the Iraqi newspapers *Al-Fourat* and *As-Sabah* in August 2004.

Qaradawi's fatwa on the murder of American civilians was published in *Al-Hayat*, September 2, 2004. The blistering response to Qaradawi by Abdul Rahman al-Rashed appeared in *Asharq Al-Awsat*, in al-Rashed's column on September 4, 2004. Qaradawi's "retreat" can be found in a dispatch in *Al-Hayat*, September 10, 2004. Ayatollah Hussein al-Sadr's remarks appeared in *Al-Hayat*, September 5, 2004.

Qaradawi's severe ruling on terror in Qatar itself was reported in *Asharq Al-Awsat*, March 22, 2005.

For Ayatollah Fadlallah's remarks on America's dilemma in Iraq, see *Al-Hayat*, September 3, 2004.

Zarqawi's audiotape on Iraq's elections was excerpted in *Asharq Al-Awsat*, January 24, 2005.

For the Druze leader Walid Jumblatt's view of Iraq, see David Ignatius, "Beirut's Berlin Wall," *Washington Post*, February 23, 2005.

On February 24, 2005, the Beirut daily *An-Nahar* published a remarkable manifesto by prominent Syrian intellectuals in solidarity with the anti-Syrian revolt in Lebanon. On Hariri's murder, and the Syrian role in it, see *Report of the International Independent Investigative Commission Established Pursuant to Security Council Resolution 1595* (2005), Detlev Mehlis, Commissioner, October 19, 2005.

The material about the corruption and waste in the Iraqi Ministry of Defense's expenditure draws on Hannah Allam's article "Audit: Fraud Drained $1 Billion from Iraq's Defense Efforts," Knight-Ridder newspapers, August 11, 2005.

For the Sunni Arab leader Adnan Dulaimi's call on his community to change its ways, see *Asharq Al-Awsat*, July 6, 2005. That of his colleague Ahmad Samarrai is from *Al-Hayat*, August 7, 2005.

Iyad Allawi's remarks equating the terror in the new Iraq with Saddam's days are from an article by Peter Beaumont in *The Observer*, November 27, 2005.

See Nibras Kazimi's view of the Iraqi elections, "A Lost Round," in the *New York Sun*, December 21, 2005. See as well Tamara Chalabi's "After Iraq's Elections," *Prospect*, January 2006.

CHAPTER 8

The quote "The face of my country frightens me" is from Pierre Rossi, *L'Irak des Revoltes* (Paris, 1962).

Georges Roux's *Ancient Iraq* (New York: Penguin Books, 1992) offered a sweeping view of Iraq's history.

Shaker Laibi's portrait of Iraqi literary life is in his book (in Arabic) *The Estranged Poet in the Strange Place* (Damascus, 2003).

Khalid al-Maali's story of the old country of the imagination appears in his essay

"The Young Poet in the Presence of the Great Poet," *Al-Hayat,* June 23, 2004.

Najm Wali's "About Exile and the Happy Place" appears in *Abwab* (Beirut and London), Autumn/Winter 2001–2002.

Salah Hassan's sad depiction of the new Iraq is in his essay "Iraqi Cultural Festivals amid Rubbish and Ruin," *Al-Hayat,* May 9, 2004.

Hayat Shararah's haunting novel *Idha al-Ayyam Aghsaqat* was published in Beirut in 2002.

Dr. Lina Ziyad on prison versus wilderness was quoted in Khalid Kishtaini's column in *Asharq Al-Awsat,* April 2, 2004.

On the Marshes, and the attempts to revive them, see Pat McDonnell Twair, "Reviving Eden," *Saudi Aramco World,* May/June 2004. Wilfred Thesiger's *The Marsh Arabs* (London: Penguin Books, 1967) is one of the great classics of travel literature, and an unforgettable encounter with a vanished world.

Shakir al-Anbari's report on Iraq's cultural fragmentation was published in *Al-Hayat,* February 20, 2006.

My own book *The Dream Palace of the Arabs* (New York: Vintage Press, 1999) provides the literary and cultural background for this chapter's concerns. The account of Buland Haidari's life and the portrait of Baghdad's literary life draw on the extraordinary letters between Buland Haidari and his boyhood friend, the Israeli scholar Nissim Rejwan. I am hugely indebted to Professor Rejwan for sharing them. For additional insight, see Nissim Rejwan's essays "Childhood in Baghdad," *Midstream,* November 2000, and "Childhood Memories: Baghdad as a Jewish City," *Midstream,* February/March 2001.

Badr Shakir al-Sayyab's poem "The Song of Rain" is available in English in Issa Boullata, ed., *Modern Arab Poets* (London: Heinemann, 1976).

For a thoughtful critique of the American mission in Iraq, see Brigadier Nigel Aylwin-Foster's "Changing the Army for Counterinsurgency Operations," *Military Review,* November–December 2005.

Acknowledgments

Iraq is a traveler's nightmare: to venture there, you must depend on the mercy of many good people. You must inconvenience them and often put them at risk. Three Iraqi leaders opened their doors to me, and this book would not have been possible without them. Ahmad Chalabi has an avid passion for all the details of his country—its history, its flora and fauna, the politics of a more merciful age—and he was unsparing with his help. It was he who gave me a memorable visit to Grand Ayatollah Ali al-Sistani, who made it possible for me to visit Ayatollah Hussein al-Sadr and to gain access to the National Assembly. Chalabi's faith in his country's possibilities is remarkable, and he communicated that sense to me. My debt to him is immense. Barham Salih opened up the world of Kurdistan to me; his generosity with his time and knowledge was boundless. I am lucky for his friendship. President Jalal Talabani reminded me always of the fellowship of people across rank and protocol. Amid the most difficult circumstances, he retained his sense of humor and his love of narrative.

Other Iraqis took me into their confidence: Interim President Sheikh Ghazi al-Yawar, the outstanding Kurdish man of letters Noshirwan Mustafa Emin, the poet Sherko Bekas, Hassanein Muallah, Defense Minister Saadoun al-Dulaimi. My friend Entifadh Qanbar took me by the hand on one of my visits, answering endless queries. The gifted political historian Tamara Chalabi knows the Shia world with depth and intimacy. She was generous with her knowledge and her material. Faisal Chalabi shared his home with me, and I am deeply grateful to him.

To know Iraq in the time of the Americans is to know the American military. Like so many others in the world of letters, I was humbled by the talent and humanity of American forces in Iraq. So many soldiers—old and young alike—lent me rides in their "choppers," talked to me about their work and their hopes for this war. My greatest single debt here is owed Lieutenant General David Petraeus. In both Mosul and Baghdad, he took me under his wing and opened his headquarters to me. I try in these pages to catch his enthusiasm and infectious devotion, but I know my account falls short of doing him justice. Major General Stephen Speakes and Colonel Lloyd "Milo" Miles are not only superb soldiers but poets as well, as their e-mails and "warrior notes" quoted in this book make abundantly clear. I am grateful as well to Colonel Stephen Ganyard, Colonel (now Brigadier General) Jon Davis, Colonel Mark Martins, and Captain Steve Alvarez of the Florida National Guard. Davis and Ganyard were students in a seminar I taught on Arab politics; they remained friends and sources of inspiration. Sadi Othman was a bridge between the American military and Iraq. I am grateful for all he taught me.

The Bradley Foundation and the Starr Foundation enabled me to carry out the travel and research needed for this book. Luck came my way as well in editors and colleagues I worked with and wrote for as I grappled with this project. I single out Paul Gigot and Tunku Varadarajan at *The Wall Street Journal.* Brian Duffy, editor of *U.S. News & World Report,* and publisher Mortimer Zuckerman have given me a home for years now, and they sponsored one of the trips I made to Iraq.

On one of my six visits to Iraq, I traveled with the peerless Leslie Gelb, one of our country's smartest and wisest foreign policy minds. To travel with him, and to be sustained by his wisdom and humor, was an experience I shall always treasure.

I was lucky to have Jennifer Gates as my agent. I can't repay her kindness and her faith in this project. She never gave up, even as I ditched an earlier project to take up this one. The editorial team of Dominick Anfuso at the Free Press had the patience of Job with me. They waited for this book and stayed with me. I am indebted to Edith Lewis and Wylie O'Sullivan for all they did for this book.

Two supremely gifted women have seen me through this work as they had through earlier endeavors—my incomparable colleague and our program coordinator at SAIS-Hopkins, Megan Ring; and my wife, Michelle. Megan did all but write this book. She will have my enduring gratitude. My debt to Michelle is known to her, and in deference to her wishes, I will say no more of it here.

This book is dedicated to my twin nephews, Chris and Jake Couch, United States Military Academy, class of 2005. Their connection to the concerns of this book is readily apparent. I saw them in the many young soldiers I encountered.

Index

About the Author

Fouad Ajami is the Majid Khadduri Professor of Middle East Studies at the Johns Hopkins University School for Advanced International Studies. Born in Lebanon and raised in Beirut, he is the author of *The Arab Predicament, The Vanished Imam, Beirut: City of Regrets,* and *The Dream Palace of the Arabs.* He has been, since 1989, a contributing editor for *U.S. News & World Report,* for which he writes frequently on Middle East politics, foreign policy, and contemporary history. Professor Ajami was the recipient of a five-year MacArthur Fellowship, an award granted to individuals of exceptional talent in the arts and sciences. In 2006 he received a Bradley Prize for outstanding achievement and a National Humanities Medal. His essays and reviews, some three hundred works over a period of three decades, have appeared in leading periodicals and papers worldwide, including *Foreign Affairs, The New Republic, The Wall Street Journal, The New York Times Book Review,* and *Foreign Policy.* He lives in New York City with his wife, Michelle Saltmarsh Ajami.